BREAK POINT

Silvester Krčméry Sr. M.D. , qui testimonium dedit Christo et Ecclesiae cum benedictione

THIS SAVED US

How to Survive Brainwashing

Joannes Paulus II
11. IV. 1995.

Qui testimonium dedit Christo et Ecclesiae cum benedictione.
My blessings to Dr. Silvester Krčméry, who witnessed for Christ and the Church

John Paul II
11.IV.1995

SILVESTER KRČMÉRY, M.D.

BREAK POINT

A Personal Account of Brainwashing and the Greater Power of the Gospel

A Crossroad Book
The Crossroad Publishing Company
New York

This printing: 2019

The Crossroad Publishing Company
www.crossroadpublishing.com

Book One was originally published in 1995 in Slovak as *...to nás zachránilo* (. . . *This Saved Us*) by LÚČ, Špitálska 7, Bratislava, and Signum, Kafendova 4, 831 06 Bratislava. Slovak Editor Gabriel Martinický. English version revised and edited by Madeleine Rivest and Benedict Hayas, O.P. Consultant: Heather Trebatická.

Book Two was compiled and edited from recordings and notes by Milada Cechová and translated into English by Heather Trebatická.

Printed in the United States of America

ISBN (13-digit) 978-0-8245-1770-0
ISBN (10-digit) 0-8245-1770-9
Library of Congress Catalog Card Number 98-73289

Books published by The Crossroad Publishing Company may be purchased at special quantity discount rates for classes and institutional use. For information, please email sales@crossroadpublishing.com.

I would like to dedicate this modest work to the Holy Father, John Paul II.

My own personal testimony of the events which took place under the totalitarian regime in Slovakia is not an exception, but is typical of what happened to so many other victims at that time.

Therefore, this book is also dedicated to so many known, but mainly unknown martyred witnesses who have not as yet published their own accounts.

And to those, who for their convictions, their faith, the Church, and human rights, underwent much greater suffering and even death, or witnessed the suffering and death of those closest to them, in the firm hope that others would be able to live in freedom, and achieve a fuller and happier life in *That which Alone does not disappoint anybody.*

Contents

Foreword: Eagles Fly High, by Michael Novak xi

Abbreviations xix

Book One
THIS SAVED US:
HOW TO SURVIVE BRAINWASHING

Preface 3

Introduction 6

The Mysterious History of My Records • The Sources of My Writings • The Pain of Remembering • The Surprise of the First Show Trials

Part I 11

Kidnapping or Arrest in the Military Zone • Solitary Confinement and Baptism by Fear • Performances by the Interrogators • Surgery

Part II 22

The First Stage of Brainwashing • Sleep Deprivation, Walking, Standing like Statues • The Interrogation Mill • Shock When the Strongest Break • How Long Can I Hang on?

Part III 32

Transfers in a "Submarine" • The Infamous Ruzyň • Convoy to Bratislava • Baptism by Physical Coercion

Part IV 42

The Beginning of My Legal Imprisonment • The Miracle of the Smuggled Bible • Brainwashing Continues, Košice State Security Police • Hallucinations, the Three Degrees of Pain, Stalin's Death

Part V 55

Back to the Familiar Ruzyň, Spiritual Weightlessness • Sophisticated Torturers, Final Refusal to Answer Questions • Stool Pigeons and Informers • State Security Leadership in Bratislava Is Supposedly Wiped Out • The Principle of Contradiction

Part VI 74

Departure from Ruzyň and the Second Move to Bratislava • The Superior Military Court and Prison in Trenčín • The Main Trial on the Feast of John the Baptist • My Final Defense

Part VII 89

My Spiritual Life in Prison • Spiritual Exercises in Solitary Confinement • Comprehensive Analysis and Personal Meditation • Themes and Ideas for Meditation

Part VIII 104

The Gulag: The World of the Condemned • Giant Cells without Privacy • "God's Mills" • Romanies

Part IX 116

Cellmates in Solitary Confinement, Traumatology • Complaints about the Prosecution • Systematic Disinformation • Rules and Regulations for Detainees

Part X 135

The Appeal Trial, the Supreme Military Court • The Prisoner Is Handcuffed, the Public Is Excluded • My Unique Family Support • Prison Uncertainty, Fear, and Constant Good-Byes

Selected Documents 144

Document No. 6 . . . 145
Document No. 7 . . . 155
Document No. 8 . . . 170
Document No. 22 . . . 180

Brainwashing Experiences and How to Prepare for Them 182

Epilogue: Thoughts on the Book, by Alojz Rakús, M.D. 187

Slovak Editorial Note 191

Bibliography 192

Notes 195

Book Two
IN PRISONS AND LABOR CAMPS AFTER BRAINWASHING

Part I 203

Mírov Prison

Part II 227

Banská Bystrica Prison

Part III 249

Bytíz Labor Camp

Part IV 267

Jáchymov District — Prokop Labor Camp near Horní Slavkov

Part V 282

Jáchymov District — The Central Camp

Part VI 299

Jáchymov District — Prokop Labor Camp (for the second time)

Foreword

EAGLES FLY HIGH
by Michael Novak

When the annals of the twentieth century are complete, one of its many great heroes — distinguished both by the purity of his mind and by the intensity of his suffering — will be the author of this book, the honorable Silvester Krčméry [pron., Kirch-máry], known to his young friends as "Silvo." To be sure, he is only one of millions who suffered unprecedented horrors of humiliation and pain in this scum of a century. Their stories have scarcely begun to be told, and their telling, were they to be narrated one by one continuously, might last till the end of time.

Even so, Silvo's story stands out. The greatest patrons of the Eastern branch of Christianity have, for a thousand years, been Sts. Cyril and Methodius, those brave young men who brought Christianity to the Slavic and other Eastern nations in 863 A.D., and named co-patrons of Europe with St. Benedict by John Paul II. Silvo has been called, with Dr. Vladimír Jukl, the new Cyril and Methodius, fathers of the new birth of Christian faith in the very bosom of hostile communism.

Because of the chronicle you are about to read, Silvo has also been called "the Slovak Solzhenitsyn."

Born in 1924 in Trnava, Slovakia, Silvo was at first not very much of a Christian — a good lad, and faithful enough, but spiritually slumbering — until a religious retreat during his seventeenth year. Walking in silence and solitude, he began to be conscious of a call to commit his entire life to God. Under the influence of a remarkable Croatian priest whose personal vocation was to carry the Gospel to Russia, Silvo joined with a small band of other young men and women who were preparing themselves for the dangerous life of missionaries in the belly of communism. They prepared themselves as lay persons, taking academic degrees in various lay professions. This small underground band worked patiently, waiting for the Russian army to drive the Germans from Czechoslovakia, so that they might find a way through the lines to Moscow.

Both in Czechoslovakia and in Russia, the communists, of course, still flush with arrogance about their own "new man," were contemptuous of these young Christians. Worse, the communists opened dossiers on them and tracked them when they returned to Prague, Bratislava, and the other cities in which they took up residence throughout Czechoslovakia. Spread through the nation, Silvo and his friends recruited and trained many other young people.

In February 1948, after abusing their party position and fomenting violence to sow disorder, the communists seized Czechoslovakia in a lightning coup. Ratcheting up their abuses, they began throwing into prison every class of leader who might oppose the communists — the clergy most of all, academics, journalists, lawyers, doctors. Almost immediately, great show trials were put on. These deserve discussion on their own.

The communist prisons were not merely holding pens depriving persons of liberty. They were torture centers designed to break the personality of prisoners and to reduce them through pain, humiliation, terror, and despair to quivering vessels, willing to assume whatever shape their now-acknowledged masters dictated. They were trained by torture, pain, and forced memorization to "confess" to the most horrible sins, to having been agents of evil foreign powers, and to being guilty of avarice, pride, deceit, sexual perversion, and hypocrisy. Their torturers especially gloated when bishops, religious superiors, abbots, and priests confessed these lurid personal crimes on public radio, to which the whole country was obliged to listen under pain of imprisonment. The jailers wished to destroy any shred of dignity and esteem the public might see in churchmen; they wanted the very thought of churchmen to incite revulsion.

The tortures applied to church dignitaries, as well as to lay activists, women as well as men, were at one level brutal, primitive, and sadistic, and at another level (particularly with coaching by experts from the Soviet KGB), scientific and medical. Sadistic beatings to put the memory of unbearable pain in every fiber of the body had two further purposes: to humiliate the recipient with disgust at his or her own broken, bloody appearance and utter helplessness, and to cause screams of agony that would be heard by other prisoners still being held in nearby cells and awaiting their turn.

Coupled with these primitive techniques were those designed by scientific analysis: prisoners were forced to stand for hours on end; to keep arms outstretched for entire nights; to live exposed for days and even weeks to unendurable cold and dampness; to bear constant light shining in their eyes, night and day, so that they could not sleep; to listen night and day to broadcasts heaping humiliating and scornful disdain on their characters and personalities, in the name of the whole nation; and to be totally deprived of any affective contact with others and any sign of human esteem. The aim of these techniques was to reduce the personality to nothingness.

Thus, for the toughest prisoners solitary confinement was the instrument most favored by their torturers — solitary confinement coupled with every technique of heat and cold, light and dark, physical agony, blasting and ego-destroying sound that evil imagination could devise.

Professional torturers took care to instruct prisoners that, at any moment, they could walk free from prison by their own choice. They pretended they were shifting the moral onus onto the prisoner. If he or she chose to confess willingly, sign before witnesses, and tell examiners what he or she knew about the "crimes" of others, out into the fresh air he or she could walk. Of course, very few were actually allowed to go free; their own "confessions," or those of others, were used to convict them of "crimes" and sentence them to further punishment, now humiliated by their own "self-betrayal."

One way or the other, virtually all except those who died under torture or broken health were crushed. Even those few who were given their "freedom" were, of course, forever compromised by the files of the police and Party; even years later (some, perhaps, even today) they were being subjected to blackmail and extortion. They could never again be "free." Besides, the memories of their agonies under torture would haunt their sleep and waking consciousness. So would the shame of having been reduced to pulp. They would sometimes wake at night screaming.

On one night alone in 1950, the communists rounded up ten thousand monks and religious and marched them to prison and labor camps, some to their deaths, all held in public disgrace. The next night, they drove ten thousand nuns and religious women from their convents. Orders were henceforth disbanded and proscribed (although some continued underground), and the few orders of nuns that were allowed to continue were forbidden to accept novices.

During the brief moment of the "Prague Spring" in 1968, before it was crushed by Soviet tanks, the communists themselves admitted to the forced imprisonment of 181,000 Czechs and Slovaks, many of whom had been sent to hard labor in the uranium mines. At that time, that was a larger population than that of any city in either country except Prague and Bratislava. In military terms, that number is equivalent to ten divisions.

In addition, the communists admitted to 240 political executions —

about one a month for each of the twenty years from 1948 to 1968 — not to mention those scores of thousands for whom prisons or work camps were also death sentences.

The aim of all of this, the communists proudly said, was to create a New Society, a New Paradise. They made no apology for killing any who stood in their way, for science told them, they said, that any morality except the triumph of the working class is false. They therefore despised everything that smacked of traditional morality, the Catholic Church most of all. As the years went on, the communists also launched waves of anti-Semitic campaigns of a new secular type, often directed against prominent communists such as Vladimír Klementis, the Foreign Minister. Their scientific theories demanded regular "purges" of foul and evil elements in society.

The grand production of public show trials was designed to instruct the terrorized population in social hygiene — in what they must learn to hate and to avoid, at all costs. Ironically, some who in the early days most avidly threw others into prison, tortured them, and purged them from the lists of the living were, by a later turning of the screw, themselves the surprised victims of purging, torture, and death. Many former communists, too, were made to broadcast public confessions.

Such social sickness is almost unbelievable. One wonders how many Americans have even now made themselves aware of this enormous civil evil, at the heart of a supposedly enlightened century. One wonders how many know the suffering that millions who shared this century with them have endured.

For this reason, the painful effort that Silvester Krčméry made to recall all that was done to him and others — the effort to endure again the nightmares and the flashbacks, the horrors and revulsions — is a great service to human knowledge. He bears upon his flesh the wounds that a so-called science inflicted. He now serves both genuine science and wisdom by so carefully diagnosing what was done to him, countering it with unprecedented effectiveness, and recording the struggle in which he was plunged, body and soul.

Silvo's advantages in this struggle were three: first, his will had been tempered to a durable steel of trust in God, well before he found himself bereft of any other strength.

Second, his mind had been trained in psychological science through his professional studies, so that he could recognize the strategies being employed on him.

Third, and perhaps most important of all, he had committed to memory nearly the whole of St. John's Gospel, and this text daily nourished his mind and furnished him with daily exercises. For example, he mentally translated it, chapter by chapter, into five other languages.

Through training of will and memory, Dr. Krčméry had already learned the arts of contemplation and had often before surrendered the action of his soul to the Holy Spirit. He had learned how to shape his deepest attitude of soul into a "Yes" to God, in union with Jesus on the cross: "Now not my will, but yours be done" (Luke 22:42). "My God, my God, why hast Thou forsaken me?" (Matt. 27:46). The symbol for St. John, the evangelist of love, in the iconography of the early church is the eagle. St. John soars, and so in his various cells — in which he also knew the terrors and the depths — did Silvo. Indeed, when many years later Silvo was able to recount to Pope John Paul II in some detail what he experienced in the attempts to brainwash him, and how he deflected them, the Pope was fascinated to learn more about the frequent sense of "weightlessness" that Silvo sometimes experienced for days at a time, particularly when he was gripped by the words of St. John.

Silvo described this strange experience to the Holy Father as — he imagined — like the weightlessness reported by the astronauts in space, except that he himself was experiencing a transformation in his spirit as well as in his body. What made him think of the astronauts was a sense, not exactly of being outside the body, but rather of body and soul being outside the bounds of their physical surroundings.

When I read Silvo's words in this book, I was reminded of Jesus, body and soul after the Resurrection, passing through closed doors, suddenly "appearing," yet offering his wounds to be touched bodily by Thomas. The state Silvo describes is not without precedent in literature. It seems especially fitting because of his daily reliance on the Gospel of "the Eagle;" for one recalls, as well, St. John's accounts of his own flights of spirit in the Book of Revelations.

Alas, most of Silvo's tale is, rather, of the suffering and the pains of the all-too-familiar body. He tells how some of his fellows had their noses pressed up against the cement of the cells, and then their jailers punched them on the back of their heads. His tales of the severe and burning cold of the prison cells hour after hour, and the glare of the incessant bright bulbs, and the horrid messages of the omnipresent loudspeaker are enough to make one want to leave one's seat and walk for air.

One can hardly imagine the courage and endurance of such men. The sweetness of temper and love that Silvo still bears are even more remarkable. It has been my privilege to meet with him more than once in Bratislava. One knows, as one knew with Mother Teresa and Dorothy Day, that one is in the presence of one in whom God is living and doing uncommon things. The presence of God surrounds Sylvester Krčméry like an unlit radiance; one feels it rather than sees it.

Silvo writes that, once he had put aside his fear of death — calmly accepted the fact that death would come any time his captors chose to inflict it — he could feel power pass from his captors to him. They had nothing with which to intimidate him. At any moment they chose, they could, of course, destroy his mind with drugs. But what they really wanted was his confession. They wanted him to defile the church, in itself and in his friends. Silvo did not want to die. But he did prefer death to betraying the Gospels.

Therefore, his jailers played the only alternative they could think of: They kept him in solitary confinement and counted on time, endless time, to reduce Silvo to despair. No human being should be able to endure without affection or contact, esteem or human reinforcement of any kind, without sound sleep or comfortable warmth, under bright lights, and with incessant propaganda designed to shame him, confuse him, disorient him, and bring him to total despair of any change for the better. Year after year, they worked on him, for thirteen years, seven of them in the department of solitary confinement. They got nothing, and at last they gave up.

When he had regained his health, Silvo once again began his missionary work, in his own country, counselling and instructing and nourishing. He is now at the center of a large and growing lay movement, dedicated to Our Lady of Fatima, who in 1917 told three little girls in Portugal to pray for the conversion of Russia. Our Lady predicted that after horrible events, unimaginable to most people at the time, Russia would return to the Faith, if many prayed for this. Silvo and his friends, in an organization now called simply Fatima, train lay people willing to go into Russia to live the Gospel in the field of their own professional expertise, and to counsel and instruct those who turn to them.

Dr. Krčméry's experience both before and after prison has drawn him unmistakably toward the spiritual destiny of Russia. From this direction, he believes that God is calling for great things.

ꟸ

What are the lessons of Silvo's ordeals, recounted so painfully in these inimitable pages? Readers, I am certain, will agree that they have never read anything like this mesmerizing story, which will strike them with awe at the human capacity to endure. The lessons they will take away are, essentially, three:

First, the human spirit must touch the ground; it must have matter to work upon, or it will fly apart. Thus, the fact that Silvo's memory was imprinted with a concrete historical text, chapter after chapter of it, verse after verse — make fun of it as "the letter of the law," if you will — anchored his spirit in the world of flesh and blood, allowed him to keep his mind "fed" with solid food, and gave him concrete tasks to work on during countless, endless hours of solitude. His enemies — even the biblical text speaks of "enemies" of our souls — did all in their power to disorient his mind. Yet his mind held firm because grounded in a concrete, finite text, a superlative text for persons driven to the extremities of the human condition.

Second, be not afraid. Especially, be not afraid of death. (Death is the gateway to our dearest love.) Fear of death is the cause of many betrayals, even of oneself.

Finally, God is love, and to tether oneself to his love, no matter how desperate the circumstance, is to be held secure to the greatest and most fundamental energy of the universe. To have everything else without God is to have nothing (like those who purged others, and then were purged themselves). To have only God suffices.

By his witness, Silvo has ennobled the entire Slovak nation, shown it new human possibilities, explored new lands higher than the snowy Tatra Mountains (in which he tried once to avoid German patrols). By his witness, Silvo has lifted up the entire human race. It is a privilege beyond desert to be chosen to introduce this overwhelming work into the English language. No one who reads it will leave it quite the same as when he first opened it.

Abbreviations

Gestapo	German, *Geheime Staatspolizei,* the German secret police under Nazi rule
JOC	French, *Jeunesse Ouvrière Chrétienne,* Young Christian Workers
KGB	Russian, *Komitet Gosudarstvennoi Bezopasnosti,* the Soviet secret police
MV	Slovak, *Ministerstvo Vnútra,* the Ministry of Internal Affairs
PTP	Slovak, *Pomocný Technický Prápor,* The Technical Relief Battalion
ŠtB	Slovak, *Štátna Bezpečnosť,* the Czechoslovak secret police

Book One

This Saved Us: How to Survive Brainwashing

"For our struggle is not with flesh and blood, but with the principalities, with the powers, with the world rulers of this present darkness, with the evil spirits in the heavens." (Eph. 6:12)

Preface

In the end, everything is only grace, that is, love. And "it bears all things, believes all things, hopes all things, endures all things" (1 Cor. 13:7)[1]

After overcoming many obstacles and restraints, including private and inner reservations about attempting this task, I am offering the public a few of my memories concerning brainwashing under a totalitarian system.

I finally decided to undertake this project since what I have to say might prove to be useful to those who may have to undergo similar trials and tribulations someday, as present signs indicate the possibility of a return to totalitarianism.

The title "This Saved Us" is intended to express the basic import of these experiences. They should, for now and the future, indicate the most effective way (see John 14:6) not only to defend oneself, but to grow, and even to find happiness as one encounters grievous situations of human hopelessness and extreme suffering.

For it is true that "our struggle is not with flesh and blood but with the principalities, with the powers, with the world rulers of this present darkness, with the evil spirits in the heavens" (Eph. 6:12). But it is equally true that "he delivered us from the power of darkness, and transferred us to the kingdom of his beloved Son" (Col. 1:13). And so "by the grace of God, I am what I am" (1 Cor. 15:10).

This way, which I seek to elaborate on in Part VII (my spiritual life in prison and my continuous daily spiritual program in solitary confinement), is the unique and only reliable key for protection. It is a key, which Jesus Christ Himself holds in His hands.

I discovered that when a prisoner lived a life centered on God, the refined brainwashing used against him sometimes led to the protection and spiritual enrichment of the tortured victim rather than to his total destruction.

The message is the same today as it was when the simple fishermen and apostolic bishops of the Church fought off evil, that is, that it is essential to listen more to God than to people (Acts 4:19). The importance of

God's Word is reiterated in Acts 4:20: "It is impossible for us not to speak about what we have seen and heard."

Apart from the tremendous gifts of God's grace and love, this book is also the result of the cooperation of my spiritual brothers and sisters, along with their on-going determination and their own personal testimonies.

In addition to my co-workers the editors, I also wish to thank my very accommodating technical associates, particularly those who do not wish to be named, for the further processing of the memoirs and other materials into the final version which you now hold in your hands.

I especially want to thank my older brother who tirelessly supported and encouraged me to publish these half-forgotten memories, experiences, and written documents even though forty years had already gone by.

ꙮ

My state of health, age, and time-consuming activities made it difficult to handwrite these memoirs so I recorded them on audio cassettes which were then used to write the initial Slovak version of this book.

While arranging and reviewing the material, I used the term "part" instead of "chapter" to clearly show that this is a closely connected and overlapping story which I divide for purely pragmatic reasons. It also makes it easier for the reader to follow the events described.

My testimony is divided into two sections:

1. Personal memories of prison
2. A selection of documents from prison

In order not to tax the reader's tolerance by presenting an unduly lengthy account, I significantly shortened all three sections. These changes should make the book more manageable and less difficult to understand for the person who has no first-hand knowledge of the subject matter.

I felt it imperative to very quickly seize and preserve the most outstanding examples of this tremendous gift which many of us have received from God. I reasoned that later, if the need arose, these cases might always be expanded upon, and testimony and data from other living prisoners and witnesses could be added. In fact, I believe that many lived through much greater suffering more consistently and much more perfectly than I did.

While working on the text, I felt a growing awareness of the inadequacy of human resources for the mastering of such a theme. But after many months of team work and consultations, I came to the conclusion that it was better to offer these memoirs now, even though the manuscript might be imperfect, rather than wait and present a more complete version at an unforeseeable time in the future.

ᢀ

I did not think it wise to avoid or leave out even the smallest personal reflection and, to all appearances, insignificant incidents, mainly those concerning cell mates and State Security men, since these people were actually there and they greatly influenced the main story. Consequently this is not a smooth literary creation, nor a stylized novel, but rather it is a factual testimony of what truly happened.

Moreover, I wanted to protect people who are mentioned in relation to the negative aspect of their activities. To maintain a certain anonymity, nicknames and abbreviations were used. However, this did not work out too well with people employed in public functions, as is especially evident in the selected documents beginning on p. 144.

I welcome any comments, critiques, additions, and suggestions and possibly permission to identify individuals and clarify abbreviations of names which are used in the text.

I would also like this book to be considered as continuing along the same lines as the work of the first lay chronicler of the underground Church, František Mikloško and his comprehensive work *You Will Not Be Able to Destroy Them! The Fate of the Catholic Church in Slovakia, 1943–89.*

This documentary was an inspiration to me, especially the introductory thought from the Acts of the Apostles:

> *But a Pharisee in the Sanhedrin named Gamaliel, a teacher of the law, respected by all the people, stood up, ordered the men to be put outside for a short time, and said to them, "Fellow Israelites, be careful what you are about to do to these men. . . . So now I tell you, have nothing to do with these men, and let them go. For if this endeavor or this activity is of human origin, it will destroy itself. But if it comes from God, you will not be able to destroy them; you may even find yourselves fighting against God."* (Acts 5:34–35, 38–39)

Introduction

The Mysterious History of My Records
The Sources of My Writings
The Pain of Remembering
The Surprise of the First Show Trials

The history of the writing of my memoirs is almost as complicated as the story itself. In October 1964, after more than thirteen years of imprisonment, I was granted my freedom.

Immediately after my release, several priests, bishops and friends strongly urged me to sit down as soon as possible and write about the realities of the many years of my imprisonment and harassment in order to preserve the exact testimony of this period. Among the many familiar persons and friends from those days a few faces stand out in my mind, namely, Father Mádr and especially Father Zvěřina. But there were also others.

They felt that it was important to document these events without delay so that the authentic, appalling deeds might not be distorted or modified by someone else in the future. I acknowledged the logic of the arguments and assented to their appeals to rouse and preserve these painful memories.

For a long time, I resisted tackling the job. But eventually, on August 27, 1966, as the date on the first page of my notes indicates, I locked myself away for several weeks and recorded the events that stood out in my mind from my years of imprisonment. When I had finished, I considered that my duty had been accomplished and I thought that I would never again have to refer to that painful and blurred story.

As time passed my notes got lost. I thought that I had either hidden them or that they had been destroyed at some dangerous moment. I saw this as God's will that I not relive the past and the anguish and reveal the dismal facts which, in any case, might not prove to be useful to anyone in either the present or the future. Thus, I considered the issue settled.

However, three or four years ago I was very surprised to hear from Rudo Mravec, a friend, who for years had been paralyzed and confined to his bed. He asked that I come to see him because he had something important for me.

I visited him in his apartment on Svoradova Street (formerly Nešporova Street). I was amazed when he said that he had some of my belongings. He couldn't recall whether someone had given him these things to hide or if I had asked him at one time or another to keep them safe for me. Because he couldn't walk, he directed me to a certain spot in the library and there, carefully concealed, were my lost prison notes. I looked at them with a great deal of interest.

They consisted in brief notes only, as I had just scribbled the most important points in a kind of shorthand to jog my memory. They were written on small A6 sheets, and including the appendices, the whole lot came to 265 pages.

The main motive for recording my memories was found in the entry dated August 27, 1966, where I had written, "After long struggles, postponements and interminable, unsuccessful, attempts to set aside time for writing these memoirs, somebody from our close circle died unexpectedly. I then felt great pangs of conscience."

There was renewed pressure, mainly from my brothers who were my closest friends and apostolate co-workers, to once again return to those times which had been dimmed by ten to fifteen years of declining memory and intense preoccupation with completely different matters.

The last two years had especially been marked by a whirlwind of activities related to the duties and work of the apostolate. I was moving around, and getting used to living on the outside which was an unknown place for me after my return from prison. It brought new experiences such as a considerable loss of concentration, peace and spiritual life. That which I had once so ironically predicted had come to pass, that is, that someday we would look back at our years in jail as a spiritually, positive, calmer time regardless of the atrocities. And I occasionally reflected on what we used to call "the golden prison times."

༄

I have relied on a variety of sources to write these memoirs.

The first source is my own recollection of the events that I experienced such as the circumstances under which I was arrested, and the places where I was taken and held for certain periods of time. This first source also contains the names of the people with whom I came into contact, that is, my fellow inmates (today with decoded names and addresses), the guards who supervised us, the investigators and prison wardens and their civilian colleagues and administrators.

The second source is my correspondence including letters I received at different detention camps and prisons and other mail I sent out and which was kept.

The third source of information consists of various court and other legal documents including acts of accusations, court decisions, appeals, grievances and the speech I made in my own defense.

(My friend and co-defendant Jozef pointed out that I had to make clear how it was possible that at that critical time those documents were rescued. This is easily explained. Some of my improvised notes, for example, and my defense plea were preserved, ironically, because they were confiscated. Furthermore, ten years after my arrest, when the political situation eased and I was trying to have my conviction revised, I was able to get access to the records and files which dealt with my case.)[2]

In the fourth source I include reflections and meditations (e.g., "Mary, The Handmaid of The Lord"), lectures, and other written materials which I concealed. (These files usually contained articles relating to subjects such as foreign medication, evolutionary theories, and other papers from my own medical field, mostly dealing with biology and other related disciplines.) In this group are also drawings, and photographs of people and camps where I was imprisoned.

The fifth source is made up of the recollections and writings of others. There is Václav Renč's writings and his entire long poem about the Virgin Mary, the *Loretan Prison Litany, May Behind Bars*,[3] which are sonnets for every invocation of the Loretan Litany. There is also a paper entitled "Traumatology,"[4] which was written by my friend Jozef Špáta (see Part IX).

The sixth source contains medical notes and clippings.

And finally, the seventh source holds summaries of my first meetings with fellow inmates, guards and prison authorities from various camps and prisons, thirteen to fifteen years after my arrest.

ꙮ

I shielded myself against writing my memoirs for so long, partly because I could not admit to my mistakes, imperfections, sins, fears, and weaknesses. And partly because it didn't seem like the right time to bring up the past, when in the present, young people were spiritually bereft and searching for support from us, and we had so little time to do everything.

Moreover, I was discouraged by previous disappointments, most importantly the destruction of the valuable Kolakovič records, and the loss of my childhood and school diaries which had been well hidden in the chimney of Julko Krébes' home, that saint-like, blind chaplain from Banská Bystrica. I saw both cases as the will of God being done.

In addition, the recalling of my experiences created serious physical and mental problems for me such as chest pains, tightness around the heart and throat, and a racing pulse, all identical to what I had felt when I was in prison. Merely thinking about my ordeal brought back splitting headaches, sore eyes, and neck and back pains. Occasional light exercise or resting on my back brought little if any relief. Those images caused back chills, tremors, and persistent insomnia.

Whenever I thought about those incredible events and divine graces, I became tense and nervous. I could not stand the pain of remembering for more than twenty or thirty minutes at a time. Sixty minutes of recollection was a rare exception. I tired easily and burned more energy during these times than during any other activity, be it physical or mental. Furthermore, I deeply felt the profound discrepancy which exists between the essence and possibilities of spirit and matter, between the thoughts that emerged and flashed through my mind and the inability to record them quickly enough.

Consequently, I could not bring myself to fulfill the promises and commitments which I had made so long ago in obedience to my spiritual brothers, and in gratitude to God for all the graces I had received.

These memories unsettled and hurt because they forced me to re-live those states of anxiety, fear and despair, and they brought forth once more the searing pain caused by human meanness. They opened old wounds and scars that had almost completely healed or at least had faded from memory and had lost their full intensity.

Because of the physical and psychological discomforts experienced, I deliberately reverted to these thoughts only when it became necessary to force myself to struggle again and again, not only to witness to the truth, but to warn against sin and the approaching judgment (see John 16:8). And through this exercise, any kind of compromise so as to be on good terms with everyone and avoid conflicts was prevented.

I particularly called upon this period of my imprisonment when it was necessary to bear witness, I might add with somewhat justifiable anger, against all those who had contributed to this criminal era of the persecution of the innocent.

I also evoked these memories when I was driven by the desire for peace, silence, and obliviousness, instead of unceasingly and indignantly speaking out, even shouting out accusations against those who continue even now, to act in this manner, and against those who are ready, willing and able to do so.

This drawing on my prison sufferings was especially important on the eve of critical trials and major interrogations which took place over the years, and also in the face of recent political events.

ꙮ

For many of us, the initial shocking events were the monstrous trials against the Church which took place between 1948–51.

The first to be attacked were members of religious orders, among whom were Fathers Urban, Kajpr, Mastilják, Dacík, and other priests and bishops. The confiscation of the monasteries quickly followed.

I remember that we were close to some pub when government propaganda broadcast excerpts and commentaries from the trials. We were shocked! It was inconceivable to us that such great, even saintly men would spread such lies to serve evil propaganda. Later, we understood that anything was possible with the proper audio equipment and skillful sound editors and directors. They could have used actors to utter the same words, but their voices were too well known.

It was nevertheless clear to us even then, that these religious men had been forced to say certain things against their will. Not only had they been compelled to speak, but they had rattled off those words and memorized phrases like robots. That was obvious, since a simple pause in their speech was enough for the head of the Senate to hastily throw in the cue to the forgotten word or sentence.

In spite of this, the majority of them were never completely broken. They were able to resist and not betray their colleagues nor the hiding places for literature, written materials, meditations, and so on.

At that time, we had no idea of what could be achieved through brainwashing or what one could accomplish with drugs, chemicals, coercion, and a complete, sophisticated array of very refined instruments and methods.

Who would have dreamed then that there was nothing in any way haphazard about these incidents, that everything was the result of a most precisely planned system?

Part I

Kidnapping or Arrest in the Military Zone
Solitary Confinement and Baptism by Fear
Performances by the Interrogators
Surgery

I was an enlisted man doing my compulsory service on a military base which was under a very strict regime and isolated from the rest of the world. There were secret Soviet Police and various other security units on this base. These factors made it possible for a person to disappear without trace.

My assignment was to the Kuřivody medical unit on Mimoň military base in northern Bohemia. This posting had its advantages. I was not involved in current events, and in my unit, it was easier to concentrate.

I was in a very strange position indeed. When I had attended the Reserve Medical Officers' School in Ružomberok, I had been demoted because along with twenty or thirty other people, I attended Mass and received Holy Communion every chance I could. Our politruks, which in Russian translates as political "guides" and our "education officers," noted all of this and took what they considered to be appropriate action.... They did not recognize my High School certificate, to say nothing of my University studies.[5]

But this decision notwithstanding, they had assigned me to medical duty. I had not been given any rank but I had to go through the Reserve Medical Officers' School anyway.

The lack of rank did not bother me, but sometimes it caused problems as I was in the company of a higher ranking medical assistant, and commissioned and non-commissioned medical officers who could approach me whichever way suited them because of their superior rank.

Then again, it was clear to everyone that, as far as the communist government was concerned, I was *persona non grata.* This was the result of an incident which had taken place when I was on a political training course in Prague at Hradčany castle, and on duty at the Dermatology department at the military hospital.

On that training course they had begun accusing the bishops of treason. During the discussion I had simply volunteered something to the effect that if they published the remarks of the prosecuting attorneys and judges, they ought also to publish those of the defense attorneys and the defendants so that the information could be objective. Everyone was genuinely surprised at my comment because at the time, almost no one would dare to even convey that much. They wondered how I could possibly risk standing up for the bishops.

From that little episode on, I was followed by negative evaluations. But first, they punished me by assigning me to Mimoň.

This post had a prison compound and a correctional facility. The forty seminarians who were being held there worked at one of the most arduous jobs. They chopped down trees under the most severe conditions, and did daily mandatory overtime labor seven days a week. They lived under a regime closely resembling a prison rule. (They called them the PTP, Pomocný Technický Prápor, that is, the Technical Relief Battalion. . . .)

Officers, including the chief officer, the majority of whom were also assigned there as a form of punishment, immediately noticed that I was a doctor without a rank. It was then clear to them that I was being discriminated against in some way since I really was a doctor, and so they showed me some consideration. The chief officer (Colonel V. if I remember correctly) invited me to a chess party on the day after my arrival and was willing to do favors for me if I needed anything.

The disadvantage of being on this base was that I became a little lazy. I relaxed, rode horses, played chess, and continued my apostolate in Kuřivody. But of all the ambitious plans I had made, I only succeeded in finishing three scientific dermatology papers which I had been working on during my stay at the Medical Officers' School in Ružomberok and which were published in the Czechoslovakian Dermatology Magazine, and another fairly extensive paper on abortion and contraception.

I feel that the dermatology papers were pretty good papers since Professor Hübschman, the great dermatological authority at that time, was one of the first to quote from them.

They dealt not only with the special variable sensitivity of the skin, but also with the entire organism which changes periodically. That explained why it was not possible to test medication based on a single time effects. Long term research needed to be done when phases of increased and decreased skin reactions were taken into consideration. Not until the doctor followed the so-called epidermal reactibility curves (that was my term) could he accurately determine what were increased, normal, and decreased skin reactions, and then judge the effects of the medication or chemical being tested.

Some of my brothers in the apostolate felt that I knew too much and that if I fell into the hands of the ŠtB (State Security) or KGB (Russian Secret Police), it could jeopardize the entire Catholic Action Movement. The situation was so tense that my friends, who repeatedly insisted on the danger, ultimately convinced me that it was possible to escape with a group of people across the border on some sort of glider.

However, nothing came of this. Later on, H. apologized and said that they had made a mountain out of a molehill. He then informed me that one of the persons in the group of people which was supposed to have flown away with us, the "granny," was really Hana Benešová, the wife of the former president of Czechoslovakia. Apparently the "Bishop" was Archbishop Beran. Both of them allegedly needed a doctor.

The whole thing struck me as being unreal. Nevertheless, I began to feel nervous and anxious at night and according to one colleague, I was talking in my sleep and grinding my teeth.

Yet, regardless of all of this, I still managed to attend a dermatology conference in Prague where the main theme was eczema, one of the most pressing problems in this specific medical field.

And on the night of July 26, 1951, a Friday, at approximately 00:15–00:30 a.m., I was arrested.

ᘓ

The entire scenario of the arrest was typical of the time. It was somewhat like a scene from an adventure movie or a cheap, exciting detective story.

I was asleep in my medical unit in Kuřivody, when at around midnight I was rudely awakened by an unidentified enlisted man or officers who urgently shouted at me, "Come on! Hurry up! An officer is dying. He's throwing up and is in terrible pain." (I later noticed that the man who had woken me was accompanied by a propaganda officer from our unit who either came from Hvězdov or Kuřivody.)

I quickly pulled on some thick socks and boots. Even though it was summer, I always wore boots, never shoes, because I lived with the nagging feeling that sooner or later, somewhere, they would grab me. I then accompanied them outside.

After a while I noticed that something was rather odd. They were calling me to a dying officer's side, and yet it was perfectly quiet outside. You could not hear a sound.

I saw a car cleverly concealed behind the building and asked one of them, "Is that your car?"

"No. No. Well . . . yeah," he mumbled.

But I already knew they were lying and that this whole business of a sick officer was nothing but a trap. I had been set up.

Suddenly, about three of them pounced on me, wrapped me up in a blanket or something of the kind, and gagged me because I was obviously screaming for help at the top of my lungs. Then they threw me into the car.

Without wasting any time, they handcuffed me and tightly fastened dark glasses (the kind worn under a sun lamp) over my eyes so that I could not see anything, and then drove off, obviously without bothering to tell me where we were going.

Such an experience can induce considerable apprehension in a person. And it was then that I noticed for the first time that in such situations, my hands would begin to tremble.

Then I heard the best joke I had ever heard in my whole life. All of a sudden the tall leader of the arresting party turned to me and said, "Don't be afraid. You're in the hands of State Security."

"Well, that makes me feel much better," I thought. "Now I'm not afraid at all!" I told myself. The fact is, that the main fear that everyone has, even today, is of the State Security force, or as people called them then, the State Danger force. Everyone was scared to death of them. People were more terrified of State Security than they were of criminals, gangsters, or thugs.

So off we went.

Along the way I tried to free my hands from the handcuffs as I had hidden some notes or addresses in the lining of my jacket, and I wanted to get at them to get rid of them. But most importantly, I was carrying a Eucharistic Host encased in a small silver plated box. I feared that the Host would be desecrated if they discovered it so I wanted to swallow it. But when they let me out of the car because I told them I was going to be sick, two or three of them surrounded me and pointed their machine guns at me. They never took their eyes off me for a second.

It is an illusion to think that everything will always work out the way we plan it. Luckily though, nothing devastating happened this time and later, God solved the particular problem of the Host in a very different way.

Through a tiny crack in the glasses, I tried, unfortunately without much success, to get a glimpse of where we were going. But later, from the conversation between the kidnappers I gathered that we were heading for Prague.

I came to the sobering conclusion that this was it for me. I was completely at their mercy and it appeared that they were on to a lot. My life would very probably end shortly. Given what I knew of their vicious but thorough methods, I had to believe that it would be difficult to avoid the worst possible outcome.

But then it came to me. Suddenly I realized that there could not be anything more beautiful than to lay down my life for God. I felt such incredible relief that I broke out in an uncontrollable fit of laughter.

But my joy rubbed them the wrong way.

"What are you laughing at?" the leader snapped.

"This whole performance," I answered. "It looks like it was taken straight out of a gangster or a cowboy movie."

"You just wait," he said. "We'll wipe that smile off your face soon enough."

&

They took me to the small, secret, military prison at Malostranské Square. The chief arresting officer insisted that I call him "Doctor." (They were very particular about titles like Professor, Doctor, and so on.)

First they searched me, which meant that I had to take out everything I had hidden, except the items in the lining of my jacket. All the things which I took out of my pockets were thoroughly examined, recorded and stored away somewhere. I had a small number of other concealed objects that they did not get. I know that I later destroyed a few American dollars which I had kept in reserve as insurance against our unstable currency.[6] I especially did not want them to find the money on me as they would surely have construed it as evidence that I was a secret agent or a spy. I destroyed other articles as well.

I later succeeded in getting into the lining of my jacket and eliminated some coded addresses. I also found a letter. It was from a fellow medical student who was in love with me and had seriously considered marriage even if it meant a missionary marriage.[7] She had delivered a message to Jenda, clearly from me, but I am not sure now if he was a friend from our days in medical school. I remember the contents of the letter because they reflected her state of mind. It went something like this, "I visited Jenda on my own so that at least, unlike me, he could be happy. Everyone on the street is smiling and laughing while my heart is bleeding. I cry constantly and go around feeling sorry for myself. Is it such a sin to love someone?

If not, then why does it happen when it is so impossible? Pray for me, so that I may learn to be brave and strong enough to calm my foolish heart and keep my chin up."

I was in the prison at Malostranské Square for a day and a night and obviously, I did not sleep at all. In the morning, the guards, or more precisely, reliable enlisted men, made me wash the toilets and urinals. They were noticeably pleased with my work. They spoke sharply and used profanity, but were otherwise not particularly abusive.

In the afternoon or early evening of the same day (Saturday) they took me across to Wenceslaus Square. By now, I could see a little bit more through the cracks in the glasses. I somehow found it terribly odd that people were calmly going on about their business, completely unaware of the other world around them, the world of prison camps, of the state within the state, the world where people suffered, were confined, and were gradually liquidated.

When the driver made an illegal turn I heard the comment, "Oh, great! Now the people from Prague are going to say that those blockheads from Brno don't know their way around Wenceslaus Square." I then naturally assumed that my arrest had something to do with Brno since our last activity had taken place in Brno. Things were slowly beginning to make sense.

That evening they took me to the prison in Brno. First, we went to Orlí Street, probably to the large court prison. It was there that I saw the list of house rules, the first civilized sign from which I could get my bearings. The prison was called the Brno-Orlí Correctional Facility.

It was then that I realized what a valuable treasure I had in the Gospel which I practically knew by heart. On the trip from Prague to Brno, I had tried to repeat the complete Gospel according to John. I knew it all except for the last chapter.

Before my arrest, I had thought that if God had protected me so far, he would certainly continue to do so. Therefore it did not appear to make much difference whether I learned the whole Gospel by heart then, or in a year from then. Memorizing the Scriptures had not appeared to be such a priority, and so I had not devoted much time to Gospel studies. And yet it had been crucial! In hindsight, it seemed as if the time before my arrest had been strictly reserved for the memorization of twenty-one chapters of the Gospel according to John.

Now, in the circumstances in which I found myself, I immediately set up my own program for Sunday: the Gospel of John. It took me about two days to repeat the incomplete Gospel.

ꟹ

Of course, the most dominant elements of my stay in prison were fear and uncertainty. Who else had been arrested? Who had talked? What had they revealed? What were they going to do to me? How were they going to torture me? What methods would they use to get me to talk?

You could not hear the slightest noise. It was dead quiet there. I remember trying to mold some figures out of bread. I had already had some practice with bread figures from my experience in January 1946, when, as a result of the Kolakovič investigation we were held in the Two Lions prison in Bratislava.[8] Bread moistened with saliva makes excellent molding material. And when it dries it is almost as hard as wood. From the bread, I molded a religious symbol, a cross (or was it a rosary ring), on which I carved an inspiring maxim. We kept this custom during the whole period of our confinement.

The words I engraved on it at that time were taken from the golden cross given to me by the fellow student who had loved me, "God's will, the highest law." But I most often quoted from Paul's first letter to the Corinthians, love "bears all things, believes all things, hopes all things, endures all things" (1 Cor. 13:7).

They took away the golden cross, perhaps in anticipation of the confiscation of all my material possessions.[9] They seized a cheap wrist watch as well and an ordinary fountain pen. These articles aptly summed up not only my own financial state, but the general economic situation of those days. I did not forget to point out these matters to the court in my grievances and appeals.

Eventually I became accustomed to various cells. There was something strange in nearly every one of them. It was graffiti, scratched by fingernails on the walls. Many of the scrawlings were of a religious nature, such as, "As long as I breathe, I hope," "I will never die completely, I will live," "Lord have mercy," and so on.

On Sunday, July 29, I mentally worked my way through Mass and the Gospel. I still was not absolutely sure why I was being held in prison but I prepared myself for the cruelest of times, including torture. I was alone.

ꟹ

On the morning of July 30, I was loaded on a metal-plated bus and driven to another building for questioning. I waited in that bus for a long time but was eventually taken into the main, underground, investigative headquarters of the State Security Force on Příčná St. in Brno.

There, I met with my first investigative officer. His name was Jan. He put on very dramatic airs as he attempted to impress his prisoner. He often wore a striking smile, one that he must have spent hours practicing in front of a mirror. At times his eyes actually glowed with affected love.

In a very oratorical manner, he immediately began to deliver Latin quotes. Most of these were from the pre-confession prayer, "Dominus sit in corde tuo et in labiis tuis, . . . " "Let God dwell in your heart and on your lips and help you openly confess everything," "Deus qui nobis sub sacramento," etc. Obviously he had memorized these prayers, but if he really was a former altar boy as he claimed he was, the sentences he quoted had nothing to do with those duties with the exception, of course, of the Confiteor.[10]

From the very beginning, he used very familiar and friendly expressions like "buddy" and you "rascal." He really wanted to overwhelm me with all of the evidence he claimed he had against me. He hinted at about seven sworn statements already in his possession. Then, the number jumped to sixteen. I think they were alleged statements from M. R., Dr. V., J. S., V. R., J. B. B. (I am not sure of this last one), and later V. J., I. S., and others.

He tried to confuse me by telling jokes and throwing in light comments, anything to get close to me. "Wow! You really get around, don't you? A real tornado! You've been all over the Republic. One day here, the next day there. Do you realize how much gas we wasted? We've traveled hundreds of kilometers throughout the whole country, just on account of you."

For the first time, I faced a real problem. How could I hinder or slow down the investigation, the admission of details, or the implication of others?

He continued with supposed records from M. B. and from a student J. K. if I remember correctly. M. was a medical student, originally from the Ukraine and J. was in High School and worked with the apostolic or biblical groups in Brno. The last time we had actually met was at a recent all night meditation, adoration, and spiritual renewal meeting at the monastery in Rajhrad.

Another name came up, Jitka, who I later learned, had not yet been arrested. She was in serious danger because they knew she was the key figure in the projected glider escape. I tried to convince them that Jitka did not even exist, that it was just a name we used as a code word, that I wanted to inform Father R. of the possibility of an escape and someone was supposed to use the code word "Jitka."

But I quickly saw what a problem these clever games like the one I had just attempted really were. In the end they arrested Jitka M. on the basis of the testimony of others and she was imprisoned. So I did not protect anyone. In fact, I did just the opposite. I ended up giving them proof that we had used conspiratorial methods and secret code names. From this, they could conclude that our apostolate was not just an innocent religious action but that our activities were truly illegal and that we were aware of this.

From then on the questioning continued almost without interruption. There usually were two sessions a day and then one again at night under a bright, glaring light. I eventually lost my appetite, probably as a result of stress.

There followed the first use of force. One was compelled to stand still like a statue all night or march. This meant that the prisoner could neither sit nor lie down, which completely ruled out sleep. Today, medical studies show that it only takes seven days and nights without sleep for a person's nervous system to completely collapse and for him to become physically drained. This condition can lead to a total breakdown of the organism and even death. That is why it is regarded as one of the most effective methods of torture.[11]

It was a terribly unpleasant feeling. I was so horribly exhausted that I practically slept standing up. To fall asleep, it was enough for me to get close to the wall or touch the radiator with my finger. Sometimes I did not even fall on the ground. The mechanism within some of the muscles definitely did not get any rest as they were in a constant state of activity.

At the slightest sign of sleep, the guards, whose responsibility it was to watch over us during these agonizing sessions, immediately began to bang against the cell and scream. They forced us to continue walking or at least to stand.

Then, for the first time, I tried to resist by refusing to answer questions. But I felt very uneasy about the whole thing.

One man, the chief of the investigative unit or the assistant to the chief, was tall and dark and, I think, a lieutenant. The closed bed was his idea. In typical ŠtB cells the bed consisted of a sheet of tin and a very thin mattress. At night, the bed folded out from the wall and during the day it was folded back against the wall and locked there. If you were not forbidden to sit, you could open up a table and a bench. In the corner stood a French toilet and above it a built-in pipe. The toilet could be flushed from the outside by the guards. There was a window very high above the street and sometimes during the day we could hear the voices of children or the ringing of bells.

The guards wore overalls and the prisoners donned very plain green burlap pants and jackets. When we were dressed in these clothes, the inspector would round us up in the middle of a room and laugh at the way we looked. Humiliation was another weapon they used to dishearten us.

&

I believe it was on August 3 that I tried to bring the cycle of pressure to a halt. In the end, I probably began to fake an illness. To this day I am not certain that I really had stomach pains or appendicitis, but I at least wanted to find out where I was and to get the message out that I was being held in prison against my will.

I was taken to see a State Security doctor in civilian clothes. This man displayed a kind manner. Apparently he had had some very bad experiences with the Gestapo. He told me matter of factly, "The Gestapo arrested us and then we arrested others."

I was quite surprised to learn that I was running a fever and that my white blood cell count had risen. These are symptoms which cannot be faked.

On August 4, they finally took me to the prison ward at St. Anne Hospital where they removed my appendix. A nun from the Order of St. Vincent was present, and Dr. Z. performed the operation. When they gave me the anesthetic, I tried desperately to scream from under the mask that I was being tortured and forced to do things against my will. I hoped that they would let others know. I thought that the nuns could get the word out, but the probability of that happening was relatively low.

I wanted to send out news about myself and warn others since most of my friends would not have known that I had been arrested. For a long time even my own family did not know.[12] I realized this because at one point I ended up in a cell with another soldier from our division in Mimoň. When he saw me he was stunned! "What're you doing here? They're saying that you deserted and fled to the west with all your military gear." (It is interesting that for two or three years they continued to question me about my "desertion." In Bratislava, a lawyer, W., wanted to put this on my record. I told him, "Look at the date when I allegedly deserted and the date of my arrest." When he discovered that both events supposedly took place on the same day he threw up his hands in disgust and muttered, "Another example of the hopeless lack of cooperation between the security branch of the military and the ŠtB.")

I also remember that S. P. from the Babický trials, who was shot in the back and paralyzed, was in the same prison ward at St. Anne Hospital. They would leave him lying in his urine and defecation.

Everyone hated Štěpánka, the head nurse. She made all of the decisions and obviously worked for the ŠtB, probably as an officer. But I got along quite well with her. I gladly followed all of the doctor's orders because issues like a strict diet after an operation did not constitute a compromise of my convictions.

At times I wished to die but only because I did not want to incriminate anyone or hand someone else over to be abused and mistreated in the same way I was.

Then the ŠtB investigators from Příční Street came to see me. "That was some performance," they said. "Or were you really sick? You see, we're not monsters or sadists. After all, we just allowed you to have an operation. But now it's time to get back to work. You've been here fourteen days already and we don't have any statement from you."

It was then that I realized that I would be better off dead than trying to wriggle out of something from which it was impossible to escape. One could only delay the inevitable.

They took out the stitches on August 9 and on the following day, they took me back to the prison with a bandage around my stomach. This time I was in a corner cell and I was not alone.

Part II

The First Stage of Brainwashing
Sleep Deprivation, Walking, Standing like Statues
The Interrogation Mill
Shock When the Strongest Break
How Long Can I Hang on?

My first cell mate was clearly put there to ensure that I would not inflict any wounds upon myself nor harm myself in any way. I was to be under constant supervision so that nothing aside of what they had planned would accidentally happen to me.

And so I greeted my first companion. At first, according to the rules, I knew him by his number only, then as Tomáš. I now know that Tomáš was actually his Christian name, and that Hradský was his surname. He had already been in the cell for ten months. Icy shivers ran through me when I learned this. I had estimated that a person could scarcely survive a week, that he would then surely die. The idea that Tomáš was still alive after ten months terrified me.

He had been a policeman in the outside world. It was said that he had hidden some weapons. At least that was the reason given for framing him. But he was a very wise and sensible person. He was a Catholic, a married man with a family, and was about forty-five to fifty years old. I stayed in contact with him after both of us were released.

He was terribly pale since he had not been outside or seen the sun for a very long time. Because he had prison experience, he spoke quite slowly and weighed everything he said.

He was allowed parcels and, once from a tooth paste tube he had, he made a small knife for cutting bacon. But since there was always great hunger, he always cut off only a very thin slice, about the size of half a little finger (2–3 mm thick), to make the bacon fat go further. The bacon was then hung on the prison bars.

Any small thing like this cheered us up a little psychologically and perhaps also physically. When the human body is in extreme distress, it knows best how to save energy and make use of even wretched food.

Less is wasted as we also found, so that a person is able to make good use of the energy provided by a quarter or even less of the food which is normally required by the body.

In the beginning Tomáš mistrusted me and the feeling was clearly reciprocal. This mutual reaction was natural and typical of every new meeting in prison. We even observed the rule which strictly required us not to give out our names to anybody. We were only numbers and that was all we had to offer anyone. But he turned out to be my first support and the source of valuable information about where I was.

He told me about individual interrogators. He nicknamed each one of them according to some characteristic each displayed. For example the head of the group was Ital, because he had a dark face and looked Italian. His deputy was "Dlháň" (Long-legs) and so on. Almost all of them were constantly smiling. Yet, they were the instigators of all the repressive and coercive methods used in that place.

Jenda R., my first (and previously mentioned) interrogator, was also a little tall, very skillful, and positively industrious. Clearly, everybody here endeavored to extract as much information as possible from the unfortunate prisoners. They did this extremely diligently either from conviction, or from opportunism, in the hope of receiving better performance evaluations as interrogators, which could mean promotion.

Jenda even allowed me a parcel. When I still refused to speak, he began to read me transcripts from Vlado J., Imro S., and Oldo, an engineer from Brno.

I was very soon transferred to a second interrogator sometimes called Gusti. He was young, smiling, and "kind." His objective was to win the prisoner over whatever the cost.

ѐ

Here, we find one of the secrets in the preparation for brainwashing. When a prisoner is alone, and has no contact with anybody except his supposedly considerate interrogator, a strange relationship develops between the two. The prisoner is afraid to remain silent or refuse to answer, because this interrogator deals with him a little more decently than the other one does, the coarse fellow. The detainee truly fears that his own interrogator may encounter problems and be persecuted for his alleged kindness.

Gusti sometimes even told me jokes, some of which had double meanings, especially at Christmas time for some reason. In this way he inadvertently revealed that their true area of interest did not lie with the good of the Church, although they all steadfastly held on to the pretense that they were believers and highly principled men of character. They would often even tell me about their marital problems or their mistakes, and asked for my opinion in the hope that I would at least be brought about to say one thing or another.

Once, to keep me from sleeping, I was taken away for surveillance and questioning to an unknown, red-headed interrogator. He was a lieutenant or first lieutenant. He went on almost all night about the differences between Christians and communists: "You see, it's said of us, that we deal harshly with people. I give you my communist word, that you won't receive even a slap in the face from us. We know what's legal and what's decent. We aren't the Inquisition, you know, like the Church had. Our communist word is different from your Christian word."

But perhaps no more than half an hour later, I had already received my first slap in the face from him. He lost his temper when I refused to give him the answer he wanted.

A more subordinate interrogator with a dark face was also present. He talked about his personal problems as well, again with the idea of forcing the interrogated person to speak. He related how his wife had died by falling off a train.... And then he reverted to shouting.

Gusti had me for a whole week. He attempted to break down my resistance by broaching subjects such as leprosy, Africa, my profession, and medical matters.

I once caught him red-handed when he was on the telephone. He was obviously being asked about the progress he was having with me and was saying, "...but, every apple has to ripen first. When it's ripe, it falls from the tree by itself." He was convinced that I would give in. He considered his tactics a most reliable method for gaining trust.

Among ourselves, we also gave nicknames to the guards so that we could talk about them, but I have forgotten most of those epithets. One guard was tall, another strong, one like a purist, another simple-minded, rowdy and coarse.

Later, it became clear that everything that happened there including the different "characters" we met and the manner in which they spoke to me was really planned in detail, and meticulously organized so that the interrogators would achieve quick and effective results.

Sometimes it was sufficient for us to give in to one of the interrogators to immediately see how all of them were closely connected with the prison guards below. The latter dealt with us a little more leniently and humanely, it is true, but they also cooperated with one another when they judged it necessary to put the pressure on and to force me to stand at attention, walk all night, or stand like a statue for hours.

Every day I got more accustomed to the abuse and I became aware that their repertoire also had its limitations. For example, once I understood that they wanted to deprive me of sleep in order to break me and make it easier for them to obtain answers from me, I endured the second night of walking much more easily. I no longer feared the unknown or the insecurity of being handed over to criminals so that they could amuse themselves with my sufferings or put me to death. I was more and more psychologically prepared.

I also realized that it was a good idea to put aside a piece of bread for evenings when unexpected things happened. It helped to be able to chew a small piece of bread and continue munching on it for hours like I would chewing gum. This activity conquered sleep when a person collapsed from weariness and his legs suddenly buckled under him.

ꕥ

The persistent apprehension of failure and the inability of some of those close to us to avoid it had the worst effect of all on us. I thought that others might be stronger than I was and when they broke, I worried that it might be impossible for me to hang on any longer. To make matters worse, in the beginning, I was misled by the relatively decent treatment by the interrogators, before we had worked out what they were up to and become aware of their inventive tactics.

In fact it is impossible to invite confidence and faith by first battering and torturing a human being and then later on conducting oneself in a more decent fashion towards him. Only the reverse is possible. Considerate treatment can win the trust of the prisoner only if it comes at the outset. After initial brutality, a courteous approach will not convince anyone that the benevolent handling will continue, and there is no knowledge of what the end results will be. Before we were arrested, we were prepared to resist, to endure beatings, blows, kicks, and any other violence with silence. But it was very difficult not to respond when questioning was done in a most civil manner.

Their apparent truth and logic also crushed us psychologically: "What can we possibly gain from keeping somebody in prison when he could be outside doing good professional work as you and all your group can do. Indeed you all have the best qualifications. So don't you think that we would be enemies of communism if we kept good workers in prison and bad ones out? We're only concerned with finding out whether, in your circles, you're doing anything against the state, whether you have weapons, explosives, and radio transmitters. We know from experience that the religious aspect is very often only a cover. Surely we have the right to find out whether somebody is collecting weapons, preparing to blow something up, launch an attack, commit murder or any other crime! But how can we be aware of this if we don't know everything about all those involved, and can't interrogate them separately. Think of Marika and the other young people who are really of no great importance to us. We'll release them if only you tell us what we want to know. Do you want the lives of these kids on your conscience? You're responsible for the fact that they're in such a nasty predicament. They could be out there studying if only you'd talk. But now, they may even be expelled from school."[13]

How perfectly logical and sensible this all sounded to one who was isolated and who could so easily be influenced! And how difficult it sometimes was to avoid and resist the "discussion and persuasion" method of brainwashing.[14]

A second problem which oppressed me was that I did not know whether or not I could continue to defy them. "They've all talked," my tormentors assured me, "but in the beginning they held out with much more strength and tenacity than you're displaying! Do you honestly think you can bear more than Father Baptista, or Jožko Š., or Father R. and the others? Believe me, when we want you to, you'll sing like a canary. Three court recorders may not be enough for you! Aren't you already climbing the walls? And you haven't seen anything yet! So smarten up and learn from those who went through this before you did and who were much more determined and more resolute than you are, you sucker, you poor wretch. . . . Look at their transcripts. They found out for themselves that refusing to answer questions no longer made any sense."

And I could not help being amazed. Did they not find anybody at all who was able to resist? Not one, single person? Then again, if someone had defied them, the interrogators were certainly not about to inform me of that fact.

One thought always haunted me: "Suppose I hold out for one or two nights without sleep, then what? What if this lasts a week, a month, a year, or even several years? What happens then?"

I did not know how long I could persist in such an apparently absurd, rigid, defensive position. I felt like some foolish Don Quixote. Maybe my resistance was irrational. Indeed other, older, sturdier and more experienced people than I were not able to stand up to this and maintain the vow of silence. I remembered how these same people had once boasted that even if they made belts out of their skin, they would not say a word.

Consequently, I was completely stunned when the interrogators showed me a letter from Father V. R. I recognized his writing. I was flabbergasted not only by the letter, but also by a confrontation I had had with him when he had tried to sway me, "It doesn't make sense. Why are you silent, when they already know everything." But I could not help asking myself how he knew that everything had been betrayed. It seemed to me that he could only know about matters he personally understood had been betrayed, but he could not be sure of anything else.

The interrogators were not always successful in their confrontations with priests. On the contrary. When Father Soukup confirmed that much had been revealed, he added, "Perhaps there are still other things where you're concerned, things which you know but did not disclose before you chose silence, but in the end that's your business." Then he quoted Matthew 7:6, and all the interrogators rushed to get the Bible and turned to the New Testament. When they saw the reading, "Do not give what is holy to dogs, or throw your pearls before swine, . . . " they started to laugh. But they also immediately sent him away. They knew that he would not cooperate with them.

Then there was Father Nováček who was perhaps a secret vicar general. He spoke very peacefully and quietly. His interrogator shouted at him, even roared for hours on end. He could be heard for whole days and nights. But Father would always calmly address him. He also told me, "Let every person speak for himself. I speak for myself, but why should I try and persuade anybody else to imitate me?" It was then obvious to me that many had maintained their intention to fight the system and to follow the truth dictated by their own conscience.

One older intellectual wept the whole time in front of the interrogator and me, "Surely you can't allow these young people, these children to suffer."[15] But this attempt at persuasion backfired as the crying man then related the defiance of his own cell mate.

He mentioned that there was a priest in his cell who also had to walk all night. This disturbed the older man who had begged the interrogators to keep a certain restraint and avoid violence, as he himself could not tolerate it. But this priest was very kind, and although he had to walk, he covered the older man's face with a towel so that the strong light they left shining would not disturb him.

The interrogators always began their questioning in the same stereotyped way, "Don't think for a minute that we're doing this for promotion or to gain some stripe or star or decoration or whatever. Sure, that's the way we used to do things. But now we're only concerned with the truth. We serve the people, that's all, and we'll be more than happy, when this sort of thing isn't necessary any more and we can go back to the factory."

They often offered me either cigarettes, coffee, an apple, or an open sandwich from their lunches as if they felt compassion and wanted to help me. When I refused to accept anything, they would immediately start, "Maybe you think we want to bribe you with these? Come on! Do you think we're such total idiots that we believe we can bribe you with a snack or a piece of bread with salami!" (As a matter of fact, my mouth watered uncontrollably after the food deprivation.)

"Go on! Take it! If you're afraid that it's poisoned, we can eat half of it first. Surely we wouldn't attempt to bribe you with such measly things as cigarettes, coffee, or bread rolls."

But I rejected these offers out of fear of becoming too friendly with them. If that had happened, it would then have been very difficult for me to go from an easy, amicable contact to a hostile approach.

Once it was possible for me to receive the Eucharist. I had it in a little round silver box which they had confiscated.

I think it was during the second examination that the interrogator took my things out and wanted to know something more about every scrap of paper there was. Then he came across the Eucharist. He pointed to it and asked what it was. I quickly took advantage of his confusion and swallowed the Host.

The angry interrogator sputtered, "How dare you! I was good enough to allow you to see your things but you tricked me! Right! It's obvious now that kindness won't work with the likes of you. . . . "

My greatest concern had been what they might do with the Eucharist, so I was very relieved when I was finally able to prevent any desecration. I might add that before being arrested, when I debated whether or not to carry the Eucharist with me, I felt reassured when I remembered that Jesus could hardly have been more abused than he was during the scourging and crucifixion but that he still had gone through it for us. Therefore, I continued to carry the Eucharist with me.

I think that Jenda, the interrogator, had once lent me my Russian copy of the Gospel of St. John for a while. When he "lent" it to me a second time, he was on the phone and so I was able to grab it, hide it in my clothes and take it back to my cell. Three or four days were enough for me to memorize the last chapter, the only one I did not already know.

ꕥ

When, during my first period of walking, I became aware of how they were able to use coercive methods (and walking was actually only a minor affair compared to everything else they could throw at us), I promptly forgave everyone I had previously judged for having revealed a lot. I had to admit that anybody who had to deal with something like this or even worse could give in. Who knows? Maybe I would end up failing too. I could not hold out forever.

After about one or two weeks, an unusual cell mate who introduced himself as F. McH., an American colonel, came to the cell. It is interesting that from the very beginning my cell mate Tomáš did not trust this man and that after his first conversation with him whispered, "You can tell that he's a mercenary." Tomáš was not certain about whether or not the man was a plant, but he played it safe, and when he could speak to me confidentially or through gestures behind McH.'s back, he warned me that I should be careful.

Later I became convinced that McH. clearly was an informer since details of certain matters which I had thrown out as a test or bait, reached the ears of the interrogator as I had expected. I had told him that I had hidden some quite valuable medical books, three large volumes of the French Encyclopedia of Medicine, Surgery, Dermatology and Venereology. After a short time, the interrogator insinuated that they knew all there was to know about me. Therefore, either we had been overheard or this was the work of our new cell mate. Later we learned that the informer, who had an unmistakable mark on his body (he lacked a toe), had introduced himself in another cell as Engineer Svozil. His real name was probably František Knesl.

He may have been their man and been threatened by imprisonment or he could have been serving a sentence for some offense or other. Then again it was possible he was actually a member of the security police and this was the way he operated. Shortly afterwards, an unexpected control by the guards confirmed that there was truly something wrong in our cell as they confiscated the Gospel hidden in my clothes....

Immediately after that incident, Tomáš was taken out of my cell. It is worth noting that any separation in prison brings on a fearful uncertainty concerning the fate of the prisoner leaving. Where is he off to? Is he going to torture? To death? To a worse prison? Is he going home perhaps? To freedom?...

ꕥ

At one time, an interrogator told me that if I was wise and came to my senses, they could reward me in various ways, like allowing my family to visit.

In any case, I prepared for a visit. With a finger-nail or a little piece of wood from the floor, I had engraved a secret message on a piece of toilet paper. This was for my family. I thought that if with any luck I ever had a visitor, I might be able to get the note out to them.

Obviously, I had to be mindful of not doing more harm than good should the note fall into the hands of the wrong people. If I wanted to indicate that it was necessary to warn someone of an impending danger, I had to do it in code.

In the end, I actually did get a visit. My father, mother, and brother Vlado came, but they did not allow the latter to come in.

They granted this visit in the hope that I would be more easily convinced to give in if I saw my parents broken and weeping. But as far as I can remember, the main theme of my father's speech was not that I should speak out and "not be stupid," or that I should value the "good will" of those who grilled me. In fact, it was just the opposite. He encouraged me to "Be brave, and act only according to your conscience."

I was shivering from the cold. When my father put his coat around my shoulders, it allowed me to slip the previously prepared note into his pocket. This note also contained a warning of who was in most danger of being arrested and asked my parents to sing the Russian student song "So Pour, Brother, Pour" outside my prison window when they found the message. They were not in fact able to do so, but in a letter they sent me, they wrote that every time they thought about me, they sang my favorite song "So Pour, Brother, Pour."

My next cell mate Jozef B. was also known by another name. He was a driver, thin, bragged about himself, and was always hungry in spite of receiving food parcels. He was the typical prisoner who was always striving to get the biggest share for himself. He suggested that we should take it in turns to have the first tin.

However, when we generously shared with him the things from Tomáš's parcel or the few potatoes we had for lunch, although we were hungry ourselves, he changed completely and was no longer interested in getting preferential treatment.

I also remember a sixteen- or seventeen-year-old boy named Oto K., from Slavkov. I think that he had "gone over the wall," that is, he had attempted to cross the border. He was in prison only a very short time, but we immediately talked to him about lay apostolate and Catholic Action.[16] His response was positive and he became very enthusiastic. Later I heard very good things about him.

Sometime in this period, I had a Yugoslav cell mate who was probably a black marketeer since he admitted that they caught him with a large number of watches.

He constantly warned us that Ruzyň was the worst prison, that he had walked barefoot there, even on snow and ice, that a person could not rest or even sit for a short while. Every activity, even eating, was done standing or walking.

I did not set too much importance on what he was saying. He even spoke of microphones and voices resounding from the walls, both day and night for whole months at a time, so that a person could eventually lose his mind. I thought that this was indulging in pure fantasy, that he was really going too far or that he had already gone a bit mad after being imprisoned for so long.

However, I began to take his words more seriously when I heard similar and sometimes completely identical stories from other prisoners, although the information always came around as second hand, never from anyone having directly experienced any of what was so vividly described.

Part III

Transfers in a "Submarine"
The Infamous Ruzyň
Convoy to Bratislava
Baptism by Physical Coercion

On the evening of Sunday, November 11, 1951, I went on my first major transport. This was a very dramatic moment for a prisoner. All the guards shouted and strove to create an atmosphere of abject terror and everything had to be done on the double which served to heighten the fear and confusion.

Individual prisoners were called according to number, not name, so that who they were would not be revealed. It was all done in great secrecy. Everyone had to give his date of birth. Thus, the guards were able to identify the prisoners and sent them from either one side of the prison to the other, or to a courtyard, through a corridor lined with guards all armed with automatic submachine guns, and dogs. As we got on the bus, we were handcuffed, usually in pairs.

I am not completely certain about whether or not it was a normal bus. I have the impression that it was not. It was more like the special closed buses divided into metal cabins, in which prisoners who were undergoing interrogation were shuttled back and forth.

These were called cupboard buses or "submarines." Once the prisoners were inside them, terror was deliberately heightened by creating the impression that they were headed for the gas chamber. Prisoners wet themselves from fear or from not being able to go to the toilet.

These transports without light, in pitch dark cabins, were also nicknamed "convoys of fear." We often heard that upon the arrival of one of these, following a freezing journey of one or two days, some of the older prisoners were completely disoriented and it was impossible to communicate with them in a normal way.

On November 12, after being isolated in the metal box or "cupboard" where I could only sit or stand, I guessed where we were: the infamous Ruzyň.

ꝏ

When we arrived, there was immediately more running and screaming around us. They took us to very small, austere cells which were obviously new. The space in each of the cells was precisely calculated to allow a person only so much air to go on living and to suffer the most, but not die. Each cell had a small chair, and a bed bolted to the wall.

Then it struck me that many of our brothers, priests, and perhaps even bishops had been there before me. The thought strengthened me.

This prison was said to be the main place of preparation for the political show trials.

At first I was alone in cell number 214 in the old building of the notorious Ministerstvo Vnútra (MV-Ministry of the Interior) Prague Ruzyň prison. And although I already knew from the information I had heard that there was a strict regime here, I began to walk voluntarily, out of solidarity with those who had had to walk before me or were doing so now. I also wanted to find out how much I could stand, and how it would end, what I was capable of enduring, and how and when I would lose consciousness.

On about November 14 or 15, I had my first interrogation session. I actually had a trump card as I knew my interrogators. Honza from Brno questioned me again, and later Gusti, my old "friend" appeared, with the phony smile still on his face.

And Honza and I clashed for the first time. He said, "If you won't speak voluntarily, we have ways of making you speak! Have you never heard of walking? Do you know what it's like when you can't sit?"

Then, and to this day I do not know whether it was impulse or out of defiance, but I shot back, "As a matter of fact, I do know what walking is. I've already been walking for three days now."

"What? And who allowed you to do this?"

"What's the matter? Since you're threatening me with it, you're using it. Why are you asking who allowed me to do it? Why can't I walk if I want to?"

At first sight, this method of not physically touching the prisoner appears fine and decent. They seem to deal with him with kid gloves. But it is a hundred times worse! In the evening the soles of his feet burn like fire and the prisoner feels the pain much more intensely than if his feet had been beaten directly with sticks or canes or even truncheons! The pain does not only last for ten or fifteen minutes. It can go on for hours, even weeks. By the first evening the feet begin to swell and everybody desperately searches for a less painful position and a place where he can support himself.

The kid glove approach may well be worse than the techniques of physical violence where a person can always tell himself, "They're striking me but I've got to hold on a bit longer. They also struck the Lord Jesus. . . ."

During the questioning, I began to suspect that even here, in this prison, they had not broken everybody as the comrades claimed with such confidence. Some of the confessions they had shown me could even be fakes. It also occurred to me that Father Ján Baptista Bárta must have really given them a hard time since they flew into a rage whenever his name was mentioned.

From the slips the interrogators had made, I also gathered that Father Oto Mádr had held up well. Perhaps these two men I knew so well were also spiritually linked with me in prayers. If they had been able to withstand all of this so courageously, maybe all the cruelty had been discharged on them. It was therefore unthinkable that I should fail to show solidarity or contemplate shirking the burden to make it easier for myself.

Fantasy was another enemy. When a bang, a cry, or a shout was heard, we instinctively surmised that one of our own was suffering or being tortured. Sometimes there was a smell of smoke or of something burning. That also stirred my imagination.

It was in Ruzyň that I first experienced a special curiosity concerning the techniques with which they endeavored to break a prisoner.

One was the so-called "Refrigerator," to which they suddenly took me. This was a dungeon without windows or fittings and with a terribly low temperature. It was probably even below zero. It is difficult to judge now, in peace and hindsight, because hunger increases the feeling of cold and causes shivering. A person cannot stop shaking. This is a defensive reflex which makes muscles work artificially to preserve at least a little warmth for the body.

Because of the darkness, it was difficult to make out the details of the layout of the dungeon. It appeared to be a concrete cell without even as much as a wooden-plank bed. One had to lie on concrete, and in the evening the prisoner even had to take off his sack-cloth shirt. He "slept," if such a word can be used here, on the concrete floor in only a shirt or underwear. So that he could not play any tricks, or attempt suicide, every few seconds a light came on like a sudden, silent flash of lightening. Then they ostensibly photographed the person or watched him.

I did some meditation then on sin, darkness, blindness, and the cold.

This very unusual experience stuck in my mind. In the morning, when I got up (obviously without having slept too soundly) I was painfully stiff, as if my body had hardened into a block of ice or stone. First I felt my ears and fingers to check whether I still had them. I could feel neither my nose nor my chin.

It is interesting to note that even after such shocks had been administered to the body in addition to the other extreme burdens suffered, I did not catch a cold. I felt frozen for whole weeks and months at a time. My feet and hands were blue and my whole body shook. However, I usually had no fever or a cold although I had often had them before going to prison. Ruzyň was quite an experience.

I especially remember November 22 and 23, 1951, when most of my interrogations were accompanied with rough treatment. It was also extraordinarily cold in the regular cell since there was a blizzard going on outside and the snow was being blown inside. It was a real Siberian winter.

Thus on the feast of St. Cecilia, and again on the feast of St. Clement, I especially prayed for help in holding out and fulfilling the will of God. I think it was also on November 23 that the glider which we had thought of using to escape was mentioned for the first time. (I have already alluded to how I attempted to turn attention away from Jitka M. who had organized everything, since the investigators always sought to arrest new people.)

ꩰ

I believe it was on December 23, just before Christmas, that I received a new cell mate. He introduced himself as František T. I immediately saw that he was a strange person. On the one hand, he complained bitterly that they were treating him badly and that he was threatened with I do not know what, because of his political activity. On the other hand, he was given very special allowances. He received double rations of food and extra parcels and the like.

I remember the first parcel he received from home and from which he offered me things. I had already been in prison for some months. My stomach was so shrunken from prison underfeeding that it was difficult for me to eat rich food. The sweets and chocolates from the parcel provided so much heat compared to the previous cold of hunger that we were kept awake at night. Perhaps this was the first time we did not sleep due to natural causes.

We confirmed that the food was the source of the warmth we felt. The organism learns to deal with food much more effectively when the body is in need. Perhaps this change of inner regulation helped to increase our immunity and so undernourishment protected us from diseases due to the cold. Apparently, an increase in certain stressful experiences and burdens may even benefit some people's health since all the defensive and immunological forces are aroused to protect the body against death by hunger or cold.

My new cell mate knew that he would be moved. He must have had some special source of information.

At first he tried to show that he had some Christian faith or at least a remnant of it. It was perhaps after a month or so, around January 30, that it came out in a conversation that he was an atheist. However, when we parted, he said in a very friendly way, "If we don't meet again, I wish you success in your education of young people so that the Gospel and good deeds from the Bible will spread among the people."

Some of my compositions and songs were written in Ruzyň sometime between January 20 and February 5, 1952. Around the feast of St. Francis de Sales, I wrote "The Conversion of Saint Paul," or "Saul, Saul, Why Art Thou Persecuting Me?" I also wrote the music to the missionary song "I'm Going to Plant the Stony Field." Since I could not make notes or write down tunes, I sometimes spent a week going over a melody again and again in my mind.

I also attempted to reach others by tapping Morse code from the cell at Ruzyň but they quickly discovered what I was doing since there was at least one guard for every two or three cells, and they were constantly peeping through the spy-hole.

The rule here was exceedingly rigorous. At night, they often shone strong reflectors in the room and the order "Hands on the blanket!" was so thoroughly enforced that sound sleep was impossible for weeks and even months at a time.

When I sometimes began to grumble a little or felt discontented and slightly inclined to some compromise, the Lord God always sent me a special sign which roused me in an extraordinary way. For instance, I was transferred to cell number 710 or 810 in the new building where isolation and solitary confinement were most strictly enforced.

Therefore, it was clearly by mistake that František Šrámek, a farmer from Roudnička, was assigned as my cell mate. According to Russian communist ideological terminology, he was a "kulak," that is, a person who owned land.[17] He had already been there for fourteen months! That really shook me up and set me back on the right track again.

I was with him for a couple of hours only and they went by very quickly. I did not expect that they would take him away so soon or I would have made better use of his company.

A prisoner cherished little incidents such as these. They brought joy and hope and would greatly hearten him.

ɛ

As far as I can remember, it was on June 24, 1952, the feast of the birth of St. John the Baptist, that we went through another transfer. Again our eyes were covered and we were shoved into a closed bus. However, this was no longer new to me, and therefore not as terrifying.

During a stop, they let some prisoners go to the toilet and, through a crack in the darkened glasses, I saw Imro S. for the first time after a long interval. His eyes were also covered and he looked very pale.

What a shock it was, after being isolated from the ordinary world and suffering in the freezer through a blizzard, snow, and frost, to catch a glimpse of a green meadow, a bit of the of the countryside I loved so much. Nature had always given me so much joy. I sometimes wondered which was the greatest penalty and the most painful for me: to be denied contact with people such as my brothers, relatives, friends, and patients, or to be separated by concrete and iron from contact with God's outdoors?

They took me to Bratislava. Once again I was following a routine of imprisonment for interrogation. On the ground floor of the Justice Palace we took back all the personal possessions which had been confiscated. Mine included a rosary made from dried bread in the form of a gear wheel with the inscription "The will of God, the highest law" on one side and "Love bears all things, believes all things, hopes all things, endures all things" (1 Cor. 13:7) on the other.

After a long time on my own in solitary confinement I got a cell mate, Pavel Valent. He was a psychiatric case but after solitary confinement a person will accept anybody just as long as one is not completely alone.

However, in the end, I even got used to solitary confinement since the Lord faithfully accompanied me whenever I was sent there.

Pavel Valent would stand at the window for hours. At times, he spent the whole night there constantly repeating, "I am Pavel Valent... I am Pavel Valent... and I am a person. I am not an animal. I am not a lamb." He would sometimes add, "I never hurt anybody" and other similar broken phrases.

I pointed out to the interrogator that from the medical point of view, this man needed treatment. The interrogator thundered: "He should have thought of that before he engaged in his anti-state activities!" and other phrases in this vein.

In the end, I thought they had finally given him psychiatric treatment since, at least in my opinion, they could not take such a person to court. Hopefully, no doctor would attest to the fact that physically he was healthy enough to be put through imprisonment, interrogation, trial, or sentencing. But unfortunately, I recently learned from a photograph published in a newspaper that my former cell mate, Pavel Valent, had been executed.

I had another great advantage compared to other people in solitary confinement. I had asked my parents to include references to little things like the calendar in their letters. Otherwise I would have completely lost all sense of time. Therefore, my mother carefully wrote in each letter such things as: "... Today, on November 30, we will remember Andrew the Apostle, and Uncle Ondrej will celebrate his name day." Soon, every letter ended with family feast days where they reminded me which member of the family would be honored. Thus I knew in advance that I was to remember Cecilia (Cilka) and Klement on November 22 and 23. And I knew where I was in time.

ꝏ

In Bratislava, I met new interrogators. They seemed bent on proving that I had been involved with the large Bratislava group called Staríček-Šmálik. Looking back now, I think they probably thought that I was their leader.

A robust chief sergeant or second lieutenant took me to the interrogation room. According to the records, I think this was O. but my brother Vlado believes this had to be D. The fact remains that one can identify this person by his appearance and the typical sayings he used such as "I... your apostle," and other various vulgar expressions. For some unknown reason, he often used the word "varnish" as in "You're only varnish!"

Typical behavior for him included grabbing a prisoner by the throat, banging the poor man's head against the wall, and then beating the prisoner's chest with his fists.

When I later had the opportunity to inspect my record, this O. was listed there as an interrogator.

It was perhaps on June 28, 1952, that is, about a year after my being arrested, that O. brought a confession for me to sign, "But there really is nothing there. I don't know why we wasted a whole year on you when you haven't confessed to anything." When I saw the confession, there really was nothing there except phrases about espionage and high treason, and it was full of broad, political comments about the Vatican.

At that time, I still did not know that they were using their current jargon and that they had instructions on how to formulate everything. From the legal point of view, it was all total nonsense, of course, since the confessions almost always lacked anything really substantial and did not prove anything. They were only a collection of political clichés.

I refused to sign the confession. It is possible that the interrogator was drunk or drugged since he instantly flew into a rage. Perhaps a few slaps in the face had usually been enough to force people to sign everything. He obviously had not expected to encounter refusal.

He began to strangle me, to beat me with his fists and smash my head against the wall. Every act of violence seemed to be allowed until eventually I fell on the floor. "So you're innocent huh! You didn't do anything, right? O.K. So write and sign this: I deny any activity which I did and I will continue to deny it."

Another meaningless and quite ludicrous sentence in terms of the law.

But in the end I signed, although later I regretted having done so. I think that on principle, I should not have accepted such lies and fabrications. We have a saying that when you give the devil a finger he seizes the whole hand. The smallest compromise may bring about the most cruel consequences and may very well prepare the way for further and more important concessions!

When they took me back to the cell I was covered with blood, so they immediately removed my cell mate. They did this no doubt so that there would be no witnesses. But later, when they discovered that this person was completely broken psychologically and actually troubled me, they brought him back.

Even though this was my first experience with this level of violent physical assault, I actually did not feel anything. Perhaps I was in such a state of shock that I was not fully conscious of the pain.

I considered the whole thing a very valuable ordeal. For hours I repeated, "Lord, you didn't disappoint us. You always promised that you would be with us, that you would never abandon us. What can I now possibly bring you as a sacrifice? Nothing hurt me. I really have nothing to offer you as a sacrifice."

Despite everything, in a sense I cherished those wounds. This was after all the only tangible, although insignificant evidence I had that I had offered Christ something.

After this interrogation I found that I had two broken ribs. I was not allowed to see a doctor but in the course of three or four weeks they healed, apparently without consequences.

A few months after this interrogator dealt with me so brutally, we heard that he had committed suicide. Almost everybody who was involved in a negative way in our case was very cruelly punished. Perhaps we ourselves would never have envisioned the punishment that O. inflicted upon himself. Colonel M., the judge in my appeals court, and colonel Dr. S., chief police doctor of Ruzyň, also committed suicide, although I must point out that Dr. S. did not record anything negative in my case.

After my first beating, when the interrogator called me in again, it was clear that he was trying to control himself. Perhaps what had happened worried him (not out of sympathy for me but only because he might get into trouble), and so he placed a more modest confession in front of me. About 50 to 80 percent of it met with my position and my answers but there were still some standard, contrived expressions. Perhaps I signed this but I do not really remember. I do know that I wanted to make it clear to him that violence did not achieve as much as normal dialogue.

ꝏ

Then Karol P. became my cell mate. I got on very well with him although I sensed that we were spiritually very different. He was Jewish and taught me Jewish prayers, so at least he had once been a believer.

We learned Hungarian songs, several Hebrew ones, and any other we could think of. They became part of my program. Sometimes, for an hour or two, I would put Hungarian, Russian, English, and other songs in alphabetical order so that I could hold as many as possible in my mind. I also endeavored to remember and complete their texts and melody. (Often these were partly my own compositions.) In this way, I arranged about forty to fifty hymns to the Virgin Mary, and about sixty to seventy Russian songs. I must say I spent many enjoyable hours humming or singing.

At that time, I also made some use of Morse code which I had learned when I was a boy scout. But when they put me in solitary confinement, I found it very difficult to reconstruct some of the letters I had forgotten. Anyone who masters this code before he is sent to prison has a great advantage.

I began to tap and reassemble the Morse alphabet with the prisoner in a neighboring cell. We replaced the long signal with two short ones close together. My neighbor signaled that he was called Sándor L., and that he would be leaving soon. They were to transfer him to Budapest since he was Hungarian.

For amusement, or in an attempt to be friendly, I signaled that I had relatives in Budapest. I gave him the address of Uncle Albín Jablonský, my mother's brother. He replied in Morse: "Don't worry, I'll do this for you. I'll bring him your greetings."

I later learned that he had actually visited them. Who knows whether or not he was only an informer. In any case, he took money, clothes, and other things from my relatives, supposedly to bring to me so that I would have an easier time in prison and be released sooner.... He was probably but a poor fellow, a con-man, or blackmailer.

Thus, I gradually learned to be more cautious.

Part IV

The Beginning of My Legal Imprisonment
The Miracle of the Smuggled Bible
Brainwashing Continues, Košice State Security Police
Hallucinations, the Three Degrees of Pain, Stalin's Death

I believe it was on August 4, 1952, on the eve of my birthday, that I was transferred to judicial imprisonment in the Bratislava Palace of Justice. Our arrest papers were there and we signed them for the first time. Up to that time our detainment had actually been illegal.

The twenty to twenty-five people from the Bratislava group stood together in a large circle in the entrance hall down on the ground floor. From where we were, it was possible to see into the upper floors.

When I was placed with my face to the wall, I tried to look to the side, and I clearly saw some of the other prisoners. Jano Gunčaga stood proudly. It was encouraging to see that they had not broken him. My brother Vlado and my brother-in-law Ferdo waved to me.

Then the most striking thing happened. Aca Šmidtová, who was quite far from me, suddenly began to shout so loudly that the whole prison could hear her, "Brothers, don't be afraid of those who can kill the body but can't kill the soul!"

About three guards lunged at her, covered her mouth and yelled out, "Are you out of your mind? How dare you! You're going to pay for this!"

And she replied, "Actually I'm not going mad at all, not in the way you guys want anyway. That's why I'm shouting."

I arrived in a judicial imprisonment cell where the rules were a little more relaxed and we were assigned new cell mates. We were not being handled any longer as if we were guinea pigs and so I had the opportunity to communicate with new people.

One of them was Janko Michalko, a Lutheran believer about twenty-five or thirty years old. He was an assistant station master from Važec. He taught us many very beautiful Lutheran hymns which were sung in a traditional Lutheran family. With time, he taught me their hymn "A Mighty Fortress Is Our God," in the old Biblical Czech.

He prayed the rosary with us, and even asked us to tell him about the Virgin Mary. He was very happy when we went over the Scriptures chapter by chapter. He taught me about the dangers that surrounded us, pointed out where the guards were, and showed me how to send out messages by hitting the radiator with spoons.

Another cell mate was older so we nicknamed him "Dad." He was called Martin Klempa, and came from Závod which at that time was one of the most important smuggling villages in Záhorie. Later, there was Šándor K. who may have been a Jew but had changed his German name.

Martin Klempa was a very rewarding cell mate. He was a typical village Catholic, pious and simple. He knew many hymns and sang them every day, in a soft, inspiring voice. We all joined in and gradually learned them. So did Janko Michalko who was Lutheran. In prison, nobody recognized any confessional differences. There was a very good ecumenical atmosphere among us, but sadly, this embracing of other religious customs was not always permanent.

From the legal aspect, the case of Martin Klempa was rather special. He was put into a large group of about thirty people among which were some who were threatened with the death penalty. His crime was that he had attempted to take people across the border.

The comrades added a connection with American spies to this accusation. In truth, the link could not be completely excluded but the motive would not have had anything to do with espionage. All the refugees wanted was to protect their lives or at least preserve their human dignity. Klempa told me how everything had ended tragically, why State Security raged at him, and why severe punishment awaited all of them.

It seems that when the whole party had gathered and was ready to cross to the other side, the leader of the group suddenly took out a machine gun from under his coat. He aimed it at the others and yelled, "Hands up, everybody! I'm from State Security! You're all under arrest! You'll all have to answer for this."

I do not know whether the next movement was deliberate or purely an instinctive reaction but Klempa's relative struck the man with the gun with his hand and shouted, "What're you doing? Have you gone mad? We're all family here, all relatives! Are you crazy?"

Then shots rang out. When the shooting stopped, two people were dead: the State Security man and a woman, also believed to be from State Security. Both had been dressed in civilian clothes.

This offense was classified in legal jargon as political or attempted murder. Some of the group received the death penalty and most of the others got very severe sentences.

"Dad" Martin was such a simple person that he had signed everything they had told him to sign without having the slightest idea of what was involved. When we asked him what he was charged with, he answered, "Weapons."

Weapons? He had had an antiquated pistol and some used up fuses for dynamite or something of the kind in his attic.

"And you signed what they gave you?"

"Of course I signed it."

"Well, O.K. But do you know what this means? All right, come on. Let's try and go through this whole thing together, step by step."

Thanks to the fact that we now had access to the Criminal Law Code, I was able to instruct him a little on how this indictment would be judged by the law. Then, I taught him how he might be able to wriggle out of it all.

Usually, the prosecutor not only forced all the defendants to confess but also obtained evidence from other people so that one betrayed the other and nobody could be set free.

At the trial, Martin Klempa was sitting about the third from the end of the whole row as he was not considered one of the main defendants. Furthermore, it was thought that his condemnation would be a very easy matter. But at his first hearing the prosecutor became aware that he had underestimated old "Dad" Martin and should have secured evidence. When they came to him they began, "You obtained a weapon?"

"What weapon?"

"That pistol you had."

"Please, that was just junk, a rusty old thing I found. I thought that the children could play with it. It couldn't be used for anything else."

The judges looked around and searched frantically but they had no expert witness or evidence of any kind. The audience began to snicker loudly.

"And what about those strings you were to use as fuses? What did you need fuses for?"

"Fuses? My wife used those strings to hang the wash. How was I supposed to know what they were for?"

"And what about the fact that you've already confessed to everything?"

"I confessed? That's the first I hear of it."

"You actually signed the confession. Isn't that your signature?"

"I'm sorry, I can't see without my glasses!"

"You didn't have any glasses then?"

"As you can see, I don't have any glasses now either."

So they gave him glasses. He took one look at the papers and denied everything.

The prosecutor raged at him, "And if I had written the death sentence there, would you also have signed that?"

"But I thought that I had to sign this. In fact I thought that I had to sign anything you gave me. You actually told me that I had to sign everything. Remember? So I signed."

Everybody burst out laughing.

In the end he was the only member of the group to be acquitted. But this was a terrible slap in the face for the prosecutor and so they did not release him although he had been duly acquitted by the court.

Then we encouraged him, "You see, 'Dad'? Now you've begun to fight. You mustn't give up. If they beat up on you or whatever else they do, you just go on repeating that you didn't have your glasses, and that you can't see."

That's how he got out of it. When he was released, he smuggled out some of my notes which he hid in his toothpaste. What is especially important is that he remembered our relationship in prison with fondness and every year he went to see my parents and encouraged and consoled them. Martin was a shoemaker and he repaired their shoes and always brought them some of his homemade wine. After my own release, we continued to meet until the day he died.

ꙮ

I also remember how, by the grace of God, the text of the New Testament reached us in prison as if by a miracle.

Jozef Slávik, a nice young man of about twenty-five, from Prievoz, I believe, was on our floor. He was accused of espionage, but considering the type of accusations prevailing at that time, I suspect that it was probably a concocted charge.

When Jozef learned through our special code that we were in prison for religious activities, he let us know that he had, hidden on him, a copy of the New Testament in the old Czech Lutheran version. During a walk, he threw it into our cell.

We had then been in prison for a year or two and had had no access to spiritual writings. Thus, we would have been delighted to read the Gospel from morning till evening and all through the night. But I was very insistent that we should also use the text in other ways. "We must divide the writings among ourselves and memorize as much as we can. Only what is in our mind cannot be taken from us!"

So we studied. I memorized ten to twelve chapters of Matthew, and others learned various texts from the Epistles or from the Acts of the Apostles. The fact that I could draw on the texts I had learned was additional spiritual ammunition for me. I added to the part of the New Testament that I had memorized by about half. And once more, I clearly felt that God was with us!

ꙮ

Whenever I had the slightest opportunity to slip or throw something to a friend, I always did so even though I risked being caught.

Then it happened. Around the beginning of January 1953, they saw me.

While walking, I had thrown Father Cibira a text from the Gospel. I believe they were chapters 18 and 19 from the Passion in the Gospel of St. John. The text was written on various scraps of paper, probably including toilet paper. I substituted Castelani's solution for ink. This was a red solution of anti-fungus medication which I had obtained from the doctor. I had shown him the peeling skin on my legs, and as a dermatologist I had diagnosed skin fungus. I mentioned that Castelani's solution was very effective, which was true. Thus, I succeeded in writing down many Gospel texts which I managed to throw to other prisoners.

Then one of the guards intercepted me. He was an otherwise very kindhearted man or at least he gave the impression that he was. (I think that he had a slightly purplish face, so perhaps he suffered from some sort of heart disease.) He may have thought we were agreeing on plots on how to answer questions or on how to commit or cover up a criminal act.

In any case he was sorry when he found he had made a mistake. But because he had already reported us, there was great alarm since we knew he could not retract his accusation. Hence, Father Cibira and I were taken before the chief.

This man was a real warden, a typical overbearing, macho type if not almost a sadist. During the investigation, the chief first began to shout at Father Cibira that he would get what he deserved for corrupting and influencing young boys (I was twenty-eight then).

I confessed that Father Cibira had not thrown me anything, but that I had thrown him something. "So, fourteen days correction!" said the chief. "Do you know what that is? You don't? Well, you'll soon find out! You're in for a nice surprise."

Correction took on various forms depending on where you were imprisoned. In Bratislava, it consisted in receiving food only once a day, and then only half a ration of bread and some slush called coffee. We were also crammed into a special cage in the middle of the cell and then had to lie on boards on the ground or on concrete.

There was an unknown cell mate with us in this crowded cage, who had allegedly called the State Security in Ruzyň "The Gestapo." His name emerges from my memory as Jozef (Sep). Father Cibira was also in the cage, and I asked him to give me some meditation and spiritual exercises to do. It was evident that the hardship we were subjected to greatly distressed him.

However, this particular punishment did not last the full fourteen days. They suddenly pulled me out of the cage and brought my personal things. such as my slippers, from the cell. When the guard handed me everything, my cell mate looked at me with envy. He thought that I was going home. I wasn't. They slapped the handcuffs on my wrists, handed me the dark glasses, and pushed me into a car.

Only then did I realize that Ferdo and Imro S. had disappeared. I knew this because at times it was possible to push open an upper tilting window in the cell and take oblique glances through the glass. Occasionally, this was enough to recognize people walking in the courtyard. A quick glance before I left the cell revealed that they were not there. I speculated for a long time on where they were. Had they been sent to another cell? Perhaps they had been released and gone home?

I was given ordinary clothes and a track suit, and for some time I thought about what was happening. Every prisoner lives with the hope of going home, "Who knows, maybe it'll be today." But when they put handcuffs and dark glasses on me, I knew that it was only a further variation of my stay in prison.

The journey by car was quite long. Two or three security officers in plain clothes traveled with me. Through cracks in the glasses, I saw that we turned south from Zvolen and went towards Detva. I mentally speculated about where we could be. Although the officers were very cautious, I still caught enough of their conversation in the car to surmise that one of their last passengers had been Imro S.

During the discussions, they suddenly began to talk to me. They said that it was a pity I was so headstrong. I think they even wanted to give me something to eat and drink. When they stopped somewhere for refreshments, they left me alone in the car without worrying about what I might attempt to do.

Finally I unexpectedly found myself in a very old building in Košice. I was put into a long cell with a man from Orava. Either he was never quite mentally healthy or he had become like this in prison.

In two days he said a total of four or five sentences. For long periods of time he simply stared into space. I mentioned to the interrogator that I was a doctor, and that in my opinion, this person was not normal. I stated that it was necessary to treat him or deal with him differently from the others. The interrogator reacted in the customary manner and roared, "He was sane enough for his criminal activities! He's got more sense than all of us put together, including you."

Once a week, they allowed us to shave with razor blades, under supervision of course.

Instead of flush toilets, the cell had a large pot which was emptied daily. The system of bucketing was quite primitive to say the least. We scrubbed and scoured and cleaned the cell every week. The prisoners enjoyed this task and looked upon it as a change of pace and the chance to do a little exercise.

But it was always very cold in there. The blankets were so thin, they were completely transparent, and gave very little warmth or none at all. The window also fitted badly. At first, we did not realize that these "accidents" were deliberate. Sometimes a prisoner came into a cell where the window had been broken in January. Then the temperature inside was the same as it was outside. At times it would even go down to below zero. Sometimes there was no blanket in the cell. When on the fifth day the prisoner complained, the interrogator would ask innocently, "Why didn't you ask for a blanket and for the window to be repaired?" Still, nothing was done about the complaint.

I tried to persuade my cell mate that we could keep each other warm at night by sleeping back to back and by sharing blankets. In such cold conditions it was practically impossible to sleep otherwise.

One night, I succeeded in convincing him but he never did so again. Either his psychological condition was the cause of his behavior or he feared reprisals if we changed the sleeping arrangements which had been assigned to us. Yet, he constantly took the better and heavier blankets for himself. In this respect at least, there was a bit of method to his madness.

ꕥ

I had a pretty typical interrogator. Lieutenant B. was between twenty-eight and thirty-two years old. He was later promoted to first lieutenant.

He began questioning in a very arrogant fashion. Like most of those who questioned me for the first time, he asked which people I knew and then went on with other similar inquiries. I hesitated to tell him which physicians I knew. Therefore, at first, as was customary, I recited known names according to the medical hierarchy of various faculties and expert institutes. But I realized that this was a mistake since the interrogator noticed that I had left out Dr. Šesták. I was deprived of food for omitting his name.

I could not figure out this interrogator's strategy. First he took away food to weaken the prisoner. This was followed on the second day by beatings, kicks to the knees and shins, and the order to stand. Later this last torment became known among prisoners by the term "statue." During the day and at night the guard provided variety by forcing me to stand first on one leg, then on the other. When I walked without being forced to do so, they were again enraged.

Another interrogator was about thirty, blond, curly haired, tall and strong. He always smoked a pipe. He also made me stand but he was more phlegmatic and did not get as angry as the one who was either a lieutenant or, I think, a second lieutenant.

ꝏ

When I stood for a long time, my feet would begin to swell. I would run a fever, tremble, and experience hallucinations or obsessions. For the first time, I became aware of how they could manipulate the mind of a person in order to bring these on and cause a mental breakdown.

I know that my own perceptions were then clear but erroneous. It is difficult to say whether I endured true hallucinations or merely obsessions. I think they were rather something in between since I maintained the conscious feeling that they were not true, but false. For example, I "heard" bells ring, when I knew they could not be ringing at midnight or two o'clock in the morning. I "saw" birds and many bugs fly around the spy hole. They sometimes appeared to be in pairs or holding hands.

During long interrogations I also lost control of my muscles and displayed odd forms of behavior. I experienced some loss of self-control. I laughed a lot, especially during lengthy interrogations, mostly when I was hardly aware of what was going on around me. This upset the interrogators the most as they always thought that I was either laughing at them, or their methods were not effective and they should try harder.

The interrogation "mill" went on day and night, night and day. Looking back, I think that once I stood for as many as 50 hours while the interrogators changed shifts after three to six hours. A dark second lieutenant, a soldier called Medik, sometimes allowed me to go back to the cell. Once he let me go there when my feet had already begun to swell. I was shaking badly and had muscle fever. Then, they were not able to wake me up. I slept or remained unconscious.

And again they began to hit me. There was a dark interrogator with a little moustache who was perhaps also a second lieutenant. He was well groomed and wore a gold watch. I could clearly smell alcohol on his breath. I think that to accomplish such dirty deeds they had to build up their courage with alcohol.

He forced me to do "squats," that is, to remain in a crouching position for a long time, or to assume the "curtain" position, which involved standing obliquely against the wall, supported only by the ends of my fingers.

I never thought that it was possible to bear so much pain.

I reflected on the psychological stages a person in an extreme state of pain and suffering goes through before reaching the limit of his endurance.

I identified a first stage where a person still defends himself and attempts to hang on for a moment, even for a second. It is already almost unbearable, but he summons enough inner strength to allow him to hold on for another minute or half a minute at any cost.

Then comes the second stage when he is so exhausted that he ceases to care. His body then stops shielding itself, submits, collapses, and he loses consciousness.

That is when many give up, including those who have bravely resisted for a long time. But now they have stopped caring about whether they say anything or not. Discernment is no longer possible. Conversely, for some, this stage may be the best. If a person is aware that it's all the same to him, why then should he say or sign anything?

This was precisely the best motivation for me: I would be silent and protect others from similar suffering, since I was already so destroyed that nothing more could be of any consequence to me.

There is also a third stage of suffering, a time of total breakdown or collapse, when the body gives up and a loss of consciousness occurs sometimes followed by death, and so the end of pain.

ℰ𝒪

The depositions began to be aimed at the people in Košice and its surrounding areas, for example at Dr. Altman, our old friend and a converted

Jew. At the mention of all new names, I was either silent or said that I did not know them.

Then I saw how they worked the documents. At first, only a slight deviation from the true statement was recorded so that the prisoner would still sign it. Then they increased the deviations. They exaggerated, dramatized, criminalized, and demonized. Then, I still did not understand the significance of the changes, when instead of the word "Church" they wrote "Vatican," or instead of "meeting" they inserted "anti-state meeting" or "anti-state act." Nevertheless there was already sufficient reason for me to stop signing the accounts. This was not always because the entire content was untrue, but it was to protest against the deliberate distortion of the answers.

Because of my noncompliance, they cut off my food. But they strongly endeavored to maintain an impression of legality, and so they did not forget to emphasize that this punishment was not due to my refusal to sign, as this, they claimed, was my affair. The reason given was my alleged rudeness towards members of the Ministry of the Interior.

This was so obviously a trumped-up charge that it bordered on the absurd. This miserable, beaten, and completely powerless prisoner had not even risked looking askance at anybody, let alone of being impudent or of launching an attack on anyone.

I am glad that I personally endured all these things. If, from the beginning, I had refused to stand or to walk, perhaps they would have beaten or crippled me or perhaps even killed me, as sometimes happened at that time, and I would not have acquired so much experience. I would not have learned to defend myself. I could not have observed these things, testified to them, or prepared other people for similar attacks.

I believed that the Lord had sent me there. He had given me appropriate medical and psychological experience, ability and knowledge, and through an unusually prolonged interrogation period with almost all its coercive variations and diversity, I received a sufficiently long preparation so that I could adapt to anything. Therefore I repeated again and again, "I am really God's probe, God's laboratory. I'm going through all of this so I can help others and the Church."

It was in Košice that for the first time they accused us of smuggling written materials through secret channels to the Soviet Union. I know that I then signed a very short statement of about one and a quarter pages but which included the hard fought for sentence, "I deny that what I did was motivated by politics or espionage." My resistance was once again rewarded with the withholding of food and all the other retaliatory measures for a few days in order to soften me up. The interrogator in this case was not Lieutenant B. but someone new.

A captain in a long coat was very familiar to me. Perhaps I knew him when I was studying medicine. When I protested against the beatings, he responded by preventing me from sitting in my cell. I could only sit three times a day at meals, for five to ten minutes.

Then, I wasn't allowed to sleep. The whole night was spent being awakened at hourly intervals. I then had to stand or wash or walk. I hardly slept at all since I constantly expected another wake-up call, banging, or some other similar commotion.

I was continually in a state of high to painful physical and psychological tension and suffered severe spasms. I was very encouraged when I found out from the tapping of prison Morse code that Vlado Jukl was there. He was in good psychological condition although they had deprived him of blankets so that he would freeze.

Screams and beatings were heard from everywhere, every night. We also often heard women's cries and the pained voices of old people.

From the depositions I was shown, and the questions asked, I think that Bishop Čársky must also have been there somewhere, or perhaps he was only brought there for interrogation. J. B. B., Ferdo, Imro S., and other people I knew were certainly there. When tapping with Vlado Jukl, we could easily recognize our motto: "I have the strength for everything through him who empowers me" (Phil. 4:13).

When disputing some answers, I was very much consoled by Vlado's denial that we met with Cyril Stavěl in Prague and other related questions. It proved that they had not broken him.

Then I got a new cell mate, Štefan Š., a teacher. He had tried to navigate through the rough waters of anti-religious persecution after February 1948. Even though it went against his personal convictions, he had eventually withdrawn his children from religious education.

In prison, he repeated almost all day long, "God is punishing me for that." He strengthened my awareness that I was not alone, and in a whisper, we sang together "Rejoice Queen of Heaven," with the same joy with which we had sung it outside.

I taught him about interrogations since I had a lot more experience in that field than he did. He told me of the shock he had felt when upon arrival in his cell, he had met with an unknown very thin remnant of a man who assured him that he was the old but strong Belo Jenčík, his favorite priest in Košice. The priest was in such an exhausted and emaciated state that Štefan had not recognized him.

ꕤ

In the midst of all of this, we learned from other cell mates that Stalin was seriously ill. He died on March 10, 1953. This was confirmed by the black bands worn on the uniforms of the guards but mainly by the complete reversal in the behavior of State Security.

There was a period of uncertainty. They no longer woke me up at night, and when a prisoner automatically stood up during the night as he had previously been told to do, they muttered a vulgar expression which in effect meant, "Forget it!"

The food was more plentiful and they kept asking, "Do you want a second helping? Do you want more?" We were totally astonished. These coarse people had become more humane overnight. We were even allowed to take baths more frequently.

ꕤ

On March 12, almost immediately after Stalin's death, we were moved back to Ruzyň in Prague. This was my second "convoy of fear" in a closed bus with very small cells. But for me it was far less terrifying and provoked little uncertainty. I had been through this before.

Everything has a tremendous effect on you the first time. Tanks and poison gas had such an effect when they were first used in battle. But man's resilience is such that he gets used to anything, however terrible, when he looks into the essence of the thing and sees the limits of its possibilities. Thus the initial moment of surprise, the fear of the unknown, of something hidden and terrifying, fades away. Soldiers have a saying, "Foreseen and known danger is not true danger."

On this journey it was very cold. We traveled in sub-zero temperatures for two whole days. During one stop, when the guards got refreshments (not for us obviously), I tried to go to confession. The Košice priest, Belo Jenčík, was in the neighboring cupboard-like cell. He would not hear my confession since under the circumstances, the secrecy of the confessional might have been broken, but he said that he gave me a general absolution.

Through the walls of the iron cells, we encouraged one another, "Hang on, brothers and sisters. The feast of Saint Joseph (March 19) is almost here. He will rescue us. Just like he did last year when they seemed to have forgotten us." This referred to the time when they had deliberately left the prisoners in isolation without any contact, not even with an interrogator, to give them the impression they had been forgotten and that there would be no end to their predicament.

But the interrogations had resumed precisely on the day of the feast of St. Joseph and had continued as usual.

During one stop on the way to Ruzyň, I began to whisper and signal to the other prisoners, "Calling Catholic Action!" There were two girls somewhere nearby. They were also imprisoned for religious reasons but they did not dare answer me. We obviously knew nothing about who anybody was inside the "submarine" or who was outside in the corridor. But Vlado Jukl, Imro S., and Belo Jenčík answered.

The guards reacted immediately, "What're you talking about?" I believe it was Belo who quickly answered, "Somebody said that he's hungry and cold." To our surprise one of the guards brought him some bread.

I turned to Professor H., who was also on the bus, and reminded him, "During interrogations we don't know each other." But he stated that he could not pretend he didn't know me since he and my father had been good friends.

He added that one could be silent only within certain limits and about very particular matters, that is, one could only go so far in refusing to answer.

Part V

Back to the Familiar Ruzyň, Spiritual Weightlessness
Sophisticated Torturers, Final Refusal to Answer Questions
Stool Pigeons and Informers
State Security Leadership in Bratislava Is Supposedly Wiped Out
The Principle of Contradiction

Two days later when we arrived in Ruzyň, we were absolutely frozen from the cold of the trip.

The system in Ruzyň was already familiar to me. Some fear remained, but I was much calmer as I now had experience and knew what to expect. I remember that after arriving, I made my bed neatly and immediately worked out a spiritual program made up of various exercises which I endeavored to complete most faithfully according to St. Ignatius. The only difference was that I spread them over forty days since Jesus had been in the desert for that length of time.

I went over the life and Passion of Christ as is set down in the Gospels. This fit in very well with Easter. I can honestly say that these were my most beautiful meditations ever on the Passion, the Easter Mystery, and the Resurrection. The meditations usually lasted about one and a half hours but with good concentration, I could extend them, as I was carried along by my enthusiasm and the love and joy of the Holy Spirit.

One could actually compare this religious experience in the confined world of the cell to a spiritual state of weightlessness, in some ways very similar to the physical weightlessness familiar to astronauts.

Sometimes it lasted for several days. When that happened, I was released, not only from contact with time, space, and matter, but also from the underlying but ever present atmosphere of pressure, terror, fear, and uncertainty. The light of supernatural love against which my persecutors vainly struggled radiated and enlightened me. I delighted in astonishment at God's eternal truth and the infinite beauty of the Divine mysteries. And changes ensued.

The crises with breathing difficulties, the times when I would struggle desperately to oppose my torturers, when I would flare up or cry out in protest, those moments when I wanted to scream or escape, punch the walls or explode, became increasingly rare. In the end they occurred only about once every four or six weeks.

I noticed that crises seemed to arise much more frequently when a prisoner enjoyed relatively good physical conditions, that is, when the quality of food improved, when he was able to sleep peacefully, or was physically fit. At the height of his suffering, a prisoner did not usually encounter such crises. Then, the human spirit's and body's only objectives were centered on holding out just a little while longer.

ꟃ

After about fourteen days, I was summoned once more for interrogation. Unfortunately this coincided with a precise time when I was feeling rather impatient. The interrogator was holding the collected documents from previous interrogations and was studying the statements of witnesses and other fellow prisoners.

My Košice interrogator, wearing the uniform of a lieutenant, was there also. In Ruzyň, there seemed to exist a stricter discipline for members of State Security. So I reminded him that in Košice I had been beaten and asked whether this had been in accordance with the law.

"Who could have beaten you in Košice?" he asked.

Then I looked him in the eye, a rather bold thing to do under the circumstances, and said, "You, for one."

All he managed to say was, "Yeah? Well, you know how cocky you were at the time. . . . "

He obviously did not remember. I concluded that as a general rule, in certain interrogation rooms, they probably used beatings or some other kind of torture routinely, on almost everybody, so that it was then impossible for them to remember what had happened in any specific case. They thought of us as so worked over, weak and utterly defeated, that it was very unlikely that the idea of one of us complaining or registering a protest ever even entered their minds.

These interrogators, criminals that they were, lied with such impudence and arrogance that the victim himself thought he might have suffered a loss of memory, if not a more serious mental or physical nervous breakdown.

The head of our interrogation team, a first lieutenant or captain (he was promoted again later), was an older man. This was the same interrogator I had had in Ruzyň. According to the signatures in the records I later had access to, he was called K. People like him never touched me and always smiled.

When I complained that somebody had struck me, or that I had been beaten during interrogations in Bratislava and in Košice, they even wrote out a report and claimed that they would intervene. But they were actually the main guilty ones, the cold-blooded and calculating authors of oppression.

The enraged lieutenant who beat or kicked me was perhaps a very minor player. He may even have been forced to do the dirty work. It was possible that real pressure from his boss drove him to take refuge in alcohol and violence. When the chief demanded results and the prisoner obstinately refused to cooperate in fulfilling what the mighty expected of him, what else could the interrogator do? He was just as dependent on authorities as we were and so in frustration he would lose his self-control and revert to blows in the hope of speeding up matters.

Once or twice he gets disgustingly drunk. However, his superiors praise him for his successes, so he becomes accustomed to dishing out beatings and becomes hardened. The top people, those who never so much as touched us and dealt with us with kid gloves, were actually the ones who bore the true responsibility for the inhumanity.

ℵ

I noticed that as a consequence of my imprisonment, I was gradually developing certain health problems and complexes. Excessive salivating was added to the constant shivering, the trembling of my fingers, hands and whole body and the persistent feelings of hunger and cold. I would feel hungry for hours before every meal and as eating time slowly approached, the secretion of saliva would begin and then steadily increase until it became uncontrollable. This would go on endlessly.

A urinary breakdown followed. Perhaps this was due to having all my movements constantly monitored with the lookouts peering into my cell as often as three times a minute. I lived in a fish bowl in an open toilet.

It gradually came to me that although I was not beaten here, I cooperated to a limited extent during interrogations. They finally had something they could use and, as can easily be imagined, they readily took advantage of it. They were well aware that although a prisoner might not say anything new, he at least confirmed what others had confessed and was bound to trip himself up sooner or later.

The food got a little better but there were still no exercises outdoors. At night they did not wake me up as often. There was only one light shining so I at least got a light sleep. Perhaps it was precisely because of these mild improvements that I sought a pretext to break off or minimize contact with them.

During meditation, I asked the Holy Spirit for discernment and enlightenment. I prayed with particular fervor around June 21, the day of the feast of St. Aloysius, the patron saint I had had since I was a boy. I asked for strength so that I could tell the truth and refute lies, and courage and fortitude to otherwise cease communicating with my tormentors. This last seemed to me to be the best way to challenge the inhumanity which engulfed me.

Finally my favorite feast day arrived, the birth of John the Baptist, June 24, 1953. Not long before, B., the interrogator from Košice, began to question me. As usual, when I did not want to sign some document, he shouted and threatened to throw the typewriter at my head. But compared with his previous methods, his verbal threats were nothing to worry about. I still refused to tell him anything, so he sent me back to the cell so that I could think it all over. Otherwise, "You'll see what'll happen to you. You'll never see the sun or anything else again. . . . "

ஐ

After the feast of St. John the Baptist, I dictated my final statement explaining the reasons why I refused to answer any more questions. The interrogator did not, as was customary, print out several copies of this document. He probably destroyed it as it was not added to my record and I never saw it again.

The statement went something like this: "I refuse to continue answering because I see that the whole interrogation process is nonsensical. State Security is in no way interested in finding out the truth. Its sole objective is the destruction of the Church. Those involved in this operation seek answers but if they find them unsatisfactory, they adapt and totally distort them. The prisoner can say whatever he likes, but the interrogators will write their own final account."

When I definitively severed all verbal contact with them, I had already come to terms with death. I no longer thought that I would ever be set free, especially since I was often threatened with the death penalty and the rope. My brother Vlado reported to me later that the comrades had stated they would have to execute somebody from the lay apostolate as a deterrent. It seemed that religious circles were increasing so rapidly that State Security could not control them. According to rumors, I was the one who had been singled out for execution.

Consequently, I lived in a state of constant expectation concerning how they would attempt to break my determination to remain silent. I waited with clenched teeth for what I thought would happen and wondered whether I would be able to stick it out. Sometimes, I was actually quite curious. I assumed that others before me had also taken such a drastic step. I felt a certain duty, as God's probe, to find out what had happened to the people who had bravely refused to say a word from the very beginning. What could they have done to them?

Strange as it may seem, I discovered that at times like these, a prisoner thinks much more clearly. The reason, apparently, is his isolation. He has no other stimuli, and so is forced to concentrate on himself for long periods at a time. Thinking then becomes unusually easy. It is exuberant, I would almost say joyful. The cause could be the absence of fear when the prisoner finally faces and accepts the certainty of death by execution. But there is also the spiritual approach of the prisoner. He can change undernourishment into fasting and thus look upon this forced hardship and all other sufferings as opportunities for purification.[18]

Ultimately, I definitively quarreled with the interrogator who to me was the representative of the persecutors of the Church. This shouting match, and the burning of bridges behind me, cutting off all possibility of escape, reminds me of a scene in an adventure movie: there stands the knight in front of the castle, surrounded by a horde of enemies. He slashes the ropes of the drawbridge, thus effectively making retreat impossible and is thereby left with two options only: he will either be killed, or he will cut through them.

When I returned to the cell, I was surprised to see a parcel waiting for me. By chance they had allowed me to have this package at the exact moment when I was most set against them, when I felt totally immune to their tactics. (Was this the carrot-and-stick strategy or a failure of the system?)

Apparently, the furious interrogator, Lieutenant B. from Košice, was reprimanded because of the position I had taken. They did not assign him to me any longer. They considered that I was silent because he had muddled things up. The whole mess was his fault. It is possible that they allowed me to have the parcel, which was in complete opposition to B.'s methods, with the thought that if the going was not so rough, I would be more cooperative.

The first few days passed in great tension. Then, as I fully expected, all hell broke loose!

They began to rotate about fifteen to twenty interrogators to question me.

In the beginning it was one interrogation after the other. They threw everything they had at me. They tried their whole range of methods: the courteous, the aggressive, the coarse, the cynical. They used threats of every kind and added more and more questions. More people from the Czech border region were brought into the discussion: Tonči Hofmanová, Lída Kopecká, Karel Komárek, and others. When all these new names came up, I clearly saw that retreat was no longer a possibility. I did not want to hurt anybody and because I was unaware of what they knew and did not know, there was only one choice left. I absolutely had to refuse to answer. There was no turning back.

The interrogators reacted with shouts and attempts at intimidation. "I didn't ask you whether or not you refused to answer! I couldn't care less. That's of no interest to me! What I want to know is whether you know Karel Komárek!" And so it went.

They tried to maintain contact by asking simple questions like, "When were you born?" But I was nothing if not consistent. My usual comeback was, "I refuse to answer." To tell the truth, the whole situation often seemed terribly asinine, senseless, and even absurd to me.

I often heard statements such as, "In the fall we had K. H. Frank here."[19] He sat here just like you, and he couldn't remember anything either. But that didn't help him. Now he's finished. He was still. . . . " This last sentence was accompanied by a meaningful gesture of hanging and wrenching of the neck, along with the appropriate screech of course.

One thing is rather fascinating. From the moment I absolutely repudiated them I felt that they could not hurt me anymore. Some limited themselves to casual browbeating to trip me up if I ever spoke. Others lunged at me and grabbed me by the neck or collar. Apparently, experience had taught them that when a prisoner stood his ground and displayed such desperate determination, they could not make him change his mind. They could only kill him.

A month after the final breaking off of contact and my unwillingness to even give them my own name, I received better food and rations. Perhaps this was after I had applied for a lung X-ray. There could have been something suspicious on the X-ray.

Interestingly enough, this improvement came about immediately after a guard mocked me when he saw me praying. (Sometimes I would join my hands and pray very openly.) But this time, even though the guards assured me that "God can't help you," they opened the door at once and I received an increased amount of food. . . .

ꟹ

Then, they changed tactics. I was moved and, much against my will, was assigned a new cell mate. I fully expected that they would plant an informer in my cell since they could get nothing out of me. But this time, as might be assumed, they did it more skillfully.

What is the best way to extract information from a prisoner with the help of a mole? When they first leave him alone for one, two, three, or more months, the solitude weighs heavily on the prisoner from the very beginning. He needs to talk to someone. But if they put in the plant or informer immediately, the investigated prisoner would very quickly find out. A liar almost always gets tangled up during repeated conversations on a variety of subjects. A connection with the interrogators can't be perfectly hidden.

I think that the most dangerous technique is when the interrogators pick out a frail and weak person from among the prisoners, one they can probably break and win over. This is easy to understand. The maneuver is based on solidarity among those who are persecuted.

With such a person it is impossible to uncover anything at first. One only knows that the planted prisoner is a little feeble, weary, and tearful. Because of this apparent vulnerability, the other cell mate is more willing to open up. Compassion becomes a trap. After months of constraining silence, it can be difficult to stop the flow of words and confidential conversations can so easily be overheard.

Sometimes two methods were combined. First they eavesdropped and then they took the planted prisoner for a grilling. They put pressure on him and endeavored to persuade him (or both him and his cell mate) to cooperate with promises of various improvements, a reduced sentence, or even release. All one had to do was to inform on the behavior, confidential admissions, or messages of the other. When they chose such fragile and easily assailed people, they usually succeeded.

In more serious cases, the planting of professional State Security officers was not excluded. These men either paid for their own transgressions in this manner or benefited from extraordinary rewards and promotion.

I would also like to mention the significant effect that the cell itself had on the prisoner. When he lost his freedom for the first time or came from another prison, he initially found the new cell very depressing. Fear of the unknown accentuated this feeling. A cell is full of special terrors. The detainee might even believe (and this is not entirely imaginary) that some sort of special radiation emanated from the walls inside the cell.

A prisoner always experienced particular anxiety and uncertainty when confronted with a change.

But his new lodging exerts this dispiriting effect solely in the beginning. When a prisoner has breathed the air in the cell and remained in it a whole day, a month, or a year, he knows every spider and beetle and every scratch that is there. Indeed, he even knows how many steps there are to the window.... In short he's in a familiar environment. After an interrogation, he is greatly relieved when he can return to his cell. It is his home.

Thus, I came to a new cell where I saw an empty-looking, thin, pale man with sad, apologetic, dim eyes. As I later discovered, this expression was typical of all long-term prisoners, especially those who had been in solitary confinement.

This was Mikuláš H., also known as S. Š. (German surname), a major in State Security, who worked mainly in the foreign department, but evidently also checked into all other matters concerning interrogations. He was a Jew who had converted, although more for pragmatic reasons than anything else. By becoming a Christian, he hoped to avoid being victimized by the persecution of Jews in the Slovak State. He had probably never really come close to anything Catholic. But his time spent in solitary confinement may have been instrumental in drawing him to the Catholic religion.

When I first spoke with him, he was not able to stop the tears. He cried like a baby and kept repeating, "Both the party and my friends have mistreated me. I've been sitting here for more than two years, staring into space. I've no hope that it'll ever end."

I am certain that God himself gave me this cell mate since I needed very much to feel shame at my impatience mingled with conceit at how long I had sat in such hopelessness. I occasionally theorized that I had little luck and that I had to expect imprisonment until the day I died or until the end of the regime.[20] And sometimes, I practically boasted that I had been under interrogation for nine months, as if I had set some sort of record. And Mikuláš had been here for two years!

But in the midst of such despair I had to admit I was still in relatively good condition. This was first and foremost due to my faith and the help of God.

Mikuláš turned out to be one of my most helpful cell mates during the period of interrogation. We immediately began a common program. He slowly freed himself of his obsession with the unknown and his inability to express himself articulately. Together, we began to make good use of our time and we studied. We concentrated on languages, especially Hungarian, but we also tackled German and even Hebrew. (As a Jew, he had been an assistant or cantor at Jewish services.) Then followed various discussions or debates.

The most beautiful evenings were those we spent sharing memories. The focal point in our daily program was the telling of our life stories, not from year to year, but more along the lines of a day-to-day basis, and at times hour to hour. It was then that I understood that the greatest, the most engrossing, and the most gripping drama of all, is the life of every ordinary individual. It provides much unexpected beauty and fascination and is most educational.

This sharing immediately created a different atmosphere in our cell. We knew instinctively what we could and could not allow during communication in this environment. We also estimated the chances of success of one or another of our protests when we tried to demand our rights.

It was perhaps two to four weeks after they began to call Mikuláš for interrogations when they most certainly asked him especially about me. And yet, although I supposed that this quite clearly was the case, I continued to trust him. By this time my intuition was considerably attuned to the people who were reliable and those who were not.

He admitted that he was considering writing a book with the title "The Conversion of a Man." It was to be his own life story including his decision to return to the Faith. He related how after his baptism he had completely distanced himself from the Church and if my memory serves me right, after 1945 he had totally abandoned all belief in God. This is indeed probable as at one time he served as a high ranking member of State Security.

He also described the experiences of his colleagues. One, a certain first lieutenant G., a Jew with a German surname, came to State Security headquarters from the training of State Security interrogators in the Soviet Union. With great self-confidence, G. boasted, "Now I know exactly how I can make any one of you confess to high treason or espionage in one hour flat." And he began to acquaint his colleagues with the so-called "discussion and persuasion" method which was the norm during interrogation sessions where strong-arm tactics and coercion were par for the course.

They had been using this approach in the Soviet Union for decades. The Russian comrades claimed without hesitation that a person would rationalize his actions and confess to anything in a final desperate attempt to hang on to whatever he could still get out of life or at the very least to protect his family. The method was so effective that the prisoner was prepared to admit to spying, high treason, and the worst crimes, even though in doing so he knew he was likely to receive the death penalty.

Mikuláš added, "Ironically, I later interrogated this very same First Lieutenant G. during confrontation sessions. He was then the same wretched prisoner I am now." And it was his turn to confess to treachery and undercover work as he had depicted others had confessed to him.

I do not remember all the names of the interrogators who had undergone the same agony they had inflicted upon others. I only know that there were many of them.

I think that he mentioned Matej B., a name borrowed from a famous Slovak historical figure. Originally Matej may also have had a German name. He was very well known as a coarse, sadistic, and very cruel interrogator. (He questioned Vlado Jukl in 1946, and wrenched his nose so badly that it immediately bled profusely.) Mikuláš said that he had also later met this same Matej during confrontations. He was then a totally destroyed, trembling old man who hardly had a single tooth left. His breath was incredibly foul because everything in his mouth was festering. Matej, the former interrogator, shivered and quaked with fear.

He had suffered the fate described in Psalm 7:

> Sinners conceive iniquity; pregnant with mischief,
> they give birth to failure.
> They open a hole and dig it deep,
> but fall into the pit they have dug.
> Their mischief comes back upon themselves;
> their violence on their own heads. (15–17)

These experiences also confirm the old Slovak saying, "He who digs a hole for another, will fall into it himself."

I remember that some of our fellow prisoners knew of people in solitary confinement, including supposedly a former commander of Ruzyň, who spent the whole day beating their heads against the wall and crying, "This is how the Lord God is punishing me for having cooperated with this monstrous regime," or "... for being too frightened to do anything against this evil."

It was from a cell mate that I later got some very shocking information about what went on behind the scenes of this effective, oppressive system.

He had previously shared a cell with a former high-ranking member of State Security who had contributed to the strategy of systematic repression of which Solzhenitsyn later gave the best analysis. At the time of his greatest suffering, this one-time Security officer had admitted,

> Some people think our repression is directed against our main enemies. This is certainly true, but most of all it is concerned with the seizure of absolute power.
>
> If we arrest and kill only those who work against us, who collect weapons and have radio transmitters, others would simply protect themselves and make sure they wouldn't get caught. But this was not our main objective. We wanted to make everybody, even the innocent, shake with fear both day and night. No one was to feel secure even if they avoided all political resistance or power struggle. We wanted to be undisputed lords and masters.
>
> Supreme power recognizes no limits. To have the ultimate control over all requires keeping everyone trembling in anxiety and fear and seeking our approval. It means forcing those who want to save themselves to report any sign of disagreement or dissenting opinion to us. It involves terrifying people to the extent that no one feels safe and no one trusts anyone.
>
> To accomplish this, we necessarily have to arrest and destroy many innocent people, including our own. Everybody! Everybody has to live in terror. All must come to believe that it is better to hand over a father, a brother, or a husband, if that allows you to save yourself.

℘

From similar sources, I also learned the very revealing story of how the members of State Security in Prague destroyed the leadership of State Security in Bratislava during the "White Legion" affair.[21]

Gradually, we the imprisoned, the interrogated, and the condemned learned that in the course of an internal struggle for position and power, various past members of the Bratislava State Security were accused either of being members of the "White Legion," or of high treason, espionage, bourgeois nationalism. They also received severe sentences.[22] We were then able to witness divine justice with our own eyes.[23]

Thus I heard how State Security in Slovakia and especially in Bratislava actually worked. State Security from the Prague contingent endeavored to interfere in every way possible in the affairs of State Security in Slovakia so that they could bring in their own people, and exercise control in Slovakia.

My informant explained how Prague had finally accomplished this. A mysterious person had come to Bratislava one day and approached a certain subordinate officer, Lieutenant Sýkora (not his real name). He identified himself, and stated that he was from the highest levels, the General Secretary of the Communist Party, and the Minister of Security. He flattered Lieutenant Sýkora by stating that the Party had great confidence in him, then asked whether Sýkora was willing to accomplish certain tasks which might at first sight appear to be incomprehensible and unreasonable.

Lieutenant Sýkora snapped to attention and promised straightaway to do everything which was asked of him. He obviously looked forward to a great career or a substantial reward. But whatever form the future compensation would take, he was convinced that the party would certainly make it worth his while. In answer to the stranger's query, Sýkora confirmed that he also knew a couple of totally reliable people who would perform any task without asking any embarrassing questions. Every interrogator had several of these comrades, real killers, whom he could trust completely.

Upon hearing this, the comrade from the Prague headquarters pulled out a long list of names and announced, "The order of the Party is that all these people be arrested by this evening. This must be done quietly and without any fuss. They must all be told to submit their resignations immediately. And you are not to question any of this. You must trust the party."

When Sýkora saw the list his face turned ashen. It contained almost all of the Bratislava representatives and functionaries, starting with the Commanding Officer. But he quickly regained his composure and resolutely said, "Fine, comrade! I'll arrange everything. You can relax. It'll all be done without a single shot being fired, without any disturbance or riot or any other sort of problem. You can count on me."

And with the utmost skill, he proceeded to put his plan into action. He announced on the office radio that he was conducting a fire-arms security check. He stated that designated officers would collect all personal weapons because they had to be cleaned and marked with identification numbers. Everyone was to hand over their weapons which would be kept for about two hours.

The men assigned to this task proceeded calmly from room to room and from office to office, and each officer gave up his machine-gun, pistol, or whatever other weapon he had. Then, two or three agents, followed by another two, went to each individual room, and ordered people to extend their hands. They slapped handcuffs on them and then assembled everyone in the same underground room where these people were accustomed to torturing others. After a while, dozens of members of State Security, from the Commanding Officer to the executive officers, had been arrested.

When the agent from Prague arrived, Sýkora declared proudly, "Comrade, the orders of the party have been executed. All of the one hundred (or one hundred and twenty) people have been secured here and not one single shot was fired."

The comrade from Prague replied, "The Party will never forget you, Comrade Sýkora. Now, let's see your hands." Before he realized what had happened, Sýkora wore handcuffs himself and was forced to join the others. "The wage of the devil is hell since the devil has nothing else to offer." Mikuláš had personally experienced such events which was why he wished to return to God.

☙

Among the State Security men and guards, there were always some who were more humane than others. I remember these beautiful exceptions. One younger guard always repeated: "Cheer up! Things will get better. You'll see." Another time, he encouraged me, "Come on. You're an old hand at this. You can still laugh and sing." Since singing was forbidden, I mostly hummed silently, so that the angry guards would not bellow at me and beat me up. They were very allergic to any kind of laughter or song.

Occasionally a tiny spark of compassion would flicker from under the ashes of this bottomless hell. I seem to remember one good and decent State Security woman. She was a nurse, very dark, perhaps Romany, and not at all good looking, rather the opposite if the truth be told. But she was very kind.

The attractive female nurses were often terribly conceited and cynical. In Ruzyň, there was a tall, plump, woman doctor, whom we named Xantipa. I had arthritis in my knee, and a damaged meniscus with blockages so that sometimes my knee stuck and I could not straighten it. When I experienced strong pains and asked to see her, she did not even bother to come into the cell. Through the spy hole in the door she shouted, "You have knee problems? Well you're not the only one! So do I!" and she slammed the flap shut. I felt shame then, not only for the medical profession, but because I myself was a doctor.

Others displayed certain signs of sympathy. One guard, a barber whose rank I do not remember, had rather dark hair. His skin had a bluish tint to it, and he had difficulty breathing, which may have indicated he had cardiac problems. Although he wore a State Security uniform, he always worked with prisoners gently, as if he were shaving the President. The other guards made fun of him, "So you'll waste another fifteen minutes on this guy and you'll probably even want to use shaving lotion?"

"Right! He sure could use it."

The decent people who sometimes crossed our paths were the ones who provided us with hope, solidarity, and compassion.

ဢ

I will never forget a confrontation which I had with Julka B. B., during one particular question round. This followed a comment my cell mate had made concerning a woman's loud and wretched moaning and sobbing which he had heard as he had started out for the courtyard for a walk.

Julka and I were to be interrogated but I do not remember who was to go first. Both of us were blindfolded. When they took away the towels from our eyes, she saw me, began to tremble, and looked away. She then slowly repeated the memorized phrases about the Vatican espionage which I allegedly had organized in Košice. When I was allowed to speak, I protested at once that I had been solely involved in religious activity and had had nothing to do with politics or espionage. She immediately turned to me in astonishment, an uncomprehending look on her face. It was clear that she thought there must be something terribly wrong with me mentally since I still dared to speak out like this. Yet, I was only stating the truth.

She was completely unbalanced. Nevertheless, after repeated grillings from the interrogator who did not hesitate to press for responses which he cleverly and forcefully suggested, she affirmed, perhaps more out of listlessness than anything else, that she did not want to change any of her answers. It is highly probable that she was not even fully aware of what was going on nor of what it was that she was actually signing. However, when she appeared before the court, she then performed very courageously. In spite of the manipulation of the interrogators, she finally appeared to have grasped the gravity of the situation.

This is but one example of what shocked me the most. What upset me even more than their unceasing efforts to convict me was what they had done to people like Julka. Some of my brothers and sisters had been so thoroughly torn apart and broken that they could no longer distinguish between reality and fiction. How had our jailers managed to bring them to this point?

At that time, another very standard part of the strategy for depressing the prisoners and demolishing their resistance was to give them forged letters from their wives. For example, "the wife" would write that she was pregnant, which meant of course that she had been unfaithful to the prisoner. But he would generously forgive her and consistently write back that he accepted everything, he allowed anything, that she must not risk killing the foetus. The phony letters would ultimately claim that she had had an abortion. Only later would the prisoner discover the truth about the letters.

On her next visit, the prisoner's wife would express shock and ask her own questions, "What's the matter with you? What are you talking about? What affair? What baby? Nothing like that ever happened! Where in the world did you get that idea? Is it possible that what they told me is true, that you've lost your mind?" Then the prisoner would realize that not only were the letters pure fabrications but that the comrades had convinced his family that he was mad.

They treated me in a similar fashion when they showed me a supposedly detailed confession from Dr. S. about our so-called visit to the "Deuxième Bureau," the espionage headquarters in Paris. This was clearly a document which had been written by experts. In fact, Dr. S. would not even have known where the espionage headquarters was located nor what it was called since this was very alien to his own sphere of interest. But the specialists in this sort of thing had drafted the text in such a manner that in the end he actually signed the confession. Challenged by the type of details which were mentioned in the document, I myself slowly began to doubt my own memory and reason.

When I got back to the cell, I did not waste any time. I cornered Mikuláš, "Do you notice anything unusual about me? Come on! Be honest! Am I still normal? Does my behavior seem peculiar to you? Am I totally off the track? I really can't tell any more whether I'm normal or whether I haven't lost it completely. Is it possible that the reason I remember so little is that I've lost contact with the past?"

The document was so perfectly contrived and ingenuously recorded in such detail that I could not believe it was all invented. Indeed, these great fictional works were cunningly interspersed with various fragments of reality from the past which made them all the more credible. They started with the fact that we had gone together to the editorial office or the headquarters of the *Jeunesse Ouvrière Chrétienne* (Young Christian Workers). S. later confirmed this when we were in the camp at the Jáchymov uranium mines at Příbramsko (Bytíz), and we could speak together.

Such written confessions plainly gave the prosecution valuable ammunition, but subsequently at the higher military court in Trenčín, I succeeded in refuting these contentions.

I pointed out the obvious contradictions in the declaration. For example, during the alleged visit to the "Deuxième Bureau" French espionage headquarters, I, an ostensibly old collaborator, had supposedly brought S. as another colleague. It was reported that we had then signed an agreement promising we would both do espionage work. I asked the military prosecutor, "O.K. So let's look at what we have here. If it's true that I already was an old hand at spying for the French, how is it that I signed an agreement to cooperate with them in the future only when S. was introduced?"

The official replied, "Details like that are of absolutely no importance whatsoever."

In Košice, they had begun to grill me incessantly with the definite objective of extracting information concerning France. Jano P. presumably had some mention of Kolakovič in Belgium in his record, and the documents in Ivan P.'s file asserted that I had smuggled espionage materials across the border in a suitcase.

I tried to figure out what the interrogators were really looking for, what could be behind all of this. I had to pay attention and stick to the facts and not agree with any variations as perhaps my associates had done.

I also inquired of the military prosecutor, "Don't you find it odd that one would send such dangerous espionage documents in the suitcase of some unknown student who could easily be beaten up or even killed and the papers taken? In fact, wouldn't it have been much more expedient, and risk free, to have sent such intelligence by ordinary diplomatic pouch?"

After my decision to staunchly refuse to answer questions or even speak to the interrogators, I began to feel that everything was coming to an end, although I did not quite know to what end. I thank God that I quickly came to terms with the idea of being executed. I was then at peace, even happy. But at the same time, I was very aware of the peculiarity of my situation.

When they gave me back my glasses, I suddenly realized how, after all this time, I had lost the habit of normal vision. Everything instantly seemed unusually large. The interrogator's strong, long face reminded me of the large head and face of Bishop Trochta.

This interrogator had black or chestnut hair. He would always copy down their usual stereotyped statements. Whenever he asked anything I would always counter with, "I refuse to answer." His reply never varied. It was always that in any case, whatever I said was irrelevant since witness so and so (and he would name either another person who was charged or a fellow prisoner) had supposedly said this and that.

They quoted Prof. V., Father H., V. J., Dr. S., Julka B., and even Bishop T. Finally, when I insisted, they handed me the document so I could read it.

But I balked at signing anything, including the statement, "I refuse to answer." Therefore all the papers had to be signed by another officer or a witness who confirmed that in spite of having received clear instructions, I had rejected any request to affix my signature to any of the statements including that "I refuse to answer."

It was then that I understood the great happiness and contentment a person experiences when he knows without a doubt that he has explicitly and openly protested against savage deeds, be it only in an insignificant way such as breaking off all dialogue with his tormentors. This action was especially rewarding to me, since it was possible to look upon exchanges with them as making a certain effort to maintain good relations so as to avoid all unpleasantness and conflict.

With this new knowledge in hand, we then added a petition for strength to remain silent to our lists of "Litany of Humility" and "Litany for Everyday Needs" which we wrote in these prisons.

After so many struggles, I now also fully understood the reasons why a person was willing to first sacrifice and suffer, then to speak, to dispute and finally to yield, in exchange for a little peace and respite from his persecutors.

However, these were clearly compromises and the kind of solace they brought did not last. I did not sleep well at night if during the day I had sought peace instead of shouting in their faces that they were criminals, law breakers, murderers, and sadists.

Indeed, their whole system was like a laboratory. But instead of experimental rabbits and mice, it contained people. The scientific practice consisted in making prisoners suffer in such a way that the agony would be maximized but they would not die. The idea was to keep them alive as long as possible. Thus, the torturing, breaking, and coercing could continue unabated as attempts were made to pump more information out of them.

The State Security people put it quite nicely. When speaking of solitary confinement they would say, "We'd like to give you a cell mate and allow you visits and parcels, but we can't. It's against the rules." Yet they themselves had devised these rules. And occasionally they did give you everything, so that you, poor anguished soul, were bound to them by gratitude.

I persevered in my daily prayers and recitation of the Holy Mass, "With you and for you, brothers!" We offered the sacrifice of Holy Mass daily and then added a personal sacrifice of the day. And we sang our song from the first imprisonment in Bratislava, "Anxiety and routine fill our days and nights. God, save us and help us!"

When I had a little free time, I used it to continue my program of recall exercises which included repeating and memorizing names and addresses. Through the whole period of my imprisonment which lasted over thirteen years, I succeeded in remembering some addresses so well that I was later able to use them to deliver messages, establish new contacts, and renew old ones.

Meanwhile, Mikuláš, my companion, was preparing for the end of his interrogations. He constantly demanded this and somehow they had actually promised him this would happen. But I began to think that I would go to trial before him. They still were not getting any information out of me and they knew that when a prisoner entered this phase of desperate defiance, they would get nothing from him.

However, they went on trying to the end. Different interrogators alternated. They used photographs. One was of my friend and colleague, Dr. Kudlička.

"Do you know them? We know that you know them. Who's this?"

As usual I said, "I refuse to answer."

And as usual the State Security man shouted, "I didn't ask you whether or not you refused to answer! I asked if you knew Dr. Kudlička!"

I was silent. I saw again how essential it was to persist in this attitude, although at first it had seemed to me to be rather discourteous. Only one thing worried me: that I had not done it consistently from the very beginning. This stance was not a problem for me when they beat me, but when somebody treated me halfway decently, I then felt that my own position was much too rigid. Needless to say, their decency was not genuine but was strictly a cover for blackmail. What a sad misuse of good behavior!

Interestingly enough, I learned through experience that whenever I would take the wildest, the most fantastic, and apparently the most unreasonable and hopelessly mad step, without any thought for the future but solely trusting in God, the better the results were. And in the end it was also more advantageous for me. I was closer to God although the devil never stopped tormenting me, "You won't really hold out you know, and then what?"

When I understood that their aim was the destruction of the Church, and that neither truth nor human life mattered to them at all, I told myself that the best course of action would be to do exactly the opposite of what they wanted me to do.

This then was my general approach: when the comrades wanted me to speak, especially during interrogations, I was silent. After trying it once, I found that it worked very well for me so I continued. I also recommended this tactic to brothers from other prisons and many of them highly praised it.

The reverse of this principle was that when they wanted me to be silent, in court, for example, where they attempted to show that the trial was fair and just, then I would again make speeches. I said aloud what they absolutely did not want to hear. Such was my defense summary, the final word at the trial.[24]

In short, I taught myself not to think rationally occasionally, but like Peter, to close my eyes and throw myself into the sea (see John 21:7). In my case it truly was to plunge into physical and spiritual uncertainty, an abyss, where only faith in God could guarantee safety. Material things which mankind regarded as certainties were fleeting and illusory, while faith, which the world considered to be ephemeral, was the most reliable and the most powerful of foundations.

The more I depended on faith, the stronger I became.

Part VI

Departure from Ruzyň and the Second Move to Bratislava
The Superior Military Court and Prison in Trenčín
The Main Trial on the Feast of John the Baptist
My Final Defense

I believe it was in November 1953 that after endless futile attempts to make me talk, they decided to move me from Ruzyň.

By the time I left, the guards had given up their nightly banging and shouting. They had also stopped confiscating my blankets as punishment for putting my hands underneath the covers upon falling asleep, something which every prisoner did almost instinctively.

When I left Ruzyň, I again succeeded in seeing a little through a crack in the dark glasses. This time I noticed a large bulk like some sort of mountain of iron and wire in the inner courtyard.

Mikuláš and I had made a bet that we would both be freed by 1958, that is, within the next five years. If this did not happen, I was to pray one "Our Father" every day for the conversion of the Jews, while, if it did happen, he was to work honestly towards his own lasting return to God.

I have to admit that it is only now that I have remembered this promise, but every evening at about 9 o'clock, I met with friends spiritually in prayer and meditation. At these meetings I used to say the "Our Father" along with the prayer "The Eternal Word," although not always consciously every day for Jews and converts. One advantage of looking again at my prison notes is that I shall be able to respect that commitment to say an "Our Father" for Jews, and I can even add a "Hail Mary" for Muslims.

ꙮ

I again found myself in the Bratislava Regional Law Courts, that is, at the Place of Justice. There we sometimes sang our refrain:

> We are faithful to Christ,
> Prison does not break us,

> We are circling round the district court,
> We are going round the hook . . . the gallows, the gallows.

In some courtyards, one could see hooks in a corner. The rumor was that they were used for hanging people. Dr. Tiso had supposedly died there.

In Bratislava, by the supernatural grace of God, I found myself in exactly the same corridor as Vlado, my youngest brother. I succeeded in throwing him a match box which held a copy of the "Litany For Everyday Needs."

He threw me a message telling me such moving details as how our parents and sister — sometimes with the latter's children — nonchalantly walked around the prison on Sundays at 11:30 in the morning in the hope of catching at least a glimpse of one of us far away behind bars. But we felt exceedingly uneasy about these attempts to see us. It was a tremendous risk for our relatives to take just to see the wave of a hand, or see part of a face passing somewhere behind a prison window. Nevertheless, they did it happily and joyfully because they thought it would encourage and strengthen us.

During these visual contacts, I had to stand on the shoulders of a cell mate, or he on mine, and if there were three of us, one had to cover the spy hole with his back so that we would not be seen by the guards.

I was touched by my father's acting abilities. He pushed a pram so that he would not attract attention. Then he would take out a handkerchief, wipe his nose a little, and at the same time unobtrusively shake the handkerchief lightly so that the screws around the prison would not realize he was signalling a prisoner in a cell.

However, these innocent exchanges with my parents only lasted until an informer from a neighboring cell spoiled it for all of us by alerting the guards. This man's action was nothing new. He had previously disclosed a lot about who came for a visit and who called on whom.

ꕥ

I believe it was in cell 214 that I had as a companion a young, rather heavy, and simple boy called F. He often pretended to accompany himself on an accordion as he performed various mimes. He especially enjoyed singing assorted love songs, such as "Jiřina." We were not together very long as after I was denounced by the man in the next cell, I was transferred to a completely different one with different windows and corridors. F. was replaced by Štefan L., an interesting lad who was either an adolescent or not much older.

Štefan L. was a typical member of the younger generation. In the beginning he praised prison since he thought that he had at last escaped his two or three girlfriends who constantly pursued him for money for their babies. He was extraordinarily skillful, although he lacked a formal education.

After several ingenious maneuvers he had managed to open the upper windows which, when placed obliquely, allowed us to catch the reflection of prisoners walking.

He accomplished this through a series of elaborate and very complicated means. First he asked the doctor to give him special boots because he had a sick and crippled foot. The doctor finally gave in and wrote out a prescription for these.

But Štefan proved to be a difficult customer. He was never satisfied and persistently complained about the boots they offered him. He griped that one pair was too small for him and the other too big. He carried on with this grumbling and muttering until he was finally given boots with metal and nails on the heels, which was what he had wanted all along.

He proceeded to work patiently on the small piece of metal on the heel with various improvised tools until he succeeded in removing it from the boot. Then he ground this small segment on the porcelain and stone of the toilet until he had made a rectangular "key" for the locks on the upper windows. And he opened the windows.

Obviously the screws were flabbergasted when they saw the open windows. "Who opened those?" they roared. "How did you do it?"

Štefan assumed a most innocent expression, "I beg your pardon?"

"We locked those windows only a moment ago!"

"You did? But, Sir, do you think we're crazy? How could we possibly open them. What could we use to unlock them?"

However, the jailers could not be dismissed so casually. They conducted one thorough search after another but Štefan always hid the key in a mattress so skillfully that only he knew where it was. And so, thanks to his resourcefulness, I was able to keep informed about the comings and goings of our imprisoned friends.

I think that it was precisely from Štefan that I also heard of another case of inventiveness. He and his friends had made a deck of cards with which they played. When they suddenly ran into a cell inspector, Štefan affected the behavior of an innocent child: "Cards? What cards?

Who would've allowed us to have cards?" This incident was followed by another sweeping search but again, nothing was ever found.

I learned that the way to hide these cards was to adopt an old trick used by pick-pockets. The cards were stuck with sticking-plaster. When a extensive check was made, the cards would be "stuck" in the pocket of one of the guards. In the hustle and bustle of the inspection, the man would be unaware that something had been given him. They would look into everything. They would turn the mattress over and the clothes inside out, and would go into a rage because they could not find anything. And just before they left the cell, the adept "pick-pocket" would slyly take the cards back from the pocket of the unsuspecting screw.

ꟿ

In the spiritual area, I used Štefan's presence to delve more deeply into the Bible and biblical history. He was a very easy pupil to teach. He enjoyed learning new things as he found that time went by more quickly when he studied. The new knowledge also provided him with more courage during interrogations. Both of us demanded that we be allowed to borrow the Criminal Law Code and Criminal Order books. I was refused. But Štefan's request was granted as they considered him a simple, harmless prisoner....

He and a friend of his who was somewhere in a neighboring cell had been condemned to imprisonment at the same time. They used their own particular code to signal each other.

Their entire alleged offense was actually quite hilarious. In a certain wood which had at one time been the war front, they had looked for old, mostly unusable cartridges from pistols, rifles, and tommy-guns. The police had construed this action as the preparation for an anti-state "armed putsch" or some other similar criminal intent....

We were finally allowed to borrow the Criminal Law Code, although in fact every prisoner was supposedly entitled by law to use this Code. If the authorities were to tamper with legal paragraphs under his very nose, it stands to reason that the prisoner should at least know what they were talking about. But the permission was only to last for twenty-four hours.

I immediately made sure that the young boys got down to reading it. I instructed them to learn it by heart. We divided the chapters and since there were a lot of pages and articles, we endeavored to mentally photograph some of them so that we would not forget anything. Although the Law Code was theoretically lent to us for twenty-four hours only, Štefan, of course, did not hand it back when the time was up. We kept on using it for a whole week, during which time we read, studied, and memorized parts of the Criminal Law Code and the Criminal Order.

ᘓ

When I had been going through preliminary investigation, I had asked for my personal medical books. But now I did not want them since I expected to be moved or put on trial and might have lost them. The problem was that we were allowed to have literature dealing with various fields of expertise as long as our books were then left in the prison library. I regarded this as extortion. To force a prisoner under interrogation to give up his own books on a specific topic was actually senseless. It was not very likely that another doctor with my specialization would go to the same library of the same prison and want the same book.

Later, in the superior military court prison in Trenčín, I was able to borrow scientific books dealing with my particular expertise. They helped immensely in stimulating my mind and boosting my self-confidence.

Although I had no patients or professional work place, I busied my mind by reflecting on how to improve present medical techniques. Interestingly enough, I later found many of these conjectured prison solutions and ideas published in foreign expert literature; for example, I read about the techniques and instruments used (which I called "Dermoexcisor") for the rapid histological investigation of skin diseases, a step which is considered an indispensable method for exact diagnosis.

In an environment which aimed at the destruction of the prisoner, I was strengthened by evidence that my ideas were not merely the whimsical fantasies of a prisoner who had nothing better to do than think up fantastic instruments. My personal conclusions included devices which were actually being patented in Switzerland and other countries.

ᘓ

At this time, I also met prosecutor W., who was known as the "bloody prosecutor." He began by shouting angrily, "You really blew it when you refused to confess! You're going to pay for it! Believe me, you're going to regret this!"

That this refusal to confess was a reaction to beatings and illegal coercive methods did not interest him in the least. "What beating? You must have been impertinent, so they beat you up for that but not for the fact that you wouldn't answer. That's your business."

Then he said that it was "senseless and impossible" for me not to answer and that he simply would not tolerate it.

The prosecutors and judges were clearly not naive people who did not know what was being done to the prisoners, but they lacked the courage and often even the interest to put an end to the illegality. Therefore, they put on their usual performance in the courtroom using the prescribed terminology.

W. had got hold of my medical articles. At first he praised them but then immediately began to cast doubt on my expertise. "You can't be a very good doctor if you believe in nonsense such as religion and reactionary ideology."

I had been silent for a long time, but that last comment was the straw that broke the camel's back. My feelings overflowed and I immediately launched into an apologetic polemic. After a while W. gave up and interrupted me, "Well, we won't bother ourselves with this now."

ꙮ

Here they also attempted to enforce the "hands on the blanket" policy at night. But they did not bang on the doors or make as much noise as usual since the political atmosphere in the country had changed.

At night when it was quiet, they could only open the cell door if extraordinary security measures required them to do so. The result was that in order to reach the dozing prisoner to wake him up or force him to stand, they had to poke him with long sticks which they stuck through the window.

During this period, we were able to improve the signalling system to our girls. Brigita Flochová, Cilka Česneková, Mária Kuníková, Mária Jakubcová, Anka Hrušovská, and others were there. Contact with the women through one or two floors to a third was very good. Tapping on the radiators was ideal but knocking on the walls was less effective.

We always started signalling with a password to identify ourselves so that the jailers could not intercept and use our code. For example, I would start out with "Long live Christ the King!" Then I would continue with "Lay apostolate here. Catholic Action. For this morning's meditation, I'll dictate a passage from Scripture. Today it is from the Gospel of John." Whoever did the tapping would conclude with "Peace be with you," or "Hang on! We're with you! We pray with you and for you, day and night. Long live Christ the King!"

This period also included the little episode of my transport to Račianska Street in Bratislava. There, they had built a faithful replica of the cold and harsh system of little cells called "rabbit cages." These were typical of the headquarters of State Security at Ruzyň during the time of scientific brainwashing.

I again experienced solitary confinement of the Ruzyň type. I guessed that in this huge complex there could be several hundred cells. The blankets were newer and better and that helped. At night, there was less banging, and more quiet. I used this peaceful time for spiritual renewal. But this system of cages also brought back memories of Ruzyň and of all the powerlessness and pressure which one felt there.

I had the feeling that I was there as a punishment from God because I had stopped protesting and I was less sensitive to the suffering of others. I had ceased complaining and had reconciled myself to the inhumanities which I saw, as long as they were not directed at me.

I stayed there about four days.

One evening an interrogator from Prague came to see me. He did not seem to know about the attempts which had been made to force me to speak and so he applied the same types of pressure again, and once more rattled off a list of names, "Do you know Kudlička? How about Nahálka Kudlička? And Botek? So, you still refuse to say anything? Are you out of your mind? When you spoke with us a moment ago, we got everything on tape. You know, we can always allow you to say that you refuse to say anything but no, you're only interested in playing the hero!"

I did not know whether or not they really used tape recorders or other machines during interrogations. The interrogator often went into neighboring rooms and that could have been to check the machines or to switch them on. Then I suddenly realized that even ordinary, rather mindless conversation was dangerous.

In Brno I had had a rather unsettling experience which might have confirmed the use of tape recorders. One night, they applied extreme pressure and threatened me. A new interrogator came in. He had somewhat of an ape's head, although that might not be too accurate a description of his features. In any case, he seemed intent on working all night to bring about a feeling of total helplessness in me.

In the end he pulled down the blinds and switched the radio on loudly so that nothing would be heard if he beat or tortured me. If I admitted anything or if I began to talk about Kolakovič, he insisted on hearing everything over and over again. However, the only result from that type of coercion was that he finally grabbed me below the throat about twice, but nothing much came of that.

Then, for unclear reasons, perhaps simply because he was under orders, he unexpectedly mastered his murderous temper. He quickly changed tactics and adopted a quite pleasant tone, as if he wanted his previous action to appear to be nothing but a simple joke. When I acknowledged that I actually counted on suffering for Christ and the Church, and that in the past I had actually had the desire to display at least some sort of solidarity with the martyrs of this age, his arrogance rapidly diminished.

Sometimes after days and months of solitary confinement, I almost longed to say something innocent and harmless so that I could learn something new about my brothers and sisters. Who else had been arrested? What had happened to them?

But, to tell the truth, even saying something unimportant always meant feverishly working out ways to say it. To consider everything so carefully presented such an arduous task that as a consequence, I suffered from insomnia and increased tension.

ꙮ

When they took me to the military prison in the district of Trenčín, they had just restored the interior of the institution. It presented a rather dismal picture. The floors in the cells were made of asphalt, and everything was terribly dirty, boarded up, and damp. The windows were all locked so that the air in the cells was stifling. They were sometimes unlocked for one or two hours for ventilation but then only on certain days.

I was alone in my very dimly lit cell where there was almost no daylight. After two or three days, at my request, they lent me a rag and I cleaned the cell and rearranged it a little.

Once, at night, and I suspect it was by mistake, I was taken to be interrogated. They covered my eyes when they took me back and forth to the interrogation room. At that time, instead of using the usual dark glasses, they put towels over our eyes inside the prison. It appeared that nothing much had changed in judicial imprisonment if they still bothered to prevent the prisoners from seeing certain things.

However, by the end of my stay in Trenčín and by complaining to the prosecutor, I did succeed in obtaining permission to sometimes take a walk.

It was at about this time that a fellow prisoner, Jožko Suchý, committed suicide. It is not clear whether he did it by hanging himself or in some other way. I only learned about this much later.

ꙮ

After about a week, I received a cell mate. As far as I can remember, it was a certain Viliam K. from Trenčín. I succeeded, but with great difficulty, in extracting at least one new Marian hymn from him. Later I met him again in the kitchen at Prokop, a penal work camp at Jáchymov. It was perhaps his second time in prison, and I think he had come to consider me a friend.

He was totally disinterested in anything aside of himself. For me, this was like attending God's school but I saw even this prisoner acquire a little more spirituality during his stay in the cell. He would desperately cry out that he had already been there for three weeks. "Can you imagine that!" he would whine. He totally ignored the fact that there were prisoners around him who had been there five or ten times longer than he. He couldn't understand why he was there at all since, according to him, he had confessed to everything and more just so he would be given a quick trial or a lighter sentence. People often had illusions about the situation.

In fact the more a prisoner asked for, the more was refused him. One had to proceed in an entirely different way. When an interrogator asked me if I wanted anything, I would ask for the almost complete opposite of what I wished to have. Thus, without their knowing, but as if on purpose, they quickly gave me what I truly preferred.

ꙮ

After Viliam K., I was given yet another psychologically very unstable cell mate, a rather naive, very simple, but excellent young man. I think Jozef H., good-natured from the bone, was a licensed driver in the military service. I did not forget him. After I was released, I stayed in contact with him.

Then the prosecutor allowed me to have medical books. He obviously felt that my case was becoming more illegal by the day, due to court delays. I believe the experts' books he permitted were Petrášek's Czech book and Kartamysev's Russian book on dermatology.

I was very surprised, when during a thorough study of these books, I saw a whole system of marks above some of the letters. I then realized that my family had very skillfully used the manuals to send me information.

From the signs on some of the pages, I learned the results of the final trials of brothers and sisters in Bratislava. Imro S. had been given fifteen years, Šmálik thirteen years, Vinco B. six years, and so on. I also worked out from the letters that Blanka was "sick," that is, arrested. I was not completely certain about this last bit of information, but it was later confirmed as being correct.

I think that it was also in Trenčín that I finally practiced medicine again. When a certain guard contracted a skin disease, they made it possible for him to meet me so that I could give him my opinion on his illness and suggest treatment.

ꟊ

I had been unable to obtain the Criminal Law Code. Later, on my first meeting with my defense counsel, I stated that even though this was a military prison and that I was being tried by a military court, depriving me of the Law Code was illegal. The defense counsel then gave me his own copy of the Criminal Law Code, but only for two days. They were afraid that I would learn too much about the law. However, they even allowed me a pencil!

I had acquired a rough idea of many legal matters in the Bratislava prison where, with those young boys, I had studied for a week to memorize a few paragraphs. I actually did not need the Criminal Law Code, but I applied for it anyway to remind the responsible officials that they had to observe the law.

ꟊ

We sometimes had the possibility to buy things. I think that my family gave me some money since the little I had had when they arrested me was already gone. In the meantime, the money had been changed. It was thus reduced to about a tenth of its former value.

Everybody was allowed to make purchases in the military prison. The withholding of this right was not used here as a form of pressure as it was in other interrogation prisons. Immediately before the trial, I was allowed goods totalling 15–30 crowns a week.

Military prisoners also appeared in neighboring cells. They were often accused of "stupidity," for example, for hiding pistols and ammunition, or selling these, or smuggling. One military prisoner from a village near Lučenec begged me to visit his wife when I was released, since he assumed I would be freed before him. This request was hilarious. For our communist overlords, my so-called political or religious crimes were far more dangerous than these military offenses.

Jozef H. and I got on very well together. To make the time go quicker for him, I involved him in study activities. He read my medical books and tested my knowledge of medicine. I would answer him according to individual chapter titles or content. We also devoted much time to repeating the Holy Scriptures, particularly the Gospels of John and Matthew.

In the evening, we often spent a little time on debates, and so we became friends. He accepted my suggestions and instructions and when they took him again for interrogations, intending to break him, he was able to defend himself very well. And in his case, the prosecutor even made a motion to drop the charges.

ꟙ

My own trial was constantly being postponed. My family privately provided me with defense counsel K., who, all things considered, was perhaps not too bad. I was against this expense for them since I knew that they had other more pressing needs, but I did not want to cause them any problems so I accepted him.

However, I knew that in this system the defense counsel actually only played a perfunctory role. He would bring up incidental, mitigating circumstances which could actually indirectly confirm that one was guilty of the criminal acts of which he was accused.

In my case, one example of this was the charge of high treason, which I of course strenuously denied. But since my counsel only raised unimportant questions concerning my work habits and omitted questions related to the charges, the impression was that I was guilty and was trying to avoid the subject. My family later told me that this lawyer had shared with them his extreme concern about my defense.

I was finally given the date of my trial. Here again I saw how God was accompanying me and literally smoothing the way for me.

St. John the Baptist was my patron saint, especially in this prison. And now, in 1954, after three years of interrogations, the date for the main hearing was set for June 24, the feast day of my patron saint, the day of the birth of St. John the Baptist.

I had previously explained many things to the military prosecutor, including what my colleagues and I had and had not done, and he had seemed sympathetic and open to my arguments. In addition, I was able to argue against all the unjust fabrications which still appeared in the records.

In a bid to win me over, he stated that I had the right to remain silent. He was suddenly most concerned with all things legal and added that should I elect to do so, I also had the right to express my opinion on every point. He said it would be better for me if the defense was not the only one to speak.

He again wrote down how everything might have happened. From past experience I knew enough to contribute to the prosecutor's interrogation only what I considered would be helpful to my case, and I insisted on the exact transcription of my own words.

He also recorded all the violence I had experienced. I almost got the impression that the political situation was improving. Later I realized that it might all have been sheer pretense of good will. His behavior could either have been to gain my confidence or to protect himself from any responsibility should any one of them be prosecuted later for illegal procedures.

ꟈ

I suspected that during his main hearing a prisoner could feel very depressed, tired, and suffer from lack of sleep. These factors could make it difficult for him to answer accusations properly, and to react appropriately to critical situations. He could easily be intimidated by the shouts of the people who had to convict him, that is, the judges, the chief justice, and the prosecutor.

Therefore, I did not leave my testimony to chance. I worked everything out in detail, especially my concluding speech, so that in the event of stage fright or fatigue, it would be enough for me to simply read what I had written. I feared that my defense counsel would be on their side. However, he at least behaved in a moderate fashion.

This had not been the case with the defense counsel which had been assigned to me by the appeals court in Prague. This man had built up his courage with alcohol and defended me in such a way that he did me more harm than good. I had had to request that he not be allowed to speak.

When they handed me the indictment, I finally learned what the charges were. I read what they had compiled from the statements of "witnesses" and my fellow accused. The actual accusation consisted of about seven or eight pages, blown up to such proportions and including such fanatically formulated crimes that I thought I would faint from shock. I was completely stunned by the extent of the allegations and the manner in which they were drafted. For a moment I could not remember anything. Then I asked, "Did I do all these things?"

After so much time spent in solitary confinement, a prisoner always has a tendency (probably psychological) for self-deprecation, especially since he knows all the sins and errors which he has committed during his lifetime. When he is in solitary confinement these thoughts persistently emerge to haunt him. As a result it is difficult for him to discern how earnestly he should defend himself.

In the first moments after receiving the charges, I was appalled. I thought, "This warrants execution! The rope! How could I have come to this?" And of course, they still attempted to convince me that I was guilty of all of this.

Then I came to my senses. The indictment was a little long for me to memorize so I read it a second and then a third time. Perhaps during the fourth or fifth reading, I suddenly burst out laughing. I had just realized how much of the information contradicted itself either directly or indirectly. After two or three hours of careful reading and thinking, I was positively euphoric. I clearly saw which facts conflicted with others. I was obviously going to use this in thinking over and preparing my defense.

ꝏ

At the actual trial, my reactions turned out to be as I had foreseen and feared. I experienced stage fright and during the hearing I was not able to react calmly and fittingly. I was suffering from lack of sleep. In spite of all my efforts at remaining calm or at least externally composed, in spite of being committed to any and all sacrifices including that of my life, at the beginning of the hearing, I answered quite hoarsely, quietly, fearfully, as if I felt guilty.

My father encouraged me with gestures and whispered, "Hang on! Don't be afraid! Why are you in such a defeatist mood?"

But after a while I rallied and caught fire. I started my rebuttal and finally I was on a roll. I could not be warded off, even during my final argument, although the prosecutor and the Chief Justice constantly interrupted me.

In a gesture of contempt, the Chief Justice allowed me to use the Criminal Law Code but only for one or two days before the hearing. He also permitted me to look at the court records for about two hours. Only now do I regard this as a mockery of justice. During that time of terror when I was being interrogated, I could view even this as a magnanimous gesture of good will. Just to give you an idea — the judgment in the "Mádr and Vacková" trial alone was about 150 pages long. I hardly saw anything of the record of proceedings against Kolakovič.

This particular system of abject terror had been conceived in a very refined way. A typical anecdote from Stalin's time shows the essence of it all. It relates how Stalin demonstrated the destruction of an enemy to his closest colleagues. First, he brought out a cage with a canary. A colleague took the bird out of the cage and began to strangle it. But the canary struggled and managed to fly away. Then Stalin said that to conquer adversaries, it was necessary to do precisely the opposite of what the man had just done. Stalin took another canary and slowly began to pluck out its feathers. He did so gradually, one feather at a time, until the bird shivered with cold and snuggled closely in the palm of his hand, grateful for a little warmth.

Thus Stalin and his successors took away all the basic human rights of their victims even up to and including basic physical needs, so that later on they could return crumbs of what had been stolen, as a generous indication of the achievements of socialism, "the new people's democracy." Stalin and his successors built, and continue to build, their personality cult on their victims' gratitude for these crumbs.

These little "crumbs" (such as the Law Code) were also there for me. I used them to show how these trials were rigged. For example, they tried two murderers with the political prisoners, just as two thieves had been crucified with Christ so that his innocence would not be distinguished from their crimes. Thus the trial of Mádr, Vacková, and Jukl also included two murderers who had had nothing at all to do with the whole religious matter.

The Chief Justice, Major M., a Moravian, appeared very elegant and jovial and behaved as if he were sympathetic to my cause. But experience had taught me that such people were the most dangerous. When somebody openly shouted or raged, one usually knew how to react. And a furious man often made mistakes.

When the Chief Justice quoted from writings during the trial (for example from our pamphlet "Inquiry") he admitted, "Perhaps you're right. At first sight, this pamphlet looks innocent enough. But this might just be sheer cunning. Who knows what's hidden there. You simply shouldn't have done this!"

But it seemed to me that he was the main initiator during the trial. He was the author of deliberate tactics which led to the predictable end. During the trial and other proceedings related to my case, he rendered the most negative and harshest judgments.

To all appearances, everything at the trial seemed to be going my way, as they were most unsuccessful in rebutting my arguments in spite of their well-prepared scenarios.

They later allowed me to speak again and argued with me, but this was only after the public had been excluded and the verdict had been rendered. The military prosecutor checked my files more carefully and also cautiously took into account as "evidence" the document from S. concerning our visit to the French "espionage headquarters." This document had about fifteen pages of information which I had completely repudiated. In the end, it was this prosecutor who pleaded for a severe sentence.

During the trial, everybody involved, including the judges and the prosecutors, acted, whether sincerely or not, as wretched individuals following the exact dictates of the Party. They even repeated standard Party phrases such as, "He never became part of the working class."

ꟹ

When my trial was over and after I had been imprisoned for almost thirty-five months, they finally allowed me the first regular visit. I was literally behind metal bars, somewhat like a wire grille or a cage. I remember that shortly before his conditional release my younger brother Vlado had jumped with joy and grabbed these bars without any regard for the risk and the consequences this move could have brought down on him.

Like others before me, I was also glad that after being sentenced, my prison life would be much more humane. In complete opposition to reason and the law, interrogation imprisonment was the cruelest. Yet, their treatment of us should have started from the presumption that we were innocent until we had been proven guilty.[25]

Long before, in letters and other ways, my father had indicated that he had placed me under the protection of St. Anne. This was the name of his oldest sister and also his patron saint, the one who had protected him, especially during imprisonment in Russia. By coincidence there was a chapel dedicated to St. Anne directly next to the prison. When he came to visit me, or brought a parcel or anything else to Trenčín, he always stopped there. He especially considered it a sign from God that I was arrested precisely in the night of her festival, July 26 to 27.

And according to the Church calendar of the time, July 27 was the feast of St. Panteleimon, doctor of medicine and martyr.

Part VII

My Spiritual Life in Prison
Spiritual Exercises in Solitary Confinement
Comprehensive Analysis and Personal Meditation
Themes and Ideas for Meditation

Every morning in prison, I began my daily program by saying, "With you and for you, brothers. . . ."

I survived and offered the whole day with and for them, starting with tidying up the cell in the morning, then following up with physical exercises, washing, and my first meditation.

I included them most especially in my recitation of the Holy Mass after breakfast. I had memorized it in Latin, Slovak, and Russian. I think that there were not four canons then, but only one, the Roman Canon. The Eucharistic prayer is the central and the most important part of Holy Mass. It was beautifully renewed by the Second Vatican Council, which gave it four main alternates.

I could usually concentrate on the Holy Mass for one or two hours. But my first meditation, a time of intense devotion, always preceded the Mass. Sometimes I made an effort to pray openly. For example, I would stand at the window with my hands joined. There were many reasons for doing this. It helped me to practice self-denial, to keep my concentration and not doze off, and was an effective exercise in courage.

But some interrogators and guards reacted quite strongly and harshly to my praying. One interrogator in Košice, a lieutenant, lost his temper, forbade me to continue and threatened me with disciplinary and repressive action. But this did not bother me too much since it was not the first time that he had lost, or pretended to have lost, his temper.

On the contrary, I was motivated by the thought that I was not adapting to these people. I felt that I was putting up a fight for at least a remnant of freedom here in prison, and I felt a bit of pride in the fact that I had sacrificed something apart from solitude and spiritual crises. I really "lacked nothing" and actually had little to bring God as an offering, except perhaps for the hunger, the cold, the fear, the brow-beating, and at some stages, the terror.

When I lacked concentration, praying the Mass might take me up to three hours. This happened especially after interrogations, or when I was in the company of others, or during the periods of "walking," when I could not stand in one place. Then, I could not finish it any faster.

I was helped by the thought that I was not alone. The majority of prisoners in the neighboring cells, the whole prison, and in all jails, were true Christians. They were people who had also been locked up, persecuted, and destroyed because of the good deeds they had performed. All of us were also united with our brothers and sisters on the outside who prayed for us. I offered this sacrifice for them and with them.

The Magnificat, Mary's song of praise, "My soul proclaims the greatness of the Lord," which "we," or which I sang with enthusiasm after spiritual communion, sometimes aloud if they allowed me, was always an astonishing source of strength for me throughout my imprisonment. "He has thrown down the rulers from their thrones, but lifted up the lowly. The hungry he has filled with good things, the rich he has sent away empty." And also, "The mighty one has done great things for me" (Luke 1:46–55).

I did some long-term meditation which I called "continuous meditation." This was free personal prayer starting with a main theme. Sometimes it could go on for a whole month, as when chapters are added to a story.

It constantly grew. Indeed, as one's spiritual life intensifies, things become clearer and the essence of God is more easily understood. Sometimes one word, or a single sentence from Scripture, is enough to fill a person with a special light. An insight or new meaning is revealed and penetrates one's inner being and remains there for weeks or months at a time.

ꕥ

I thought out the rest of my daily program in detail. To be idle is very dangerous. It is possible to sink into depression because of an inadequate blood supply reaching the brain due to a lack of activity. As far as I know, experiments have now confirmed this theory.

My meditation was often so deep that later, as I have already mentioned, I called it a "weightless state." I would lose contact with the material world. Once, I heard noise from the corridor indicating the serving of food. I was surprised. "Is it time for breakfast? I thought I'd already had breakfast. Am I losing my sense of time?"

But there was a mess-tin at the door, with lunch! For four to five hours I had been elsewhere spiritually. I had gone to another, more beautiful world, the spiritual one, equally real, but purer than the physical, morally deprived one in which I found myself. And there, I had lost my awareness of prison, time, and space.

This was not an escape to a substitute universe filled with fantasies and dreams. It was easy to tell these two worlds apart as one knows a tree by its fruit. On the contrary, I experienced the highest level of concentration as I actively searched for a moral solution to a problem where I was physically powerless. The state was similar to that of a typist whose concentration is so riveted to the dictated text that what is happening outside the office is not perceived.

During the day I stuck to a program of meditations lasting from one to two hours.

And I endeavored to exercise my knowledge of languages. I began to translate texts which I had memorized (mainly the Gospels) from Russian into German, then into French and other tongues. I continued to arrange foreign language dictionaries in alphabetical order, especially when I could not remember a certain expression. When praying, meditating, and during periods of intellectual recollections, I tried to use a different language every day of the week. In this way I was able to practice Slovak, Czech, Latin, German, Hungarian, French, English, and Russian.

Thus, I actually filled my program, and at the same time escaped depression and extended my knowledge of languages a little. In silence and solitude, texts which I had long ago forgotten came back to me.

ℵ

I think that the most valuable knowledge I acquired in prison was self-discovery. A person finally got to unearth his main shortcomings there. Obviously, this could not always be entirely objective, especially with regard to self-accusation, which a prisoner, particularly a Christian, was inclined to suffer through.

Everybody makes mistakes. But when interrogators and screws turned on the pressure and claimed that you were a criminal and had done evil against the working class and the poor, a prisoner tended to exaggerate his own faults.

The interrogators could not have regretted the time and efforts some of them had put into their study of morals and theology, since this allowed them to more easily manipulate believing prisoners into false "pricks of conscience."

I understood people who "confessed" to crimes they had not committed, since their own pangs of conscience went on to include transgressions which the interrogators forced upon them. At such time, a person could easily admit that he had done something wrong. However, I personally always emphasized that my failings were certainly not the ones of which they accused me.

I determined that my main sins and defects were: self-interest, pride, unwillingness to suffer, lack of confidence in God, and excessive concern about my own future. In addition to other related matters, I felt a suffocating fear because of my uncertainty about what would happen to me.

I believed, and in the end experience confirmed this at least to me, that I was destined to play the role of the "experimental rabbit." I especially wanted to experience the fear and apprehension for myself. For example, I wondered whether I was not actually increasing my suffering by making up a program from morning to evening. What if I tried giving up and reducing my life to that of a vegetable, to mindless existence? What if I did not fight the accusations? Perhaps it would be better if I used my intellectual capacities only during interrogation and trial.

I tried it. I can say that I attempted to live a few days entirely without a program but it did not work. When I thought that I would only vegetate for the whole day, and just rest, that is when there were the most crises.

I again felt burnings and tightness in my chest as if I were bound in iron hoops. I felt like smashing through the walls, shouting and roaring. I was very agitated and raged, not against God, but against these criminals, against the wretched people who had established this regime and served it.

I told myself that I had committed many sins for which I needed to do penance and that I needed to suffer a little more. First, to compensate for my weaknessess and transgressions and those of my friends and enemies.

Second, to heal myself and face the persistent challenge of human love and its inherent problems. Although I had long ago decided on celibacy, I still had the impression that I was sometimes inconsistent in my behavior towards women. For example, during a stay in Prague, a women had fallen in love with me and I was not indifferent to her either. Consequently, I did not put a stop to it in time or make it clear to her that there could not be any further contact. Unfortunately, it did not turn out well and I was the cause of much unnecessary emotional suffering.

And third, as a doctor, with a practical knowledge of psychology, I actually had a certain clinical preparation for becoming "God's laboratory," as I mentioned above. I could observe matters from an expert, scientific point of view, more easily than other prisoners. I understood what could be achieved by silence, the effect total isolation could have on a person, and the results of lack of sleep, fear, shouting, terror, cold, and hunger.

ꕥ

After an unsuccessful experiment at vegetating, I therefore returned to my daily routine where the priority was my spiritual life.

Apart from prayer and meditation, singing always had a very good effect on me. I sang religious hymns and after Easter I added secular songs.

Singing in the spirit, softly or aloud and the rhythm of the music itself, brought me great joy. These musical sessions would soon culminate in an explosion of confidence that this terror would come to an end and that God would ultimately triumph.

I also tried to "conduct" a choir or orchestra. The guards interrupted me once since they thought I had gone mad. However, I was only composing an oratorio, something like "Abraham's Sacrifice of his Son Isaac," for example, or trying to come up with something equally dramatic.

I made the best use of my daily spiritual program when I was forced into solitary confinement for long periods of time. This was especially true in Ruzyň where I was isolated from January to June 1952 and again from March to July 1953, and at several other times for one or two months for a total of about fourteen months. All in all, during my thirteen years and some months in prison, I was in some degree of seclusion or in solitary confinement for about seven years.[26]

At those times, my all-day spiritual exercises program would last at least four weeks. Once or twice they went to six weeks.

I would take half-hour or one-hour breaks and try to relax the muscles in my body, exercise, or walk. In times of spiritual weariness, I spent these rests in "half-sleep." With a great deal of effort, I trained myself to be unaware of my surroundings even though my eyes were open. This was necessary as the moment a prisoner closed his eyes, a guard immediately made a lot of noise such as banging, knocking a chair or table against the wall, or something of the sort.

I usually did three meditations before lunch and often a fourth after lunch or while walking. When I was nervous, I paced almost all the time, like a lion in a cage. The speed of my stride was automatically determined by my state of uneasiness or concentration.

Between meditations, I prayed the rosary, the stations of the Cross, the litany used in Church, and our improvised prison "Litany for Humility" and "Litany for Everyday Needs." Since then, I have also used the latter for special examinations of conscience.

Along with these exercises I also took an evening break. Then, for about an hour before supper, I devoted my time to more intellectual problems from the fields of medicine and scientific discoveries, and thought about suggestions for improvements in these areas. I considered the feasibility of a single international language, and busied myself with world problems and reforms.

After the evening meal came one of my most beautiful hours of the day, a time for memories and examination of conscience. Sometimes it lasted longer than an hour. My memories, especially from recent years, were quite detailed. Up to bed time I reviewed the past, month by month, week by week. I was often seized then by feelings of great joy and overwhelming gratitude to God. In the end I always told myself, "We really did all this. It's good to be imprisoned and suffer, whatever happens." Only one thing saddened me, and that was that we had not done even more and what we had accomplished had not been better. I considered work in the apostolate to be clearly the best way of life, the best job to have.

During these times of recollections my feet and hands even became warmer for a while. Perhaps this was the result of a change in neurovascular tone, an opening up of the vessels where nourishment could flow more easily. But for whatever reason, I at least briefly lost the sensation of having frozen extremities.

For meditation I chose various themes. During exercises according to St. Ignatius I especially concentrated on its basics and principles; why man is created, the use of worldly goods, the principles of detachment, independence and freedom, that is, the avoidance of emotional and material ties. A person needs to acquire this disinterestedness in order not to become a slave to sin, to anyone or to anything, and then find that he is unable to free himself.

Further themes were original sin, death, eternity, and hell. I also meditated on the life of Jesus, especially His suffering, and all sections of the Gospel which concerned the Resurrection, at least those parts I knew.

The core of my meditations and spiritual life were the texts of the New Testament which I had memorized. Prior to my imprisonment, I had learned most of the Gospel of John by heart (the Russian version, the Synodal Orthodox translation), and had completed it in the interrogation prison in Brno.

In November 1952, in prison in Bratislava, I memorized about eleven chapters of Matthew, the Lutheran version from the Kralická Bible, written in old Biblical Czech.

For meditations I also drew on the Epistles I had partly memorized. I especially liked 1 Corinthians about the mystical body of Christ, "But one and the same Spirit produces all of these, distributing them individually to each person as he wishes. As a body is one, though it has many parts, and all the parts of the body, though many, are one body, so also Christ" (12:11–12).

And ever since I was a boy, even before my complete conversion, I had roughly known the part about love (1 Cor. 13).

Also of great interest were:

- 2 Corinthians 11:21–33 and 12:1–10, which deal with the sufferings and revelations of Paul.
- Galatians 3 and 4, "For all of you who were baptized into Christ have clothed yourselves with Christ. There is neither Jew nor Greek, there is neither slave nor free person, there is not male and female; for you are all one in Christ Jesus" (Gal. 3:27–28).
- Colossians 1:12–13 about Christ the King (which I had learned from Professor Kolakovič), "giving thanks to the Father, who has made you fit to share in the inheritance of the holy ones in light. He delivered us from the power of darkness and transferred us to the kingdom of his beloved Son. . . ."
- Romans 13:11, "And do this because you know the time; it is the hour now for you to awake from sleep. For our salvation is nearer now than when we first believed."
- 2 Timothy 4:6–7, where St. Paul, in prison, says good-bye to life, "For I am already being poured out like a libation, and the time of my departure is at hand. I have competed well; I have finished the race; I have kept the faith."
- And the letters of John, especially 1 John 3 and 4, and "let us love not in word or speech but in deed and truth" (1 John 3:18).
- I believe it was from Karol Maník's copy of the New Testament that I learned the Slovak text of Matthew 12, when I was in the penal labor camp at Bytíz.

At "Prokop," my last camp at Jáchymov, when someone smuggled in further fragments of the Gospels for me, I memorized Matthew 23 and

24, "Woe to you, scribes and Pharisees" (and, I might add, hypocritical Christians and Catholics). These chapters also deal with eschatology, the last things, and the final judgment.

In addition, I recited the Eastern Liturgy.

Memorizing texts from the New Testament proved to be an excellent preparation for critical times and imprisonment. The most beautiful and important texts which mankind has from God contain a priceless treasure which "moth and decay cannot destroy, and thieves break in and steal" (Matt. 6:19).

A person who follows up on this suggestion has a much clearer and stronger foundation for a program of prayer and meditation, and he feels closer to God as God is present in his Word.

Solitary confinement was extraordinarily alleviated by my knowledge of the Bible. And it dawned on me that I had at my disposal one of the most effective means of defense against brainwashing.

ᢀ

In addition to praying for support in our prevailing difficulties, I reserved one day every week for special intentions:

Monday was for doctors, medical students, nurses, hospitals, and the sick. I added prisoners and jailers to this list since I considered them to be "sick," and all prison camps, the suffering, and those who caused others to suffer.

Tuesday, as far as I remember, was for workers, the apostolate among them, the proletariat, and social concerns, for the conversion of businessmen, traders, financiers, for the appropriate use of financial resources, for my immediate family, and our Kolakovič "Family." ("Family" was the title given to the group of about 80 to 150 people of all professions and layers of society who were the closest associates of Professor Kolakovič).

Wednesday was for technicians, technology and the mass media, radio, film, and the press.

Thursday was for teachers, lawyers, and all scientific and technical branches and groups, the apostolate of youth and children.

Friday was for the begging of forgiveness for my own faults and sins, for the sins of others and the whole world, and for reconciliation with the Heart of God. I pleaded with God to free me from my many transgressions. I asked Him to grant me and those close to me time for a joyful and thorough preparation for death. I prayed for the Slovak and Czech nations, for new saints and martyrs in our nations and for the strength and courage to sacrifice my life should that become necessary.

I devoted Saturday to the Virgin Mary, and pleaded to come to imitate her in her humility and chastity. I asked for her intercession for sinners and those tormented by problems related to sex, for prostitutes, the young, homosexuals, and the apostolate among them. I prayed for our chastity. Saturday was also always reserved for Russia, communism and especially its supporters such as Stalin, Khrushchev, all dictators, the KGB and State Security, communist China, Mao Tse-Tung, Deng Xiaoping, the camps and all those suffering in them, and for Soviet youth.

Sunday belonged to the Church. I prayed for the Holy Father, the enemies of the Holy Father and future Popes, for the cardinals and their colleagues, the bishops, new vocations and members of the priesthood, religious orders, missions and missionaries, lay people and doctors for the missions, and for our community. I begged God for cooperation, mutual respect, love and unity among all religious orders and communities in Slovakia and in the world.

ꟸ

My most profound and engrossing meditations were when I followed up on old ideas which came out of Kolakovič's spiritual exercises. Then I created my so-called comprehensive and personal meditations.

The comprehensive meditations consisted in tracing one subject in different places in Scripture. For example, the theme of the Holy Spirit. At Pentecost, or for a whole month (usually June) close to the feast of the Holy Spirit, I meditated on the Christian hymns "Veni Sancte Spiritus" and "Veni Creator Spiritus," and all the texts of the New Testament where the Holy Spirit was mentioned. In the Gospel of John, He is referred to in almost every chapter, and after the Last Supper, several times in every chapter. Other topics were God the Father and the Holy Trinity.

Each month I liked to concentrate on certain saints. In June and August, it was mainly St. John the Baptist, and in August, Peter. In May and October, I meditated on Mary, who after Jesus is the most rewarding theme among the individual people in Scripture. In June and January, Paul filled my thoughts.

These specific, focused meditations were to avoid abstract, theoretical reflections. It was important that in the Scriptures I find personal applications to my own life. What did this mean to me? How could I relate this to my own sins, defects, errors, temptations, tendencies, and desires?

ꟸ

My personal meditations tackled a variety of issues:

Death and Me

I looked at how I felt when I stood alone before death and when I experienced the death of others. I scrutinized the reasons I sometimes feared death so much. So many around me had already died. What messages were they giving me?

I thought about all the deaths among my relatives and friends. I pondered over the number and the sorts of deaths I saw now, and how I viewed them, both as a doctor and as a prisoner. These observations of death were important for me because all encounters with it are actually anticipations of our own death. They pointed to the fact that this was a very personal problem which I would have to solve alone soon enough.

Relationships

Personal meditation included relations with my friends and the graces and gifts which I had received through them. During these recollections I felt like John, the disciple Jesus especially loved. What a great number of remarkable gifts I had received since childhood!

I meditated on my family and my nephews, my parents, brothers and sisters, cousins and uncles. I recalled my educators, teachers, and spiritual guides. What an elite! What a group! What guidance and protection I had received from all of them!

Success and Me

I reflected on what I had achieved through God's grace. I looked at my qualities, my character, and the assistance I had provided in the conversion or vocation of others. (But then, whom had I actually helped to come to Christ? I felt I had done a lot of work but the results did not appear to reflect that. And the failures! Where were the people I had previously helped? Had not some of them already divorced, separated, fallen away? I remembered boys from my first group, not long after my complete conversion.)

I considered my journey through life and its main milestones:

My Personal Vocation

My consecration to God and the Virgin Mary, and the basic direction of my work in the future. I made a very conscious, definite, and final decision to live a consecrated life in celibacy and chastity. (I was aware that had I married, I would have very much affected and burdened my family.) I renewed this commitment or vow especially to St. Agnes of Bohemia, on March 2, 1952, and 1953.

Medicine

I loved medicine and regarded my profession as God's will for me, as the area in which He wanted me to work. I meditated on healing and on freeing myself from any desire for gratitude or reward. I reflected on how to renounce a scientific career, how to sacrifice everything and be thankful that I could help somebody. I saw that I could also provide spiritual assistance in many serious matters since medicine by itself is not enough in the healing process.

I returned to the problem of leprosy which had previously left a strong impression on me. Twenty million of my brothers and sisters were in constant pain and dying. It was a very slow death, with gradual disintegration of the eyes, face, and body. During my medical studies in Paris, I had seen lepers and this had helped me choose dermatology as my specialization.

After practicing in a lepers' hospital at Fez in Morocco, I decided on a lifetime of service on the island of Molokai reserved for lepers. I wanted to contribute at least a little to continuing the work which Damien de Veuster had started.[27] Hundreds of thousands of these poor people had not seen a doctor in years!

The coming to power of communism and my subsequent arrest frustrated my ideals of becoming a medical missionary. (On the other hand, when they put me in prison, my mother was, paradoxically, relieved, as she thought that I might not be lost to her completely after all.)

My Other Missionary Aspirations

These included the evangelization of the USSR, the liberation of Russia and the East from communism, socialism, and violent atheism, or more accurately anti-theism. I had to prepare for apostolate work, to confront the sacrifices it entailed and pray that I would be able to accept the challenge.

Therefore, I practiced Russian texts. Within this context, China's needs also began to emerge. I grew to willingly accept personal sacrifice, to give up my own country, the little nation which I loved so much, for the spiritual redemption and protection of Russia and China. Later, in one of the camps, I received Chinese books or texts but I only succeeded in learning eight hundred Chinese characters.[28]

The Apostolate

I was especially interested in the apostolate and missions to young people. Then I thought, "But, even now, I can go out into the whole world. I can do it through these walls and bars! I can begin here and now with prayer and sacrifice. I do not have to waste any time waiting for ideal conditions somewhere, sometime in the future."

Sacrifice

I wanted to be able to give up everything, even my life, to accept everything including suffering and my great fear of it. But how was I to do that when sometimes I could not even endure lesser miseries?

Our Spiritual Family

I thought about our society, which we called the "Family," especially my closest friends, and Vlado J. in particular.

ꝏ

There were many other main ideas and themes for meditations and spiritual renewal. The quotations are approximate since in prison we did not always have access to the Bible text.[29]

- "From his fullness, we have all received, grace in place of grace" (John 1:16). Everything is truly only grace!
- "When Simon Peter heard that it was the Lord, he tucked in his garment, for he was lightly clad, and jumped into the sea" (John 21:7). This particular verse was a great inspiration for me. When the Lord is present, a person should have no fear of drowning. He knows that Jesus will not leave him in distress. Today I use this thought for meditations, especially with young people.
- "No one has greater love than this, to lay down one's life for one's friends" (John 15:13).
- "Love covers a multitude of sins" (1 Pet. 4:8). We cannot minimize, erase, or retract sins once they have been committed, but we can find forgiveness through greater love and good deeds.
- "Her many sins have been forgiven; hence she has shown great love" (Luke 7:47).
- I meditated for a long time on the Annunciation as described by Luke in 1:26–42, "But she was greatly troubled at what was said and

pondered what sort of greeting this might be. Then the angel said to her, 'Do not be afraid, Mary, for you have found favor with God' " (Luke 1:29–30); "Most blessed are you among women" (42), that is, you are chosen, you are called, God bestows his grace on you.

- Mary protests, "How can this be, since I have no relations with a man?" (34), that is, how can I possibly do this? (I often asked myself that very same question where my situation was concerned.)
- The angel continues, "The Holy Spirit will come upon you, and the power of the Most High will overshadow you. . . . For nothing will be impossible for God" (35–37). That is, this will not be your work. It will be the work of the Son of God. Mary's answer also became my own, "Behold, I am the handmaid of the Lord. May it be done to me according to your word" (38).

Then it hit me. I finally understood these so often repeated words, not only with my mind, but with my heart. I had prayed the angel's greeting and each Hail Mary carelessly, but I suddenly grasped its full meaning, that is, that this prayer is actually the model of acceptance of a vocation! And nothing is impossible to God, not even deliverance from prison, from death, and from this whole diabolical system. "Blessed are you who believed" (45).

℘

Another theme was Jesus himself, and I pondered the following verses:

- "Jesus knew that his hour had come to pass from this world to the Father. He loved his own in the world and he loved them to the end" (John 13:1). He loved them even unto his own death. And he laid down his life for our salvation.
- "If I, therefore, the master and teacher, have washed your feet, you ought to wash one another's feet" (John 13:14); "I have told you this so that my joy might be in you, and your joy might be complete" (John 15:11). It was from this verse that we got the name of our first samizdat[30] song book *My Joy*.
- "for I know him in whom I have believed, and am confident that he is able to guard what has been entrusted to me until that Day" (2 Tim. 1:12).
- "It was not you who chose me, but I who chose you" (John 15:16).

- “Man, what do you have which was not given to you, and if you have received it, why do you act as if you had not received it?” (1 Cor. 4:7).
- “I have the strength for everything through him who empowers me” (Phil 4:13).
- “I have told you this so that you may not fall away” (John 16:1).
- “But beware of people, for they will hand you over to courts and scourge you in their synagogues” (Matt. 10:17).
- “In the world you will have trouble, but take courage, I have conquered the world” (John 16:33).
- “And do not be afraid of those who kill the body but cannot kill the soul.... So do not be afraid; you are worth more than many sparrows” (Matt. 10:28–31).
- “They will expel you from the synagogues; in fact, the hour is coming when everyone who kills you will think he is offering worship to God” (John 16:2).
- “So they went and secured the tomb by fixing a seal to the stone and setting the guard” (Matt. 27:66). (In prison, the stone was replaced by bars and concrete and the seal was the official sentence. Furthermore, just as Roman law had backed soldiers in Jesus’ day, so now State Security violence was sanctioned by law, and the prison guard stood now, as he had done in Roman times.)
- “Grant me justice, God; defend me from a faithless people; from the deceitful and unjust rescue me. You, God, are my strength. Why then do you spurn me?... Why are you downcast, my soul? Why do you groan within me? Wait for God, whom I shall praise again, my savior and my God” (Psalm 43, originally the standard introduction in the opening prayers of the Holy Mass).
- “And when he comes, he will convict the world in regard to sin, and righteousness and condemnation” (John 16:8). This verse inspired me to think about the importance of evidence, sin, and judgment in this world. It is easy for us, and without much risk, to witness to the truth. But it is much more difficult to testify to the sins of the powerful of this world and warn them of the coming judgment. Nevertheless, we have the responsibility to do so. All Christians are

committed to this task by the Holy Spirit. John the Baptist was a clear and excellent example of one who understood and did this.

- "Saul, Saul, why are you persecuting me?" (Acts 9:4). Silvo, Silvo, why are you persecuting me with every one of your sins? From this arose the song "Saul, Saul," which my father set to music, according to a melody composed in prison, and it appeared in the illegal songbook *My Joy.*
- Mary saw the stone was rolled away, so she ran to the apostles and cried, "They have taken the Lord from the tomb, and we don't know where they put him" (John 20:1–3). (See Emil Boleslav Lukáč's book: *Where Have They Taken Him? Essays on the Divisions among Christians.*)[31]
- "But Mary stayed outside the tomb weeping. And as she wept, she bent over into the tomb and saw two angels in white sitting there, one at the head and one at the feet where the body of Jesus had been. And they said to her, 'Woman, why are you weeping?' She said to them, 'They have taken my Lord, and I don't know where they laid him'" (John 20:11–13). I must have an intimate and close relationship with my Lord. Otherwise, nothing makes any sense and all that is related to faith is only theory.
- "Stop holding on to me, for I have not yet ascended to the Father" (John 20:17). I interpreted this as meaning that worldly concerns and affairs are not to divert us from our prayers and meditations.
- "Jesus said to her, 'Mary!' She turned and said to him in Hebrew, 'Rabbouni,' which means Teacher" (John 20:16). With such joy will we rush to embrace our families and friends when we leave prison.

Part VIII

The Gulag: The World of the Condemned
Giant Cells without Privacy
"God's Mills"
Romanies

I question again and again the usefulness of rousing these unpleasant and painful memories, especially when I am not totally convinced that this is God's will, since I lost many of my previous notes or they were destroyed. But perhaps I can continue at least for myself as penance for my sins, or in thanks and praise for the many gifts and graces the Lord Jesus has showered upon me.

Perhaps the voice I hear is that of Satan who would like nothing better than to divert me from fulfilling God's will and revealing the deft methods used for destroying souls.[32]

Following his arrest, but particularly after the first trial, a prisoner suddenly enters an entirely different world, as if he were on another planet.

Today, from Solzhenitsyn, we have the term "Gulag" (the Russian Gosudarstvennoje upravlenie lagerej or State Administration of Camps). He also later called it an "archipelago." This was an entirely other world, a state within the state. Although a person might only have a vague knowledge of it, he could not dismiss the fear and apprehension which this thought pressed upon him. It had existed for years, completely separated from the rest of humanity although physically only a few meters away. It was a world with its own completely different population, territory, problems, tragedies, tempo, and breath.

℘

About fourteen days after the main trial and after thirty-five months of imprisonment for interrogation, I was about to leave solitary confinement, the latter in itself being an even greater distinct society from the rest of the prison. I was to be transferred to the world of those already tried and convicted, which meant new people in addition to new walls and fear.

On the road from the prison of the Superior Military Court in Trenčín, I was again jolted around in a cupboard bus, which we called a "submarine." I had already been tried which meant that I was between the first court and the appeal trials. While I was still stuck alone in my own little "cupboard," several other convicted prisoners were less isolated and normally sat together in another corner of the bus. For a moment, their being together appeared to me to be pure happiness, an impossible dream. Imagine that! To be able to communicate with people again....

Ilava, to which we were transferred, was like a transit station out of hell: trucks, ordinary and cupboard buses, and cars stopped here. There was shouting, the constant clinking of keys and chains while they shipped out a browbeaten, humiliated, and terrorized mass of human beings.

Since I no longer had to wear dark glasses I could make out new faces, especially when I was in the ordinary non-cupboard bus. Many of the prisoners wore the civilian clothes into which they always changed when they were traveling.

There were rather comic contrasts here. In the middle of a hot summer one could see people in heavy clothes, coats, furs, and ski boots which they had worn in the winter when they were arrested.

On the other hand, in the winter, women shivered with cold in the light dresses they wore when they were snatched from life in the summer months. Some of them looked as if they had been grabbed straight out of the swimming pool.

During long stops and constant moves, there were also "filcungy," that is, searches which sometimes involved having to strip naked. During these searches, I attempted to protect or hide something which had either been smuggled or allowed, such as a medical book, the summary of my judgment, or at the very least the bread rosary and little notes written on toilet paper. What was found during these inspections was put in a bag and left outside in the corridor, or immediately destroyed. The standing order was, "You can only take soap, a brush, and bread with you."

And so, after endless, repeated checks, registrations, and calculations, I ended up for the first time in a large, musty, and what appeared to be an underground transport cell, with bunk beds stacked in threes. In the prison in Ilava, there were about fourteen people to a cell. At the time, it seemed impossible to cram so many into such a small space. But I learned about, and later personally lived in, cells where there were forty to fifty prisoners jammed together.

I actually looked upon this crowded space as a great gift from God, an unbelievable joy. Suddenly I could communicate with so many new people and get information from practically all the prisons and camps. From this point of view, transports provided a source for news and a bringing up to date of the situation.

But disadvantages immediately surfaced: it was the end of concentration, meditation, and prayer. If a person really wanted to reserve a quiet time to be alone with God, he could only achieve this through great ingenuity.

Since meditation was best done at night when others were sleeping or at least were not up, we used a simple trick to wake up: we drank so much liquid that we had to get up to go to the toilet. Then we did not lie down but only sat on the mattress. I would then have a half hour or an hour to myself and I would pray until weariness overcame me.

This was the end of peace and the beginning of enforced coexistence with a family not of my choosing. The members were remarkably varied and often exhibited the worst natures and characters. The living quarters gave the effect of living in a submarine.[33] We also felt we were inhabiting a common toilet. Under the "bucket" system, there was only an improvised toilet in the cell, a large pot with the predictable smell.

Again, I witnessed how many equally suffering people will immediately seek to establish what they consider to be their rights and privileges. They threw themselves onto the lowest or best bunk beds in efforts to occupy the most advantageous positions.

Later I understood this behavior, at least to some extent. For years on end some had been allocated the worst treatment, been shoved aside, and had had to yield to other forces. In prison, their lives risked being even more bitter and the suffering more intense. So they sought to improve their lot by grasping at any little thing. For example, one lacked adequate ventilation when one was far from a window or, in the winter, it was better to be away from a broken window; one attempted to avoid ending up with a worn blanket, or a bed with a missing stick or board, or a shaking bed. (When a bunk had three levels, at every roll of any of the prisoners everything moved and creaked and woke up those around it.) In addition, one had to contend with dirty, smelly neighbors, people in the upper bunks who wet their beds at night, and a myriad of other endless frustrations.

Thus, I even surprised myself when, in an almost childish way, I began to offer others spare pieces of bread, provisions, bits from parcels, tobacco and cigarettes. As a result many considered me naive and crazy. But, far from refusing, as I expected they would, at least out of courtesy, they sometimes lunged at whatever was offered.

On the second or third day, I suffered the consequences of this generosity. I had no food while others ate a lot, but hardly anybody offered me anything. They even refused to share when somebody literally begged. The situation with tobacco was similar to that with food. "Let me roll a Taras Bulba cigarette, . . . " (a sharp smoking tobacco).

In prison, any type of chemical dependence of a person is a double punishment. Even well-educated people such as university professors, would kneel in front of a guard, and ask, or even kiss his boot, just to be allowed to pick up the few cigarette butts lying in the corridor. Obviously, there were also exceptions.

But sometimes, my generosity (difficult as it was for me to practice) prompted charity in others as well. There were some, both from the cell and the camp, who quietly began to give away what they had.

ꝏ

At that time, there were the non-political prisoners among us and the number of criminals which began to increase.

I especially remember, but only dimly I must admit, a certain selfish dentist. He constantly talked about his personal problems. His life revolved solely around his own petty affairs. This was rather typical of all criminals. He was fat, and moaned endlessly about how he had been wronged and been sentenced to twenty-five years for simple gold speculation. He eventually appealed and the sentence was reduced to five years, but he continued his appeals.

This drastic change in his sentence surprised me. Who knows. Perhaps he had done the interrogator some service. Even before he appealed, he theorized about how he might gain protection, or get out, so that he could go on earning money from gold.

He tried to get in my favor, too, and commented that I could have a very easy time in prison, since almost all health workers have the chance to work in the infirmary at one time or other. His chief consideration was how to exploit prisoners for the professional help he gave them. Black marketeering, speculation, and self-interest remained firmly in his blood, and in prison, these weaknesses were even more apparent.

ꝏ

Those prisoners who had lived through and bore the marks of immense suffering disturbed me greatly and provided me with considerable food for thought.

There was a certain Dr. Oto. If my information was correct, he was a deputy of Laco Novomeský, the Commissioner for Education. Dr. Oto had been condemned to death but was not immediately executed. He had waited for mercy in a special cell on death row for nine months. One could see that he was not normal, that he now lived in his own, entirely different world. He appeared lost, was pale, tearful, and stared into space. What a terrible tragedy this was. I realized then how insignificant my suffering was compared to this. I had to be ashamed of myself.

Somebody also told me about a completely opposite case. It seems that after being condemned to death, a certain man by the name of Lančarič had waited for mercy on death row for two years. I thought he might have been the man who had interrogated me with decency, during my first month of imprisonment, in 1946.

They accused him of "Titoism." It was customary at the time to accuse the person they wanted to execute of collaborating with an enemy movement or government. Tito of Yugoslavia had lost all favor with the communists. But after two years of waiting Lančarič had been executed. How unpredictable and dreadful human justice often is!

Of course, if we see it, we can only see it from the outside.

ꙮ

And then there were God's mills. They grind slowly but surely. I often saw that they really did exist.

Later, after I left prison, I was able to speak with a man who had been one of the inspectors or State Security men when I was in prison. I knew I had seen him before.

He came as a patient where I worked as an X-ray technician after my release from prison. He could have been the same person who had rolled up his sleeves and had interrogated me and perhaps also beaten me in either Bratislava or in Ruzyň. I couldn't remember exactly where it had been and it was already a bit difficult to identify him. I had not got all the information concerning those times. I wondered if it had really been him who had beaten me, or whether it was somebody else. However, his answers to my questions confirmed that he had at least been one of the interrogators as, among other things, he stated that he had worked for State Security.

If I remember well, at that time, X-rays were done in a dark room. He dug his fingers into my arm and cried, "Doctor, it isn't cancer, is it?"

This attitude was typical of those who had been the roughest inspectors and interrogators. They were the most cowardly and tended to get hysterical where their own health was concerned. These fellows all reacted in the same way, "It isn't cancer, is it?" they lamented.

In this case, the diagnosis was merciless: lung cancer, probably with secondary tumors in the oesophagus.

I wanted to show him that I had forgiven him everything long ago. But he evidently did not recognize me. Nor did he appear to suffer from a guilty conscience or have the courage to say, "Don't be angry with us for hurting you."[34]

ဢ

Outside prison, many State Security men played the good guy with great self-righteousness: "I never injured anybody in my life. If I couldn't help or do some good, at least, I never hurt anyone in word or deed." Or, "Sure, I was a partisan, and I never harmed anyone. I actually helped a lot of people." This sounds almost unbelievable but it was typical behavior for the greatest sadists.

I have already mentioned God's mills. They grind slowly but surely. They are reliable, not like a State Enterprise run by the builders of socialism.

Then, friends at Bytíz or some other camp assured me that now, God's mills were not grinding slowly but quite fast as if powered by electricity or nuclear energy. They certainly ground quite thoroughly, not omitting anybody.

I commented that, "In my case they also caught everybody except this lieutenant from Košice. As far as I know, he is still a first lieutenant." Then somebody asked, "What's his name? Who's that?"

After listening to my description, one person said, "That's surely Lieutenant, or First Lieutenant B., who later received fifteen years for some violent act or murder. In the context of 'liquidation of the personality cult,' they took him to Jáchymov as a prisoner. The prisoners there recognized him and beat him so badly that they cracked his skull. Apparently he went blind in one eye." But the rumor was that the doctor refused to admit that there was anything wrong with him. Obviously we could never wish for nor condone such punishment.

This kind of information circulated in the transit transport cells, where a prisoner sometimes remained for several days or two or three weeks or a month.

There was a young priest in Ilava, from whom I wanted to obtain additional details concerning the texts of the Holy Mass. I think he was given eight years. He was short on enthusiasm and, I suspect, even on mental stability. This priest thought mainly about amnesty and when it would be granted. I was surprised, but then I would often see such cases.

Now, I am not shocked by the behavior of older prisoners worn out by long struggles and suffering. Their philosophy and physical makeup are quite different. They live in a totally separate world where reason and prudence have priority over enthusiasm and feeling. It is a change caused by age, life, and the impact of prison.

ꕥ

Two young students imprisoned for activities in the lay apostolate, chiefly Catholic Action, and I prayed the Holy Mass, but with difficulty. If I am not mistaken, I met them again later, after my release. I recognized them immediately because of their fine, decent, normal, cheerful faces. The young almost always immediately depended on me when they found out the reasons for my arrest and the sentence I was given as punishment.

They hung on my every word. These two also remembered a certain girl, a student. Apparently she had not been beaten. But the interrogator drew all sorts of pornographic pictures and forced her to look at them. He was coarse, obscene, and used dirty language. This was perhaps the worst kind of suffering for our sisters.

I also found those methods unpleasant but they never used them on me. They assumed that this approach would have no effect on a seasoned doctor.

ꕥ

A prisoner from a certain labor camp once talked about the situation there and I found myself envying those who were in a working environment. What freedom must be provided by labor even if it meant the grind of uranium mines.

Everybody also began to warn me about informers, stool pigeons, and spies among the "mukls." The term "mukl" referred to an old prisoner or a man destined for liquidation. Another term "bonzák" (plant) was also new to me, although I knew such people from the interrogation prison. It alluded to those who could really make life miserable for prisoners.

It was obvious that transit areas and transport cells or escorts were also the best places for "mukls" and screws to gather their information. But the regime soon changed and these large cells were replaced by smaller ones which could accommodate one, two, or at the most four prisoners.

One prisoner at Ilava who acted as room commander was probably an informer. He had already been in prison for nine years and may have been a war criminal.[35] He even warned me against spies. However, the greatest informers were often the ones who would pretend to alert us to be cautious. In this way they diverted attention from themselves and won the trust of new prisoners.

The showy heroic radicals were always the most dangerous. They spread hatred and revenge, "All communists must hang!" Nevertheless, after a short time, they almost always proved to be the main informers and collaborators of State Security.

When it was time to clean, I would be the only one to sweep the floor. It was an opportunity for physical exercise, service to others, and sacrifice. Quarrels always erupted when it was time to allot tasks to be done. Arguments would break out concerning who was the youngest, who had been in prison for the shortest time, and such. It was a rather sad example of how people found it difficult to reward a good deed with another good deed.

ꝏ

Each day brought with it orders to do ordinary jobs. There were the usual lengthy waiting periods for guards who had the keys and the name lists. The prisoner had to give his date of birth and was then hustled along roughly with shouts and the use of truncheons. Other people would again disappear into the unknown, either to isolation, solitary confinement, or a transport. Nobody knew exactly where they would end up and that was precisely the worst of it. The not knowing.

On the afternoon of about the second day I was in Ilava, while doing some heavy work to which I had been assigned, I was again taken away on a transport.

I thought of the terrible transports of Jews. Ours partly resembled theirs with one of the differences being that there was no famous Auschwitz orchestra playing. When the transports had arrived at the death camps, the Jews had been forced to play marches or cheerful waltzes and popular hits such as, "O Donna Clara."

But here, although there was no music, there were also guards everywhere, with tommy-guns, murderous faces, dogs, and shouting.

They drove people with truncheons or with the butt ends of tommy-guns: men and women, young and old, the sick and the blind, often people with amputated legs, and even those in wheelchairs. The prisoners were usually shackled in twos. At Pankrác, there were sometimes women with children and even babies who had been born in prison, although this was clearly illegal.

ꕤ

This time, they were very thorough. They shoved us onto elegant buses. After being convicted, we were no longer moved in closed cupboard buses or "submarines." Anyone who only had a prison uniform was seated in the middle of the bus so that the grey prison garb would not be seen by the public outside. Handcuffed hands had to be kept down so that people outside would not guess that these were prisoners. If somebody lifted or moved his hand no matter how slightly, it was enough for the guards to hurl themselves at him and for the metal to dig more deeply into his wrists. These were the famous American Ralky handcuffs which the prisoners considered the cruelest of all. They were clearly a hard currency import.

Policemen, always in pairs and wearing civilian dress or in uniform, were at the front of the bus. They checked everything from front to back and even kept a close eye on people's lips so that there would not be any whispering or speaking. And they always shouted.

From the outside, this looked like a chartered bus for people on vacation. It often had the sign "Excursion" on it to convince the public that this was so. During short stops or at crossroads in towns, we sometimes heard envious remarks, "Look at them living it up at our expense and sweat! They've got it made!"

On this particular transport, I met a very intelligent person (he may have been a lawyer) about thirty-five years old. He showed a little more courage than the others and took things quite sportingly. Again I learned a bit more about Ruzyň and the terribly stringent sections there. He said that there were cells without toilets where a prisoner had to live and sleep with his excrement, and others where the prisoner could not even sit, since the cell was filled with water and dirty mud up to a certain level. There were other similar "improvements" on the ordinary cell.

ꕤ

Olomouc was another transit stop. Jožko Suchý and I were once more in the solitary prisoners' area. I think I got a brief look at him. There was also an unknown woman there. During walks, I attempted to say a few words, both quietly and aloud, "Catholic Action. Christ the King. Do you have any information?" But I did not succeed in finding anything out, including which of our people were still imprisoned.

In Olomouc, I was handcuffed to a certain Dr. Ch., who added to the information I already had about various innovations in his branch of medicine. I learned about a new medicine for tuberculosis: INH Nitrazide.

Later I was astonished to learn that this doctor also collaborated with the prison regime. How could a respectable, intelligent person do such dirty work?

Unfortunately, this experience was repeated throughout my imprisonment. Intellectuals in particular seemed to have a great propensity for playing this double game. Simple people could not pretend and role-play like this, and neither could criminals and thieves. But then, there were few of these.

ꟈ

Thus we finally came to Pankrác.

At first, hundreds of prisoners stood holding their possessions, in a corridor in the basement. Who was that standing near me? Was it Vojto M.? Really? I scarcely recognized him, with his downcast face and his bulging eyes. His eyes had always protruded a little, but now there was no light there. Anybody could see that he was taking all of this badly and that he was angry and irritated. He had not smoked for a long time so I gave him my last cigarettes, perhaps a hundred of them. This was quite a large amount of property, under the circumstances.

Only then did I understand why I had kept them, although I did not smoke and so did not suffer from that addiction. However, tobacco was the universal currency in prison, even for those who did not smoke themselves.

A few encouraging words were enough to strengthen Vojto M. "Have you been convicted? What's happened to the others?" But then they immediately separated us.

I was issued a bowl and assigned to a military escort section with large cells. As I have already mentioned, military personnel were sometimes imprisoned for minor offenses, stupidities, and breaches of military discipline such as sleeping on guard duty or desertion.

On the second and third days, I and others were brought to the prison office and store. There they issued us new prison rags. Although clothing varied, after conviction they were better and warmer since the interrogators did not need to use insufficient clothing as a method of coercion. Now the regime mainly needed labor productivity from the prisoners.

Prisoners who were assigned to work in the store were immediately after cigarettes. They endeavored to make deals or exchanges, even offering better clothes. Since I did not have cigarettes anymore, I could not bargain for any improvements. I accepted this as an obvious indication that I was not meant to have anything better when it could be given to somebody else.

ꕥ

I suddenly saw Karel Komárek in the corridor where the offices were. He was a good friend, a worker and apostle to workers from the area below the Krkonoše Mountains. He waved to me with enormous joy and showed through enthusiastic gestures that he was all right. He had got ten years. What incredible luck it was to greet him among the thousands of prisoners who were there! How was it possible for us to meet at all?

Then they put the two of us in separate cells in the basement in what they called solitary confinement, although in fact there were two to four people confined together. It was possible to receive several publications there and we could even read foreign language books in German or Hungarian, although the general content was usually communist propaganda. However, at night, rats sometimes came out of holes or lower cellars. A coat which I had against the cold was very useful.

Here in Pankrác, I also drank water from the toilet, as I had learned to do when I was in the Palace of Justice in Bratislava. Where there was a flush toilet, water was always available and appeared to us to be cleaner than the water in the pails in which we did not have much confidence.

I could speak freely with somebody again. My cell mate was Stanislav S., a confectioner from Prague, and a typical follower of Masaryk, who was a humanist and a liberal. Stanislav had offended the communist regime with his pub conversations. He spread a multitude of criticisms and jokes in pubs, and the comrades turned these into anti-state meetings. He did not know how to extricate himself from the mess he was in. Unlike us, he was unprepared for the refinement of the interrogators, or for solitary confinement. They broke him.

At his trial, he caved in because the prosecutor (and apparently his own lawyer) threatened him. In a conversation, he was told that he would be executed if he did not answer according to what the interrogator had put in the record.

ꕥ

Romany women and men often sang at night. It was not possible to keep them quiet. But sometimes the Romany singing actually reported who had betrayed what, and counselled on what to say in the future.

Then, one night, around midnight, an older Romany woman began to bang on the door and shout, "Mr. Jailer! Mr. Jailer! Come quickly! Come quickly!"

When the guard came running, they were disappointed, which could also be heard through the wall.

"So what do you want, you old witch?!" They shouted at her, "Why aren't you asleep? What are you howling about?"

"Mr. Jailer, Mr. Jailer, do you know how the President is? Isn't he sick? Will there be an amnesty?"

And I realized that there were many people who did not sleep at night, because the president (at that time Gottwald) could be sick and dying, and there could be an amnesty.

Part IX

Cell mates in Solitary Confinement, Traumatology
Complaints about the Prosecution
Systematic Disinformation
Rules and Regulations for Detainees

After five or six days, I left the basement and went up to Department 3A. I had a cell opposite death row. There was a special routine for prisoners there. When they went out for walks, interrogations, or any other kind of contact, each one was accompanied by two screws, and the prisoner was handcuffed to one of them.

There was no hope here. There were no more interrogations. The prison was overfilled, and the solitary confinement cell which had originally contained a single prisoner under interrogation now held four people.

Again, as whenever there was a change, I was aware of the accompanying hustle and bustle. Agitation, trembling, uncertainty, and nervousness increased. The screws were amused when they saw how a humiliated prisoner shivered uncontrollably. It was very difficult to stop the shaking, since one often suffered from malnutrition which increased the feelings of cold. And the guards were not about to pass up an opportunity for sarcasm, "It's too late now for your conscience to bother you! No use shaking! You got your just punishment!"

Here, on death row, I saw those who had been condemned to death. They waited for execution, twenty or thirty at a time, but in individual cells. Sometimes I got various information about executions. It was said then that there were police executions which had not been preceded by trial or judgment. Sometimes we did not even know who it was. We only heard someone shout, "Long live freedom!"

We usually learned about an execution from old cell mates, or prisoners who cleaned the corridor in the execution section who guessed what was going on. A quiet drumming on cell doors usually accompanied prisoners who were on their way to execution. Drumming in time, in the morning, was also a clear sign that somebody was going to their execution.

ꙮ

I came to a relatively clean cell with three cell mates. There was Karel V. from some group called the "Faithful Dog" and a member of "Sokol,"[36] an old man, a follower of Masaryk and a typical liberal Czechoslovak. Then there was Helmut U., an atheist, who was extradited from East Germany, and Jozef Špáta, an extraordinary man, who contributed much to my spirituality. He was a convert, and had survived the Traumatology Department (a pseudonym considering what really went on in there), that is, a division in Ruzyň where electricity was used. He could describe everything in detail. He gave an authentic report of reality as it appeared to him, without any distortions or additions. Nevertheless his was a subjective truth. He spoke about matters as he perceived them behind the walls of the prison.

The following description may seem nonsensical and absurd, but not only for the reader. It also appeared so both to him and to me even then, in the 1950s.

An interest in various experiments with the human psyche is characteristic of the dismal period when attempts were made to destroy the human personality. Špáta found out how far supporters of such an inhuman ideology, without conscience and moral restraints, could go, thanks to totalitarian forces.

He experienced everything they were able to think of to humiliate human beings and cause unspeakable sufferings to one's fellow men. But he did not cultivate a personal hatred towards anybody who had caused his torment, as he believed that following a thorough investigation, these matters would eventually be cleared up.

At that time he said to me:

> Before my arrest, it was a public secret that in some prisons, they did things which had nothing to do with the investigation of a criminal activity, or with the carrying out of a punishment. How this came about, I don't know. I mention this so that I can show the poverty and wretchedness of this period, the age of the triumphant establishment of "scientific materialism."
>
> I come from a family which left the Catholic Church in the 1920s, and whose political leanings were to a socialist democracy. We never supported the communists, but we understood them. When I was in the resistance I didn't distinguish between right and left. It was all the same to us. In spite of this, in the 1950s, I was put on a list of people who had to be liquidated.

I was arrested on July 10, 1951. The interrogation to which they subjected me in the first weeks in Ruzyň was no different from the current approach of the time. The interrogators dealt with me harshly and unjustly, coarsely distorting my claims and words. They accused me of crimes which I had never committed, but in spite of this, they still treated me as a human being. Then they led me to a certain dark cell in the old wing of the building. A gallows could be seen behind the window.

I found myself in the factory of psychological injuries.

In the summer months of that year, from the window of my cell, I watched them complete the work on a prison building which they later taught me to call "Traumatology." I saw miniature cells in the building and was interested in the large copper plates in the corners of some of the cells. Sometimes my cell mate and I joked about how they were preparing this dovecote for us. When the building was finished, they moved us there.

My first impression was one of horror. My whole body knew that it was in an environment which it had never known before. The dreadful power of electricity completely crushed me, but the cries from the neighboring cells, and the terrible curses of my suffering fellow prisoners, reminded me that I was not alone in my misery.

The effect of the charged energy was absolutely obvious. If the joint of a finger touched a metal object, there was pain, like receiving an electric shock. The intensity of the current varied: sometimes it was increased to an unbearable level and at other times it completely stopped, as when the lights in the whole building were turned off.

Severe shaking accompanied the pain, and the victim usually suffered a drastic weight loss. I quickly shed about thirty of my eighty kilograms.

Listening and loud speaker devices were installed in the walls between cells. Other prisoners also learned beyond any doubt that this was true. The prisoner already traumatized by electric shocks was now submitted to sound effects.

They left me alone in a cell.

At first several tones of an unpleasant level began to be heard simultaneously. A person then became nervous as one does when he hears the whine of a circular saw for a long period of time. Several "circular saws" screeched and screamed here, day and night, for whole months at a time. It was extremely depressing.

Then monotonous blows like the beat of a kettle drum were added to this set of sounds, and again with brutal regularity, and without stop. The prisoner walked and breathed to the rhythm of these blows, and perhaps his heart also beat to it. It was a state similar to hypnosis.

We couldn't sleep. There was bedtime, and if I was not at night interrogations, I could lie on the bed. There were the usual admonitions, "The face must be turned towards the door and the head kept uncovered!"

If a person moved a little in his sleep, there was immediately harsh knocking on the metal door and they took the blankets away. There was always some movement in the long corridor and there was noise all night, "The hands must be uncovered and on the blankets to above the elbows!" When sleeping or because of the cold, somebody always moved his hands under the covers. Then the knocking on the door and the general racket would begin.

The prisoner desperately wanted to sleep but there was the screeching of circular saws, the beating of invisible drums, the guards shouting, knocking and bellowing, and a light mounted above the bed shone in his face all day and all night. The light of a filament bulb is still bearable, but oh, how the prisoners suffered under the glare of neon lights for whole days and nights. I was lucky, mine was only an ordinary light.

Absurd and senseless stereotyped phrases coming from invisible sources would then be heard, "You idiot, you idiot. . . . " This would go on endlessly and when they faded away, some sort of contraption in the corridor made a low noise and they immediately started up again. In my case, there were two idiotic themes: "Are you Joshua or aren't you Joshua?" This was the first theme. The second was: "You're Žingor in your very core!" I don't know why they pestered me with this precisely since during my whole life I had never had anything in common with Žingor.[37]

What was terrible was that the voices did not come from all sources simultaneously. There was a difference in time, a slight delay. They formed a monotonous whisper, somewhat like several echoes joining in at various moments. This significantly undermined my weak and weary mind.

I looked like a ghost. But even at the worst of times, I maintained a spark of critical reason untouched by all the madness, and mentally recorded all the forms of evil and my reactions to them.

When I was in this psychological state, they began to take me blindfolded to a new chief and interrogating officer. "We have summarized all the previous documents, and have found a common denominator: Zionism." I refuted the charge. "What do I have in common with Zionism? I'm not even a Jew, and the interests of the Jewish nation are foreign to me."

"Zionism or Gestapoism," continued the chief with a meaningful slashing gesture at the throat. It was interesting that the interrogators insisted on being addressed as "Sir," and got very agitated if a prisoner called them "comrade."

They began to throw the usual accusations and totally absurd "facts" at me. In the beginning they came up with the idea that during the War, I had had contacts abroad with a certain American diplomat with whom I had remained in contact after the War when he was working in Prague. Why this diplomat had a special interest in me remains the official secret of this chief interrogator of our State Security.

If a person in his weariness and perhaps also naivety decided that it made no sense to defend himself against the nonsense, and signed something which, in his opinion, was an innocent little thing, they immediately brought a whole repertoire of absurdities to be documented.

I went along with this for a while, then disgust got the better of me, and I declared that all they were saying were lies and refused to continue. "So then you lied? Three days in the dungeon and a fast!"

History repeated itself three times. I was in the dungeon more than in my cell. In the dungeon I slept on bare concrete and received a little food every third day. When they saw that I was not compliant enough for their purposes, they increased the pressure.

The voices in the walls started up again and to my weary mind repeated the long history of my alleged collaboration with the British secret service. It was an absurd, but expertly assembled story, loaded with perfect English secret service terms which I had never heard before, and precise "facts," with the full names of the "participants."

When a person was in complete isolation and under constant mental coercion, supplemented with "evidence," the inventions did not appear as absurd as they do now. I often tended to doubt my own memory and mind, and resisted more out of instinct and intuition since I felt it a duty to struggle against evil. The worst was when the fantasies included some core of reality from which they had started and then twisted. It showed once again that a partial truth is more dangerous and seductive than a complete lie.

The story was that during the War, I had got into contact with the British secret service, and that after the War, I had organized a network for them in the Balkans. After several days I had memorized this recorded tale. Then the interrogator summoned me, looked at me triumphantly with a hypnotizing look, and asked encouragingly, "So, is the conscience working?"

He eagerly drew something on a sheet of paper. Then, without a word, he turned the paper towards me. There was a British flag on it. But I did not react to this nonsense.

"You're in Traumatology," announced the interrogator. "Trauma" means injury. This was actually an establishment which deliberately produced psychological damage for mysterious aims, which had nothing at all to do with the security of our state. This was criminal experimentation with human beings who were exposed to the tortures described here and certainly many others. They searched the psyche of a person, intentionally driving him mad, as a scientist dissects and studies the gland reactions of a dog.

It was in these terrifying cells that, for the first time, I really wanted to die. To my way of thinking, death meant the end of all this suffering. When the interrogator gestured at the neck indicating the possibility of execution, I did not look upon this as a frightening threat. Perhaps I initially experienced relief. I saw a chance of escaping, an end, a way out. I eagerly asked, "Really? When will it happen?"

I do not know what I would have given then to bring death faster. I understood why they took such drastic measures to prevent attempts at suicide. They did not want any of their guinea pigs to escape. People were put in cages and allowed a precise amount of food, oxygen, sleep, and psychological perceptions to keep them alive so that they would endure the maximum pain, fear, and suffering. At the same time, as much information as possible was wrung out of them so that it could be used both against them and others. And I understood the reason that at their trials, many paved the way to their own hanging and willingly confessed to contrived accusations.

I became more and more like a puppet without any will or thoughts of my own. Only the tiniest spark of my ego was left to flicker in the profound darkness of spiritual desolation.

A voice of authority ordered me to stretch out on the floor of the cell as if I were dead. It promised me what I most wanted, death. After a while, a guard came into the cell and a kind human voice asked, "What! Are you crazy? Stand up or I'll tie you up!" However, the other commanding voice insisted, "Don't move!"

They dragged me to a cell in a distant wing. The suit which I had worn when they arrested me was hanging on a coat hanger on the door. It was dark in the cell. On the right was a toilet and on the left, the ceiling above the horsehair mattress was quite low. The cell had no window. It was a dusky grave.

"You can go to the john if you need to!" I tried to urinate.

They put me in a straitjacket. They bound me with leather straps up to the neck, hands and legs included, and left me on the door-mat. I could not move at all. Then they turned the light off and slammed the heavy door. Only a little blue light penetrated past the door into the dense gloominess of the cell.

But I was happy for a while. Above all, I enjoyed the real, true, dense, black darkness! This was bliss for my weary eyes! There were no voices here! There was perfect, blessed silence except for the chirping of birds. I had a feeling of there being a muffled choir in the water pipes, but I was aware that this was only my hypersensitive hearing reacting to genuine, true silence.

Then again, shadows and tranquillity. After a few hours, I wanted to go to the toilet. I called and shouted but nobody came. A long time later I woke up from a deep sleep, as wet as a baby.

And then they took me back to the terror-filled trauma section.

I sat in the corner of the interrogation room and because I had a headache, from time to time I would move my hands and massage my temples to alleviate the pain. "Stop that!" roared the interrogator. I stopped. After a while the pain increased and I unconsciously moved my hands again. "I told you to cut that out!" shouted the interrogator.

After a while, they brought out two huge pigskin gloves which they put on my hands and secured with a lock. They left me tied up to this rack of madness for about six weeks. The skin between my fingers was inflamed and my hands became numb. When I had to go to the toilet they freed one hand for a while.

Sometimes a Gypsy was on duty. He only stared impudently through the little window and never did anything for me. Because I could not use my hands, I urinated in my trousers. That humiliation was even greater than the pain in my hands.

After six weeks they took the gloves away and brought a young Croat to my cell. He looked at me with frightened, frantic eyes, then he reached out to touch me and asked, "Are you a ghost or a man?"

"A man," I assured him.

He had been in a straitjacket for perhaps three months, or even longer. He showed me the unnatural position he had been in. He had had to hold both his hands behind his head for a whole month. They wanted to hypnotize us as they would hens.

Everybody, everybody was broken. But our Croat stood firm, apparently because he believed in God. Did he pray? No, he could not. He could not even say the Our Father. But he constantly called out, "In the name of the Father and of the Son and of the Holy Spirit!" This saved his life and his sanity, in spite of the devils around him. He did not fear them. When they were most enraged he pacified them. "Don't be afraid, comrade. No matter what efforts you put into this, you'll never be a marshal!"

He knew about traumatic illusions. "Josip, you know the devil has a radio," and he pointed to the invisible listening apparatus in the walls.

The interrogator with the sadistic face was not happy with me, but I was not exactly clear about the cause of his dissatisfaction. Nevertheless, first, he slapped my face. I willingly offered the other cheek. He then smashed my head violently against the wall. I did not stop him because I knew that he only wanted to provoke resistance on my part so that he could go on tormenting me for months.

In the cell, my whole world dissolved into a feverish haze. I did not know where the circle of terrors ended and where my own madness began. In my greatest need, I turned to the only person who was available, the guard who looked through the little window every minute.

"Help me! I'm going crazy here! I can't stand it anymore!" An eye looked at me for a long time and then painfully looked away. Another eye was hard and angrily turned away. One guard opened the door and whispered, "We can't help you. Pray!"

What kind of advice was this? Prayer was for old women! What was prayer to me? I rejected this idea. After all, I was in favor of progressive thinking.

Then the pain increased and I asked myself, "What if I tried this prayer thing?" I thought about it. It could do no harm. Only I did not know how to pray. I knew a little of the Our Father but was not sure whether or not it was correct. But I decided to try it anyway. To my astonishment I found that after a short time of prayer, the pain eased a little.

"Glory be!" I exclaimed and almost forgot to continue praying. When the suffering increased, I tried it again. Once, the words of the Our Father and Hail Mary resounded from a neighboring cell. I learned them and my sick soul finally had a good weapon.

But I am not a good warrior. I am too much a victim of my education and progressive prejudices. I struggled with God and about God for whole months. I really did not want to believe.

On the night of June 13, 1952, my suffering climbed to its highest level. All those sounds danced around in a sick twirl in my soul. I felt that I would die.

The intense pain, like that from inflammation of a nerve in a tooth, penetrated my eyes and sleep. I was a wretched ruin of a man moving to the rhythm of a drum, pipe, and siren. My body was weak and death threatened. I could not think. I was a robot waiting to be worn out and broken.

Then a tiny ray of light which had not yet been entirely extinguished in the depths of my soul began to burn intensely. "If such terrible evil exists, there must also be absolute Good! It is necessary to believe!"

A fighting, joyful mood then permeated my whole soul and thought. No, I was not healthy. The screeches of the external and internal world still pressed upon me. Pain still shook me.

But now it all meant nothing to me. I was convinced that I was protected, that someday I would be a person again. And I was filled with joy at the knowledge that the rule of evil is not unlimited. I was certain that God would not abandon anybody who called Him, even such a wretched creature as I was.

The next day, I asked to see the interrogator. I declared his documents to be nonsense and I behaved like a reborn person with human awareness. In the following days, I surprised them with my very energetic, rational speech.

And their reaction to this? They stopped torturing me. The doctor prescribed a health package. They considered my case as settled. I categorically refused to sign the final document.

Once they took me to a smaller hall where about twenty members of State Security were sitting. (My commanders and interrogators were not among them.) They asked me a great variety of questions which I calmly and factually answered. They laughed among themselves and commented, "They didn't succeed, ha ha ha!" Someone else added, "This doesn't apply to our people." He obviously had the famous "Traumatology" in mind.

The forces of good and evil, between the supporters and enemies of traumatology, were a little confused. One uniformed member of State Security with the rank of captain (his colleagues called him "Jozef") worked in the prosecutor's office and prepared notes for counsel. Once he summoned me, and with a lordly tone, ceremoniously proclaimed, "State Security as such has no objections against your saying and writing about what was done to you here, whenever, wherever, and before whomever you wish."

But my commander advised otherwise. "That is the prosecutor's opinion, but our people will be in the courtroom." He was right. The judge in my case was the famous Dr. Rudý.

On January 10, 1953 (Imagine that! After all I had gone through, I still followed precise dates in the calendar), a guard came to me and announced, "Pack your things and come with me!" I was given ordinary clothes. The commander came to say good-bye, "But leave electricity alone, it could harm you!" I replied, "I'll talk about it since that is the will of God!"

When I signed the release form in which I declared that I would not betray state secrets which I had learned during interrogation imprisonment, I asked the commander, "Is the electric treatment also a state secret?" "No, it isn't," he answered. "Your signature does not apply to that."

Immediately after arriving at Pankrác, I asked to see the prosecutor. He recommended that I make a complaint to the General Prosecutor. They sent a certain high ranking officer who listened to me very carefully. After he had questioned me, he addressed me by name and said, "This had to happen to you so that you would believe in God."

The rumor was that in the fall of 1953, the traumatology department at Ruzyň was closed. After certain alterations, the former house of fear began to be used for other purposes. . . .

I have limited myself to a rational, comprehensible description of what truly happened. But my experience reaches beyond this. You must understand that my conversion to Christianity was achieved in complete isolation. I could not draw on sources of information from the past. In spite of this, I became a Christian to such an extent that everything which my Christian fellow prisoners did for me later appeared completely acceptable, clear, reasonable, and entirely appropriate to me.

The internal struggle which led me to faith surpassed in its completeness my entire earthly, human nature, and I lacked the intellectual abilities to express it even to myself. In essence I resisted faith because I considered it irrational. I believed when I understood that our human reason is imperfect and that there exists a superior rationality which surpasses it.

For long months, I was on death row in Pankrác. This meant that every day, I looked into the faces of people who were going to their deaths. I know the stark terror of those places.

For long days and long weeks, I was in the cells of madmen, exposed to their rage. I was also the witness to how people were rendered unconscious by injections, and subjected to recorded interrogations while unconscious. And I know that on the basis of confessions obtained in this way people were convicted of serious offenses.

I know from talking to cell mates that the illegal actions which prison officials committed in interrogation prisons, and which I described here, are not unique. There is good reason to believe that they also used drugs with psychological effects. Complete breaking of prisoners suggested that scopolamine, which has a narcotic effect, was used. Extravagant colored visions described by some prisoners suggested that mescaline, which causes hallucinations and aberrant conditions, was also used.

I also know other terrors. I know the terrors of returning to ruined houses, and although I was not directly at the front, I know the terror of war at close quarters. But what I experienced in Ruzyň was the worst terror, because there, the torture penetrated into the innermost spheres of the human soul. In Ruzyň, they conducted experiments with something to which another human being never should be subjected.

The reason I must testify is not to emphasize the described suffering. I know testimony of Bolshevik and Nazi concentration camp victims which is much more rending.

But in Ruzyň, under the brutality of violent men, those were human beings who died, regardless of how wretched some were. In Ruzyň, the evil was organized in a more refined way, with kid gloves,

> but was even more satanic. Poor puppets, from whom everything human had already been stripped away, went to their death.
>
> I was sentenced to twelve years in prison. During this time, I passed through various institutions which were filled with people who had met with similar or even worse fates.
>
> I promised these poor tortured wretches, many of whom already could not speak, that I would not be silent about their suffering, that I would appeal to peoples' conscience about them.

I was ashamed when Jozef told me about all the things he had survived. If I had not known him as a very serious, honest person, and if I had not already known about the "radios" allegedly concealed in the walls of underground cells in a special department in Ruzyň, from the above mentioned Yugoslavian and other prisoners, perhaps I would not have believed him. I would have thought that he was crazy, that he had simply lost his mind. In fact, in the beginning I did not believe the Yugoslavian man and others. I considered their accounts to be hallucinations and illusions caused by nervous or psychological disorders.

I was very glad to have Jozef in the cell, especially when I wanted to rouse myself a little, on the eve of a trial or before interrogations, and when I needed additional courage, righteous anger, and an uncompromising attitude. Then, I needed to hear again about the inhumanity of the methods used against prisoners.

I would ask him to relate his testimony once more, particularly when I was due for a court hearing. Then he always repeated everything so that I was freshly aware of the foundations on which the whole monstrous system rested, and would not be appeased by the appearance that there was also a little humanism there or a true attempt to administer justice.

Jozef and I shared a spiritual life which consisted in prayers and sometimes songs. Later he memorized the prayers of the Holy Mass which I had taught him. He had previously shared a cell with an older parish priest for eight months. But the priest had not memorized the Holy Mass, like the majority of those who had not prepared for prison.

We began our joint studying of a chapter from the memorized Gospel. The courage with which Jozef testified constantly put me to shame. Where was I compared to him! He never stopped reminding them of their Gestapo-like behavior in their torture and inhumanity towards prisoners, and he steadfastly refused to sign anything.

I adopted the same attitude where confiscation of property was concerned and, when after three years they handed me an arrest warrant, and so on, I refused to sign whatever they put in front of me.[38]

Jozef wrote a complaint to a higher authority almost every week, but he told me that I was the first person who ever supported him. Others attempted to dissuade him, including General B., with whom he had previously shared a cell. They claimed there was no sense in it since nobody took our testimony seriously, and we might even cause ourselves more harm. They thought it would be best to protest later, at another time, when we would be able to speak openly about everything.

However, Jozef and I thought that when such a time did come, our testimony would not be needed. And so I also wrote various complaints on hidden scraps of paper. I wrote protests in accordance with their own communist laws, the ones which they had passed but refused to observe whenever it suited them.

I constantly claimed that the chairman of the Supreme Military Court of the Military College should hear me. The chairman, Colonel M., did listen to me but it was on the day before the trial and when I was in irons. In a harsh tone he threatened to tame me if I was so impertinent as to appeal to the law. "You're not going to teach us our own laws!" It was as if their laws were only to allow prosecutors and judges to kill people, and were not for the protection of the accused or of all citizens.

I think that the chief guard with a mustache who took me in irons to see M. was at least internally inclined to support me since on the way back, he treated me very decently and courteously.

One morning, I wrote a document entitled "Complaint about the Violation of Laws in the Practice of Interrogations and Trials." This had been written in an empty cell on death row, where the section commander would usually allow a condemned prisoner one hour to write official letters. He would give him a pen and ink but not a pencil, so he could not break it and use the pieces. . . .

I had written notes but it still took me about three to four hours to write the text, during which time the commander of the department heaped insults on me. This was the only official protest which disappeared and may not have reached its destination. All the other complaints went to their intended places and many were even effective, although in general the answers were always negative.

Later we found out that some of our protests and comments were used to make amendments to some of their laws, for example, the definition of high treason. I had argued that the whole Criminal Law Code was redundant since that paragraph covered everything. The article stated that any action committed "out of hatred for the people's democratic order" was automatically considered high treason.[39]

ᴕ

Strange things were going on in this prison. We were not allowed to take walks very often, the family photographs which I had been allowed to keep vanished, letters were lost, and when the prisoner did write, he was afraid to mention anything that was happening. When making purchases from the prisoners on duty in the corridor, a person could receive a comb or a tooth brush when he had ordered bread.

A prisoner who was said to be a sadist or a murderer was assigned as barber and librarian. He earned extra from bribes on the side. He handled books and purchases according to the size of the payoff. We refused to pay anything so we were often given the worst books. I argued a little about this with a friend. He considered the bribes to be the lesser evil. He thought it was better to pay up rather than have nothing to read and remain constantly idle. The books we received were mostly communist propaganda, but we also got Hungarian and German books which we used to study German and for discussion sessions with cell mates.

Two of us were Christians, and two were atheists. Compared to us, the atheists in prison were poor fellows lacking the joy and trust which faith in God gives to believers.[40]

Sometimes, while cutting hair, the barber threw out scraps of news but the information was always false. We called these "latrines." They included the news that Chiang Kai-Shek[41] had dropped an atomic bomb on northern China and was marching against the communists. When these rumors came from all sides, it gave them a ring of truth.

The reports, especially the ones concerning amnesty, were often spread by commanders and informers. It was another way of applying psychological pressure to disarm and paralyze detainees. When a prisoner expected that at any moment there would be an amnesty, a war, the end of the regime, or the end of the world, he stopped making complaints, and laid aside all protests and conflicts. The "latrines" fostered the passiveness of the victim who counted on outside intervention, but this reliance actually bound his hands and mind.

Therefore, when I heard these reports, I consistently emphasized the strict truth, regardless of how bitter it was. Dreamers who were seduced by these alluring fantasies were disappointed when they did not materialize. They even thought that I was siding with the authorities, since I did not concern myself with the reports with as much enthusiasm as they did.

According to them, that meant that I wanted to stay in prison endlessly, and might even be an informer.

However, there is nothing worse in prison than being constantly disappointed. When that happens, a prisoner loses faith in everything, gives up, becomes a pessimist, and goes under. He seeks protection under the guise of humiliation and subservience.

This barber also said that Father M. had been executed the previous day and that fear had caused him to soil himself with excrement. That fear had been a reason for the defecation was already suspicious to me, since I was aware that muscles are not always under the control of the will, but that such reflexes are influenced by various other factors. Obviously what they said was pure invention, but this was how authorities would break a prisoner's brother or best friend.

ꝏ

Signaling to other prisoners did not work very well here, but often during a walk, somebody would throw something. The sick and those who feigned illness were sent to a slower internal circle within the larger circle of walking men. There, if the guard was a bit lenient, it was sometimes possible to exchange a few words or to place a scrap of paper or something similar on the ground when one was pretending to adjust a bandage or tie a shoelace, or straighten socks or fumble with clothes while kneeling.

There, I saw F. again, and we were able to talk a little. After I described how I refused to testify, I was surprised by his view that it was nonsense to make useless efforts. Why should a prisoner "bang his head against a brick wall" needlessly at every obstacle he faced when he could go around most of them or easily conquer them by either waiting or using dynamite? Why surrender immediately?[42]

I also saw "báťuška," that is Dr. Šesták, from the Russicum, but only twice, and then he completely vanished.[43] I learned about Father Konopa, a priest from the Russicum, but I did not know him at this time. And because I misunderstood, I thought we had been trapped by an informer.

During a walk, I once risked calling, under the women's windows, "Catholic Action here. Long live Christ the King. I'm Silvo." I then heard, "I'm Anka," and a few words about the Bratislava group. Those who had appealed were now clearly here. Perhaps Imro and some of Šesták's group were also here. Helmut had a brother in the underground to whom he had given messages but the latter suddenly disappeared. Then when Helmut began to demand a trial and justice, he also disappeared. It was said that as a taxi driver he drove somebody in the direction of the Slovak border. Suddenly they arrested him, took him away, and brought him here. His protests were useless.

They also transferred Karel V. He got about ten years. Somehow we later quarreled because of Hus and the Church. He was a follower of Masaryk and isolated himself from the rest of us, but I had my share of responsibility in the dispute.

Their whole secret organization was called the "Faithful Dog" and was probably a State Security set up, as the police were not above staging anti-state groups.

"Somebody" would get a car for them, and perhaps a transmitter (and then they were seen among State Security). State Security was able to persuade them to make long lists of new, reliable, "secret" ministers, and looked for codes and transmitters from "trustworthy" State Security men. They had even prepared armbands with the inscription "National Guard" on them for the future revolution. This was obviously most useful to State Security, since it made it easier for them to get more evidence about anti-state thinking.

But he loved his dog. He dreamed about it a lot, more than others did about their children.

ꕥ

At the beginning in prison, I felt like a complete novice, a "simpleton," needing to be taught by everyone. But with time I matured into an "old hand." Among the prisoners in the cell, I was the one who had been in prison the longest. Sometimes I took pride in this, but at other times I was again impatient about when and whether this would end at all. When would they assign me to the camps?

It was especially difficult for me to see so many people leave. They were going to a freer environment in camps or perhaps to freedom. I had seen so many go, and I always remained alone.

I must mention that I also quarreled with Jozef. This concerned his fasting. As a convert, he offered a strict Friday fast, actually a hunger strike, a full twenty-four hours without food, as a penance for his previous life. But I noticed that he then became a little yellow and rather weak. His breath acquired the slight sweet smell of acetone, not an artificial one, but a biological one. For a doctor, this is a symptom which confirms an honest hunger strike, when a person eats or drinks nothing at all.

I rebuked him, and forbade him such a strict approach. We had a heart-to-heart talk and I stated that at his first confession, he should tell the priest my point of view as a doctor and a Christian, which was that especially here in prison such drastic fasts could damage his health. I know that at Mírov he succeeded in going to confession, and the priest enjoined him to discontinue this kind of sacrifice.

But during our quarrels I suspected, with a certain envy, that he was progressing faster than I was, that he was way ahead of me in spirituality, and living his faith better, offering more. I always had to struggle with these human weaknesses and jealousies.

Then another prisoner came to our cell. I think that A. T., a social democrat, had got twenty years.[44] He was a good man but a little sensitive to various minor medical problems such as hemorrhoids. And like almost every introvert, he had great doubts about the Church. We decided that he was divorced since his reservations extended most particularly to the area of marriage and sexuality. His positions were substantially opposite those of the Church. But in spite of this we became quite close to him.

Then we acquired another excellent cell mate, Václav Věříš, a pilot, about twenty-three to twenty-five years old. He was still an innocent boy, brave and enthusiastic. Although he was originally an atheist, or rather indifferent and unaware of religious matters, he very soon joined us. With my help, he learned about ten chapters of the Gospel of John in Russian. It was obvious that faith transformed his life.

After that I lost contact with him. I only knew that he had been moved, perhaps to Leopoldov, on the same day we were moved. He apparently stayed there for some time. Only now, in January 1994, Karel Komárek found out that Václav's name was on the list of the "Organization of Political Prisoners." He got perhaps twenty years and was last seen in the Jáchymov camp. Apparently he is now dead.

ȣ

I had been taken to Pankrác for my appeal trial which, as it turned out, was postponed several times. Sometimes I really had the impression that it was deliberate. This was the simplest way to unnerve the accused who was in isolation. He constantly waited for something to happen, but again and again, he had to experience disappointment from endless postponements. Such a prisoner would not demand details in writing or insist on checks, whether to correct some illegality, or perhaps actually to protest. Even if he was not given a pencil and paper, the Law Code, or the possibility of a defense counsel, he would put up with everything just to be left in peace.

It is an exceedingly nerve-racking situation in which to be. Although at the time I was still quite a young, quiet person, the constant waiting, pondering matters over, loss of sleep, and repeated postponements, week after week after week, took its toll on me.

They left the prisoner, as the saying goes, to stew in his own juice, until one day he just did not care about anything. This corresponded to my three stages of pain, experienced during torture, including "walking," which on the surface seemed like such a comfortable, kid glove approach. They did not even touch a person, yet perhaps he suffered more than if they had beaten the soles of his feet, not only for a few minutes, or one or two hours, but for a whole day, a whole week, or a whole month.

It never stopped. It went on and on and on, without limits, without the slightest hope that it would finally end, that there would be some sort of interruption or way of defending oneself. That was the worst feeling of all.

I have already mentioned the local regulations for interrogation. The list was hung somewhere high up so that a prisoner could not damage it. "When the door is opened, the prisoner will announce . . . Number 2309 . . ." (I think this was my number in Ruzyň) ". . . cell 214." Later 710, or 810. "All's well."

Everything is fine. . . .

With this declaration, the comrades actually verified how far they had already broken a person and whether he was now submissive. For many prisoners, this rule provoked a cry of desperation, so that the guards immediately knew whether he was still normal or not.

For whole weeks, I heard the cries of beaten, broken people, "I'm a person not an animal!"

The rules also stated, "Stand by the window." That is, farthest away from the door. "It is forbidden to: write on or mark the walls, or damage the equipment in the cells, address the guards without permission, sleep, or take a nap anywhere except on the bed, sit on the blankets or mattress, speak to other prisoners or otherwise establish contact with them, sing or behave in a noisy way, reject food."

As far as I remember, the rules even stated that it was forbidden to "sleep with the head covered, or with hands and forearms covered."

However, the latter was not to prevent suicide attempts by the slashing of wrists, veins, and arteries. All this was a cunning way of limiting the amount of sleep one got. Since when sleeping in the cold everybody naturally automatically stuck their hands under the blankets, a very normal reflex action, the roaring of the guards did not stop all night.

In addition, we were not permitted to present group complaints and requests, only individual ones.

This also was ludicrous. When they opened the cell doors in the morning, the supervising officer always called out, "Requests and complaints!" But the prisoner knew that whatever he had to say, even concerning violations of the law, would be reduced to asking for toilet paper or soap.

Part X

The Appeal Trial, the Supreme Military Court
The Prisoner Is Handcuffed, the Public Is Excluded
My Unique Family Support
Prison Uncertainty, Fear, and Constant Good-Byes

In the end I was assigned a lawyer or defense counsel because I did not want my family to incur additional expenses. He introduced himself as Dr. K. He smelled of alcohol. Members of State Security were not the only ones who had to drown their consciences in alcohol. These actors, supernumeraries from the great political theater, did the same thing.

I knew that we could not come to an agreement even though we quarreled for ten to fifteen minutes. He kept repeating, "Leave this to me! Take my advice! You haven't any experience. You're in prison for the first time! I know how it goes. Don't try and defend yourself. You'll only get a heavier sentence, nothing else!"

"But I didn't commit high treason!"

"That doesn't matter! What's important is getting a reduced sentence. That's the most vital thing."

"But I don't want a reduced sentence," I insisted. "I want the truth."

During the trial he only requested the reading of the evidence. He did not summon witnesses, even though I maintained that he should do so. Perhaps he truly believed that this was the best thing to do, or from his professional point of view, the most effective approach to take. He may not even have been aware of the consequences of this procedure. It meant that the legal defense was badly limited if statements which had been acquired under duress were read but there was no possibility of cross-examining witnesses and refuting their statements.

In the end, I had no choice but to turn to the prosecutor and ask, "Is there no one at all to defend the law before the court?"

I requested that my own defense counsel should not be allowed to speak. He was basing the whole defense on mitigating circumstances, the fact that I was a good worker or an honorable citizen, but this actually indirectly indicated that I was guilty of high treason, which I had never committed. Mitigating circumstances are needed by a guilty person, not an innocent one.

The appeal trial was finally held on August 12, 1954. The chief justice of the Supreme Military Court, Dr. M., a colonel, who later allegedly committed suicide, feared something in my case. Therefore he thought of a very good tactic. He called for exclusion of the public. I protested against this, especially because the trial was not about new and therefore secret matters but about charges which were already three or four years old. Since the first trial had been public, to insist on a closed court now was total nonsense. In the end he called for a vote that confirmed the exclusion of the public.

In accordance with the law which I had previously studied, I requested two assistants. Colonel M. seized upon this and said, "The law says this may be granted 'only if the prosecutor has no objections to them.'" And he turned to the prosecutor, to ask whether he had any objections to the people I had requested.

One of the two assistants was my father. In the judgments (Personal Characteristics of the Accused and his Family) he was highly evaluated. Maybe it had been for my sake that he had tried to get such a good reference. The other was my brother Vlado. I thought he had been released by the court. I did not know whether or not he had been convicted. This turned out to be very interesting as the prosecutor seemed to be taken by surprise and was unprepared. He made no objections to what I had asked.

Then Chief Justice M. made another illegal intervention, "The court will consult...." As far as I know from what I learned in the Criminal Law Code and procedures, the court does not have the right to exclude attendants completely. But in my case, it did. The courtroom was emptied. My parents, brothers, and sisters also had to leave, and as far as I remember, so did old Mr. Vaško and Mrs. Vašková, and a certain older, plumpish woman. Later I remembered who she was and got confirmation that she was Mrs. B., mother of B. B.

ꙮ

When they emptied the courtroom, I was alone, with four or five against me, since my defense counsel actually created obstacles for me. Colonel M. folded his arms and smiled triumphantly as if to say, "So now, lad, you can speak and say whatever you like." He gave the clear impression that he would not listen and was not at all interested in what I had to say.

I cannot remember now whether it was during a visit, or after my release, but my family later told me that once on a sudden opening of the door, they heard my voice, "...And so I submit this criminal complaint against the agents and members of the Ministry of the Interior, who examined witness S., and skillfully prepared and produced his false statement about espionage, especially the section dealing with the alleged French intelligence, Le Deuxième Bureau."

The chief justice even wanted to move the reading of my appeal document to the final summation. I insisted that according to the Law on Criminal Procedures, the appellant first had to submit the reasons which were the causes for lodging the appeal action. He then allowed me to read the defense which I had prepared. The reading of the document with the appropriate emphasis and comments took about one, one and a half hours (see document no. 8).

I again felt a surge of strength and all the extreme tension of the last month somehow left me. Again, as had happened during the first trial, I had the impression that one of the judges, I think he was a major, was beginning to sympathize with my cause. He followed my words very carefully. His gestures and nods gave me the impression that he understood and agreed with me. The others were bored, and gave an overall impression of total indifference. I think some of them entertained themselves by reading newspapers. This was the typical circus, the theater symptomatic of that period.

When I finished reading my defense, the prosecutor had to speak. He did not concern himself at all with reacting to my arguments and conclusions. He uttered a few unconnected words to the effect that the verdict of the first court was justified and there was no reason to change it. He did not address the actual charges or any of my contentions at all. He was a young, new, very smooth second lieutenant or major, flaunting a gold watch.

He only protested when I spoke about the physical violence, the broken ribs, and other coercive methods, "That is defamation of state institutions!" He said he would check into everything, and then threatened to add to the charges against me because of my insolent and nonsensical accusations.

But he did not do anything. The charges were not increased since he knew very well that I was telling the truth.

Again, to all outward appearances, the whole trial seemed to be going my way. Nobody contradicted me, hindered me, or objected to what I said. This, of course, is the easiest approach: do not quarrel, just expedite proceedings with an all-inclusive verdict against which the person will not be able to defend himself.

According to what was said at this trial and the many which had taken place before it, they should have released me. I had refuted the previous verdict point by point but nobody paid any attention to this. Nobody contested anything from my statement.

I knew what the political situation was. I had no illusions. However, I strongly felt it was my duty to testify, to speak until they silenced me, so that it would not be said later that I had wasted an opportunity to defend myself or had been silent out of cowardice. I did not want the comrades in power to say, "They didn't know what they were doing." I wanted them to hear, face to face, that they were committing unjust, illegal acts, and that they were guilty of judicial crimes. It would not be said later that during those "courtroom comedies," I played a passive role and helped the criminals to put on their act and make a mockery of justice.

Their behavior then and later was fairly typical. They did not have the courage to react to the truth. They chose to speak only when the negative verdict was rendered and when I was not allowed to speak at all. Then the chief justice launched a vigorous and out of place polemic against me.

In one of their innumerable complaints, my parents skillfully dealt with the fact that my doctorate had become the main argument of the case. The claim was that I must have known that I was committing high treason since I was a university graduate. However, no one ever enlightened us on what it was in my actions which could be considered as high treason. The fact that they lacked any substantial proof whatsoever of a criminal act (a legal concept also known to writers of cheap detective stories) did not bother them at all.

The testimony of Bishop Trochta suffered the same fate. There was no substantiating evidence in either his files or mine involving me with Bishop Trochta. Nevertheless, my name was mentioned in the testimony. As far as I was concerned, that was illegal. They blatantly proceeded in the same manner to render my own verdict.

ꙮ

After the trial I was allowed a visit. There was no reason anymore to keep me isolated. The visit was again behind bars and wire grids and along with the shouting; it lasted about ten to fifteen minutes. We really only got a brief look at one another. (And in the corridor outside the courtroom, we exchanged a little smile, a few gestures, a wave, and an unambiguous "Hang on!")

I was truly under God's protection. I found great support in my wonderful, steadfast, and courageous family. Many prisoners lacked the love and strength of a family. My chief backing came from my father, who never, at any time, ever encouraged me to make compromises. On the contrary, he would often send me messages stating that he was proud of me.

The appeal trial was followed by more long weeks of routine life in a cell in the company of the same individuals. Our motto from the song "In anxiety and routine pass each day and night. Strengthen us, God, and help us!" was very appropriate.

Under normal circumstances, a person's hope is usually focused on one moment, event, or desire. When the long awaited moment finally comes, it may ease the tremendous tension a little, but nothing is actually solved. Prisoners were no different except that their hope was mostly in the trial.

We were still in prison, waiting for a miracle, for something extraordinary to happen. Only now we had a legal basis for this expectation, a verdict, a piece of paper, in my case, confirming that fourteen years were to be spent in prison. It was as if we had been told that there were no grounds for our frustrations now since we had been deprived of our freedom and were left at the mercy of violence, because following an inquiry, we had been found guilty and had been condemned.

ည

Prison life was rather complicated and unreal. People developed a dependence on apparently insignificant little things. It was a reliance quite incomprehensible to those who had not experienced this way of life.

For example, when, because of the librarians' laziness it took two weeks to do the inventory in the prison library, that was enough to greatly increase the suffering of the prisoner who could not read for even a few hours during the day. Or there was the little matter of the guards who took eyeglasses away, not in the evening, but in the afternoon, so they could have peace for the rest of the day. For the prisoner, that meant an afternoon of eye pains and a headache in addition to not being able to read.

On the other hand, small occurrences could ease the life of a prisoner. For example, a chalk-written sign on the outside of the cell door about the return of glasses or other things brought considerable joy.

Prisoners were very susceptible to any chance happening or little deed. They learned to quibble over all sorts of things in the quest to make their lives easier. It was especially difficult to give up little perks to which they had become accustomed, although originally they had not even dreamed of them. An example of this was being allowed to buy things after the trial. Previously, much worse things, such as solitary confinement and isolation, were taken for granted and the possibility of relief was not even considered. But now, when somebody acquired something, it was extremely difficult for him to give it up. Thus, in the end, ironically, prisoners were gradually being enslaved by minor alleviations and improvements.[45]

Then there was the confiscation of property, or money from accounts. It was cruelly ironic and absurd. In fact it was not our own property, but the money of relatives, saved with difficulty, or lent, only so that it could enable the prisoner to buy a little bread or hygienic necessities. Jozef had been right about this when he had said, "You must spend everything. Don't keep anything." I contributed to the many complaints which he constantly wrote concerning illegal practices.

The routine confiscation of property, including personal valuables without giving out receipts or keeping records, was actually opening the door to theft on a large scale. After my first complaint, as if by accident, they began to exercise more control in the administration of personal property. I suggested that they give purchasing priority of confiscated effects to relatives of prisoners. Otherwise this led to the expropriation of whatever was most advantageous to authorities and would lead to their own personal enrichment.

Later I learned that during this period of absolute political irresponsibility, some prisoners were convicted and sentenced but their sentences did not take into account the time they had already spent in prison. Sometimes this not only meant many months, but several years of interrogation imprisonment which were not deducted from the penalty because these prisoners did not protest. This took place in spite of the fact that their previous imprisonment was not only similar, but they had actually been under a much more severe regime when they had been in the interrogation prison. They had already suffered much more than they would in the course of a normal sentence.

ꟈ

One day, we were joined in our cell by a thin young man of about seventeen to nineteen years old. I do not remember exactly whether he was a painter or an electrician. He was in prison for moonlighting and bungling his work, and was sentenced to about three to four months. He was a typical product of the new society.

His entire sphere of interest revolved around money, entertainment, women, girls, clothes, fashion, various eccentricities and accessories. We tried without success to introduce him to higher and deeper thoughts but he would have none of it. However, it was through these new cell mates that we could at least keep up a little with what was happening on the outside.

He was only with us for two or three days so we did not attempt to acquaint him with our spiritual program.

Jozef and I did not want to give up our "Holy Mass," prayers, songs, and readings from Scripture or debates because of him. However, we had to take into consideration that they might use him as an informer. If information got out about what we were doing, we both risked its being recorded in our files and our being sent to a closed prison, not a camp. In a camp, life was better and there was more freedom. But we knew that the regime would not look kindly on the influence we could exert there.

ꙮ

With regard to the day of transport, the prisoner would usually already know something was up from fragments of information which he succeeded in getting if he was not completely alone. The greater bustle in the corridors immediately sharpened everybody's attention. In a few days the cry would again resound, "Take all your things! Take everything with you!" The prisoner was always at the mercy of change, though essentially change brought on by the same despots. They pestered him without any inhibitions and only minimal observance of the law.

He then became hypersensitive to the messages from his subconscious. The results were persistent feelings of fear, anxiety, nervousness, and cold aggravated by intense shaking caused by three years of undernourishment. These reactions appeared even when he expected and had an idea of what was about to happen to him, what the next stage of his life would be like.

The uncertainty of being given up into the hands of totally irresponsible people henceforward remained for many the worst feature of imprisonment, the highest form of terror. I think fear in itself is much worse than any physical and perhaps even psychological pain.

In the interrogation prison, we were repeatedly astonished when we discovered that we considered beatings or other forms of physical coercion to be better than constant inactivity and waiting. When somebody beat us, that was a change. Unfortunately, I could not get rid of this idea, although I know that this was surely due to a lack of faith, trust, generosity, and willingness to sacrifice and suffer.

I was not able to completely change my way of thinking about fear, even after many years of imprisonment, many repetitions of these certain, constant moves, and even after legal procedures and general conditions improved.

I often endeavored to hide this from fellow prisoners and especially screws, who took great pleasure in amusing themselves with such taunts as, "You're afraid, aren't you? Is your conscience clear? Don't you want to know what'll happen to you next, where you'll go?"

A great friendship, a common life with friends, contact with a good or even saintly person often ended with the words, "Everything with you." A brother who helped in hard times was closer in suffering than the closest relatives and friends outside, often on a permanent basis. Sometimes it was a last look, or a handshake, perhaps before going to one's death by execution or suicide or to a permanent separation for the rest of our lives.

In a moment, the family atmosphere in the prison changed into consternation, desolation, loneliness and despair. Separations were often just as difficult as the original arrest: a sudden loss of human consideration, security, freedom, dignity, known soil under the feet. We had to live through that again and again. If a person is not alone on the road to the unknown, it is immediately different. This is true even if there is only one other, not completely unfamiliar and strange person.

ꕥ

And now, if I remember well, Jozef and I were about to be transferred together. To which camp? Leopoldov, Ilava, Jáchymov, Mírov. . . . All these prisons or camps had reputations, some worse than others. What awaited us? Was it there that we would end our lives? A prisoner could never be surprised by anything.

First of all we went to a transport room. It is already difficult for me to remember the details of that particular room. Altogether, there were about fifteen to twenty men there. We could talk freely, and our eyes were not covered. I attempted to establish human contact, to get someone's attention. I had always longed for the moment when I could talk freely, and even choose the person to whom I would speak. Perhaps many did not feel this way or did not attach any importance to it.

I always threw myself enthusiastically into contact with people, but I was disappointed with most of them. The older prisoners in particular had little inclination for making new contacts. They were more interested in "latrines" or "Těšín apples,"[46] as we called them. These were "guaranteed" gossip about amnesties. Prisoners often put all their hopes in illusions.

ꝏ

I found that since the periods of solitary confinement (In Ruzyň in 1953, and Trenčín in 1954), I had neglected to do the evening examination of conscience of my life, hour by hour, and the daily evaluation of my faults, good deeds, and meditation on the gifts and graces which I received from the Lord.

During intensive communal life, my original monthly spiritual renewal sessions changed into an occasional event, something I did on special days such as the feast of Christ the King, Christmas, Good Friday, Holy Saturday, Pentecost, and others. At those times, I would arrange for someone to wake me up. I also slightly neglected the learning and memorizing of addresses, the categorizing of everything I had in my memory, the visualization of ideas, and spiritual connections with friends and acquaintances. I already could not rouse and ponder these numerous experiences and so I forgot a lot of them.

From this long journey to an institution, I only remember a few people, although we were together for about three days. There was General K., in uniform, and I think it was then that we saw our girls in the courtyard. Jitka, Milada K., and others were there and they happily waved to me enthusiastically and unrestrainedly in spite of the rules and the presence and shouts of the guards. These little, chance meetings stirred pleasant memories and provided me with so much joy.

I think that we again went through Ruzyň, through disinfection searches, and to the new world of the Gulag Archipelago....

At that time I did not know that it would be another ten years before I would be set free, but with God's grace, I was determined to face anything and everything.

Selected Documents

Introduction

Unfortunately, the transcripts of the proceedings of that time were greatly distorted and did not reflect events as they truly happened.

The chairman of the Senate was the one who decided what went into the transcripts. For the most part, neither the accused nor those convicted ever had the opportunity to correct or add anything even to what was purported to be "their own statements." Decades later, they were still not allowed to see what was in the records.

I am including these transcripts (with their many distortions) more as a testimony to the times, as a reflection and indictment of the legal system of that period. The content of the legal documents is really a form of political enlightenment. Similarly, the objective nature of accounts related by the various witnesses as formulated and transcribed in their records, is very suspect, if not totally worthless.

After reading Part I of this book, it should be clear how those regarded as criminals were treated and records forged. The witnesses were usually fellow prisoners or other people who had been convicted in the same way, and who had been subjected to the unrestrained whims of investigators operating in the overall atmosphere of brainwashing.

Moreover, even according to the law, the accused's statement need not be true and the court was expected to regard it in this light. Many people retracted their supposed "statements," rejected, or changed their formulation or transcripts and disclaimed their signatures at the very first opportunity, in spite of the threat of further reprisals for themselves and their families. My quotations from Scriptures were always only approximate, as I remembered them, because I had no opportunity to check them. I did not always wish to change and substitute words borrowed from Czech and German, especially if they were part of the documents of those times since they were often the result of the long-term influence of particular social and linguistic environments.

S. Krčméry

Document No. 6

The Superior Military Court, Trenčín June 24, 1954

The accused:
Private Dr. Silvester Krčméry

The final stage of the *defense before the District court*

As I have been allowed "the last word," I must immediately emphasize that I shall in fact put forward nothing in my defense. What I wish to state is merely to uphold the facts and the truth. I should like this to be understood so that what I say may not be considered in my favor or construed as mitigating circumstances.

The reason I have refused to make a statement over these two years of so-called investigation was mainly because I could see that those conducting the inquiry did not want to know the truth, but on the contrary, wished to distort it.

I do not wish to "get or wriggle out of" anything I have done, or lessen my responsibility for it, because I am convinced that with regard to what I am accused of, I have a clear conscience before God and our fellow men. I did not wish to harm anyone, and I have not consciously done so, to say nothing of human society or even one particular "class."

If, then, I am to be punished for what I have done, that is, for goodness, truth and Christ, then I do not wish a lesser punishment, but rather a greater one, and I should be happiest if I could even die for Christ, although I know that I am not worthy of such grace. For this reason I do not wish any extenuating circumstances to be taken into account, just as I cannot apologize for having done what is good.

Naturally (and unfortunately) I am not a "saint." I have my own faults and sins, mainly before God, as each of us has and maybe far more than others. For example, I lack humility and self-sacrifice. I am negligent as well as complacent and am guilty of self-interest, insufficient spiritual purity, poor concentration, and perhaps also considerable inner selfishness, and many other weaknesses. But my general purpose was clear: to follow Christ, to spread the love of God and love for one's neighbor, so that everyone might be happy on earth (and of course even more so after death), as I have been happy from the moment of my inner conversion when I was about seventeen years old.

L. N. Tolstoy wrote somewhere about a mysterious magic wand buried deep in the earth. It contained the greatest secret in the world, that is, the recipe for human happiness. When, after considerable effort, it was found and dug out, there were only three words from Scripture written on it, "... (dear sons!) Love one another!" Tolstoy added that it is only when you live for others that you yourself will live. Your happiness will come from making others happy. This appears to be a baffling contradiction, but try and experience it and you will be convinced of its truth.

This is why we, too, have lived entirely in the service of God and our fellow men. We have not needed property or rewards, or even minimum pay, most of which we gave away anyway. That is why in our movement we have long (1945–47 and earlier) been in favor of the abolition of private medical practices and privileged rewards for healing pain and suffering, for we were happy to be able to help our neighbor, and our greatest reward was the thought that we were at the same time serving God and were doing his will.

And vice versa: by serving God and man, we were serving society, and in the terminology of today, "the working class." We do not divide people either according to class, property, appearance, race, or birth, because for us, every person is a second Christ.

This is why you will not find in either our jobs or our work the slightest reason for complaint, because I believe that each of us did more than was his required duty or at least decidedly more than the majority of his colleagues. For we look upon our work not just as a source of income, a career or an interesting hobby, or sport, etc, but as putting Christ's message into practice in our daily lives.

Obviously, our behavior could be judged more objectively by our superiors, colleagues, and subordinates, as well as our patients, and no doubt they have already done so. Perhaps it is a sin and again a lack of humility which makes me dare to mention this at our trial, especially since I know that all the brothers and sisters in our group would receive an even better evaluation of their work. Yet, most of them do not even mention it. But this is also due to my eternal (maybe Utopian) optimism, that I long (again because of a lack of humility) for us to be understood at least a little, even by unbelievers.

Our work was not a strategy, as many people nowadays would like to suggest, in order, they say, to cover up our treasonous activities. It is the very foundation of Christ's teaching, "Love your neighbor" (Matt. 22, Luke 10) ... and when he washed his disciples feet, "... for not even the Son of Man came to be served but in order that He might serve others," and, "the higher a person is among you, the greater a servant he should be to others."

If, however, our deeds are not enough to prove our positive attitude towards people, society, and the state; if we are required to renounce our Church (that is, the Vatican) and Christ, unconditionally, without the possibility of criticizing (which can be likened to renouncing reason and humanity); if we are to accept all the objections to the Church and the bishops, and instead of faith in God, we are to embrace philosophical fiction, a theory based on a philosophical error or on political compulsion (force or dictatorship), then we cannot reply otherwise than Peter and John did before the high court about nineteen hundred years ago, "God must be obeyed before people."[47]

For Christ clearly said of the Church, "Whoever obeys you, obeys me" and, "he who receives any messenger of mine receives me" (John 13:20; Matt. 10:40). And ,"who will not even obey the Church, let him be a pagan and toll man" and, "Whatever you allow on earth will be allowed in Heaven, too" (Matt. 16:19). We therefore go to prison with pride and joy and if necessary, to the gallows. If God in His inconceivable providence and mercy has chosen us, unworthy and sinful as we are, we will follow Him into prison and onto the cross.

We can serve God even in prison, and maybe we will do so in a better way and more sincerely than if we are free. We can care for our fellow men at least to a certain extent, though perhaps not as well as we could if we were not in prison. Of course, it is impossible to save a person against his will. We can only minister to one who allows and accepts it.

We do not pretend to be indispensable. We know that others will replace us. You yourselves will have to find those who will replace us in our secular jobs, and God will call upon others to fill our duties as apostles, just as He called on us and transformed us literally from nothing, even from the dregs of human society.

After all, I myself did not inherit my faith, nor did I win it in a lottery, or pick it up on the street. I had to fight hard to acquire it. God helped me when as a youth I experienced difficult inner struggles, doubt, pain and suffering, in my work and in the study of various world outlooks, including Marxism, Leninism, Islamism, Buddhism, and Judaism, as well as most other Evangelical beliefs. God gave me everything I have and now that I face persecution because of Him and am called on to profess my faith in Him, should I now pretend I don't believe? Should I hide my faith? Should I deny Him?

Religious groups will continue without us. Others will follow us and their numbers will increase. That is already obvious in the preparation of other investigations and trials.

They will survive as long as the Church does, that is, to the end of time. Most of them will function publicly if they are not persecuted, and secretly or privately if they are, not because it is dogma, or the Church could not exist without them, but because as long as the Gospels are read in the world, there will always be people who will believe and learn from them and they will build communities and groups as Christ and St. Paul did.

We will not allow ourselves to be led to hate, to rebel, or even to complain. There are already hundreds of people who can testify to that. That is where our strength and superiority lie. We know how to return good for evil and we know that all our brothers will work harder and more selflessly than others (just as Christ taught us). After all, we are following an old tradition. The first Christians who were persecuted under the Roman Empire, though imprisoned by the hundreds, tortured, and crucified, were the most self-sacrificing workers, even after they were imprisoned and sent to hard labor in mines. There is no record that we know of which states that they organized any rebellion.

That is why anyone can persecute us without any risk to themselves. Other political prisoners are sure to repay their opponents — with interest — at the very first opportunity! And us? It is quite the opposite. From the very outset we have been praying every day for all of you, and not, as one investigating officer ironically put it, "so that the devil will take you!"

On the contrary, we pray that God may forgive you all your faults and sins, for you do not really understand the consequences of what you are doing against God and the Church.

I prayed for you as well, sir (addressing the prosecutor[48]), although I had not yet seen you or made your acquaintance. I also prayed for those who beat us, degraded us, confined us, and made us suffer, using methods of nervous and mental duress, subjecting us to long periods of solitary confinement, not allowing us to work or read, or walk outside, to receive visitors or write letters, sometimes even restricting sitting and sleeping in attempts to bring about a nervous and mental breakdown, and to force out of us distorted or false testimony against Christ and the Church, or against our friends.

I should be prosecuting you, not you me!

But no one will escape God's judgment.

The reason I did not conceal these things and reported them to the prosecutor was certainly not because I wanted revenge or that I was filled with hate. We were happy and grateful for every blow we received and we forgave everyone a long time ago. However, I spoke of it out loud only because it seemed to me that perhaps it could be stopped, and therefore I felt a duty to protect others.

At our trials, it is in fact the Church which stands accused, in other words, the Vatican. But the Vatican is not here and is not being given the opportunity to defend itself. This is a violation of a basic, fundamental right and human principle which has always existed, namely, that the other side has a right to be heard.

What in fact is the Church? From the religious point of view it is the mystical body of Christ, the organism, the continuation of Christ (1 Cor. 12)! From the human point of view it is a voluntary community of Catholic Christians, which is "not of this world." This society is in sharp contrast to the state, as the Church has no prisons nor security structures nor human means of coercion, nor physical power, that is, weapons, with the exception of a couple of historical halberds. Anyone in the world can leave it at any time, without being harmed by man. The total opposite is true of countries which, under threat of many years in prison, force their citizens to remain there against their will! (see article 95 of the Penal Code).

Therefore, both the people and democracy in the Church have much greater weight than counterparts in other human societies. Furthermore, the people support the Church through their membership. Even today, in our country, the Church has the backing of at least 80 percent of the population. If, therefore, these attacks on the Church were founded on truth, most people would already have left the Church, especially when subjected to such great pressure.

The Church does not interfere with the internal affairs of the state, but only defends itself against the intervention of the state in its own affairs. Is it a sin to want to live? It has been condemned to annihilation by a few people who do not know it or who hate it. Is the Church then expected to approve or applaud such considerations?

You say the people want this approach? Then let the people freely express their opinion! In fact they have already done and continue to do so by their membership and by filling the churches.

You say Christians are not persecuted in this country? That depends on how you look at it! From the point of view of those who do not know Christians or who hate them, there is religious freedom for one is allowed to go to church. However, the true freedom here lies in attacking, defaming, and persecuting religion. But Christ did not come into the world only so that people would go to church! "I am the way, the truth and the life!" (John 14:6).

To live their faith: that is what religion and the Church are not allowed to do! The religious press (in Slovakia alone, about two hundred to three hundred different good books and roughly thirty-five religious journals used to be published), the monasteries, seminaries, theological faculties, pastoral activities, church organizations, religious movements, and associations, mainly of young people, have all been abolished.

And above all, you decided that the head must be removed! The episcopacy has been destroyed and contacts with the Church cut off! The argument that it is because of its relations with the West is just an excuse, because communication with Christians and churches in the East are made equally impossible. In accordance with a program set in advance, three wedges have been driven into the body of the Church: first, between the leadership of the Church (the Vatican) and the bishops, second, between the bishops and the clergy, and third, between the clergy and believers. Therefore, from the point of view of believers and Christians, there have been persecutions in this country since 1948. That is not only shocking but illegal! While it is true that everywhere in the world some sort of anti-religious propaganda can be found, nevertheless in other areas, it is at least possible to reply to it!

But that is really nothing new. Christ Himself was hunted and persecuted all His life even though He clearly rejected all political actions: "Pay Caesar what is due to Caesar..." (Matt. 22), "Sheathe your sword" (Matt. 26; John 18:11), "My kingdom is not of this world" (John 18:36). Even as an infant in the time of Herod (Matt. 2) He was considered a threat to the powerful of this world and thus became the youngest refugee. Immediately after He left His country, because of Him, an infant, the first bloody reprisals took place. Dozens of innocent babies were massacred in accordance with the principle of collective punishment ("all for one!") as is always the case with every persecution. Christ was not killed, but the hands of the powerful of this world were stained with the blood of the innocent.

In the Gospel of John, we read that during his public ministry he fled at least eight times, and there were many attempts made to arrest and kill Him. In the end He was also declared a traitor and executed in the most ignominious way, for "no one has a good word for it" [His teaching], and for supposedly inciting people from Galilee to Jordan to riot, telling people not to pay taxes, and claiming kingship, "Whoever sets himself up as king is an adversary (rebel against) Caesar" (John 19:17).

The same persecution and death awaited his disciples: Paul was beheaded for treason, Peter was crucified upside down, James beheaded, Andrew crucified, Steven stoned to death. Thousands more were tortured and hanged. Christ's religion was "opposed everywhere" (Acts 28:22). And Paul received thirty-nine lashes, was three times beaten with rods and stoned once, all for Christ (2 Cor. 11).

The first Christians suffered a similar fate. From the very beginning, and then for another three hundred years, they had to hide in underground cemeteries called catacombs. It is almost impossible for people to understand how the greatest legal system of the time, that of Rome, could act so lawlessly and ruthlessly towards Christians.

Under the Caesarean despots Nero, Decius, Domicius, and Diocletian, Christians were dragged into circuses and stadiums, given as food to wild beasts or crucified. They suffered all of this because they would not sacrifice incense to Caesar, which meant that they did not confer divinity either on the Emperor or the state. Because of this, they were accused of rebellion, revolution, and what was even worse, treason.

Such was the fate of about thirty of the first popes who were tortured or executed.

Is this what is called Christian passiveness? Hardly! This is a fight without bloodshed, or at least the blood which is spilled is not that of others. It is the sacrifice of one's own blood and own life.

And in spite of this, slavery was abolished, as was the despotism of Caesar, of the Romans, and other empires. They were abolished without the shedding of blood and without the sword. This was not the case in Egypt, Africa, China, and other lands where Christianity did not exist.

It is useless to try and pretend that the Church is reactionary. History shows quite clearly that wherever there was the presence of Christianity and the Church, culture and literature, art, schools, universities, and social institutions flourished. There were hospitals and old people's homes, something which was unknown among pagans.

By accepting Christianity, the barbarian nations of Europe became bearers of great progress and civilization. This was not the case of the highly cultural pagan nations which had been far ahead of other states. By not accepting Christianity, Mesopotamia, Phoenicia, Egypt, and China fell far behind and declined, and even now, find it difficult to catch up.

To this very day we all depend on and benefit from the social and cultural activities of the Church. The Church is responsible for the Old Slavic alphabet, and the literature and culture on which all the old Slavic cultures are based. Even the Soviet historian Derzhavin admits this, as do those who defame Christianity most vigorously such as Nikolskij in his work "The Origin of Religion."

Every priest and student believer could easily reply to the kind of science that dismisses Christianity as a whole, and Christ and the Church in particular, by ridiculing everything as idolatry and primitive religion, but they are not allowed to do so! Even the Bible has been taken out of libraries and confiscated. But I think it was old Ampčre who said, "If one day a savage stops kneeling to wooden idols, it will not be because God does not exist, but because He is not made of wood!"

From the very beginning, the Church has come into conflict with every dictatorship, including that of Napoleon, Bismarck, Henry VIII, Joseph II, Hitler, etc., and for the very same reason: it refuses to offer incense, that is, it does not bow to Caesar as God, nor to the state as God. And it does not submit to anyone "unconditionally" ("...his generation....They are like children sitting in the market-place and...shouting at each other: 'We played for you and you did not dance...'" (Matt. 11:16–17). "What did you go out to the desert to see...? A reed swayed by the wind?" (Matt. 11:7).

The Church is not a prostitute or a shameless woman, as her adversaries tried to paint her (Voltaire, "Écrasez l'infâme!"), who would submit to anyone, but is a true bride of Christ and therefore similar to Him, "one, holy, universal, apostolic, and persecuted," just as Christ was.

Of course, no tyrant has yet admitted that he is persecuting anyone for their religion or their beliefs. Christ suffered under all sorts of pretences including stating who He was, that is, Christ, "You have heard his blasphemy!" (Matt. 26:65). Other excuses were, "If we leave him alone, all will believe in him, and the Romans will come and take away both our land and our nation" (John 11:48); "You see that you are gaining nothing. Look, the whole world has gone after him" (John 12:19). Then after those condemning words of Christ, repeating "woe unto you" eight times to the Pharisees (Matt. 23), Caiaphas declared, "It is more to your interest that one man should die for the people, than that the whole nation should be destroyed" (John 11:50).

Many first Christians also died when under Nero, they were accused of setting fire to Rome. Others were executed for the alleged ritual murder of babies ("they drink the blood of children"). Most recently, Christians and priests were sentenced by Nazi courts for exerting a bad moral influence on young people, the same charge which had been leveled at Socrates so long ago. (These Nazi moral trials as described by the left-wing press have now been completely forgotten.) Then, there was the trial of Mádr-Jukl, where two murderers were judged along with the members of Catholic Action (just as two criminals had been crucified with Christ), to emphasize that the Vatican would even stoop to murder in order to conceal their guilt.

Christ himself foresaw all of this when He said, "I am sending you out like sheep among wolves, . . . they will hand you over to their courts, they will flog you . . . you will be brought before governors and kings, for my sake . . . " (Matt. 10:16–18); "all will hate you for your allegiance to me (Matt. 10:22); "When you are persecuted in one town, take refuge in another" (Matt. 10:23). He was always on the run, as were Peter (Acts 12) and Paul, as is stated in Acts 9 and many times after that. "Do not fear those who kill the body . . . " (Matt. 10:28); "If the world hates you, it hated me first. . . . As they persecuted me, they will persecute you . . . on my account . . . " (John 15:18–21); "I have told you all this to guard you against the breakdown of your faith. They will ban you from the synagogues (the churches); indeed, the time is coming when everyone who kills you will suppose that he is performing a religious duty. But they will do all these things because they do not know either the Father or me" (John 16:1–3). "How blessed you are, when you suffer insults and persecution and every kind of calumny for my sake. Accept it with gladness and exultation, for you have a rich reward in heaven; in the same way they persecuted the prophets before you" (Matt. 5:12).

But whoever is beaten arouses sympathy (which is why the suffering of the Jews under Nazism inspired such sympathy).

The Church has no prisons, police, nor physical power. Therefore, from the human point of view, it is an unequal fight, as it is easy to silence the Church which cannot defend itself. But from God's point of view, "the gates of hell can not triumph" — never! For God exists and Christ truly rose from the dead!

People are particularly sensitive about freedom of belief and of conscience and that is why there is such resistance to oppressive measures. The people, the masses, Christians, all think as we do, but today they are continually educated in the art of deceit and are forced to be hypocritical. That is why many will say what they think only behind your backs, or when they are at home or in their cells, or they will say nothing at all. They are waiting. . . . These people are often regarded as more reliable, whereas others who openly say what they think are persecuted as traitors and hypocrites!

Why do we say what we are saying now, when of course we are aware that we may be doing ourselves great harm?

1. Out of hate? The reverse is true. We feel no hate for anyone, only love. Although you may not realize it, we even have much in common with you, in the fight against abortion for instance.[49]

2. That we expect it won't be long before things change? That there will be a war? No, quite the opposite. We have always put our trust in God and not in arms and atomic weapons, let alone wars.

3. Perhaps out of futile heroism or martyrdom? Unfortunately, I am too sinful a person and therefore I could only be a caricature of a hero or a martyr of whom the Church would always be ashamed. We certainly did not willingly get ourselves into this situation, nor did we arrest ourselves and offer to go to prison. We did not humiliate or accuse or judge ourselves. Even Christ did not appear before the Council or walk the way of the Cross of His own accord. For us, it was even less so. Nevertheless, He in fact chose us (John 15:16), "You did not choose me, I chose you, I appointed you to go on and bear fruit." Without knowing it, you are actually carrying out some of His exact instructions or doing what He allows.

4. Do we speak out of fanaticism? No. We are not religious fanatics or blind extremists. We are simply Christians. But we have never shut our eyes to other faiths, world views, or science. Furthermore, we have sought and learned without prejudice, and we are still studying other philosophical and religious trends. We acquired our convictions through study and through hard work and by the grace of God. Real fanatics are, on the contrary, those who reject God and Christianity without knowing them or without having examined them.

5. Are we mad? Many people have already declared us to be so and to be believers in Utopia, because we refused to take money or rewards for healing, for helping others, or when we claimed that prostitution could be wiped out and prostitutes reformed. Other beliefs and suggestions of ours were greeted in the same fashion. But we are not ashamed of them. Paul was also proud of being "a madman for Christ." They even said of Christ that "he is possessed, he is raving. Why do you listen to him?" (John 10:20). Not that we would compare ourselves to Christ, but, like all other Christians, we wish to follow Him. (After all, according to some, even Lenin was a believer in Utopia, and Dostoevsky, along with many others, was mad.)

6. But I have decided to bear witness out of a sense of duty. I must testify to the truth, therefore I must speak out! I cannot be silent! (Long live Christ the King and His Church!)

You have power in your hands, but we have truth!

We do not envy you your power, nor do I have any desire for it. The truth is enough for us, for it is greater and stronger than power. Whoever has power in his hands often thinks that he can hide the truth, suppress, kill or crucify it!

But the truth has always risen and will rise again from the dead! (As it does — sometimes — even on the third day.)

Declared, with the help of improvised notes and with interruptions from the prosecutor, at the main hearing in the military court in Trenčín on June 24, 1954. Parentheses indicate that I am not sure whether I used those exact words.

Document No. 7

T16/54
Rectangular stamp
The Superior Military Court in Trenčín
C O P Y

The Verdict

In the Name of the Republic!

The Superior Military Court in Trenčín held public proceedings on June 24, 1954, in the criminal matter against Dr. Silvester Krčméry, a soldier in the reserve service, and against Eng. Josef Suchý, a soldier in the reserve service. Both were accused by the superior military prosecutor in Trenčín of high treason according to Paragraph 78, Articles 2(a), sub 1(c) and sub 2(b) of the Penal Code.

According to the indictment they have committed the crime of high treason insofar as:

From 1945 until his arrest in 1952, in following instructions given to him by Vatican Catholic Action, the accused, Krčméry, founded seditious groups called "The Family" in Bratislava, Košice, and other cities of the Republic, and directed their activities according to the instructions of Vatican agents Kolakovič, Schützner, and Mádr, to whom he also transmitted seditious information for hostile propaganda, and, in 1951, with a certain Staríček and Jukl, negotiated an illegal departure to hostile countries, where he intended to continue his subversive activities against the People's Republic.

The accused Suchý was in charge of propaganda for this Center of Illegal Groups from the fall of 1951 to January 1952, both in Bratislava and Prague. He prepared treasonous leaflets and distributed treasonous publications, participated in the drafting of hostile reports for Vatican propaganda, received instructions for further activities from Mádr and seditious propaganda material from a certain Tomek.

After the introduction of evidence, the Court accepted as proven that:

in the present struggle between two causes — the cause for peace and democracy led by the Soviet Union on the one hand, and the cause for imperialism led by the United States on the other hand — divisions which have characterized the international situation since the Second World War, the Vatican stands unreservedly on the side of the imperialistic camp.

This, however, is nothing new.

During the whole of its existence the Vatican, led by the Pope, has been the enemy of progress, and has stood on the side of reactionary classes, since they, by their very reactionary character, corresponded best to the Vatican's aim of dominating humankind to serve its own interests.

Therefore, it greeted the Great October Revolution with the same hatred as it did the Great French Revolution. It saw in fascism a force which was capable of leading the struggle against socialism, and therefore in the Second World War, it stood on the side of Germany and Italy.[50]

After the Second World War it combined its interests with those of American imperialists, preparing the third world war against the Soviet Union and the countries of the People's Democracy. With all the means at its disposal, it supports treasonous and espionage activities against these countries, actively participates in them, taking full advantage of the influence which it has acquired over the centuries through a gigantic and widespread propaganda apparatus.

To carry out these activities it chooses various methods.

Thus, according to Vatican instructions, the clergy, with the assistance of laymen entirely devoted to the Vatican, organized within the framework of the so-called Vatican Catholic Action, various theological groups which, following the model of the JOC organizations, attempted to lead citizens away from loyalty to the People's Democratic Republic and from socialist convictions. They abused the people's religious beliefs, to win them over to the politics of the Vatican, which, with the help of imperialists, is trying to restore capitalism in the Republic and to overthrow the government by the people.

While doing so, they covered up their real intentions with the pretext of religious activities. An important role in this treasonous action was played by the so-called Central Catholic Office in Bratislava, which directed and coordinated the activities of these groups in Slovakia, and passed on to the Vatican reports on conditions in the Republic, cleverly obtained by means of questionnaires distributed among its members.

Both accused collaborated with this agency, and after its abolition in 1948, when its activities against the People's Democratic Republic were discovered, they both participated in organizing and directing new groups, in which, as indicated above, they were encouraging young people to oppose the People's Democratic institutions.

They distributed leaflets and publications issued by the Vatican, hostile to the People's Democratic institutions, and were in contact with those who organized this destructive activity against the People's Democratic Republic according to the instructions of the Vatican. Many of them have already been judged as traitors and sentenced (Mádr, Razík, Jukl), while others, who succeeded in escaping from the Republic, have, according to reliable information, continued abroad as Vatican agents in their treasonous espionage activities against the People's Democratic Republic (Schützner, for example).

In 1943, the accused Krčméry came into contact with Father Kolakovič, who was already preparing and securing the establishment of this activity by organizing groups called "The Family," because he knew that communist ideas would also influence developments in the Republic after the end of the war. By organizing these groups, which were formed according to JOC concepts, they intended to use personal contacts to influence the faithful to be loyal to the Vatican. The groups were based on the cell system. The cells were organized according to professions, as a hierarchy (second and third order), and even prior to 1945 were not reported to the authorities.

The activities of these groups, organized within the framework of Vatican Catholic Action, were intensified and began to be fully operational after 1945, following the establishment of the People's Democratic Republic. They then began to fulfill their true purpose, that is, under the pretext of deepening religious faith, to ensure that believers would remain obedient and loyal to the Vatican, which from the very time the People's Democratic Republic was instituted, was preparing in every possible way to overthrow the People's Democratic institutions.

The accused participated in the activities of the group mainly in Prague, where he was studying. He was present at meetings at which Kolakovič discussed the JOC concept with leaders of the groups. The accused himself formed such groups at the medical faculty in Prague and participated in meetings of "The Family" at the home of a certain Vacková.

When in 1948 a meeting of the group leaders was arranged in Litoměřice to coordinate the activities of the Slovak and Czech groups, he took part as one of the leaders. He also attempted to set up groups in Litoměřice and Ústí nad Labem.

In December 1949, he was present at a meeting in Dolný Smokovec, called for the purpose of extending the activities of the groups, weakened by the closing down of the Central Catholic Office in Bratislava, which had previously directed activities, especially in Slovakia.

On the initiative of the accused, another meeting took place in 1949 near Lubietová, which was attended by group leaders from all over the Republic. The purpose of the meeting was to direct the activities of the groups throughout the whole of the Republic.

After the closing of the Central Catholic Office in Bratislava in 1948, the so-called Central Group was formed. Its job was to replace the Central Catholic Office and direct the activities of all the other groups in Slovakia. The accused participated in secret meetings of this group, where one of the leaders, Šmálik, gave instructions on how to extend the group's activities.

The accused was also in close contact with other leaders of Vatican Catholic Action whose operations were within the Republic, namely, Mádr, Jukl, Razík, and Tomek. He had secret meetings with them, where they coordinated group activities and agreed on further tasks. Yet, he was aware that these men were in contact with the Vatican, that they were carrying out this action according to its suggestions, that they also used literature and leaflets published by the Vatican and which were hostile to the People's Democratic Republic.

In 1951, he also knew, and informed Jukl, that Mádr and Tomek planned to escape abroad. From 1948 on he was in contact with a certain Schützner, who worked in the group and who, he later learned, had escaped to a foreign country. In May 1951, when he was informed that Schützner had returned to the Republic from abroad, he met with him, and they discussed and decided on further plans for the actions of the groups.

Through his activities in the groups, he was in contact with Reverend

Baptista, who was also one of the leaders, even though he knew that Baptista was hiding from the police. When later in the second half of 1951 the leaders of the Central Catholic Group and Vatican Catholic Action were arrested, the accused, together with others, prepared and arranged his own escape across the border through Father Holub. He was aware, and informed Jukl, that both Mádr and Tomek were also planning to escape in May 1951.

In 1948, the state discovered that the Central Catholic Office was a center of hostile activities directed by the Vatican against the Republic, and closed it down. The accused Suchý then became a member of the so-called Central Group which had replaced the Central Catholic Office, and which coordinated and directed other groups (in Slovakia), all within the framework of Vatican Catholic Action. He was the treasurer of this group. The financial means entrusted to him were used to purchase propaganda material and to support weaker groups financially. He was also given the task of mimeographing pamphlets and printed matter, mainly published by the Vatican and hostile towards the People's Democratic Republic. To accomplish this, he was provided with a mimeographing machine.

The accused knew that in November 1950 there was a meeting of group leaders from Moravia and Slovakia in Brno. Following this meeting, he and Porubský, who was also at the meeting, were entrusted with the task of studying Papal encyclicals. The position of Vatican Catholic Action towards new social conditions in the Republic was to be worked out on the basis of this study. This was to be sent to the Vatican for approval.

The accused was also aware that in the Spring of 1950, there was a national conference of university group representatives, in Prague. The purpose of this meeting, where the Central Catholic Group was represented by a certain Helena Schmidtová and Ján Gunčaga, was to coordinate activities.

Written material was submitted by Staríček, Jukl, and other leaders of Catholic Action to the Central group and then mimeographed and distributed to other groups by the accused.

For instance, he mimeographed and distributed Pope Pius XII's "Christmas message," "Antireligious Propaganda," "Teaching about the Sacraments" and, in the summer of 1951, "Mádr's Message." The latter contained an appeal by Catholic Action leaders to form additional groups, as well as seditious reports against the People's Democratic Republic.

In 1949, while a student, he founded a university group which he led until he was called up for military service in 1951. The group had four members and worked under the direction of the Central Group.

He also knew that in May 1951 a meeting took place in Professor Šmálik's apartment. Leaders of Catholic Action attended this meeting where Jukl and Tomek asked those present to see to it that the groups collect information and reports for the Vatican.

In April 1951 he was sent to Prague by Jukl to meet with Father Mádr, the leader of Vatican Catholic Action, who acquainted him more closely with the Action's activities. Father Mádr stressed that it was first necessary for the group to win over young Catholics, then to establish groups on the basis of professions, and then to expand them even further.

After Staríček and Jukl were put in prison, the activities of the Central Catholic Group somewhat slowed down. At the beginning of 1952 the accused then contacted other members of this group with the intention of reviving its activities. A meeting was then called in the apartment of Cecília Česneková, and led by the priest Nahálka, whom the accused knew was hiding from security agencies. This meeting did actually discuss reviving the activities of the Central Catholic Group.

These facts the Court considered as proven for the following reasons:

From the verdict of the former State Court, Department Brno 6 Ts 1–41/52, it was established that Otto Mádr, Vladimír Jukl, Václav Razík, and Růžena Vacková were leaders of Vatican Catholic Action, within which framework they founded groups working under Vatican authority to subvert the People's Democratic Republic.

From the evidence submitted by Mádr, Jukl, and Razík, both before investigating agencies as well as before the Court, testimony which was taken as a basis for this decision, the accused was allegedly in touch with the witnesses and worked with them closely as one of the leaders of this Action. The above were condemned for high treason according to Paragraph 78, Articles 1(c) and 2(a) of the Penal Code, and also for espionage according to Paragraph 86, Articles 1, 2(a), (b) and 3(c) of the Penal Code, since it was demonstrated that they passed on espionage reports to foreign countries (document of the former State Court in Prague, 6 Ts I 41/52/).

From the testimony of Růžena Vacková it was ascertained that the accused participated in founding groups, took part in their activities as one of the leaders, that he himself founded and directed several groups on his own, that in 1948, in Litoměřice, he attended a meeting of group leaders from the Czech countries and Slovakia, whose purpose was to coordinate the activities of groups in all parts of the Republic. The witness, after being condemned, explicitly stated that the activities of the groups were hostile to the People's Democratic Republic (Article 52).

The testimony of Vladimír Jukl confirmed that the "The Family" was founded by Tomislav Kolakovič, and that the purpose of this association was to prepare devout Catholics to be faithful to the Vatican.

The witness further confirmed that the accused Krčméry was one of the leaders of this organization and that he participated in 1949 in a meeting in Dolný Smokovec, called for the purpose of revitalizing group activities, especially in Slovakia, after the Central Catholic Office in Bratislava was abolished.

From the testimony of this witness it was evident that the accused Krčméry knew that one of the leaders of this movement, Schützner, had left the country to live abroad. Later, when Schützner came back, he was in touch with the accused and in June 1951, the accused told him in private that Mádr and Tomek had also tried to leave the country, but had been intercepted.

He further stated that the accused confided in him that he too intended to leave the country and live abroad, because the leaders of Vatican Catholic Action had been arrested and imprisoned. The accused said that he had the possibility to go abroad through the assistance of Father Jiří Holub and suggested that the witness should flee with him. He referred him to a certain Anna Gubová, who would give him further information about escaping to a foreign country.

The witness further stated that at the end of March 1951, he gave the accused Krčméry letters for Mádr, which contained news about the religious situation in Slovakia. This procedure was arranged during a meeting in Professor Šmálik's apartment, with the accused Krčméry and Mádr present, and it was agreed that they would send him an assessment of the church situation in Slovakia. It was also stated that religious Jan Baptista, who was hiding from security agencies (Articles 24–27, 59–66), was present at the meetings of group members held in Prague at the apartment of the accused.

Witnesses Šoltés, Trochta, Jenčík, Baníková, and Komárek also confirmed that the accused Krčméry participated in nationwide group activities as one of the leading officials, and that he himself founded new groups and directed their activities (Articles 20, 30, 55, 65, 67, 72). Witness Staríček confirmed this and added that he gave the accused reports about conditions at the universities and at the Theological Faculty in Bratislava. These reports were destined for Mádr.

As for the accused Suchý, witness Staríček declared that Suchý was a member of the Central Catholic Group in Bratislava and, after the closing of the Central Catholic Office, was entrusted with directing the activities of other groups in Slovakia and with mimeographing various Papal encyclical letters and messages which were distributed through the Central Office.

The testimony of witnesses Schmidtová, Porubský, and Krajňák also confirmed that the accused Suchý was a member of the Central Group, that he held the function of treasurer and Public Relations officer, and that this entitled him to use a mimeographing machine to make copies of Papal encyclical letters and messages, which were distributed to other groups by the Central Catholic Office under his direction and supervision.

Witness Schmidtová further testified that the accused Suchý was asked to study the Papal encyclical letters (1 T 25/54 Articles 830–58, document of the Regional Court in Bratislava).

The testimony of witness Čavojský further substantiated that the accused, before leaving for military service, left him a mimeographing machine and several publications which he had as an officer for Public Relations of the Central Group. The witness also stated that the accused Suchý attended and invited him to take part in a meeting held in January 1952 in Cecília Česneková's apartment, where it was decided to continue the activities of the groups (1 T 25/54 Articles 830–58).

The testimony of Cecília Česneková further confirmed that such a meeting was held in her apartment and that it was also attended by Dr. Nahálka (1 T 25/54 Articles 830–58 — documents of the Regional Court Bratislava).

From the decision of the Regional Court in Bratislava (1T 25/54), it was established that Staríček, Šmálik, Porubský, and other members of the Central Group which directed and supervised the activities of the groups in Slovakia, were found guilty of the criminal activity of high treason according to Paragraph 78, Articles 1(c), 2(a) of the Penal Code, as well as of espionage according to Paragraph 86 of the Penal Code, since it was proven that they were sending espionage material abroad.

From the files confiscated from the Central Office in Bratislava, it was asserted that the office acquired reports about the economic and political situation in the Republic through a survey using questionnaires. These reports were sent to foreign countries, as was also confirmed during the main procedure of the Supreme Court against Josef Tomanóczy, Doctor of Theology, and other co-defendants (1 T 25/54 Article 643 of the Penal Records).

Finally, the Court also considered the testimony of the accused who, on the whole, confessed to having taken part in the activities brought before the court, Articles 75, 104).

Krčméry admitted that he participated in Vatican Catholic Action, a framework from which groups known as "The Family" were formed. He admitted that he participated in meetings of group leaders from the Czech lands, Moravia and Slovakia, and that at one of the meetings the religious Baptista, who was hiding from the authorities, was present. He also admitted knowing that one of the group leaders, Schützner, had gone abroad and that he had returned to the Republic secretly in 1951, and he admitted that he himself had intended to go abroad with the assistance of Father Holub.

However, Krčméry stated in his defense that in the groups in which he participated and helped to form, as well as in the whole activity of Vatican Catholic Action, he only saw a means of deepening his spiritual life, that his activities were not motivated by political considerations, and that although he knew that those activities were directed by the Vatican, that fact in itself did not convince him that they were aimed against the People's Democratic institutions.

The same defense was put forward by the accused Suchý, who added that charges of his participation in the preparation of hostile reports against the Republic were not founded on the truth.

In evaluating the defense, the Court found that the Prosecutor based his accusation solely on the confession of the accused to the investigators, a confession which the accused later repudiated. Since there was no testimony from other witnesses and nothing in court records to substantiate the charge mentioned above, the court exonerated the accused from this criminal activity according to Paragraph 162(c) of Criminal Procedure.

Otherwise the Court did not accept the defense of the accused.

In weighing their activities as well as their defense, the Court was of the opinion that the behavior of the accused had to be judged within the context of actual, contemporary developments in the world, particularly taking into account the efforts by the Vatican to destroy the order of the People's Democratic Republic, and then to examine whether the accused consciously contributed to these efforts.

There can be no doubt that the so-called Vatican Catholic Action as well as the various types of JOC activities are some of the techniques used by the Vatican to overthrow the People's Democratic Republic and to give back to the Vatican the same international position that it once held.

In the present international situation, the Vatican stands unreservedly in the camp of the enemies of the Soviet Union and the People's Democratic Republic, and uses all the means at its disposal to overthrow them. It does so because it is interested in bringing about a change in political systems and replacing the People's Democratic State by a regime which would make it possible for the Vatican to regain its former influence in these countries to the greatest possible extent.

The methods chosen by the Vatican for this destructive activity are varied, as was established in many trials before the Courts of the Republic. From sedition and terror they then engage in more polished forms of destructive activity, one of them being Vatican Catholic Action.

Vatican representatives are fully aware that under the guise of religion, it is especially easy to influence people's reasoning and submit them to Vatican policy. Thus, they are among our main enemies, trying to disrupt democratic order and instigate the citizens against their Republic.

According to the Court, the accused, who have a university education, were sufficiently politically aware of the present international situation to be able to discern and understand the true Vatican Catholic Action objectives, in whose achievement they very actively participated.

In the first place they should have realized that this activity was performed without the knowledge and consent of the state, since the meetings were held in secrecy. Furthermore, if they had really been interested in a true expansion of spiritual or religious life, without hostile intentions towards the People's Democratic Republic, they could have fully participated in the existing framework of spiritual activities which are carried out with the knowledge of the state, and which are not in any way restricted.

The accused understood that this movement was directed by the Vatican, that its purpose was to gain devoted followers to the Vatican, and that Vatican Catholic Action leaders worked according to Vatican instructions.

The accused, Krčméry, was further aware of the fact that one of the leading officials of this movement, Schützner, had left the country without permission and gone abroad, that he had later returned and given further instructions for this activity according to the experience he had gained abroad. Both accused then distributed several Papal encyclical letters and other letters to other members of the groups. These letters were hostile towards the development of conditions in the People's Democratic Republic, and the accused knew that the state forbade their distribution.

They also knew that many leaders of this organization were hiding from the authorities (Krčméry knew about Baptista and Schützner, Suchý knew about Nahálka), yet, in spite of this, they remained in contact with them and acted according to their instructions.

They knew also that this activity was spread all over the Republic, that it was thoroughly organized, and that the leaders of the groups from different regions held meetings to coordinate their activities.

For these reasons the Court did not doubt that the accused were aware that this action was directed against the People's Democratic Republic according to instructions from a foreign country.

This conviction of the Court was further substantiated by the fact that the accused, Krčméry, talked about and prepared to escape to a foreign country, and taking into consideration his personality and activities which made him one of the leaders of this association, the Court did not doubt that he would have pursued his activities abroad.

Our Constitution guarantees religious freedom to all men. But the state is fully justified in reserving the right to ensure that the Church and religious life develop in accordance with the Constitution and the principles of the People's Democratic institutions. Only thus can the state safeguard the right of religious freedom for every citizen, based on the principles of religious tolerance and equality of all persuasions, as guaranteed by the Constitution.

Within the framework of Vatican Catholic Action, whose real goal is a widespread movement directed against the People's Democratic Republic, groups were formed which were not under the state's control and which were in fact uncontrollable, groups among different sections of the population, which were to be won over to Vatican policy and thus put into opposition to the People's Democratic Republic, a movement which is the continuation of other forms of disruptive activities of the Vatican against the People's Democratic institutions. According to the Court's opinion, the accused were no doubt aware of this, but nevertheless joined this movement and became part of its leadership.

That is why the Court found the accused, Krčméry, guilty of high treason according to Paragraph 78, Articles 2(a), (b), 1(c) of the Penal Code. He conspired to disrupt the People's Democratic Republic, and to fulfill this task he was in contact with foreign agents, as was the traitor Schützner, whom he knew had reentered the Republic from abroad without permission so as to coordinate Vatican Action activities according to instructions which he had received abroad.

On the other hand, the accused Suchý was found guilty of high treason according to Paragraph 78, Articles 2(a), 1(c) of the Penal Code, since it was not proven that he was in contact with foreign agents in the sense of Paragraph 78, Article 2(b) of the Penal Code. As concerns his contact with Mádr, the leader of Vatican Catholic Action, it was not established that he was aware that Mádr was sent from abroad to our territory as a hostile agent.

From his personal documents, it was ascertained that Krčméry comes from a family of office workers and that in spite of his advanced age, his father is actively involved in the building of socialism and is an excellent worker in his factory. The accused also performed his duties adequately at his work place and there were no complaints against him, even during his period of military service.

The accused Suchý is the son of a Greek-Catholic priest. He studied at the University of Economics and was then employed as a commercial engineer in various organizations. He has no previous convictions and there is nothing to show that during his military service, he had acted in an openly hostile manner towards the People's Democratic Republic.

Under the leadership of the party and government, the working people of our Republic are endeavoring to bring about economic and social change, with the aim of building socialism. At the same time the state fully respects all opinions and views, and in particular religious belief. Freedom of religious belief is guaranteed to all citizens by the Constitution itself and the state also gives all churches financial support.

Freedom of religion cannot, however, be understood to mean freedom to take part in any treacherous or subversive activities against the People's Democratic Republic. This would make religion a force that would slow down the building of socialism. However, the accused, under the influence of Vatican reactionary forces, became involved in subversive activities against the People's Democratic Republic, activities which were carried out on a large scale.

That is why the Superior Military Court decided as follows:

Silvester Krčméry, M.D., a soldier in basic military service, born in Trnava August 5, 1924, resident of Mimoň, son of an office worker, a physician, whose last residence was No. 1 Pilárikova Street, Bratislava, and at the present time is UVV Trenčín,

committed

high treason according to Paragraph 78, Articles 2(a), (b), Article 1(c) of the Penal Code, as, since 1945 until his arrest in July 1951, he founded and directed in Bratislava, Prague, Košice, and in other places in the Republic subversive groups called "The Family," within the framework of Vatican Catholic Action, whose goal it was to evolve according to Vatican political directions and activities which would lead to the disruption of the People's Democratic institutions; he coordinated the activities of these groups according to other Action leaders' orders, namely, Kolakovič, Mádr, and Schützner, knowing full well that they were acting under Vatican instructions, and also being fully aware that Schützner had entered the Republic from abroad with new orders for Vatican Catholic Action; he gave Mádr, and later, through Staríček, sent him malicious information to be used as enemy propaganda against the Republic; in 1951, when he learned that the leaders of Vatican Catholic Action had been arrested, he, along with Staríček and Jukl, negotiated an illegal departure abroad, where he planned to continue his disruptive activities against the Republic;

AND FOR THIS HE IS CONDEMNED

to 14 *(fourteen) years of imprisonment* according to Paragraph 78, Article 2 of the Penal Code.

According to Paragraph 47 of the Penal Code, his properties will be confiscated.

According to Paragraph 43 of the Penal Code, he will lose his civil rights; the temporary loss of his civil rights is set for 6 (six) years according to Paragraph 44, Article 2 of the Penal Code.

He is responsible for and must pay half the expenses incurred by the State for these penal proceedings.

Josef Suchý, a soldier in basic military service, born September 15, 1924, in Prešov, member of the military artistic ensemble in Bratislava, a commercial engineer, son of a Greek-Catholic priest, last domicile, Gunduličova No. 4, Bratislava, and at the present time UVV Trenčín,

committed

high treason according to Paragraph 78, Article 2(a) and Article 1(c) of the Penal Code, as since 1950 until January 1952 he was a member of the so-called Central Group in Bratislava which, after the abolition of the Central Catholic Office, was to coordinate and direct activities of the groups founded in the framework of Vatican Catholic Action in Slovakia; he held the position of treasurer and public relations officer in the Central Group; he distributed to other groups various Vatican publications which were hostile towards the People's Democratic Republic; he received instructions for further activities from Mádr, the leader of Vatican Catholic Action, and propaganda material from a certain Tomek. After several members of the Central group had been arrested, he participated in a secret meeting in January 1952. The accused knew that Father Nahálka, who chaired the meeting, was hiding from the authorities. The purpose of this meeting was to revive the activities of the Central Group;

AND FOR THIS HE IS CONDEMNED

according to Paragraph 78, Article 2 of the Penal Code, *to 10 (ten) years of imprisonment.*

According to Paragraph 47 of the Penal Code, his properties will be confiscated.

According to Paragraph 43 of the Penal Code, he will lose his civil rights; the temporary loss of his civil rights is set for 5 (five) years, according to Paragraph 44,, Article 2 of the Penal Code.

He is responsible for and must pay half of the expenses incurred by the State for these penal proceedings.

After the evaluation of the danger to society of the defendants' criminal activities as specified above, the Court, in making its decision, considered the circumstances which spoke for and against the defendants.

It was for their own benefit that the defendants partially confessed, since they admitted de facto activities.

The Court further considered the fact that they lived orderly lives of working people, since it was not established that before committing these criminal deeds they had acted with enmity towards the People's Democratic Republic, or had failed to fulfill their civil duties properly.

While Krčméry, together with Kolakovič, was active in the founding of the groups in 1943, at which time he was a juvenile, in the Court's opinion it would be impossible to allege with conviction that he was at that time aware of their true purpose and goal. However, it is against the defendants that they continued these activities during a lengthy period of time, that they introduced them to other persons, and then made these people members of the groups.

The Court also considered the fact that they themselves entered into these activities under the influence of other persons and that of their own religious upbringing, which strengthened in them the feeling of dependency on the high church hierarchy and on the Vatican.

Considering their class origin, the Court came to the conclusion that it could safely assume that adequate sentences could reeducate them to the point that they would bring their religious convictions into harmony with the principles of the People's Democratic Republic.

Since Krčméry's activities were more widespread, he received a more severe sentence. But even in the case of the accused Suchý, the Court did not consider applying Paragraph 30 of the Penal Code, taking into consideration that the accused did continue in his activities even after some members of the Central Group had been arrested; on the contrary, in 1952 he again participated in a meeting dealing with continuation of these activities, so that he too received a severe sentence as a corrective measure.

The declaration about the confiscation of property is based on the ruling of Paragraph 78, Article 4 of the Penal Code.

Through their criminal acts, the defendants demonstrated their hostility towards the People's Democratic Order, and the Court therefore deprives them of their civil rights for an adequate period of time. In view of their dire circumstances, they are released from paying financial penalties.

The declaration on the reimbursement of expenses is based on the ruling in Paragraph 68, Article 1 of the Penal Code.

On the other hand, the defendant J. Suchý is

acquitted under Paragraph 162(c) of the Penal Code, since it was not proven that he had committed a criminal act, insofar as it was claimed that he participated in 1950–1952, in Bratislava, in drafting hostile reports for Vatican propaganda, an act of high treason already covered under Paragraph 78, Articles 2(a), (b), and Article 1(c) of the Penal Code.[51]

Instructions:

It is possible to appeal against this sentence.

The appeal has to be filed within three days.

The accused can, during this period, request a written rendition of the verdict and should he do so, the above period will then start from the day the verdict is delivered to him.

A duly filed appeal has a delaying effect.

Trenčín, June 24, 1954
President of the Senate:
Chief Justice Antonín Merta Ph.D.

Document No. 8

Copy

Private Silvester Krčméry, M.D.
Appeal against the verdict of the
Superior Military Court pronounced on June 14, 1954
(Ref. no. T 16/54)
Delivered to me on July 1, 1954

Trenčín July 3, 1954

To the Supreme Military Court

Prague

If I have decided after all to appeal against the verdict of guilt pronounced against me, I am doing so only in order that I may never be reproached for not having taken advantage of all the possibilities that contemporary human justice boasts of, although I think that after being kept in custody for almost three years (and after my trial), I have, justifiably in my opinion, lost even the little that remained of the trust I once had in human justice.

If the court is merely an agent of the powers-that-be, that is, the state is solely a machine for oppressing people and an instrument of the ruling class as was emphasized, and if the accused is automatically relegated to the class which must be oppressed (not on the principle of truth and justice and a priori open-mindedness towards the matter being discussed, as in my case, the Church), then the court is really superfluous, for this task could easily be carried out fully and adequately by police departments.

However, in that case it would be pointless and impossible for citizens to try and obey the laws, if for the slightest offense they could be accused of high treason and sentenced accordingly. The rest of the Penal Code is also expendable if every punishable offense is to be considered as an attempt to overthrow the regime, that is, as high treason.

I believe that the court must always show impartiality, even if the accused were the state itself.

Paragraph 78 of the Penal Code, which deals with high treason, especially Article 1 c, is, in my opinion, very vague and open-ended. That is why one and the same activity, the existence of religious groups for example, is sometimes defined as high treason, or conspiracy against the republic, or sedition, or undermining state supervision of the churches, or even as an offense against the police for not having reported them.

Nevertheless, the law requires proof or evidence that there was an attempt at a coup d'état. However, we never intended anything of the kind, never talked about it nor acted in any way to bring it about, and we never accepted anything from anyone who could have been involved in such an action. On the contrary, we always emphasized that our activities were purely religious, spiritual and apostolic, and clearly warned against engaging in any political, disruptive, espionage, or other similar activities.

We therefore do not understand on what grounds we have been sentenced and on what evidence religious groups have been declared treasonous or having treasonable intent. We refused to confess to this crime because there simply is no truth to the charge. The testimony of the only witness brought before the court (Staríček) corroborated what we declared as to the aims and mission of Catholic Action and of the groups. No other significant evidence concerning this aspect of our activities was ever submitted.

It is not possible to refer to other verdicts in accordance with Paragraph 5 of the court regulations, because that would mean punishing the accused simply on principle. Such a procedure would suggest that on the basis of one person's mistake or unjust verdict, others could be similarly condemned ad infinitum. Yet it is well-known that not only are trials occasionally reviewed, but whole trends in society's way of thinking may be revised. Moreover, we were not even allowed to be present when these verdicts were rendered, to say nothing of being permitted to express our views about them or defend ourselves. These verdicts are therefore incomplete and totally biased against us.

With reference to the first part of the verdict (pp. 1–3) concerning the Vatican, I should like to point out that it was not "after submitting evidence" that "the court took as proven" certain actions. The court only made a general statement at the hearing to the effect that the matters concerned were "generally known" and "would not be discussed." When I tried to express my opinion, I was interrupted with the warning "not to use the court as a platform and not to act as an advocate for others."

We did not work for the Vatican itself. We love truth and are against every confusion and distortion of concepts. We worked only for Christ and the Church. Your term "Vatican Catholic Action" is a pleonasm, a redundant expression which is intended to hide the heart of the matter. Catholic Action cannot be both Catholic and non-Catholic at the same time, that is "non Vatican." It cannot be Catholic and not follow the Vatican.

Catholic Action was officially set up by the Church around 1920, not as something new, but as a continuation of the spreading of the faith by Christ and His apostles. The Church has been proceeding with this, its mission, in various ways for the past two thousand years.

When, in 1941, as a sixteen- or seventeen-year-old youth, I began to work for this organization, it was not on the basis of any political instructions from the Vatican, but because of the Gospels and the Acts of the Apostles, that is, Scripture, which were then at least tolerated and allowed by the state. Alleged treasonous activities by Catholic Action must first be made evident before a verdict is pronounced. As far as Catholics are concerned, no one ever received any directions or guidelines aiming at the destruction of the state.

The phrase "renewing capitalism in the republic" sounds particularly strange, as it is generally known that the Church in its encyclical Rerum Novarum, totally rejected exploitative capitalism as long ago as 1890. Professor Kolakovič himself was strongly against it (see his books "The Main Features of Human Order" and "We Want Peace," published in Ružomberok around 1947). Furthermore, we and the Central Catholic Office did not distribute any sort of illegal questionnaires or leaflets.

Of course, if by "the Vatican" one means the Catholic Church or its leadership, then we, by the very fact that we are Christians, may be said to have worked for the Vatican.

When reciting the "Our Father" or participating in the Mass we do indeed fulfill the "instructions of the Vatican." For that matter, the whole of the Catholic faith is based on obedience to the Church in religious matters. We differ from other religions in that we recognize the Pope as Christ's true representative on earth, a fact which is clearly stated in all catechisms and confirmed throughout the Scriptures. The state, if it recognizes any church whatsoever, must at least respect its rules, teachings, and faith. It cannot casually dismiss and outlaw 10 million Catholics in our republic for "loyalty to the Vatican."

Therefore, it cannot be said that we somehow joined up with the Vatican, for we are bound to it and members of the Catholic Church from the moment we are baptized. The fact that we, as millions of other believers in this country, have not left it even after it has been so seriously attacked (although anyone can leave the Church at any time, anywhere in the world without the least fear of being harmed) shows that we support the Church. We are making it clear that we will not give in to these persecutions. In this sense then, one can say that I have worked for the Vatican[52] since I have propagated the Catholic faith.

But our laws and our Constitution clearly allow and guarantee the freedom to engage in religious activities, "both in public and in private" (Paragraph 16), that is, secretly. The fact that these groups were not registered in the Slovak State, that they existed and were organized in some form in all countries, under every regime, is the best proof that they were always simply looked upon as being part of religious life. Consequently, their purpose could not have been to overthrow the present system.

At the hearing, an attempt was made to interpret the Constitution in such a way that religious freedom would be defined solely as religious services or the teaching of religion in schools, while apostolate work would be illegal. But the Constitution is very clear and explicit and we have not broken any of its laws dealing with morality and civil order.

I have tried in vain (both while in custody as well as on April 1, 1954, from the chairman of the Senate) to obtain permission to look at the law or directive which actually forbids religious groups. Obviously any such regulation would be in direct conflict with the Constitution as a whole and more specifically with Paragraphs 15–17, concerning religious freedom and creative spiritual activities, and Article 24, referring to freedom of assembly. Thus, according to Paragraph 172, such a law is invalid.

According to the Constitution of this country it is not religious groups that are illegal, but their persecution and the classification of religious activities as high treason. If religious freedom as laid down in Paragraphs 83 and 234 of the Penal Code still exists, then by law the spreading of religious hatred and restrictions to religious freedom are punishable offenses.

The mission of these religious groups has always existed. It did not suddenly appear only after 1945.[53] If the groups expanded more rapidly then, it was because the war ended and many of them became part of established Catholic associations and institutions. I do not think there was really any feverish increase in groups, as one might conclude from the reading of the Verdict (see "meetings in order to intensify and spread the movement"). To a certain extent the spreading of the faith was always spontaneous, as the occasion arose, and, like every other human activity, sometimes grew in strength and sometimes declined.

As far as my contacts with Mádr and Jukl and my superiors[54] are concerned, these were not clandestine meetings with "Vatican agents," but merely normal gatherings of believers, priests and people who held similar interests such as to follow Christ, spread His teachings, His love, and to grow spiritually.

If any one of them was in contact with the Vatican, it was as a Christian with his Church, just as the apostles were in contact with Christ or with one another. Furthermore, if they distributed any sort of printed leaflets,[55] one can safely assume that these were on religious themes and not "seditious," for I knew them as people who love truth. (I should like to point out that it was Kolakovič himself who said, "If the devil himself were to speak the truth, we should have to accept that he had done so.")

As far as I remember, I was able to tell Jukl that Mádr and Tomko had "disappeared" because no one knew whether they had been arrested or had gone abroad. In my opinion, neither Schützner nor Vacková ever played a key role in Catholic Action. I met with Schützner in August 1950 (not in 1951, since I was already in prison by then)[56] and we did not agree on anything of importance. On the contrary, I recall that we differed about some things, but I did not have the slightest impression that he had any special instructions from abroad. Baptista was, I think, in hiding, but not on account of any treasonable activities, but because as a Catholic monk he was being illegally persecuted.

For the sake of accuracy I will add that I was imprisoned before the arrest of the Central Catholic Group (if the Bratislava one is meant by this) and I was not present at the meeting between Mádr and Šmálik in Bratislava,[57] nor did I pass on a written message to Mádr, to say nothing of a seditious one.

My intention to go abroad was momentary and not fully thought out. It was a deviation from my own personal policy and motivated only by a passing fear of (illegal) arrest and a desire to continue my study of leprosy (I refer to 1946). But I myself came to terms with these motives and gave up the idea of leaving. The whole affair was nothing but pure fantasy, without any realistic or solid basis in fact (no "gliding" machine of Holub's as was discovered during the inquiry). Therefore, there can never be any question of my being motivated by a desire to work against the state from abroad or at home.

I should also like to comment on the "evidence" given on page 6[58] of the Verdict. I speak from experience when I say that State Security [the police] does not keep a record of the voluntary statements of detainees. However, it uses all possible methods, in order to try to force from them statements against the Church or in agreement with what "they have already found out." These methods include stretching out the supposed "investigation" period over many years; long-term solitary confinement with deliberate and systematic withholding of any form of employment, reading, visits, and often even outdoor exercise and sleep. These are strictly against Paragraphs 107 and 296 of the Penal Code, which attest that the accused can only be subjected to such restrictions as are essential to prevent him from interfering with the criminal prosecution.

It is therefore not possible to consider as reliable evidence the statements of either witnesses or the accused obtained and signed under such duress. A continuous atmosphere of nervous and mental anxiety inevitably leads to a nervous breakdown, and in many cases, to madness or a state very close to it. (For example, I experienced hallucinations even though I had very strong nerves.) It is far worse than the physical coercion which they did not hesitate to use when they deemed it necessary. (I was beaten in both 1952 and 1953 and suffered two broken ribs during an interrogation.)

In my case it was often stressed, even two years after I had been taken into custody, that they would never allow me to go before the court, even if it were to take ten years, until I had confessed, that is, until I had given the official what he wanted, for I had admitted belonging to religious groups from the very first day.

That is why as early as April 4, 1954 (that is, three months before the main hearing) I requested, as is also in the records, that witnesses for the prosecution be heard in court if the indictment differed from my conclusions. I wanted to question the witnesses at the hearing in order that arguable matters be clarified. This was in accordance with Paragraphs 151 and 154 (and 161?) of Court regulations which state that only statements made before the court may be taken into account.

During the main hearing, I repeated my request but the court (with the exception of Staríček) again rejected it. They cited Paragraph 157, but that was incorrect since according to that paragraph, the accused must agree that no witnesses will be presented before the court, and I had not agreed to such a procedure. Furthermore, since all the witnesses were prisoners, their presence in court would not have caused undue disruptions.

Upon questioning Staríček, the extent to which he was in disagreement with his previous statement taken down at the police station was immediately obvious. (This was not surprising. Once mental stress was eased, prisoners usually recanted and totally rejected the evidence they had previously given.) In order to illustrate the point, I asked that Staríček's declaration before the court be compared with the one he had given at the police station, and the records in my court file. However, the request was again denied with the comment, "It will be looked into."

If the Supreme Court is truly interested in discovering the truth about the alleged anti-state and treasonous aims of the Catholic Action groups, then I request that the following people be present at the appeal hearing and their testimony heard by the court: Otto Mádr, Vladimír Jukl (with regard to messages and Professor Kolakovič), Růžena Vacková, and above all, Bishop Štefan Trochta, Jozef Šoltés, Vojtech Jenčík, and perhaps Baníková, Puobiš, Komárek, as well as all the other witnesses for the prosecution, insofar as they disagree with my statements.

Staríček should also be recalled, since at the main hearing he declared that he could no longer remember the content of the messages and that they could well have been of a purely internal nature. He spoke about them so vaguely that it is not clear whether he passed messages on to me or I to him. Yet, the verdict is based on his obscure affirmations (bottom of p. 7 and p. 13 of the Verdict).

I cannot objectively comment on the written material from the Central Catholic Office,[59] or on the trial of Dr. Tomanóczy, as neither has anything to do with my case.

However, the fact that I admitted to participating in religious activities, a freedom which is guaranteed by the state, should be added to my supposed confession.[60] Catholic Action (along with the whole Catholic Church) is, and always has been, under Vatican authority. That is clear not only to me, but to all Catholics. In addition, since the state has, until now at least, recognized the Church as a legal organization, there cannot be anything treasonous in its being lead in religious matters by the leadership appointed by Christ, that is, by the apostles and their successors, for the Church cannot be lead otherwise if it is to be Christ's church.

The assertion in the Verdict[61] that "there can be no doubt" is misleading, as it was never proven that we engaged in anti-state activities. After all, we know that we never received any instructions from the Vatican to overthrow the Republic. Actually, we have never even heard that the Vatican looks upon the West as an ally.

On the contrary, the Vatican clearly stresses its neutrality in political conflicts. That is why it chose to be a miniature (symbolic) state, that is, a small urban district with extraterritorial rights. In doing so, it avoided other countries putting pressure on it and exerting political influence on its religious activities.

The Vatican has not become hostile to us. The truth is that it cannot become hostile towards any state because it cannot be regarded as an equal. It has no means (army, weapons, etc.) to carry out hostilities nor is it interested in acquiring any.

To describe Catholic Action and the apostolate (the fundamental activities of every religion) "a cunning form of subversive activity" would mean that religious freedom guaranteed by the Constitution is not taken seriously in our country.

The fact that our activities were carried out without the permission of the state[62] is by no means proof that they were not religious or were treacherous. The law certainly does not define high treason as "secret activities."

Why are we therefore not accused of having perhaps broken some regulation about registering groups? (As previously mentioned, we have repeatedly asked to be shown such a law, if it does exist.) After all, nowhere are the Bible, or Our Father, or any other religious services or prayers ever actually mentioned as being allowed. They are taken as a given, obvious aspects of religious life arising from the freedom to carry out ceremonies, either privately or publicly, connected with the faith of any religious denomination (Paragraphs 16 and 17 of the Constitution).

Neither Christ nor the apostles ever reported their religious groups, because these were not organizations or associations in the narrow sense of the word. In a sense, they were much like other groups who centered their activities on some common interest such as study, science, sports, or philately, and so on.

All religious societies have existed "within the framework of religious activities" with the knowledge of the state.[63] Nevertheless, they have all been disbanded and forbidden, even those which after February submitted their statutes (some even had "action committees"). The ban included prayer groups (centered on the rosary or the Eucharist), Marian groups, and others. Thousands of Catholic monks were suddenly illegally sentenced to indefinite prison terms (which meant for life) without any court proceedings whatsoever, merely because they were members of orders or institutions. It did not matter that the latter were "recognized by the state within the framework of religious activities carried out with the knowledge of the state."

As far as "various Papal encyclicals and letters" are concerned,[64] they could of course have been circulated among group members. This does not mean that the main function of the groups was to distribute materials, since this literature was also available outside the groups and was read in churches. We are human beings and Christians, and have therefore always been interested in life, and above all, religious problems. It is therefore quite normal that we would wish to know what the Church and the bishops have to say about these things. Our interest is not solely in the attacks on them.

Nearly half of the New Testament (the most important part of the

Bible) is made up of such so-called "inflammatory pastoral letters" beginning with the letters written by Peter, the first pope, and on to those of the first bishops, the apostles Paul, James, John, Jude, etc.

As far as I know, apart from those dealing with strictly religious matters, these letters were only concerned with the internal affairs of the Church, or with the rebuttal of some accusation against the Church or the bishops.

That the other side should be heard is based on a very natural human principle, one which is also found in our Constitution and laws, which guarantee every accused person the right to defend himself. It certainly is not considered high treason! (Circulus viciosus: the letters are treasonable even though they only reject the accusation of high treason). I am not aware of the slightest distortion of the truth or display of an allegedly "hostile attitude" in their content. I ask that any letter that we are said to have circulated be presented in full and that it should be shown in what respect it went beyond the limits of religion.

Certain events which took place in our country (and which are widely known) aroused the indignation of believers for the very reason that they are in direct conflict with the Constitution and our laws. These included the abolition of the Greek Catholic Church, declaring religious activities to be high treason, the imprisonment of thousands of monks without court proceedings, the liquidation of the episcopacy, the disbanding of Catholic societies, the ban on Catholic newspapers and journals, the state Catholic Action, Dechet,and others.[65]

Responsibility for this righteous anger lies with those who carried out these deeds and who, either from ignorance of religious questions or hate for the Church, have dragged the state into such an impossible predicament. This dilemma is unacceptable not only to every believer but intolerable for the state itself. It is a situation similar to the times of the greatest religious persecutions.

It stands to reason that those who protest against this crisis cannot be blamed for its occurrence. I also wish to emphasize that the Church does not incite its followers to acts of rebellion. It has never done so, even during the worst persecutions. Our dedication to social services is most obvious and the best testimony to the fact that even under the present circumstances, we have not allowed ourselves to be goaded into engaging in any treasonable activities or feelings of hate (in accordance with Christ's principle [Matt. 5:44]), nor have we incited others to do so. On the contrary, dozens of people can testify to our goodwill.

I think it is time people and their relations to others and to society were not judged by whether or what they believe, or their claims about who and what they are, but by how they work for their fellow men. And our work speaks for itself.

"On instructions from abroad"[66] is indeed a compelling comment. However, if we stop and really think about it, the Gospels and Christ himself, and even our own culture, all have foreign origins. Therefore this does not constitute proof that ours was "an action aimed against the republic." If the state demands control over the Church in order to ensure "legal religious tolerance and equality among all denominations,"[67] I think that in that regard not the slightest objection can be brought against us.

As for the conclusion of the Verdict,[68] I declare that the aim of Catholic Action was not "in accordance with the political directions of the Vatican to develop activities leading to the overthrow of the people's democracy." Furthermore, I maintain that I did not establish "seditious groups," and that when it is stated that all Catholic religious activity is organized "in accordance with the instructions of the Vatican," this simply means that it is according to Christ's teachings.

Unfortunately, I do not have the education nor the eloquence of a lawyer (nor access to materials and the law), nor the ability, nor even the competence, to adequately defend the Church, because I have never been good at making speeches and putting forth arguments. But I wish to say that our strength lay in our work and service and love for our fellow men.

In conclusion, where the appeal hearing is concerned, I wish to make the following requests and suggestions:

1. that other prosecution witnesses and the following people be heard before the court: Mádr, Jukl, Vacková, Staríček, Trochta, Jenčík, Šoltés, and Komárek;

2. that the pastoral letter or a similar decree, which we were supposed to have circulated, be quoted in full, and that it be pointed out where it was against the law or was not in accordance with the truth;

3. that where other verdicts or decisions are quoted, similar documents and witnesses in favor of those being tried be presented as well; this would include a prisoner's personal evidence and comments (such as Kolakovič's) and thus ensure a complete record and total objectivity;

4. that, according to Paragraph 66 of the Penal Code, I be allowed to take a closer look at all the penal records that will be submitted at the hearing so that I may copy excerpts;
5. that I be permitted to see the directives which forbid religious groups, and other laws and regulations connected with religious matters;
6. that I be authorized to borrow the Penal Code and explanatory notes, amendments and additions to it and to the Constitution, insofar as they pertain to our cause, a pencil, paper, and my notes;
7. that I be given copies of the Indictment, the Verdict, as well as copies of all other decisions taken by the prosecutor or the court (in accordance with Paragraph 29 of court regulations).

Trenčín July 3, 1954
S. Krčméry

Document No. 22

Horní Slavkov October 21, 1964

Convict Krčméry, Silvester

Statement concerning the hearing for *conditional release*

In order that my point of view concerning the hearing for my conditional release may not be presented in a distorted or inaccurate form, I am submitting a written statement.

I have not requested conditional release and I do not even know how it came about that this question should be discussed at all. I have never applied in any way for mitigation of the punishment assigned to me and I have rejected the possibility, for one reason: in my opinion, a condition for the fulfillment of the legal criteria for conditional release from prison is that the convicted person has broken the law and that his deserved punishment has effected a reformation and rehabilitation.

As, however, I never committed treason and the punishment of fourteen years in prison to which I was sentenced lacks any legal basis whatsoever, I have had no opportunity to "reform myself" and begin to live the "proper life of a working man," because I have never stopped living such a life, as all the testimonials submitted to the court by my superiors and colleagues have confirmed. For this reason I have always considered the verdict declared against me as one of the illegal expressions of high-handedness so typical of the era of the so-called "personality cult."

I must therefore regard the conversion of the remaining part of my sentence to a conditional one as an attempt to put the whole matter in such a light that my conviction would appear to have something in common with the law.

However, for the past thirteen years and more that I have been in prison, I have been trying in vain to get an objective and disinterested re-examination, according to the valid laws, of the charge of treason brought against me! And the fact that I have rejected any mitigation of the sentence or personal privileges is perhaps also proof that I never committed treason, and that even after so many bitter experiences, I have not learned to pay lip service, to hide my thoughts, or pretend, and that even after all that, I have not ceased to believe in truth and justice.

Acceptance of conditional release could therefore, from my point of view, be understood as an acknowledgment of the justification for and legality of the verdict, and for this reason I reject this hearing and I will not accept conditional release.

At the same time, I stress that as a Christian I have no feelings of being insulted, of bitterness or hate. I have long since forgiven all those who have trespassed against me at any time and in any way. My standpoint is not based on any feelings of superiority or personal perfection, on dramatic holiness, heroism, or a desire for flamboyant martyrdom. As a person, I am no doubt full of faults and sins, to a far greater extent than many others.

This attitude does not originate from hostility or blind fanaticism. But rather from the fact that I consider it my human and civic duty to protest against lawlessness, and to fight with every legal means available for the strict observance and strengthening of law in the spirit of the Constitution, without regard to nationality, race, or religion.

At the same time, I urge that there be a re-examination of my detailed complaints about infringements of the law, which I submitted to the Supreme court through the Ministry of Justice in June this year, and which, in themselves, offer more than enough evidence for the invalidation of the verdict in my case.[69]

Horní Slavkov, October 21, 1964
Convict Silvester Krčméry

BRAINWASHING EXPERIENCES AND HOW TO PREPARE FOR THEM

To describe brainwashing, its effects, and how to resist, I rely on the following: Edward Hunter's classic description of brainwashing, domestic sources of data from Jiří Šulc[70] and a group of doctors from the Institute of Aeronautical Health, experiences of some Catholic bishops who were tortured by this system in solitary confinement in China for thirty-eight to forty years, and some of our own partial experiences.

The expression "brainwashing" was allegedly introduced by Edward Hunter in Hong Kong by translating the Chinese "hsi nao" (to wash the brain) or "K'sai tao" (ideological reform). The process was an attempt at breaking into pieces and destroying the personality and identity of a person, his reason, will, memory, and feelings by subjecting him to long term isolation, exhaustion, and extreme suffering. Then, on this "clean slate," one would write new "thoughts" of a different personality, which would "rationalize" or completely change the brainwashed person's views and positions.

Brainwashing is a comprehensive, varied technique, applied on an essentially individual basis. Therefore defense against it must also be personal and individual.

Apart from a physico-neuro-psychic power of resistance, what are essential are spiritual preparation and capability. A motivation which is stronger than usual is necessary to overcome and break physical and spiritual isolation, extreme suffering and exhaustion, deprivation of sleep, and especially increased suggestibility.

Therefore I consider Part VII, on my spiritual life and spiritual program in solitary confinement, to be a key part of my memories. It is about a sort of charging up of oneself with spiritual energy and spiritual ability. It is even about their growth and enrichment, precisely because of what should have led to their total destruction, that is, isolation, silence, forced undernourishment, and the cold. These factors are then replaced by meditation leading to a "weightless state." In similar extreme situations, spiritually motivated people have extraordinary possibilities for resistance and growth and the accumulation of spiritual capital."We know that all things work for good for those who love God. . . . " (Rom. 8:28)

The word of God in one's mind is priceless! (see John 6:63).

I will try to give at least a summary of some practical experiences, and I would be most grateful if readers, especially former prisoners, would add or bring corrections to these.

Preparatory Stage

In this phase, security agents put the person under surveillance and search for as much information and "proof" as they can get about his contacts with relatives, friends, hobbies, work, and so on. The agents want him to feel insecure and afraid, therefore some of the surveillance is done in a very striking and dramatic manner.

Defense

The victim should then take the precaution of cleaning out his table and study, skillfully concealing, or better still, destroying notebooks, addresses, and telephone numbers. He should take the possibility of wiretapping into account, end or significantly reduce correspondence, telephone calls, meetings, and visits.

On the other hand, it is necessary, paradoxically, to avoid complete isolation, fear and depression, or minimalize them mainly by engaging in an intensive spiritual life of prayer, including receiving the sacraments and studying the Bible with the memorizing of the most important texts, especially those from the Gospels. They can protect against thoughts of and attempts at suicide, and spiritual crises. They can also be the most valuable material for meditation in approaching isolation. It is especially strengthening to meditate on Jesus' last evening and agony in the Garden of Gethsemane, his suffering and resurrection, and on Paul's wounds and defensive actions.

However, when there is the danger of a nervous breakdown, it is imperative to do everything to break the isolation and feeling of despair, even at the cost of personal risk, that is, arrest of oneself or with other friends.

Practical Matters

Read the Penal Order and Criminal Law codes, especially the sections dealing with the police and human rights, even if it is only to acquire information. Relearn the basic signals of the Morse alphabet in its prison modification, that is, when tapping, use two rapid dots instead of a dash. Reread the samizdat instructions (Basic Rules of the Game, Self-defense I–II) and get advice from the more experienced.

First Stage of Brainwashing

This is the phase immediately after arrest when one is in a state of spiritual shock and disorientation.

There now begins about one week of adaptation and acclimatization. This will be followed by a stage of repeated aggressive interrogation sessions, each one lasting perhaps one or two months and sometimes much longer. Its aim is to generate feelings of guilt and then confession.

This is where many people who recognize that there is a moral code but do not have a clear relationship between it and their behavior succumb. Then it is good to do the following things:

1. *The Conscience*

Where your conscience is concerned, face the fact that you have done things which are wrong, but that you have not done what they are accusing you of, and offer God your sincere repentance (Rom. 8:1–2, 33). Then, since we all aspire to God's divine forgiveness, let us forgive those who harm us. A clear conscience and faith will renew one's relationship with God, who is the source of all strength, peace, and love for everyone, even enemies. They also give one the belief, along with a childlike certitude and joy, that one can prevail.

Struggle against fear and depression with the help of constant prayer, love and the power of the Holy Spirit, and spend time in "adoration" even if it is done at a distance. The "Instructions to the Apostles" before they were sent out (see Matt. 10:16, 26–31, and many other places in the New Testament) show the Gospel as a great source of power and courage, especially the triple exhortation, "Do not be afraid. . . ." But the most effective protection against fear are love and growth in love, "There is no fear in love, but perfect love drives out fear. . . ." (1 John 4:18). In addition, any kind of physical action, such as walking, exercises, repeated washing and cleaning should not be underestimated as weapons.

2. *A Daily Program*

Establish a detailed daily program with only short intervals for relaxation and exercise; include walking, "singing," at least in your mind, and time to ponder memories. Some things are especially important such as spiritual exercises lasting from four to six weeks, spiritual renewal with prayers, particularly meditation based on memorized texts from Scriptures, praying the Holy Mass, examining the conscience, that is, evaluating one's life in the past, present, and future, and a program for the day, week, and coming years. Accept even this most difficult stage of interrogation as a grace from God, use it towards a complete conversion and spiritual growth, gather a treasure consisting of prayer, silence, sacrifice, and fasting.

3. *Practical Preparation for Interrogation and Accusation*

Have a good idea of the position you will adopt, beginning with the decision to react slowly, in a well thought out way, to only give a partial answer or to totally refuse to answer. If possible, decide not to sign anything, or only sign the exact answers you were allowed to give in a free and weighed manner. Do not fall into resignation, nor rely only on human skill and evasion. Adopt a basically apostolate approach towards the aims of those who are enemies of the Church, of humanity, and of democracy.

Check the three stages of pain and suffering and know their limits (maximum resistance), for example, when a person falls into unconsciousness. Write the minimum in any curriculum vitae, and be fully aware that everything will be misused against you and your "brothers," and will be the basis of accusations.

Second Stage of Brainwashing

This is the phase of interrogation, the concoction of evidence, the establishment of guilt, and the possibility of indirectly giving evidence against brothers.

Do not violate confidentiality, either agreed upon or derived from the nature of the matter. Appeal to their own laws and the protection of human rights, that is, the right to silence. Christ did not answer the accusations of Annas (John 18:21) and Pilate (John 19:9–11). Lying is not the only or the greatest sin. Judas did not lie when he told those who pursued Jesus, "The one I kiss is he, . . . " but he violated a trust and in doing so became partly responsible for murder. "We must obey God rather than men" (Acts 5:29). Conversely, remember that every contact, even with an enemy or spy, can be a unique divine opportunity for loving, spiritual service, all the while keeping the required caution and protection of others in mind. Do not neglect any opening for spiritual service. That is true apostolate work.

Third Stage of Brainwashing

This phase is the preparation for the trial and main hearing. Here it is still possible to bear witness to Christ in a meaningful way while at the same time put up a good defense. But do not rely solely on a great spiritual state and readiness. We are responsible for what can be foreseen. Therefore it is necessary to earnestly prepare the appropriate spiritual and legal passages we are to use. This was what Christ and the Apostle Paul did.

A thoughtful and prayerful defense is also a defense of truth, love, and the Church, but it cannot be calculated and egotistical and done at the expense of others. Even when the public is excluded, the trial may provide a once in a lifetime occasion for the judges and guards to receive important testimony (see 2 Tim. 4:16–19).

The period when we thought the sequence of events and experiences was only an accidental series of events and isolated drastic measures, when we did not fully understand the precise, focused, organized, and progressive nature of these incidents, was the worst. It seems to me that the most important thing for escaping fear of the unknown and the feeling of horror of brainwashing, is to be fully aware that it does exist and to grasp its essence, possibilities, and limits.

We are so often naive in our thinking. We live, contented and safe, with the idea that in a civilized country, in the mostly cultured and democratic environment of our times, such a coercive regime is impossible. We forget that in unstable countries, a certain political structure can lead to indoctrination and terror, where individual elements and stages of brainwashing are slowly implemented. This, at first, is quite inconspicuous. However, after a very short time, it can develop into a full undemocratic totalitarian system.

Epilogue

THOUGHTS ON THE BOOK
by Alojz Rakús, M.D.

It is not easy to add an epilogue to the book of an author whose captivating personality along, with the destiny and values which helped shape it, had a great deal of influence on the development of my own spiritual life at a very critical age, that is, the period when I was a student at the university, and then again later.

However, it is precisely because of this (and partly also because of my personal knowledge of the author) that I have taken leave to divide the epilogue into three sections, three aspects of the book as its reading evoked them in me. In this sense it seems to me that it would be useful to try and understand this book first as a *story,* second, as *evidence,* and, third, as a *spiritual message.*

The Story

If we look at this book as the telling of a particular personal story, then the central, indeed, the turning point of this story appears to me to be where the author dictates a statement to the State Security interrogator, "I refuse to continue answering, because I see that the whole interrogation process is nonsensical. State Security is in no way interested in finding out the truth. Its sole objective is the destruction of the Church. Those involved in this operation seek answers but if they find them unsatisfactory, they adapt or totally distort them. The prisoner can say whatever he likes, but the interrogators will write their own final account."[71]

Alojz Rakús was born in 1947. He is a psychiatrist who also specializes in biomedical cybernetics. He is head of the Department of Psychiatry at the Institute for the Further Education of Health Workers, and of the Psychiatric Clinic of this institute in Bratislava; Chairman of the Psychiatric Society of the Slovak Medical Society; and a member of the New York Academy of Sciences.

From July 1990 to June 1992, he was Minister of Health for the Slovak Republic, and is Chairman of the Union of Christian Doctors and Health Workers.

The central and crucial nature of this event is not only connected with the fact that it shows a strong, naturally willful decision by the victim of arbitrary and cruel persecution not to continue in a further "interrogation game" (and that this paradoxically had some positive effect), but it is especially important to note that here, the hidden meaning and essence of the whole persecution is precisely diagnosed and identified, that is, that *the concern is not with discovering the truth but only in destroying the Church.*

In fact, *war against religion and the Church* is an integral part of the totalitarian communist system and one of the deepest rooted features of its ideology. There were so many purely political and administrative steps taken against the Church up to 1989, that their mere enumeration far exceeds the framework of this account.[72]

However, the story in this book is an actual, irrefutable document of what a merciless and brutal form such a war can acquire. It is good for this story to be made available to the public, since it at least partly lifts the veil of anonymity, vagueness, and uninvolved amazement. The true stories of many distinct individuals are hidden behind it, people who had to bear unspeakable suffering or death at the hands of an inhuman tyranny, in the interrogation facilities of State Security, or in the prisons and labor camps of a totalitarian regime, on the sole basis of untrue, contrived crimes, while in reality they were being punished for their religious convictions and faithfulness to the Church.

Evidence

The second aspect of the book indicates that the author wants to provide evidence about his experiences in prison with brainwashing, the method which the totalitarian system developed and used to justify itself and evoke the appearance of "legality" for the persecutions, condemnations, and imprisonment of innocent, falsely accused victims.

Let us note that the real motive for these accusations and persecutions of people living under a totalitarian communist system is the intrinsic *paranoia* of its ideology. In it, the world is understood as a struggle between "us" and "them," and the only way to escape from the threat of "them" is an "implacable struggle" until a complete victory over "them" is achieved. Thus, a totalitarian system will not stop short of physical liquidation.

Brainwashing is a violent, coercive method for controlling people. Its aim is to fragment, disorganize, and destroy the identity of a person, so that, being in conflict with the truth, he will satisfy certain demands, for example, sign a false confession, give false answers (admit to guilt) before the court, and even change his convictions.[73] Prisoners are forced into acts of self-preservation which they would not normally resort to, and as a result they then change their views, so that they can justify their behavior to themselves.

According to E. Schein,[74] the process of brainwashing has three phases: the breaking of a person (so-called thawing), the indoctrination process (transformation), and finally, the construction and strengthening of a new manipulated identity (re-freezing).

During the process, methods are used which affect every aspect of a person. These are some of the techniques used: lack of sleep, hunger, cold, pain, physical overloading (forced walking, standing like statues, and so on) torture, isolation, humiliation, insufficient and controlled information, disinformation, evocation of fear and ideas of guilt, continual uncertainty, etc., up to the inducing of a mental breakdown or states similar to a trance, with the help of various refined hypnotic means or drugs (for more on this, see Part IX, "Traumatology").

Although the term *brainwashing* (a translation from the Chinese *hsi nao*) appeared for the first time only in 1951 in connection with the practices of the North Korean and Chinese communists, methods of brainwashing[75] were undoubtedly already used during the period of the Stalinist terror in the Soviet Union before the War. Let us remember, for example, the answers which were given and the false confessions of guilt which occurred in the famous show trials of that period under the direction of the KGB. This book is evidence that methods of brainwashing were really being applied in our country, at least in the interrogation practices of State Security. Many people succumbed to their aggression and were broken, but the author notes that after experiencing these methods himself, he forgave everyone anything they may have said under pressure.

This book is also proof that it is possible to resist brainwashing, that one does *not have to yield to it.*

Although it is above all the personal testimony of one specific man, it is written on the basis of such scientifically precise observations and with such penetrating psychological intuition (undoubtedly with the support not only of the whole spiritual "armory" of the author, but also his medical expertise), that the extent of this evidence fulfills the criteria for more general validity.

Spiritual Message

So then, *how was it possible to avoid being broken? What is the weapon against brainwashing? How can one defend oneself against hopelessness and resignation? How does one find support for oneself? Where can one look for strength?*

A special, central, so to speak, key part of the testimony (Part VII) answers these questions. It is the core of the book's spiritual message.

"Come to me, all you who labor and are burdened, and I will give you rest" (Matt. 11:28). This challenge of Jesus, although the author does not directly quote it, represents a sort of summary answer to these questions, especially, "Take my yoke upon you and learn from me, for I am meek, and humble of heart; and you will find rest for yourselves" (Matt. 11:29). This is the precise origin of the "charging" with spiritual capacity and ability which the author mentions.

If we learn to draw strength from this source, perhaps we will also be able to say at difficult moments in life, "This Saved Us."

Slovak Editorial Note

Other memories and testimony about life in the prisons of a totalitarian state have already been published. This one differs from the others in one essential way. The author did not face and survive interrogation imprisonment and all the coercive practices of the totalitarian regime as an unprepared victim caught unawares by the violence of the regime.

He viewed his experiences from the point of view of a doctor. This enabled him to understand what was happening, find connections between the various incidents, and recognize the sophisticated criminal system for what it was. Therefore, he describes not only the painful experiences, but above all the discovery of how the system works and how it is possible to defend oneself against violent manipulation.

Therefore we emphasize the author's competence and his professional qualifications. His testimony is all the more valuable because he was in interrogation imprisonment (that is, in a prison where they attempted to brainwash him in preparation for a show trial), for three years, which is an extraordinarily long time.

Dr. Krčméry often emphasizes words and passages by using single inverted commas, quotation marks, or italics. In the epilogue, Alojz Rakús used italics to emphasize words or indicate special terms.

Bibliography

Andrew, C., and O. Gordievskij, *KGB: důvěrná zpráva o zahraničních operacích od Lenina ke Gorbačovovi.* Czech language edition East Art Agency Publishers, 1994. Eng. orig.: *KGB: The Inside Story of Its Foreign Operations from Lenin to Gorbachev.* London: Hodder & Stoughton, 1990.

Baštecký, J., S. Šaulík, and J. Šimek. *Psychosomatická medicína* (Psychosomatic medicine). Prague: Grada-Avicenum, 1993.

Frolík, J. *Špión vypovídá* (Confession of a spy). Prague: Orbis, 1990.

Hassan, S. *Jak čelit psychické manipulaci zhoubných kultů* (How to face psychic manipulation of destructive cults). Czech language edition Brno: Nakladatelství Tomáše Janečka, 1994. Eng. orig.: *Combatting Cult Mind Control.* Park Street Press, 1990.

Hlaváč, Š. *Po priamych cestách* (On straight roads). Verona: Dobo, 1986; Bratislava: IKAR, 1990.

Hunter, E. *Brainwashing.* New York: Pyramid Publications, 1958; 5th ed. 1968.

Kaplan, K., M. Bulinová, M. Janišová. *Církevní komise ÚV KSČ 1949–1951* (Church Commission of the Central Committee of the Communist Party of Czechoslovakia 1949–1951). Praha-Brno: Nakladatelství Doplněk Brno, Ústav pro soudobé dějiny AV ČR, 1994.

Kaplan, K. *Stát a církev v Československu 1948–1953* (State and Church in Czechoslovakia 1948–1953). Praha-Brno: Nakladatelství Doplněk Brno, Ústav pro soudobé dějiny AV ČR, 1993.

Kolakovič, T. *Božie podzemie* (God's underground). Bratislava-Nitra: Fatima sek. Inštitút, 1994.

Korec, J. C. *Po barbarskej noci I–III* (After barbarian nights I–III). Bratislava: Lúč, 1990–93.

Lenin, V. I. *O náboženstve* (About religion). Bratislava: SVPL, 1954.

Lepp, I. *Cesta do Damašku* (The road to Damascus). Nové Město n.Met.: Signum unitatis, 1991.

Lepp, I. *Psychoanalýza súčasného ateizmu* (Psychoanalysis of contemporary atheism). Toronto: Dobrá kniha, 1972.

Lifton R. J. *Thought Reform and the Psychology of Totalism.* New York: W. W. Norton, 1961.

London, A. *Doznání* (Avowal). Prague: Československý spisovatel, 1990.

Mikloško, F. *Nebudete ich môcť rozvrátiť* (You won't be able to undermine them). Bratislava: Archa, 1991.

Pachman, L. *Boha nelze vyhnat* (It is impossible to expel God). Prague: Vyšehrad, 1990.

Pius XI. Encyclical *Divini Redemptoris.* Lidové knihkupectví a nakladatelství v Olomouci, 1937.

Schein, E. H. *Coercive Persuasion.* New York: W. W. Norton, 1971.

Špáta, J. "Traumatológia" (Traumatology), *Mladá tvorba* 6/1968, pp. 29–35.

Špáta, J. "Ruzyňská trauma" (Trauma of Ruzyň). *Bratislavské listy* 7–8/1991.

Šulc, J., J. Dvořák, and M. Morávek. *Člověk na pokraji svých sil* (A man at the breaking point). Prague: Avicenum, 1971, pp. 132–65; only the 1st ed. contains the part on brainwashing.

Tomin, J. *Eurointerlingua.* Private ed., Bratislava, 1994.

Vaško, V. *Profesor Kolakovič* (Professor Kolakovič). Bratislava: Charis, 1993.

Notes

Please note that unless otherwise indicated ("SE," Slovak Editor, or "EE," English Editors), all notes are the author's.

1. All Biblical quotations are taken from the *Saint Joseph Edition of the New American Bible* (New York: Catholic Book Publishing Co., 1992).

2. See Document 6.

3. In Slovakia, people pray the Loretan Litany daily during the month of May. Because the author and his friends were in prison in May, they called their particular Litany "May Behind Bars." (EE)

4. At the request of the chief of State Security in Mírov, J. Špáta informed higher authorities that there existed a section in prison where, among other staggering horrors, prisoners were subjected to electric shocks. Špáta sent letters dealing with these matters to the General Prosecution service in the first months of 1953, and to the Central Committee of the Czechoslovak Communist Party in 1956. What you read in Part IX of this book is only the tip of the iceberg. It reveals but a few of the types of inhuman torments inflicted on inmates. These tortures were described in the declarations which Jozef Špáta sent to various government agencies after his transfer from Ruzyň to Pankrác. In retrospect, it is truly amazing that these incriminating documents were delivered at all to the people to whom they were addressed. In 1968 and 1991, the letters were published in the Czechoslovak press.

5. A man who joined the army after graduating from High School was automatically assigned to the military college for non-commissioned and reserve officers. There were no exceptions to this rule. The punishment thus clearly went against well established state and military practices. It would also deprive one of the possibility of ever attaining a superior rank.

6. Shortly after assuming power, the communists carried out a monetary reform which effectively wiped out the savings of most of the population.

7. A missionary marriage implies that both husband and wife would agree to work as missionaries once they were married. (EE)

8. Kolakovič, a Croatian and former Jesuit, was the head of the Catholic Renewal Movement (in anticipation of Vatican II). In 1946, the communists were looking for him but they could not find him. Therefore, they arrested some of his followers, of which I was one. When Kolakovič heard of this, he gave himself up and they released the rest of us. This incident was indicative of the more serious, out and out persecution which would begin in February 1948 following a communist putsch.

9. Apart from a prison sentence, almost all political prisoners also bore the additional burden of confiscation of property. This meant that after the appeal trial, when the judgment was final, legally valid and enforceable, the prisoner was then equally deprived of money in bank accounts, any remaining money he had for small

purchases in prison, and personal objects such as watches, fountain pens, crosses on chains, rings, etc.

10. "Deus qui nobis sub sacramento, . . ." God who to us in the sacrament. . . ." These words are part of the prayer repeated at a Catholic Mass at the moment of Consecration when the bread and wine are changed into the body and blood of Christ. Thus the interrogator used words which he may have memorized but did not truly understand. The "Confiteor" (I confess) is the confession of sins which is said by the congregation at the very beginning of Holy Mass.

11. J. Šulc, M.D., quotes research on sleep deprivation where the people subjected to experimental sleep prevention had breakdowns in their perception of time, shapes, and sounds. After forty hours without sleep, 75 percent of 350 people experienced hallucinations. (SE)

12. According to the law, the family of a detainee is to be informed within fourteen days of his arrest.

13. The same state government agency was responsible for expulsions from school, State Security, and political arrests. (SE)

14. "Discussion and persuasion" was one of the methods of applying psychological pressure on those being brainwashed. It frequently led to people confessing to crimes which they had not committed. But according to Vyšinský, the supreme prosecutor of the USSR, a confession of guilt, regardless of how it had been obtained, was the final and irrefutable proof needed to condemn a prisoner. In the Soviet legal system of the time this procedure led to mass liquidation of the innocent.

15. Compassion with a neighbor's pain is commendable, but the man did not realize that they used this compassion as one more way of inflicting torture on their victims.

16. According to Pius XI who initiated the project, *Catholic Action* is the Catholic laity working in concert with the apostolate of the hierarchy. The so-called *State Catholic Action* which surfaced around 1948, was the work of the persecutors of the Church. They forced some of the weaker priests and faithful to launch complaints against the bishops duly appointed by Rome and attempted to form a fraudulent "patriotic" apostolate. It ended rather embarrassingly when it was revealed that a large number of the names of members had simply been taken straight out of the telephone directory and included the names of dead priests. The founder of State Catholic Action then went to Rome and used Vatican Radio to do public penance and bring to light the false State Security documents.

17. Many landowners were killed under Stalin in 1929. (SE)

18. A. T. (see Part IX) also focuses on his difficulties, but the result is different. When a person is under pressure, the things he values the most come to his mind. These thoughts can either help or hinder depending on the values of the person involved.

19. A leading Nazi condemned to death and executed.

20. Later, in prison camps, the typical response to the question, "How long did you get?" became a cliché. The prisoners answered "UER," that is "Until the End of the Regime." Everybody knew that people who had strong views of their own would not be freed even after serving their sentences.

21. The "White Legion" was at the time the name of the main anti-communist organization in Slovakia and abroad.

22. Lenin stated that to abolish classes would entail a long and difficult struggle which would not end after eliminating the power of capitalism or after breaking down the bourgeois system. The struggle would only change its forms and become in many ways even harder. In fact, some of the initiators of these class struggles actually became victims. (SE)

23. Of course, with the beginning of the political "thaw," these party colleagues were among the first to be released and rehabilitated. Obviously, the freeing of their victims took a bit longer.

24. See Document 6.

25. According to articles 107 and 296 of the Penal Code, the prisoner who is interrogated can be subjected only to those pressures which are unavoidable to prevent him from frustrating the criminal proceedings, for example, to stop a prisoner from bargaining with his fellow accused (see Document 8).

26. This involved solitary confinement or isolation in a miniature cell in the interrogation prison. According to international humanitarian principles, solitary confinement is considered an unacceptable mental torture. In the overfilled prisons, four or five prisoners were pressed into single solitary confinement cells. The law also states that interrogation imprisonment could last no more than three months, but as can be seen from my case, that law was ignored since my interrogation imprisonment was automatically prolonged to a number of years.

27. Damien, Joseph de Veuster (1840–89), was a Belgian priest who dedicated his life to lepers on the island of Molokai in the Hawaiian islands. He contracted the disease and died in 1889, surrounded by the lepers he had loved. (EE)

28. Departure for missionary work (for example to Molokai), also meant irrevocably giving up one's country so that others would find life. "Whoever loses his life for my sake, will find it" (Matt. 10:39). (SE)

29. Most Bible quotes have now been corrected.

30. "Samizdat," Russian, refers to clandestine literature.

31. Emil Boleslav Lukáč was a Slovak writer who translated philosophical and religious classics into Slovak.

32. God gives man freedom of choice. He directs him towards the good but does not limit him nor impose His own will on man's will or reason. God's will is not aggressive nor authoritarian. On the contrary, He blesses those who do not yet believe. Knowledge of truth increases as man struggles with doubts in order to believe God's word, to differentiate between truth and illusions, and to be purified from sin which clouds his reason.

33. The "submarine effect" is the psychological reaction of people who are forced to live together for a long time in a small space. As a result, special tensions arise among them, they become oversensitive and have strong negative reactions to trivial things. For example, the way a colleague puts a spoon in his mouth may become intolerable. This was observed among submarine crews and members of polar expeditions separated from civilization for a long time, and in other similar groups. (SE)

34. According to psychosomatic medicine, psychic mechanisms of repression (in this case, remorse) are one of the causes of cancer. (See Bibliography, *Psychosomatická medicína,* J. Baštecký, M.D., S. Šaulík, M.D., J. Šimek, M.D., pp. 316–17. (SE)

35. Courts were created after the Second World War to judge political crimes and crimes against humanity.

36. "Sokol" (falcon) was the name of the largest physical exercise society in the Czech lands. It was less popular in Slovakia. It organized mass performances of exercises for tens of thousands of people in Prague. The spirit of this patriotic organization was liberal, prevailingly atheist or at least secular.

37. Žingor was a legendary captain who led a partisan struggle against the Nazis, mostly in the Turiec region, entirely on his own initiative and long before the Slovak National Uprising. When the "liberation" of Slovakia led to communist dictatorship, he returned to the mountains and renewed the armed struggle. He was betrayed by "fellow fighters," and finally condemned and executed.

38. Details are included in unpublished documents 13, 15, 17, 18.

39. See Document 8.

40. It is also necessary to understand letters to the family in this context. The joy about which the author writes was not a sham. It flowed from his faith in God which is greater than any oppressor and which cannot be surpassed in generosity. God sacrificed his Son for us, which is incomparable with what a totalitarian regime offered us. One can imagine how the comrade censors must have raged when they repeatedly read in letters, "I am happy and well." On the other hand, for the family, this was highly encouraging. (SE)

41. Chiang Kai-Shek was a Chinese general who ruled in China before the rise of communism. Mao Tse-Tung's red army pushed him onto the territory of present day Taiwan.

42. It is a historical fact that over the ages, people built walls to isolate their fellow-men. Could one literally "beat his head against the wall"? Of course. But walls, whether it be the Great Wall of China or the Berlin Wall, have been conquered by people who used their heads for thinking. The best example is the destruction of the walls of Jericho. The Israelites walked around the walls without hammers and ladders, but with trust in God. They blew trumpets and the walls tumbled down. The powerful build the most perfidious walls in the heads of their victims. They conceal the fact that the head is for thinking and they give it only the function of a hammer. Thoughts which lead to God hinder two things: the destruction of true altars and burning of true books, and, at the same time, the construction of altars to false gods and spreading of false hopes. (SE)

43. The Russicum, a college attached to the Oriental Institute in Rome, was founded by Pope Pius XI, as an institute to prepare missionaries for the USSR. Its first rector was a Slovak, P. Vendelín Javorka, S.J., and the majority of students were Slovaks.

44. See end note 18.

45. J. Šulc, M.D., says that during the Korean war, among all the prisoners of war, Americans most frequently succumbed to indoctrination since they were suddenly torn away from an environment which had made their lives easy, down to the smallest detail. When the structure of the social group to which they were bound broke down, they were not able to find their way in this completely different system of authority. They were psychologically unprepared for the special method of imprisonment, had less resistance to climatic conditions, and suffered up to 35 percent of losses. In the same prison camp regime at this time, not a single Englishman or Turk died. Indoctrination clearly failed with 13 percent of prisoners. They were people

either with extraordinary strong characters or people who had never recognized any authority. (SE)

46. The concept of "Těšín apples" was not derived from the town of Těšín but from "tešiť sa" which means to be glad, to enjoy oneself, to rejoice, but, here in prison, in vain.

47. At this point the prosecutor or the assessor interrupted my speech with the comment, "But this is absurd! Is he going to engage in treasonable propaganda here of all places?" or something to that effect. However, after a brief pause and a show of phony indignation, the chairman said something like, "But we'd better hear him out, because otherwise someone is sure to complain that we didn't allow him the opportunity to have the last word."

48. At this point he smiled for the first time, albeit ironically.

49. At that time abortions were still illegal in our country and in the USSR, almost on the same level as murder. When I was in the Banská Bystrica prison, around 1956–57, there was a fellow prisoner there, a doctor, who was apparently sentenced to eight years only for carrying out abortions without any complications or harmful after-effects.

50. This is an obvious lie. On March 14, 1937, Pope Pius XI issued the encyclical "Mit Brennender Sorge" (With Burning Concern). It dealt with the position of the Church in Germany under Nazism, and on March 19, 1937, he issued "Divini Redemptoris" (Of the Divine Redeemer), about atheistic communism, where he condemned the errors of both related systems. The communists knew about the last encyclical and imprisoned people for having it in their possession. (SE)

51. Such "cosmetic" dismissal of charges in unimportant matters served only to give the public the impression that the court was objective in its dealing with the defendants.

52. See Document 7.

53. Reference to the Verdict. See Document 7.

54. See Document 7.

55. See Document 7.

56. See Document 7.

57. See Document 7.

58. See Document 7.

59. See Document 7.

60. See Document 7.

61. See Document 7.

62. See Document 7.

63. See Document 7.

64. See Document 7.

65. A problem priest, Dechet, was assigned by the state as administrator of the diocese of Banská Bystrica after the death of Bishop Škrábik.

66. See Document 7.

67. See Document 7.

68. See Document 7.

69. Sent prior to the hearing, and read at the court hearing in the Ministry of the Interior's reform center (Útvar NZMV) "PROKOP," Horní Slavkov, Sokolov district. The work at my last prison labor camp in the Jáchymov district was considerably

reduced at that time. No mining was being done in the uranium mines. The jobs consisted mainly in working with gangs of construction workers, and even those were later completely disbanded.

70. See Bibliography.

71. See Part V.

72. Soon after the "February Victory" of 1948, on April 25, 1949, the Presidium of the Central Committee of the Czechoslovak Communist Party appointed the members of a special secret agency, the so-called "six." Its role was the political direction of the secret police and other power instruments during the liquidation of the Catholic Church. Historian Karel Kaplan, Cardinal J. Ch. Korec, and F. Mikloško also mention events and documents from the years 1948 to 1953.

To achieve its goals and ideas about the transformation of society, the Communist Party showed great ability in finding, educating, and using a special type of person. Under its patronage, these servants built their cases on countless lies. They used all the pressures possible and even phony love to bring the victims to "confess" to crimes which they had not committed. (SE)

73. After reports on brainwashing reached the public, some who felt threatened (such as Cardinal Mindzenty) immediately advised people that whatever the Police would claim he had said or signed should be regarded as having been done because he was brainwashed. (SE)

74. E. H. Schein, *Coercive Persuasion* (New York: W. W. Norton, 1971). (SE)

75. R. J. Lifton, *Thought Reform and the Psychology of Totalism* (New York: W. W. Norton, 1961); see also the work mentioned in the previous note. (SE)

Book Two

In Prisons and Labor Camps after Brainwashing

"He has rescued us from the power of darkness and transferred us into the kingdom of his beloved Son, in whom we have redemption, the forgiveness of sins." (Col. 1:13)

Part I

Mírov Prison

After the appeal before the highest military tribunal in Pankrác prison, I was transported to Mírov. I think we went once more via Ruzyň, the crossroads for journeys to the GULAG prisons and camps. (GULAG is a term introduced into literature by Alexander Solzhenitsyn in the title of his book *The Gulag Archipelago.* It affirmed the existence of a "state" within the totalitarian state, consisting of a hermetically isolated system of prisons and forced-labor camps. "Gulag" is an acronym, based on the initial letters of GLAVNOYE UPRAVLENIYE LAGEREI MVD. . . . Main Administration for Corrective Labor Camps of the Ministry of the Interior.) There we underwent a "delousing and frisking" procedure. This thorough examination came as no surprise, but it was always a tense moment, because every prisoner had something to hide; an improvised "knife" made out of an aluminium tube of toothpaste or a piece of string. On that occasion I wanted to keep some small books, a rosary made from bread, and a rather nice chess set, also made out of bread. My father had made a similar chess set from wood when he was imprisoned in Siberia. I think we still have one knight even now.

When I was changing my clothes I immediately came into conflict with the guard in the storeroom, because he took a fancy to this miniature chess set. Of course he confiscated it and I couldn't get him to give me a receipt. I pretended to be naive, because if something was confiscated, by law a receipt had to be given for it. By that time I already held firm to the principle that one should fight against evil however and whenever possible, in order to bring it to light and not allow it to be hushed up and kept secret (glasnost, i.e., publicity—was the first step to democracy).

But not everyone understood my attitude; they laughed at me and were amazed that although I had been shut up for so long, it seemed I didn't know I couldn't achieve anything anyway. They told me that I would experience far worse things, I would see people killed, and there would be no use protesting or invoking the law. Nevertheless, I believe that one of a Christian's most important duties, even in prison, is to testify to the truth.

I think we left Olomouc in a small Black Maria (which here is actually a green police minibus without windows) in isolated compartments, blindfold and handcuffed. I had the impression we were heading north-east, and therefore probably in the direction of Mírov, not far from Olomouc. That is where we found ourselves towards the end of October 1954. Behind several security lines, barbed-wire fences, which may possibly have been electrified, and an open strip of ground guarded by watch-towers. Right in the center of this fortress. Although I lived there for about a year, I never saw the place from the outside. In fact it was even stranger in Ruzyň and all the detention prisons, where we could only catch a chance glimpse of the "iron exterior" while being escorted there. At such times we were not allowed to talk or look out of the window. Only straight ahead, at the guard in charge, accompanied by a dog. He would shout from time to time and deal out punishment without warning, with a blow from his baton, or in some other way.

Whenever I could, I watched the streets and the people, in order to return to normal life at least for a moment. To that old world, which carried on as usual. That carried on without the slightest sign of awareness, to say nothing of feelings of sympathy or solidarity with the people who, one by one, were disappearing into another world. I still had the naive illusion that I might see someone I knew and would be able to give them a sign, even at the cost of repressive measures.

After informing us about the more stringent rules and regulations applied during transport, the commander of the escort always warned us that the guards would shoot without prior warning. Ostentatiously, even provocatively, they loaded their automatic rifles and machine gun, let the dogs loose and took their muzzles off. They would say cynically: "If you behave yourselves, you'll ride like royalty. You can even smoke, it all depends on you. But you'll pay for the least little mischief, you'll have it written down and at the place you're going to they won't let you forget it for a long, long time."

We arrived at Mírov around Friday. We were kept in the escort cell for three days, because no one was particularly interested in us on a Saturday and Sunday. There were about fifteen of us.

In solitary confinement, in interrogation cells, people more often turned to God, prayer, or conversation about spiritual matters. In prisons like this, at least for the most part, people did not have the right conditions or were not even interested in praying together or reciting the Mass. Their first concern was to find a good bed. On that depended whether you were permanently short of sleep, aching all over, or in conflict with psychopaths and vicious neighbors, or had a bed-wetting fellow prisoner in the bed above. Quarrels would begin about who was to fetch the lunch, who should empty the rubbish bin, or clean out the cell. Although before, when someone was in solitary confinement, he would have given anything just to be able to do something, or at least see someone, to say nothing of being allowed to live in the same cell. A certain willingness and feeling of solidarity lasted for no more than the first few days.

I should like to mention one of my fellow prisoners from that period, an editor about thirty years old. He was an uncertain atheist at that time. He told me about some very strange experiences he had had in Ruzyň. He almost seemed to be talking about experimental or empirical proofs of the existence of God, or of some kind of "higher power." I can clearly remember him telling me: "When I was in Ruzyň (which meant in the strictest isolation), I had doubts about God's existence, or maybe about my own atheism, and I thought to myself: Well, Lord God, if you exist, perform a miracle, to give me a clear sign, so that I can believe you exist. And then I laid down well-thought-out conditions. What if all the lights in Ruzyň should go out at midnight?" In interrogation cells prisoners have to sleep under a very strong light, almost like a searchlight. The prison has its own generators, in case the normal power supply should fail. "Later I had almost forgotten about this arrant nonsense, but I couldn't fall asleep and about midnight suddenly — at first I thought I was dreaming — all the lights went out. It sent shivers down my spine. I began to reproach myself for my effrontery: How can you lay down such conditions for God, if He does exist? However, the next day this was quickly followed by fresh doubts: it must have been a power cut. It could be mere chance. But if God did exist, He could do something even more surprising or more unlikely — such as making all the lights in Ruzyň go on exactly at midday. You won't believe me, but that very same day, at exactly midday (we knew it was midday, because food was being served), all the lights suddenly went on." His vivid experience surprised me greatly and left a deep impression on me. I asked: "So do you believe now?" "Yes, but not entirely. I still need something more." Once more the truth of the apostle's words were confirmed, that many find God without miracles, but for others not even a miracle is enough.

In Mírov the anonymity of the prison staff more or less came to an end. In the investigation prison, we were not even allowed to say our names, just our numbers, and their names could only be found out by chance. To make it possible to talk about them, we gave most of them nicknames, taken from some typical or even comical characteristic. In

Mírov we came to know the great majority of the names of the guards, officers, and prisoners — with just a few exceptions.

The general atmosphere of the prison began to change quite considerably within a few months, when a wave of hunger strikes and riots broke out in the labor camps around Jáchymov (a large complex of about fifteen forced-labor camps mainly in north Bohemia, where the majority of the prisoners worked in the uranium mines). All those who participated or were active in any way were brought to Mírov in ones or twos, in handcuffs. They were then given a particularly hard time. This was how hunger strikes and riots were stamped out.

One day I was suddenly taken from the escort cell by a "medic" — a warder, Warrant Officer G. They had just thrown out Dr. Franto H., an ear, nose, and throat specialist and they wanted a replacement for him. In spite of my protests that I knew nothing about ear, nose, and throat medicine, they took me up to the surgery. The other prisoners naturally envied me my somewhat privileged position. From the material point of view they were right. We were in the hospital itself, about eight of us to one room, but in a relatively hygienic environment. The patients, however, some of whom were seriously ill, lived in cramped conditions, with as many as twenty to a room, so I was decidedly better off. We had the same food as the staff in the infectious ward, known as diet N8 — a fattening diet, really rich, with milk and plenty of eggs. We even lost a taste for it sometimes and instead of rolls we helped ourselves to bread. We took the rest and shared it out, so the others had some advantage from it, too.

Mírov was organized like a closed prison. At that time there were about eight hundred prisoners divided into six to eight departments, strictly isolated one from the other. People from each department were kept separate, even when out for exercise. They only met at their places of work, if they had one, and were kept isolated from each other even as patients.

There were several workshops of different kinds. A locksmith's workshop, where locks were assembled, then one for making paper bags, a carpentry workshop, and so on. The maintenance work in the prison was done solely by the "Alsatians," that is, by criminals, not by political prisoners. They had lighter sentences on the whole, too. At that time they were better off than the political prisoners. They could move around freely, especially in the front courtyard, and most of them abused their privileged position. They were in fact murderers and thieves. "Gang leaders" were often chosen from their ranks to supervise work, and they had almost a free hand to put people under a stricter regimen, in the punitive unit, or to beat them or punish them in any other way. Rather like in the Nazi concentration camps. Of course, after the change of course, when the dictatorship began to ease up, the other prisoners paid many of them back with interest.

News always spread in advance of the arrival of informers and stoolies. The *mukli* (prison slang — an acronym for "muži určení k likvidaci," i.e., men destined for liquidation) had very good information services. That is why everyone knew, even a day before their arrival, that a "bloody" informer was coming to the labor camp or prison and they prepared a welcome for him. In our prison, for example, at the initial dental examination, when people's arms were usually tied to the chair, it went something like this: "What's your name?" The person in question said his name. "Ah, you were in Leopoldov prison in 1951?" At this he would turn pale. "So you don't know me?" Whack. He received blows on both cheeks from D., the dentist, and then from others. In fact that dentist didn't have the best of reputations himself, either, at that time. These lay, prison trials were altogether very dubious.

The toughest and most isolated department was that for priests. It was only possible to meet them by chance, in the cinema, for example, when we managed somehow to mingle.

Many political prisoners boycotted these communist, ideological films the whole time they were in prison. The priests used to go there, though, so they could give the sacraments whenever they got the chance. It was also possible to meet them in the hospital or out-patients' department, when they came in contact with the medical staff, which I tried to make the most of. I very soon drew attention to myself, though. It was not so much the medics, warders G. and G. who noticed me, because they couldn't care less about anything, including their patients, who suffered as a result, because they didn't get the attention they should have had....

But I drew the attention mainly of the stoolies. In particular of "The Scribe" — H. J. He must have held an important position in the secret police, because even the warders were afraid of him. His services were worth those of five or ten of such prison guards. He had eyes everywhere and also friends, who kept him informed. He was egocentric and sometimes very aggressive. Anyone unwilling to kowtow to him, fawn on him, usually had his name blackened and had to suffer all kinds of repressive measures. Few people dared to boycott him openly, which was the main weapon of the *mukli* against informers at that time. They wouldn't speak to them and therefore they could only talk among themselves. This caused many of them to have nervous breakdowns, and some of them even tried to commit suicide. Sometimes in the labor camps they could be rescued from the anger of the prisoners only if a scrupulous commandant or political officer shut them up in a correction cell for a long stay, with all the "advantages" that went with this.

Another such informer was our colleague, Dr. O. L. He always used to introduce himself by his full name. A Mohammedan or Muslim, said to be the only one in Czechoslovakia. He made a show of his conversion to Islam, often boasting about it and expressing himself very cynically about Christianity. He was egocentric to an extreme. This was how dangerous people could be most reliably recognized — informers, included — by the fact that they were egoists. If someone was an egoist and not yet a stoolie, he would soon became one, because egoism can only find expression in one person living at the expense of another. He didn't understand much about medicine. There were even anecdotes passed round about how he prescribed PAS (a new medicine for TB: Para-aminosalicylic acid) that was then administered in doses of fifteen, twenty, twenty-five tablets a day, in order to have the required effect. He used to prescribe one tablet a day. When it had no effect, he increased it to one and a half, and so on. He usually tried to cover up his lack of knowledge by callousness and pretended unscrupulousness, an authoritarian manner that would not tolerate discussion. It even seemed that, after the priests, those he hated most were his own patients. The only person who knew how to stand up to him or prove him wrong was our dentist, Jarda Novák. He claimed that all his stories about the tropics and journeys through Indonesia and Africa were "a load of rubbish."

Meanwhile I had studied some practical psychology and acquired a nose for stoolies. I sniffed them out before they could get up to mischief or do anyone much harm. I could tell them by their egoism, by the privileges they thought they had a right to, and mainly by the self-confident way they railed in public against the regime, in order to provoke others. After all, they knew nothing would happen to them. That, however, was true only for as long as the authorities needed them. Sometimes they went too far in their demands and began to annoy the warders, too. Then they were brought to us in the surgery after such a cruel beating that I had to feel sorry for them.

O. L. was under the protection of the deputy warden, but the latter lost patience with him when O. L. even began to be aggressive towards employees of the Ministry of Interior. It was said he had attacked Dr. K. and almost killed him. The most remarkable thing about O. was not what he himself was, but the way in which people around him were forced to reveal their own characters. Unfortunately, almost all those who hated him and cursed him behind his back, flattered him to his face or said nothing, in order to be left in peace. Except for Jarda Novák. On one occasion I could stand it no longer, either, and after he had blackened someone's name, I told him outright what he had done. He immediately began to threaten me and accuse me of telling lies, even of being an informer myself. A tactic typical of stoolies.

From that time on, he was even more against me. Jarda Novák was the only one who stood up for me on that occasion. All my colleagues kept their distance and even F. Ž., a senior consultant, for whom I had the most respect, rebuked me: "What came over you? How could you do something so stupid? You've been in prison long enough. You know how it is here. How could it even occur to you that you could win against him?!" As if the important thing was to win. As if they didn't know what harm that man did people. Or they pretended not to believe it. The day after these quarrels I was very pleasantly surprised when one of our warders brought me an apple from his elevenses — it was a great luxury in prison at that time — and praised me for my "courage." He obviously knew about O.'s activities as an informer from the other side, the side of the prison management.

How easy it would have been to win the favor of these people, as others did. At least by keeping my mouth shut, not boycotting them, or even better by supporting them in some way. It was not difficult to find the weakest side of each of them and use it to win their favor. But it didn't seem right to me, I thought it was weak, immoral.

The most likeable person in our room was Jarda Novák. He was an excellent dentist. He very soon became a good friend. He was sincere, somewhat sharp-tongued, but a man of principle. He was the only one who remained courageous and uncompromising and at the same time good-hearted. We got on very well together. More than anyone else in our room, it was he who gave me moral support. When I arrived, he had already been there several years. We often discussed the political situation together. Unfortunately he was not a practicing Christian; like many, he was christened, but that was all. And like most people, he expected social problems to be solved by politics, by the West, or by war, by the atomic bomb.

At Easter we got to the point of agreeing that he would set his spiritual house in order and go to confession. He said: "It's true that after all these years, I myself feel everything's not as it should be. After Easter

I'll go, I will, for sure." But then another strange thing happened, which really shook me. I believe it is generally true that in prison God intervenes in a supernatural way more often, because people need Him more. It is more likely and easier for us to understand God's intervention in times of extreme need, than outside, where in the bustle of life and under the burden of everyday cares we very often overlook these miracles and they go unnoticed.

Once when we were walking outside, I suddenly said to him: "And why do you want to go to confession after Easter, if you consider it useful? Why not right now? You never know what might happen even in the next few days." "Huh, what can happen, for goodness' sake? Don't be so fanatical. It's waited long enough! Years. Can't it wait a few more days? Don't worry, I'm fine. I'm absolutely fit. And it will be better if I prepare myself for it more carefully. Nothing can happen to change things so much in just a few days. Yet three days later he was dead. If I remember rightly, it was a Wednesday. On Tuesday morning or even Monday evening, he suddenly got terrible pains in his stomach. All the tests were negative. He remembered he had had something like that several years earlier, but it had passed. There seemed no reason for the high level of sedimentation in his blood. Some people even considered it to be a result of nervous strain, oversensitiveness of the nerves, or hypochondria. But by midday there were about five doctors around him all the time. He could hardly have had better care. In the afternoon a senior consultant, F., mainly on account of that high sedimentation, urged that he should be sent to hospital. Unfortunately, prisoners were sent to Brno and not to nearby Olomouc, because the hospital in Brno was the only one with a prison ward. However, it was a three hours' drive away. When they left he already had acute pains. Dr. Ž. gave him morphine for the journey, making a note of it to inform his colleagues.

We heard that Jarda turned yellow by morning and he died the following day. I don't know to this day whether on the operating table, under an anesthetic, or how. And to this very day, when I think about that terrible finger of God, I do not know where I went wrong. Whether I should have urged him to go to confession at a time when he may not have been quite decided. Or was I not forceful enough, as sometimes happens with me. Maybe if I had been more insistent, he would have gone to confession without delay. After all, there were ideal opportunities just then. I still remember this much, that before his departure, when saying goodbye, I reminded him in no uncertain terms of this confession: "You see, you could already have had it. But in any case, when you return, or if you can, when you are there, don't put it off an hour longer. And at least put yourself in a repentant frame of mind!"

For a long time after that I carried with me a needle he had made of bone for threading laces or elastic. Later I passed it on to someone else.

Good, conscientious doctors, who did what they could to help their patients, were not difficult to find in prison. In fact, here every *mukl* was in some way gentler, more sensitive. It was probably thanks to the feeling of solidarity and the awareness of being under a common threat, of suffering together, that we had in prison. People were generally better than they were when they were free. Maybe it was just that the better ones were put in prison. Sadly, however, when they later returned to ordinary life, they grew self-indulgent, resigned, they lost interest in people. After several years of freedom, I couldn't even recognize them. In prison they were good and sincere, now they only live for themselves. They used to take the sacraments every day, and now they hardly go to church on Sundays. Once self-sacrificing apostles of Christianity, they have forgotten about other people, about the younger generation. At the most they devote their attention to their own families. And those who were converted? So many of them have slipped back! They live for material things, for the body. Some of them have even got divorced. And although they were christened in prison in all sincerity, once free, they were suddenly ashamed to be believers. One such good doctor was Ž. He became an expert both in radiography and internal medicine. Even so, he did not manage to build up a close relationship with his patients. This affected his work to some extent, as well as his relations with people. Sometimes he went astray and acted in a friendly way towards those in power, that is, the warders or informers. He picked up all the "latrines," as we called misleading rumors, about amnesties or divisions of the Wehrmacht that were going to invade us in the near future. He seemed to give priority to his friends and acquaintances when it came to assigning hospital beds.

It was said that people got into hospital in return for cigarettes, which were the main form of payment. I was against this, from the point of view of medical ethics. For that reason I gave up smoking altogether and refused to accept anything. I was very strict about that. I could see how it always began in a seemingly innocent way, by offering cigarettes or sweet things. Then a box of matches or cigarettes followed, out of friendship. Finally it led to different treatment, especially at the dentist's, according to what the doctor received, or what he could get. Some people even said quite openly that you could go to hospital for seven days in exchange for a hundred cigarettes.

Another doctor was O. P. I came to like him, too. He was quite a good doctor and he continued with his studies; he did not allow himself to become resigned and easily depressed. It was not hard to persuade him to take the sacraments, but I don't think it meant enough to him. In prison I had learned that people could treat the Eucharist far too lightly. In the case of Dr. O. P. I realized that he had never asked to take the sacraments of his own accord. So I soon stopped offering them. Later, he disappointed me greatly during the inquiry into the affair of the American leaflets, which I shall come to in due course. I think it was mainly because of the way he behaved on that occasion that many people didn't want to have anything to do with him. While in prison, I often saw how people can change overnight, from one hour to the next, when they are hard pressed. In this case, too, it could be seen that it is not "opportunity that makes the thief," but it only shows what is in him.

As soon as I came to work in the hospital Helmut — our "Scribe" — asked me, as he did everyone, what kind of trial I had had and made a note of it. This was obviously part of his role as an informer. When I told him it was a military tribunal, he said: "That means a political trial. That's good. We don't want any thieves among us." Such a silly pretence. But the young boys in the laboratory, Arnošt, Emil J., and above all, the two Honzos, Honzo J. and Honzo S., whom I met after we were released, asked me more confidentially. "What are you here for? Catholic Action? Who was with you?" And before you knew it you were screened from all sides. There was no chance of pretending then. Emil: "Don't you happen to know Vlado Jukl?" "Sure." "He's here." "What?" "Do you want to meet him? "Of course, I do!" So he arranged a laboratory test for me (a two-hour test on the gastric juices).

What a joy that was! Who could have imagined that, without realizing it, the powers-that-be would bring us together, even in prison. Later he was moved to Bytíz, where we met for a second time. These boys also arranged a confession for me. It was often done during physiotherapy, diathermy, and so on. You had to let them give you radiation or sunray treatment, let them warm you up or cool you down. Sometimes meetings could be arranged, for example, in the form of a gastroscopy: sitting for two hours with a tube in your stomach, through which gastric juices were extracted every few minutes. "If something is important to you," this young male nurse used to say, "you must be willing to suffer for it. If you want to meet someone, it's not free of charge. You must be willing to have your stomach pumped if necessary." That was also one of the best ways of arranging a confession.

The best thing about Mírov was that we had the sacraments. And at least brief contacts with priests and with great, even saintly, people.

One day old Vaško was brought in under guard. I tried to give him a sign that I knew him. What joy that was, when we could hug each other behind a cupboard in the laboratory! He was also sentenced to fourteen years, like I was. For being nominated leader of a new, secret Christian-Democratic party. He had high blood pressure. I exaggerated it a bit and managed to get him taken into hospital. I learned from him that his son was doing time in Leopoldov. And also, how he had cleverly managed to get among the priests. The work committee, which assigned prisoners to different jobs, asked him: "Why did they shut you up?" He said: "For the lay apostolate." "And what's that?" "Spreading the Gospels." "Hm. Something like a preacher or catechist?" "Well, not quite, but similar." So they sent him off to solitary confinement, probably in handcuffs, straight to the "Vatican." In this way he managed to get access to the priests and therefore to the sacraments as well.

I myself was able to receive the Eucharist through our pharmacist H. J. I received it behind the shelves in the pharmacy every morning before 7 a.m. Before surgery hours. Later I took a small square of transformed bread or roll to my room in a cup. I realized later that there was a risk it would be desecrated, although there was no way of telling the Eucharist from ordinary bread. Or maybe just because of that. So we wrapped it in thin cigarette paper, which we swallowed with it.

We got the wine from raisins, sometimes with great difficulty, by picking them out of cakes (from our parcels) and then pressing the juice out of them after they had been soaked in water in a little bottle. At other times, Honzo or the priests in isolation cells already had small supplies of this "wine." Sometimes the guards ferreted it out, though. Of the 150 to 200 priests, three of them were unreliable. The best known was U., who was believed to be there for immoral behavior. I also heard that some Hosts were once found in a book, maybe unconsecrated, but I don't think they were desecrated. I therefore came to the conclusion that it was best to carry the Eucharist with you all the time, so that you could consume it when being searched, especially when you were not allowed the slightest movement.

The most self-sacrificing of our colleagues was Honzo Sloboda. He had been in prison from about the age of seventeen. He was accused of collaboration with the Germans, or rather of being active in the Czech societies which the Germans set up at that time. Originally, he had been sentenced to death by hanging. Then this was converted to life imprisonment. He served eighteen years altogether. I can imagine what those boys suffered. The threat of execution hung over them for months or even years before they were given a reprieve and life imprisonment.

Working as an orderly, Honzo cared for every patient conscientiously and distributed the Eucharist along with the patient's medicines. The younger generation in general can be said to have acquitted themselves creditably in prison. Older people were more cautious, more timid and what's more, they could be calculating. That is why intellectuals and older people aroused a feeling of distrust in me from the very beginning.

It was in Mírov that I spent my first Christmas in four years in the company of others. Of course, in our room Christmas was spoiled considerably by the comments of Dr. L. There was a patient who used to come to help us in our laboratory, who had Ehlers-Danlos syndrome — a total defect of the elastic tissues and ligaments, so that all his joints were loose and they would slip out of place. In spite of this, he was an excellent violinist. When he was in Ilava prison he was given 30 days in one of the worst punishment cells for playing Ave Maria on Christmas Eve, as others were for singing even the shortest carol or Christmas song. At that time such punishment also meant having a ball and chain fastened to one's leg. But it was there, he told us, that he had experienced his most wonderful midnight Mass, because the punishment cell in Ilava was directly under the church. In this way he could at last hear and take part in the whole Mass.

I wanted to organize a midnight vigil, at least with prayers, or with the Eucharist, but I only managed to win over Jarda, the dentist, and a few young assistants. None of the doctors would join us.

Anyway, my memories of Christmas in prison are very vivid. It was in fact a real Christmas, much nearer to that first one, which was neither sumptuous nor merry as they are nowadays when Christians wish each other a happy Christmas by shaking hands and by drinking the usual toast. On the contrary, "He came among his own and his own received him not." It was a poor, lonely Christmas, with the lowliest and most deprived.

Occasionally they herded us into the cinema. For the most part, the films were superficial, full of propaganda. They enraged many of the prisoners. The newsreels, for example, would sometimes show painful scenes, such as of a bishop at the so-called peace conference in Helsinki, which had a very depressing effect on the prisoners. Especially when there were declarations about building a happier future for freer individuals in a freer world. Some films, documentaries or extreme criticism of the West, of the conditions and persecutions there, even sounded comic to the audience and were greeted with bursts of muffled laughter.

In spite of all this, I liked going to the cinema. For one thing, it made a change; for another it was an opportunity to meet and talk more freely with certain people, which we always prepared for carefully beforehand. Of course, things didn't always go as we had hoped and it was only a waste of time. Apart from that, I was of the opinion that every book or film could offer something, whether it taught you something or amused you by its absurdity. Even a bad example gives us a chance to reflect how we should or should not be. In fact some films were good, or at least positive, from the human point of view. For example, *Prelude to Fame* at Easter in Banská Bystrica, or *Man on the Rails* or *Eroika,* about Beethoven. Many people reproached me for going to the cinema. Some of the old prisoners boycotted every film and every cultural program to the end of their time in prison.

As doctors, we took it in turns to be on duty at night. As we all slept in one room, those who got up to take their turn unintentionally woke all the others. But we eventually learned to sleep through these disturbances.

There were some serious cases in the hospital, but the death rate was relatively low. If I remember rightly, even though we had at least five cases of heart attacks that year, not one of these patients died. There were so many stressful situations, though, it is amazing how few ended tragically. I think there were far more cases of suicide. There were also patients there with very serious injuries resulting from torture or beatings. One prisoner, R., had a fractured spine with paralysis from waist down, so he was practically confined to a wheelchair. Others were tortured on their genitals and so on. One poor man, I think his name was Fišer, had a leg amputated, hemiphlegia (paralysis of one side of the body), and advanced arteriosclerosis of the brain, with spastic weeping and laughter, therefore practically forced to behave abnormally. He was an old sailor from Boka Kotorská, at one time sentenced to death for mutiny. He was very fond of me and would cling to me.

I remember one unexpected death during cardiazol shock, probably due to pulmonary embolism. This upset our head physician Ž. very much, because he had (probably rightly) considered the patient — otherwise a well-known informer — to be a malingerer.

On the other hand, another patient was brought to us from Pankrác prison on the verge of death. S. was about twenty-five years old, supposedly severely epileptic. He was so thin, cachectic, that he weighed only thirty to thirty-five kilos and had enormous bed sores. When seized by a fit, though, he was suddenly so strong that it was more than five men could do to hold him down. He even bent the iron beds. The strange thing was that the fits came on regularly at around seven in the evening. Dr. Ž., an old, seasoned neurologist, thought this didn't fit the diagnosis. Once, we had ourselves locked in the room where he was lying. (There was a lock-up system even in the prison hospital and the doctor's rounds had to be done with a warder, who carried the keys.)

Around seven o'clock we were sitting quietly at a side table playing chess, when S. really did get a severe fit. He screamed the way epileptics usually do and arched his back. We all ran over to him and tried to hold him down so he wouldn't hurt himself. At this moment Dr. Ž. suddenly yelled at him: "Are you going to stop this nonsense?" and gave him such a hard slap on the face that it jerked his head round. The man hesitated for a second. Then the "fit" continued. But it was enough to convince us that it was not a genuine fit, in a condition of deep unconsciousness. He must have been aware of what was going on around him for that slap to have such an effect on him. Everyone pounced on him and began to beat him up for letting others wait on him, wash his dirty underclothes and bedclothes, for being sick over everything, and so on. The next day he did have another "fit," but a weaker one this time, and in the end they disappeared altogether. So it was really a case of hysteria, which can sometimes be worse than epilepsy, or some kind of fit that he could bring on himself out of a desire to be set free or to stop them punishing him, as he was ill. But it had gone so far that we did not expect him to live for more than two or three weeks at the most. He was no longer taking infusions or injections. I believe it was Dr. Ž.'s slap that saved him, because it was then he took a turn for the better. He gradually began eating again and even worked as an orderly. But there were also rumors that he was an informer.

I can still remember a young priest, Vašek Řiha. He often had constricting pains around the heart, as is usual in conditions before a heart attack and stenocardia. But the staff and warders were reluctant to believe him. I don't think even I was convinced about the diagnosis, though I stood up for him because he was a wonderful person. He clarified many things for me, especially questions of morality. We used to have long discussions. Nevertheless, I did think that his problems were more a result of the severe hardships in prison and a strong tendency to neurosis. It therefore pained me considerably to hear later, when I was at a camp near Jáchymov, that he really had died in Mírov of a heart attack.

Another, in fact even earlier, victim was Father Kajpr, a Jesuit priest.

He had suffered greatly in a German concentration camp. Then he became an editor of the Czech weekly, "The Catholic." Father Kajpr died in Leopoldov of a ruptured heart, that is, a very extensive heart attack where the heart is torn apart. It literally broke. He had survived the cruelty of the German concentration camps, but the further cruel conditions of the new totalitarian regime were too much for him. Later, Bishop Gojdič also died, but it is said his body was never handed over. Where we were, a priest of the name of Jakubec died of cancer of the tongue. As far as I know, the bodies of priests were never given to their relatives, in order to avoid large funerals. All such embarrassing and sad cases had to be hushed up. In the tuberculosis ward there was a much hated member of the Gestapo, an SS man. I think he was very malicious, an embodiment of evil. He was so unscrupulous that he made life difficult for everyone. Even here he informed on people and was on the side of the authorities. Everyone said that if anyone deserved the death sentence, it was certainly him. Then on a couple of occasions we saw him walking with Father Urban. We all bet each other that he was preparing another crime and we waited to intercept the priest. But he calmly said: "Let's wait and see what happens." What a shock it was, though, when someone came across him praying. Later he began to speak politely and to help people. No one believed that someone like that could be converted. But it happened. What a holy priest and holy man can achieve! And as if by another miracle, his hopeless lung disease stopped spreading. I can remember well the huge cavern the size of a man's palm that I saw on the X-ray. It got rapidly bigger, nothing could stop it, so in the end we gave up and stopped giving him therapy, in order not to provoke a turn for the worse with the chemicals themselves.

After May 1955 all those who had previously spread panic with the idea of an atomic war did an about-turn and grasped at the idea of an amnesty. In the end, in spite of all the rumors about the forthcoming amnesty, only five to ten people out of a hundred, or even a thousand, were sent home from prison. Moreover, practically all of them were from the front courtyard, from among the "Alsatians" — the criminals. Only one or two political prisoners. In contrast, there was a great movement of German "retributionists," prisoners sentenced after the war for allegedly committing punishable offenses during the German occupation. They clearly had better patrons in countries abroad with which our state wished to have better relations. We carried out dozens or even hundreds of medical examinations on such prisoners who were being discharged. They were not only set free, they were sent straight back to Germany.

The amnesty was a farce, enacted more for the journalists and foreign countries than for the prisoners. Old *mukli* say that every amnesty hurts. Not simply because it passes you by — after all, some of us had even rejected the opportunity. It hurts because it takes your best friends from you. One begins to feel like the last madman who is still going against the tide, while the others enjoy better or more human conditions.

Many of the guards in Mírov, even the officers, were known for their despotism and cruelty, bordering on sadism. If any of them had a pinch of good in them, they were afraid to show their sympathy for those who suffered, so we often didn't know of their existence. Perhaps the only exception was Sergeant Matýsek, who once brought me that apple.

One of these brutes was the "education officer," more exactly, the censor. He could also decide what to do with our letters. Once he called me into his office and asked me: "Do you know a Miss R.?" "Yes, I do." "What is she to you?" I thought this was going to be a new kind of inquiry, because they had already tried that on me here, but it always ended in the same way, with me refusing to answer questions and them threatening further interrogation, hard labor, mining in the uranium mines, and all kinds of other "improvements." This officer even inquired once whether I would like to go home, saying there was a pardon on the way for me. He was terribly surprised when I declared I did not want it and I would not accept it. That I didn't want to go home under those circumstances. "Well," he continued, "an acquaintance?" "A friend." "Why are you laughing?" For I had laughed. It always infuriated them more than anything if a prisoner managed to laugh. "Is she a relation of yours?" "No." "And who is Imro?" At this point I became alert. "I don't know." I don't think it actually occurred to me immediately that they were referring to Imro Staríček. "Then she's writing about someone involved in your case. That's forbidden!" Then this churlish fellow hesitated. "Well, here's your letter from R. And you can send an answer, but nothing about prison or about your accomplices."

That is how our correspondence began. She applied for permission to receive answers from me and under the guise of love letters, she tried to inform me about "the Family," about our main central group, about Imro Staríček and various trials. I answered her and later she found out my address in Banská Bystrica and wrote to me again. At a later date she even managed to get permission to visit me. This made possible a certain link between the closed prison environment and the outside world.

For the last three or four months in Mírov I took over the tuberculosis ward from Dr. O. L. He was released during an amnesty, which at that time revealed much about his character. Soon after, however, he apparently died of TB in Bulovka hospital in Prague. Things were in a terrible state in the ward I took over from him. It was called the "tropical" ward, because he used to go there every day to lie on the divan in the surgery and rest. It took a long time before I managed at least to separate the infectious BK-positive patients (with Koch's bacillus) from the negative ones.

In the Autumn of 1955 we learned about the widespread hunger and other strikes of the prisoners in the Jáchymov district. They began them on account of the starvation diet, but I think it was also already a reaction to the news that was filtering through about attempts in Hungary, East Germany, and Poland to free themselves from the straitjacket of the dictatorship. There were riots in most of the camps, not only around Jáchymov. Where we were, they resulted in severe repression. About fifty to a hundred prisoners from Jáchymov were assigned to us. All of them hard, seasoned men. They were put in strict isolation, in the textile workshop owned by the firm of Moravolen. There were very old machines there and working conditions were very tough.

It was then that, after many talks and meetings between Eisenhower and Khrushchev, a lot of rumors started going around among the prisoners about possible amnesties. Later, however, they poured curses on Eisenhower for selling them down the river yet once again, remarking that he and Nikita had just patted each other on the backs and bowed to each other, although "all we needed to set us free was the sixty to one hundred divisions of the Wehrmacht (the German army) lined up along our borders. After all, if only on account of their fellow Germans, they would not stand by idly, but would be willing to intervene." How much unpleasantness and ridicule I had to put up with from my fellow prisoners when I refused to collect these dubious sensations and pass them on, which I did only perhaps on exceptional occasions, when I saw that someone was very depressed. But I certainly put no faith in them. I always put my faith in God, in his power, greatness, and love. In the end we agreed that if the situation could be settled without conflict, even at the cost of further years of imprisonment or even of our lives, we were willing to sacrifice ourselves, just to avoid an atomic war. We would be happier to go home last or even be the only ones to remain. It was wonderful to raise our spirits like this, but it was harder to bear when we gradually lost all our friends, taking leave of them as they were gradually released into normal life. And we, like fanatics, were left still more isolated.

Some of the prisoners refused to do any work on principle and often went on hunger strike. As a doctor, I was called on to feed them artificially through a tube or by injections. I refused outright to do this. Most of the doctors did it, though, on the grounds of saving life, and they tried to persuade me to do the same.

Attempts to escape formed the most fantastic chapters in the story of every prison or camp. It is an interesting fact that no prison could be made so secure that no one ever managed to escape from it. Some of them had complex, well-guarded security systems — Ruzyň, for example. But at Bytíž there was a Slovak working with me who had managed to escape from Ruzyň. Leopoldov had electric fences. Even so, although it seems incredible, there were successful escapes. The prisoners were capable of scratching a hole in the walls with their fingers and various makeshift instruments, such as spoons, toothbrushes, toiletries. They would undermine the floor, flushing away the fragments of mortar and rubble, in this way making unbelievably long tunnels.

Yet for the most part these plans were betrayed "just before the escape." I write this in quotation marks because the preparations might have been observed some time before or one of the planners might have tried to save himself from punishment at the last moment. In fact there really were more of those who paid dearly for it than of those who succeeded. Often it seemed that in their desperation they planned their escape so that the matter would be settled one way or the other — either they would be shot or beaten to death. Many of them certainly did pay for it with their lives. If they were brought back after running away, they had to wear special green armbands on their left sleeves and had a stricter regimen. Those who had been shot were often paraded in front of everyone. In Jáchymov the whole camp had to march past those who had been shot or wounded while trying to escape.

Here at Mírov people used to talk about how the warden arranged for a stricter regimen. With the help of informers and stoolies, they organized an attempt to escape with the most unflinching, most resolute prisoners, who could not be broken or bought off. During this attempt they lay in wait for them at night with machine guns and shot down the best, most courageous, and most persevering prisoners. Then, as a warning to others, the warden, with the approval of his superiors, is said to have introduced a very cruel regimen, for which he was decorated, as it prevented escapes and riots. After that no one could be certain he would live to see the next morning.

Nevertheless, there were many whom the repressive measures could not break. Our Oto Mádr was one such person as was Felix Davídek, a thin little priest. He was well known as an invincible, tough man, who had survived about two hundred days in the punishment cell and had hardly spent a whole week in a normal prison cell.

When we had him in hospital for a few days, Oto even told me about his well-thought-out plans for organizing Catholic Action in the future, after he was set free. Even with the structure of a future Catholic university and Catholic organizations and institutions in general. On account of these plans many people said he was a utopian. When Oto came into hospital he was little more than skin and bone, he was suffering from nervous exhaustion, and his hands shook (as mine did later). When I saw him then, I told myself that martyrdom does not only result in bloody wounds and stigmas, it leaves scars on the nerves and spirit, too. What a joy it was to meet each other! However, for safety's sake, we had to suppress and hide our feelings of happiness. In front of others we behaved with reserve, like doctor and patient. The same was true with Father Urban.

The new warden, S., came straight from training in Russia, having been promoted, and as "a new broom" he began to introduce order in many ways. He even required the prison guards to answer the prisoners' compulsory greetings. It raised our hopes for an improvement in our lot, because order in prison is sometimes to the advantage of the prisoners, too. Especially where disorder has concealed the overbearing behavior of the strong, the bullying, the clans of convicts used as guards, and other criminals. Where I worked, a systematic examination of outpatients was introduced, one department after another. This meant that the departments were isolated even more from each other and there was more work for the doctors. I was given the priests, intentionally, I presume.

I had a severe complication with one patient, when one of the informers, orderly U., who watched my every move, put a different ampule among the strophanthin ones, maybe by accident or out of carelessness. I injected an old priest with it. Fortunately all turned out well, but it could have ended very tragically.

At that time the chief medical officer—junior lieutenant Ga., was always breathing down my neck, even though he was not the worst one. There was a priest who had eczema of the lower limbs. When I recommended sick leave, Ga. "magnanimously" crossed it out. I asked him how, then, in his opinion, was I to treat the patient. Without a moment's hesitation he told me I was to apply ointments in the out-patients' room. This I did. A few days later the patient came with such exacerbated eczema that I immediately showed it to Ga. He bit his lip and asked coldly: "What do you suggest, then?" "Now, twice as long in bed — at least five days." "Give it here." He signed it without a word.

At last I have got to one interesting episode which influenced my further stay in prison. From time to time we heard bits of news that American balloons released from the United States or from German territory were dropping leaflets, newspapers, and other material published by Radio Free Europe. There were rumors that some people had seen them pass over our prison. As usual, I was sceptical about such news. Then one day a colleague, Dr. O. P., appeared with a leaflet, which he said had been found in a bush in the yard. He said it had been dropped by one of Radio Free Europe's balloons and that it had been passed to him by S., a cook he felt sure he could trust.

I didn't like it at all. Especially as he didn't read the leaflet himself, but gave it to Honzo J. to read aloud. There were some witty things from our press. For example, a caricature of Tito, which portrayed him as a bloodthirsty executioner with an axe dripping blood and then, after a change in policy, another picture from the same newspaper and a quotation referring to Tito as a great genius and a statesman whom all our leaders embraced. Then there was muscle-flexing data about what big, powerful planes and rockets the Americans had. But otherwise nothing special, certainly nothing seditious; it was more ironical. A lot of the text was in Slovak, which is why they passed it on to me to read. I didn't want to disturb the atmosphere of trust, so, out of solidarity, I finished reading it aloud. Then O. P. took it and burnt it in the toilet, or so he told us.

I had no idea at that time how such a trifle could have such a profound influence on our lives and, above all, on our relationships. It is indeed only in need that one discovers who one's friends are. About fourteen days later a nervous atmosphere developed among the prison staff, especially in the kitchen, and the interrogations began. Some people were sent straight to the punishment cells, apparently on account of some leaflets. Among them, we heard, was L. S., the cook already mentioned. Later I learned that Dr. P. said he was an informer. We tried to come to an agreement: "O., you brought it here and you took it away or destroyed it. You didn't give it to anyone. None of us know anything about it." To this he replied: "No one knows about me, either. We'll keep quiet. The person who gave me it won't give me away. And if he does, then I simply destroyed it and that'll be that."

But, as is usually the case (and as usually happened during interrogations), the next day O. looked pale; they kept calling him upstairs and he no longer told us what they asked him or how it went. In the afternoon he didn't come back. They began to round us up and escort us upstairs, to a special office. I knew by this time that things were looking bad, that someone had given in or that the whole thing had been set up and we were in the soup. I was kept isolated for hours in the library or in the corridor. Occasionally I heard a shout or a blow. To emphasize the seriousness of it all, they put me in handcuffs. It occurred to me that they could beat me better like that. It was evening when they led me in. They were all there. Dr. Ž, Dr. P., Arnošt S., Honzo J. The warden, a plain-clothes man with sleeves rolled up, and the guards were striding up and down in a furious mood. It was clear they already knew everything, but even so I didn't dare spoil our solidarity. "So how was it with those leaflets? Why did you read them?" "What leaflets?" "None of that lip. You think you can tell outright lies. They'll all tell you to your face." To this I said, "Then let them tell me. I refuse to answer questions." My usual tactic during interrogations. At this he raised his arm, but, if I remember rightly, he didn't hit me. Someone did grasp me round the neck, though. "Then call Dr. P." With eyes downcast, the latter told me: "It's no use. They know everything. Tell them how it was." "Well, does that convince you?" "Yes," I replied. "Are you still going to tell us that you didn't read anything?" "I didn't say I hadn't, I just said I wanted them to say so." They led Dr. P. out and brought in Arnošt. "Tell him he read it out." "Why should I tell him? Let him say so himself, if he did." "Do I have to go about it differently? Did you read the leaflet, or didn't you?" I remained silent. That was enough for Arnošt. He stuck to what he had said. The warden flew into a rage. I think he hit me, but I don't remember exactly.

"Take him away!" But an hour later, when they led us away to the punishment cell, he seemed fed up with the whole affair. He was no longer fuming. We got five days in the punishment cell, which wasn't so much for such a thing. Honzo S., Honzo J., Arnošt, and I. I was the only one of the doctors. Dr. Ž. apparently stuck to his version that he hadn't read any leaflets and took no notice of what others read. He only read his own books. In this way he avoided punishment. But I was told Honzo Svoboda said the same, but it didn't help. Which only goes to show not everyone got the same treatment. Dr. P. was spared punishment, clearly for squealing on all the others. Later he said he did it because of his family, as if others had no families. His main excuse was that it was nothing of importance. He said we should have confirmed that he burned the leaflet. As it was, the warden could think he had hidden it somewhere or passed it on to someone. I have mentioned this as a typical example of many such episodes in prisons. It is pretty well impossible to rely on any prior agreements.

I have another experience from the punishment cell. The one in Mírov was notorious. We sometimes used to get patients from there who were in a state of complete exhaustion, in danger of their lives, with inflammation of the pleura or acute rheumatism and huge swellings of the joints. The walls of the correction cell were about three and a half meters thick. It was known as the ice cellar, it was so cold. Even in summer, to say nothing of autumn. Punishment there was really by freezing, even though the regulations didn't allow that. There was one positive thing about it. I was able to renew myself spiritually at least for a short time, which previously in a room together with seven or eight medical assistants and doctors was not possible. This renewal was disturbed to some extent by the shouts from nearby cells, when the guard left us in the afternoon or evening and we were left alone. Then it also had the advantage that I got to know the young medics, the orderlies, better, Arnošt in particular. His opinions about faith were quite different from mine and he had always been nearer to Dr. Ž or Dr. P. Now the situation changed completely.

By doing time in the punishment cell I also won great respect from the prisoners. I made friends with the tough convicts from Jáchymov who were in the cells around and could not be broken or forced to work, but who never stopped protesting. On the other hand, I realized how I had wasted my time in Mírov. I had had wonderful conditions in the hospital and I decided to renew both my spiritual program and my medical studies. To withdraw for a while from openly spreading the Gospels, because all the stoolies and many of the guards picked on me. I was drawing too much attention to myself and maybe even needlessly revealing my contacts. After all, in many wards I had managed to plant good male nurses, who could move about and pass on news, themes for meditation, and even the Eucharist.

Father Urban had already asked me on an earlier occasion to be more discreet, because the role I played was very important. At that time I had taken over the tuberculosis ward from another doctor, as I mentioned, and I could devote more time and energy to the seriously or hopelessly ill patients. (Grof Esterházy, for instance, died one or two months after my departure, or so I was told.) I could also cover up for less serious cases, such as Father Milan and Father Urban. After my departure all these tuberculosis patients could be in danger.

On my return from the punishment cell, I was surprised to find that they didn't put me in a department where I would have to do hard manual labor, or in isolation, in solitary confinement, where some of the old communists were, even founding members of the Communist Party and Gottwald's colleagues. Instead, the medic said to me in an almost friendly manner: "You've done your time, so why should we get rid of you?" Meanwhile, however, some changes had taken place in the hospital. My friends were subdued, they were scattered around in different rooms, and the stoolies began to behave in a self-assured, aggressive manner. Relationships in the doctors' room were strained and painful. I was not surprised, therefore, when about ten days later Junior Lieutenant Go. told me: "Pack your things." I was convinced that I was being put in isolation as a punishment, being sent somewhere unknown. When he said goodbye, however, he was quite reasonable and told me: "You see, this needn't have happened. You brought it on yourself." "Where am I going?" "I don't know." But later I learned that I was going to Banská Bystrica. They had asked for a doctor and in Mírov they took advantage of the fact that I was a Slovak. They gave me all the medical books I had bought and which Go. had of his own accord stamped with the mark of Mírov prison. At the time I had vainly protested, but now he even gave me a paper confirming the books were mine. There was no sad parting from my friends because I was not allowed to see them again. All I could do was to send them greetings through some of my colleagues or orderlies.

Once more an escort, the changing of clothes. I think they sent my ordinary clothes home at that point. (When my family received them, they had quite a shock, because they thought it meant I was dead.) To give it a favorable explanation, maybe it was so that I could keep my good prison clothes and shoes, because at each new place a new prisoner was always given the worst. I was taken by a smallish prison bus to Olomouc and from there on the next or third day to Ilava.

Every time I traveled under escort, I literally hunted for people I knew and for information, because it was really the only opportunity to come into direct contact with the world, or at least the prison world. I found it fairly easy to make contacts, especially with new prisoners, because I already had three or four years behind me and therefore I had acquired a certain amount of authority. But I came up against various prisoners, including coarse criminals. One of them spat at me: "Ugh, didn't I tell you, he'd be another political one?" Prisoners like that looked down their noses at us. It became more and more difficult to come across old political prisoners or others of good character. When we did, however, they stuck with us immediately and tried to keep as close to us as possible.

This time I wasn't put in a large, common cell, but in a smaller room for four with two bunk beds. For the time being this was the end of my time in large mass cells with several other prisoners, which could otherwise be very useful for getting information, but were sometimes physically quite unpleasant. I tried to change cells with other prisoners in order to get into a cell with a priest, but I was not successful. By that time I knew that prisoners traveling under escort didn't have particular cells assigned to them. So with a degree of courage and daring, it was possible to take a risk and try to be at least for a while with whoever one needed. At least until they found out. One was beginning to learn how to do things in this world of the *mukl,* of the condemned. Nevertheless, I managed to meet a good priest and at least he heard my confession.

I spent three weeks in Ilava, because the transports were held up, the camps and prisons were overcrowded. As it was, they took me among the first, because they needed me in Banská Bystrica to replace a colleague, V., who had requested a transfer to Bohemia. In the end I shared a cell with a swindler, a black marketeer, who had testified in Ostrava against an officer who was mixed up in the same affair. Theft by the watchdogs was common and they used to be sentenced for such offenses. This informer knew Banská Bystrica and even the camp in Senica. He praised it highly as a suitable place for a doctor. Otherwise he was a typical criminal, who just wanted to spend his time having an easy life lying low and pretending to be ill. He was only interested in sex and immorality, which in time even led me to a certain sexual temptation. I felt so bad and ungrateful before God that it even made me cry. As always, and especially in prison, punishment followed.

Part II

Banská Bystrica Prison

It was about the end of November 1955 when I was taken to Banská Bystrica. Not to a labor camp, but once more to a closed prison and, what is more, one where people were kept on remand awaiting trial. It was evening when we arrived in Bystrica. The town brought back to me many memories of my childhood and adolescence, years spent here as a schoolboy and a Scout. I sometimes used to claim proudly that Bystrica was my real home town, because I was only born in Trnava.

I remember well how, as a child, we occasionally passed the well-known prison with its high walls, behind which I now found myself. We used to see the convicts in grey uniforms sawing wood and picking up cigarette ends to smoke. Now I would go into town in just such grey "rags," deliberately putting on the most tattered I could find. Accompanied by a guard, I would push a cart for the shopping or medicines and watch to see how people would react to me. My teacher, M., for example. I was standing on the pavement with a group of prisoners and when I greeted him, he turned away. He was clearly very embarrassed, mainly because of the company I was in. To be honest, though, I cannot be absolutely sure that he recognized me. Maybe it was just a reflex or intuitive reaction.

Others did quite the opposite. When we stopped at the pharmacist's, at the foot of the town's main tower, where the Flittners used to live, whose descendants had returned from German concentration camps, they went out of their way to help me. Some people, whether they knew me or not, tried to give me an apple, chocolate, a piece of bread, or cigarettes — even in the presence of the guard or through him — but I refused. I have a vague picture in my memory (though maybe it was only something I heard) of a little Czech girl saying to the prisoners: "Mr. Thieves, Mummy sends you these cigarettes and she says you are to share them with the other Mr. Thieves." Really endearing, so typically childlike, simple and warm-hearted.

That first evening I was put in a solitary confinement cell for those on remand. There was a dirty straw mattress and broken window, no doubt to "cool" people off a little. The blankets were torn, the cell stank of dirt, there was a bucket for bodily needs. All this had a very depressing effect. Especially when I realized that it was obviously deliberate and maybe even sent by God as a punishment for being disloyal and not sticking to my principles. Maybe I would be there for a few months, or perhaps for the rest of my life. But in the morning the warder in charge of that wing had me moved to another cell.

I found myself in a cell reserved for the maintenance and prison service workers. The cell was a bit cleaner. There were iron beds, mostly old and broken, with bent bars and large holes in the straw mattresses. The worst thing, however, was the company there. Seven or eight people in one room and not a political prisoner among them. Political prisoners were scarce by this time.

For the whole of those two and a half years in Banská Bystrica, I did not have the fortune to live with anyone who gave serious thought to anything, or was willing to stand up for anything of a spiritual nature. They were almost all delinquents, often young boys, inconsiderate and selfish. Only on rare occasions could one meet someone a little more decent, who would show some respect for others. I had no privacy any more for reading or study. If I opened a book, some people seemed to enjoy disturbing me. Or did they really want my company? It was also unbearable there because so many people smoked, which was later officially forbidden, but no one ever kept to it. It was impossible to breathe the air in the cell, impossible to sleep, partly because no one had any consideration for anyone else. Some of them would talk or shout to each other all night.

At this point I have begun to think about why I sometimes demanded physical labor outside the doctor's surgery. It was clearly not just a stubborn wish to sacrifice myself in order to demonstrate solidarity with the political prisoners, the religious ones in particular, by joining them in their hard and often dangerous manual labor, such as working in the uranium mines. Nor was it a desire to renounce the privileges of a cleaner and more attractive job in the prison surgery or hospital.

I think it was partly my old egoism, which intuitively wished to avoid the prolongation of the period of isolation forced on a prisoner in pretrial detention. After all, I had already spent a total of about seven years in solitary confinement cells, although occasionally I had been given a cell mate. The latter, however, was usually a carefully chosen informer or a cruel agent provocateur, planted to help guard me and to enforce my isolation. So even after being convicted, I was treated like a detainee, in fact guarded even more closely in my free time and private life, with no opportunity to meet other prisoners — or only under observation, While other convicts could meet each other fairly easily, without surveillance, in their sleeping quarters or at their places of work, or anywhere in a labor camp.

My first cell mate was Milan S., who was serving a sentence for fraud. It took me quite a long time to discover that everything that seemed good in him was just pretence. He knew how to get what he wanted. Perhaps the only person worse than him was Franta M., an old lag, a recidivist, who died during a football match when, I'm told, the main coronary artery, the aorta, burst. He used to tell horrible stories and everyone had to listen to him. They were mostly boastful and sexually perverse. I tried to put a certain barrier of decent people between myself and these two. One such decent person was a strongman, Jano K., who was known to break shackles and chains, but was unfortunately in the grip of alcohol. Otherwise he was a sensitive person and I was very fond of him. I think he had fought back when some policemen broke through the barricaded door into his flat when he was quarreling with his wife. He wasn't ashamed or afraid to seize them and give them a beating.

One person who has stuck in my memory was "Uncle" Žiga, a "kulak" (a communist term for someone who owned a largish farm) whom I cheered up when others were unfair to him. The name, or rather insult, "kulak" was really a made-up term for every hard-working or prosperous farmer, or simply for a person to be hated. I didn't agree with this, although I also strongly disliked that kind of "kulak" self-centeredness. Maybe it was the fight for survival in that lawless jungle that made them like that, but they were often incapable of sharing with other people as wretched as themselves, with the exception of myself. Sometimes not even when food they had saved up went bad and they had to throw it away.

At least I could pray sometimes with "Uncle" Žiga on our Sunday walks, or even sing the Mass. When he was released he didn't forget to visit my family several times.

I also came to know a teacher of physical training, P. He had been shut up repeatedly for homosexuality. Such people found it very hard to cope with their problems, but they could always be "improved" a little, if they nevertheless had a longing for good, truth, and beauty. Maybe I achieved a good deal by being the only one to respect them and defend their human dignity. When we began of our own accord to do some physical exercises after our walks, he became our trainer. We exercised with persistence and enthusiasm, but only when it wasn't forced on us. Compulsory physical exercise quickly became a source of the worst bullying and therefore the prisoners did everything possible to get out of it.

Later, when I managed to get a smaller cell, at the beginning of the corridor next to the warder's office, I was alone for most of the time for the next two years. The people in charge didn't want to give me decent company, only informers. They didn't want to let me join the other prisoners or the gangs of laborers, either. Mainly so I could not influence them and in order to keep me absolutely isolated. Which I used as an excuse from time to time to urge them to transfer me to a camp or to physical labor.

I shared this little cell for quite a time with B., a fanatical Hungarian. A quick-tempered man, who had sued the authorities about thirty-eight times before they managed to get him put behind bars — and that only by a swindle, he claimed. I greatly admired his doggedness and his refusal to be daunted. He didn't spare even those in uniform, especially if they broke the law. We had a warder the prisoners nicknamed "horse head." This Hungarian called him "ády húgyi köves ember," that is, "a man with kidney stones in his head." He filed suits and complaints one after the other, mainly against the prosecutor, who he claimed had broken up his marriage. He had seduced his wife and then had him shut up for insulting a public servant or for "raping" his own wife, I can't remember which.

The warden, old Captain M., seemed quite a pleasant man at first. He always emphasized order and justice and showed quite a bit of respect for me. But when I was there longer, I noticed that he behaved differently behind my back. On occasions when I refused to confirm that a prisoner was fit enough to be sent to the punishment cell, or I recommended some alleviation in their work or regimen, he often didn't make sure that the regulations were strictly observed. Once I happened to hear him say behind the door: "Let him drop dead!" He was talking about a boy with an aching tooth that I wanted to extract, but I didn't have the necessary tools. On Sunday, when he was howling with pain, I had asked for him to be moved to the dental ward and the warden suddenly showed himself to be a callous man.

The governor's deputy, T., if I remember rightly, didn't devote so much of his attention to the prison. He was always occupied with some pastime; he used to assemble or mend various instruments or shoot at the sparrows in the courtyard with his small-caliber gun. The security officer, a lieutenant, reminded me of a fox, because he was always very kind to your face. At the same time, however, he kept a much closer watch on me than anyone else did. The stores manager was a typical lout, who often told new prisoners: "You thought the republic was a cow you could milk and use for your own ends without being punished." In fact, I heard they checked the stores later and arrested him immediately on account of a deficit and missing items.

Some warders were very coarse and loudmouthed. One dog-handler, a youngish sergeant, was very uncouth. I considered him to be one of the roughest because of the way he yelled at the women prisoners exercising outside, but when he escorted me to Bytíz, he chatted with me so freely that I had the impression that he was really quite good-hearted. But maybe he only had a personal liking for me.

The warder in the workshop was a leading corporal, a short man nicknamed "Little Key," because he always carried a bunch of keys with him and he admitted that he loved locking and unlocking doors. He was said to have lived through all the regimes, the Hungarian included. He said he would live through all those to come, too. He knew how to keep in the background and serve everyone and anyone, so no one really knew where he stood. Personally, I think he wasn't bad, even though he wouldn't help anyone if it meant taking the slightest risk.

It's an interesting fact that I occasionally met really good-hearted people even among the employees of the Ministry of the Interior. It's true that this might have been because the prison was run like those for pre-trial detainees, which means that the prisoners were kept in isolation for most of the time and didn't have the opportunity to get to know the staff and see through them as one did in various stressful situations in labor camps. Warder M., an amateur artist, was one such good-hearted person. He very much wanted to leave the service and he often came to my window to chat. The leader of the shift, Junior Lieutenant H., was an agreeable, decent man. But at the final body search he made me strip naked, even though others had long stopped doing so and were more considerate. I am told he shot his own wife later, when he caught her in flagrante delicto and he was given five years. They say he was a good prisoner and even became a good Christian.

Another leader of the shift, a leading corporal known as "The Pilot," disappointed me when he wouldn't put off the initial medical examination of a new prisoner so that I could go to see a film, which was a rare cultural event once a week or a fortnight. He lost his temper and suddenly seemed quite a different person.

Some of the women warders who used to come to the window in my cell door for a chat behaved in a similar way. Sometimes they would suddenly put on an official face and you didn't know what to think.

One young-looking woman warder in particular spoke very coarsely to the women prisoners, although they weren't choosy about their language, either.

At the end of 1957 or the beginning of 1958, a new, agreeable regional warden arrived, a great sports fan, especially when it came to football. He liked the prisoners to think he was fair. Maybe he really was, but I was afraid to let myself like someone, after having been disappointed so many times. In his time there I began to go on voluntary Sunday work shifts, twice a month. For the most part this was hard, physical work, digging a ditch for the new sports stadium or regulating the River Hron with huge angular boulders.

I decided to take part in these shifts mainly because of the opportunity to come into contact with people more freely and the change of surroundings. The monotony of the prison walls began to get on my nerves as the years went by. For me physical work seemed like recreation. Sun and fresh air at last. Another reason was the money it earned, as for these six hours twice a month one could earn more pocket money than for a whole month's service as a doctor, including night duty, and in addition one received a large ration of cigarettes or tobacco and beer, which it was possible to exchange for other favors.

As soon as I arrived in the cell for those employed in the running of the prison, I was visited by a medical officer, Pavol F., an oldish sergeant from eastern Slovakia. He was an astute, experienced man with a nose for trouble, capable of making all kinds of deductions, and with a mechanical smile. He was not one of the worst, but like all medical officers, employees of the Ministry of the Interior, he was self-important and he despised other people so much that he just didn't care what happened to them. We often used to come into conflict. He wanted to make decisions like a doctor and in fact I complained about him a couple of times, in his presence, of course. When I refused to give hunger strikers intravenous nourishment, he did it himself.

I must admit that even for me it was a hard decision, especially if the patient himself requested a doctor and refused to have a medical orderly because the latter did it roughly, without consideration, in order to make him change his mind. However, I refused to do this to hunger strikers as a matter of principle, because it was a coercive method used to silence their protests by interrupting their hunger strike. These protests were often justified. Some wanted to force an interview with the prosecutor or higher authorities, or to make someone respect their justified complaints. However, I sometimes explained to the hunger strikers that they could do themselves lasting, irreversible harm within a matter of two or three days. Even on the second day of a genuine hunger strike it was possible to smell acetone in the person's breath. Dormant or half-cured tuberculosis often took a turn for the worse, and so on. However, explanations were useless for the most part, as was the argument that they would do themselves more harm than the thing they were trying to achieve was worth. Some of them even went on hunger strike for no better reason than they had not received enough cigarettes or someone was not willing to give them sick leave. Many of them were just chronic complainers and bad-tempered fellows.

I remember a typical case of an old man who was sentenced to fourteen days in prison. At that time such a sentence meant that he really couldn't have done anything serious. Most punishments were for many years and only exceptionally for a number of months. Apparently he was there for illicitly slaughtering a pig, or something of the kind.

At first glance I could see that he was suffering from an advanced stage of arteriosclerosis, but otherwise he was in fairly good shape. Others were of the opinion that he was fit enough to serve his sentence. "If he was fit enough to commit a crime, he's fit enough for prison." Wonderful logic! On just the second or third day I suggested his sentence should be postponed and that he should be hospitalized, because he had diarrhea and couldn't find his bearings. When they examined him they found he had feces in his trousers. All the others reacted: "Ugh, you filthy old man!" A typical human, malicious judgment. When I urged hospitalization once more, the medical officer declared: "He's got more brains than all of us put together." Infallible people.... The next day the old man was too weak to move and the medical officer quickly rushed him off to hospital, where, seeing his condition, everyone wanted to get him off their hands.

That is a typical sin of doctors. From the internal ward they bundled him off to neurology, from there to the infectious ward and, of course, each time he lay for an hour or two in the corridor. No one wanted to have him. In the end they took him to the tuberculosis ward, where he died of tuberculosis of the meninges, that is, of meningitis. I blamed myself very much for not having been more energetic, or not going on a hunger strike. I made such a fuss about how the medical officer had dealt with this case that in the end, to my great satisfaction, they transferred him to another prison. But later I heard that the real reason for his transfer was apparently some moral offense with a married employee of the Ministry of the Interior.

After a time I was joined by another medical officer, Leading Corporal Ján R., who aroused considerable hope on account of his good-natured appearance and behavior. But only up to the moment when he was given the post he wanted. Even so, I have experienced worse. However, he did not respect the rule that only a doctor was allowed to be present when women were checked for lice. He removed the screens, arguing that "he was also a health worker" and ignoring the prison regulation that said these examinations should be carried out by a woman. At least the previous medical officer had respected this, even thought he grumbled about it and at me, too.

At about the beginning of 1958 a Ukrainian, Dr. A. P., was sentenced for carrying out abortions. At that time it was a punishable offense. I think he was given eight years. That was not a heavy sentence, because abortion was regarded then (as in the Soviet Union) as being almost as bad as murder. He claimed he only did it when his patients begged him to and he never had any complications, nor financial rewards. Otherwise he was a decent, elderly man. He was assigned to me as a male nurse, as he had only about a month still to serve, but they didn't allow us to live in the same cell.

This doctor was perhaps the only good company I had during my time in the prison surgery. When we were out exercising, I could test my memory of the Russian Gospel of St. John that I had learned by heart and correct my pronunciation. He admired me very much for this, but we didn't get any further in the spiritual sphere. Like most of the others, he would cry for his family. He was proud of his son, who was a doctor. I still have a shaving brush with an "amber" handle that he gave me. It was the first of my prison shaving things.

At the beginning they took everything away from us and we would be shaven once a week, or sometimes even a fortnight, by a prisoner, a barber from the detention wing. At Mírov we used to call the barber "Dr. Soaplather." He was a very good young boy, a believer, and he shaved us whenever we needed it. In Banská Bystrica they were keen for me to shave myself, like other convicts. This was a new practice, probably designed to isolate me from my last contact, the barber — a Jehovah's Witness, with whom I had at least a little in common. He was a German and he had got about two years for refusing to do military service and carry a weapon, as well as for propagation of his religion. I used to enjoy learning the books of the Old Testament from him, in so far as he could remember their division and contents.

My last decent cell mate was H., a man of about thirty, whom they had transferred from Kamchatka. He had worked in the gold mines after being dragged off there from Slovakia as a prisoner after the war. The poor man had survived ten years in terrible conditions and when he was about to be set free, the Slovak authorities refused to count those years and not only didn't let him go, but they even wanted to bring him up for trial all over again.

For the time being he cleaned the corridors in a new two-storey building with about thirty little cells on the ground and first floors, built exactly in the same way as Ruzyň. The majority of the political detainees were kept here. For example, there was one named Ď., arrested for sending a letter to the United States embassy. Later they were joined by most of the detainees from the emergency services of Hlinka's home guard, who were once more a target for political reasons. They included priests and one monk with huge calluses on his knees from kneeling at prayer. I was told that General Turanec was there with high blood pressure, Hedera, a priest and several others, who I heard were later condemned to death. When they were executed, however, some of them were said to have cried out, "God is my witness, I am not guilty!"

Upstairs there were the offices where interrogations were carried out. It was here that one lieutenant, whom I had also treated as a patient, "went to work" on me. He obviously wanted to force me to stop refusing to testify, although there can't really have been much point in it for them any longer. Above all, he wanted me to stop refusing to accept a pardon, amnesty, or the like. Even though he made quite an effort to control himself, it was possible to see he was one of those overbearing despots. He stubbornly denied any beating or torturing of prisoners, or if he allowed it might happen, then he excused it with the old phrase: "Because they were aggressive." Or: "A policeman also has the right to defend himself, if someone jumps at his throat." Nevertheless, rumors still went around of beatings and the use of physical force during interrogations. Shouts and blows were to be heard from time to time. Then they would hurry most of those who worked on maintenance back into their cells, and "Little Key," the warder, became very irritable. Once traces of blood were to be seen in the snow and on the path, but they could have been caused by accidental injury or a suicide attempt.

It was in Banská Bystrica that my first and maybe only patient died. It was, however, questionable whether he was a patient, or whether he was already dead when I was taken to him. I didn't succeed in reviving him, in bringing him back to life. He was a twenty-year-old who had committed suicide by hanging himself. He had been known as a rather unpleasant, restless, quarrelsome grumbler. He had tried to hang himself on several occasions, but clearly in such a way that they would find him before it was too late. This time he had miscalculated. The guard he was perhaps relying on had stopped to talk to someone or gone somewhere. When they brought me to him, they were just cutting through the noose. He had hung himself in a half-sitting position by fastening his belt somehow to the radiator. He was completely blue. The warder made a hopeless gesture: "It's all over, he's cold. He's had it." "How can you be sure? You mustn't lose nerve or give up. Quick! Artificial respiration and everything possible." He was immediately given the kiss of life, then heart massage. When all this failed, I gave him an intracardial injection — straight into his heart, to activate the adrenaline. However, uninformed people sometimes think the doctor is "piercing" the heart, in order to make sure the patient is dead. . . .

This episode disturbed me considerably. I couldn't get over it for at least a week. I asked for a postmortem. I think it was in fact carried out by another prisoner, Dr. Vápeník, in the camp in Senica. The autopsy revealed a small heart with some fibrosis, that is, with scars left by a heart attack or by myocarditis — inflammation of the heart muscle. All these had clearly speeded up his suffocation and death. People around me, both warders and prisoners, reassured me: "You did all you could. What more do you want? No one can perform miracles. Anyway, he got what he wanted." Others said: "I didn't tell him to hang himself or eat nails." The usual phrase of the warders and chief medical officers was the saying: "If that's what they want, let them have it." What struck me and pained me about these reactions was the indifference to human life. They were more worried about the long reports they had to write and the administrative duties involved. I openly criticized the chief officer on duty, because I had been with him to see this prisoner only the evening before. He refused to allow him something and immediately led me away. I couldn't even talk to him at length. Maybe his problems could have been solved by discussing them. Or all that was needed was a more human approach.

It was here I was fortunate enough to meet a priest, Father T. He was kept in relative isolation in the detention wing, but as I lived there too, we could at least see each other when out exercising. The governor usually allowed me to walk with him and occasionally with some of the detainees, but only in the inner circle. Once I used this opportunity for a confession. At least a fragmentary one. The Lord arranged it for me wonderfully, just at a time when I was under pressure from temptations and problems. On another occasion, I wrote a confession in Latin. I slipped it through the window in his door when I was distributing medicines. He returned a gesture of absolution. He was not afraid to give the sacraments and also protested against his illegal conviction with a sentence of about eighteen months, for so-called "incitement to revolt." At that time sentences were getting lighter, and it must have been some triviality, because when they sentenced me, a minimum of ten, fifteen years was usual even for something trivial or for nothing at all.

One person I came to like in particular was a thin, pale, pleasant young man, J. T., an idealist who stuck to his principles. We managed to exchange a few words during his medical examination on arrival. He had refused to do military service and returned his "certificate of citizenship" — his identification card. He asked to be allowed to leave the republic because of its disrespect for the law and persecution of decent people who believed in democracy. He wasn't a Jehovah's Witness or a member of any other sect. He was a lone runner, he had formed his own outlook. He wasn't a Catholic, either, at least I don't think so, rather the contrary. He accepted my Catholic convictions, maybe even admired them. He was inspired by Leo Nikolayevich Tolstoy, Gandhi, and other such people.

He was almost always on a protest hunger strike and I, of course, refused to feed him artificially. But once, when he was very weak, I at least persuaded him not to continue. I urged the warden's office to hear him out or allow him to lodge formal complaints, which he had a right to, and which could do no one any harm. After all, the complaints were handled by them anyway. I was very sad that I could not come into closer contact with such people, talk to them at length, or even live in the same room with them, even though we were under the same roof. I tried to get him assigned to the prison surgery as a nurse or assistant at least for a few hours. What a pity I shall never see him again. However, by some miracle, he managed to catch my name and he visited my parents when he left prison.

Later I managed to get permission to have political newspapers — communist ones, of course. According to the regulations, prisoners have a right to them. But in my case, although I was a doctor, and therefore also a prison worker, they hadn't wanted to allow it. I got access at least to "Práca" ("Work" — the Trade Union newspaper). I read it from cover to cover behind closed doors in the surgery and then I had to return it. In spite of the political phrases, the cult of personality, and the distorted, one-sided reports, it did enable me to keep contact with the outside world. Even though one's only hope was really in God.

At the beginning everyone believed the regime must collapse, but eventually we had to take our "DKR" (do konca režimu) sentences seriously. After all, we didn't want a war or a bloody revolution and, our attitude being what it was, we could not rely on an amnesty or even on being released after we had served our sentences. We had already had experience with that. We had heard that Father Botek, for example, had served out his sentence but had not been released, and they even wanted to give him a further sentence. Almost all the Jesuits were imprisoned for years, even decades, even without trial.

Then suddenly — I didn't want to believe my own eyes — this miracle began. First some criticism of Stalin. Exactly what we had all felt and often talked about among ourselves, but couldn't say out loud. Then came the condemnation of the cult of personality. This was followed by a wide-ranging amnesty in Poland. The governor told us to ask our families to send us some ordinary clothes. This caused panic, not only among our families. Some people thought they were going to bury us and that they needed our clothes to put on our dead bodies.

Time and time again on occasions like this many people were overcome by optimism, a feeling that their dreams were coming true, which was very hard to resist in prison. Especially when this mood was actually encouraged by the political chiefs in the prison and sometimes even had some real justification. At such times they would usually answer our questions enigmatically: "We don't know yet exactly, but there will definitely be an amnesty and all those wrongly sentenced will be released in turn or have their cases reviewed." We had already heard this, and not once, and we knew who they meant when they talked about "those wrongly sentenced." But on this occasion, we heard that in Poland all the political prisoners had been released. We grasped at any news about amnesties and reforms abroad, especially in the satellite countries. How misleading it all was! In our country amnesties were mainly for criminals and only a very small number of political prisoners who had less than six months to the end of their sentences or were seriously ill with cancer, pregnant women, and so on.

From time to time we received some Hungarian prisoners, too. I remember one very beautiful young woman, whom they had caught trying to escape with her husband through Czechoslovakia. Then there was a group of four sportsmen in skiing boots. Next a period of great confusion. The guards were nervous, sometimes over-willing and gentle, which was always a suspicious sign. This was very soon followed by a consignment of prisoners from the nearby camp in Senica. They divided them up among the cells, without work and without interrogation. This is how they isolated prominent prisoners they were afraid could influence others. Zdeněk, who shared my cell, suddenly began to read aloud from a newspaper about the chaos in Hungary. It was a miracle we had received it, obviously only by mistake. For we usually knew that something extraordinary was going on in the world outside by the fact that they kept back all the newspapers and turned off the cable-piped radio. Three days later there was a coup d'état in Hungary. Suddenly they stopped letting us out of our cells. More tension, speculation about what would happen, what was going on.

Time and again in one's imagination, one packed one's things and fell into the arms of one's parents, relations, friends, brothers. What was going to happen? Would we live through it? Many of the guards or instructors made no secret of the opinion that we were not there in order to have our freedom restricted, but were destined for liquidation, for execution. We were worse than the worst murderers or criminals who harm one or two people, because we had spiritually ruined a whole generation. There was only one thing I couldn't understand: why the Hungarians didn't safeguard themselves properly from attack and how they could quarrel over details when nothing was yet at all certain. My fears about the traditional disunion of good people were immediately confirmed on Sunday, when my father whispered to me during his visit that the Soviet Army had occupied Hungary.

A new phase immediately followed. They began to transport Hungarians to the prison in Banská Bystrica. They were said to have been on the run from the Russians and crossed the border, or maybe they were literally kidnapped and brought here. I think the latter was true in most cases. First there were soldiers, army officers. They didn't know what to do with them, but in time they treated them as normal political detainees. The Hungarians protested in vain, or went on hunger strike.

I wasn't allowed to come into contact with them, even when distributing medicines to the cells, and the medical officer began to carry out the initial medical examinations by himself. But as he was afraid of the responsibility, he eventually roped me in and so I was able to gather some fragments of information. A few artists and writers arrived, along with a couple of very young students, almost children. One man was from Catholic Action in Budapest. They kept them for about a month in isolation and uncertainty, in fear of the Russians, and then they transported them to the very place they were most afraid of. Some argued in vain that they had nothing on their consciences, that they had fled before the reactionaries. They probably transported them back to Hungary or to the border. But where exactly, who knows?

Many people, mainly Romany women, but young prostitutes as well, came to the prison in a terribly neglected state. After "civilizing" them in prison and releasing them, they would return a few weeks later in the same condition. I remember one young woman, A., who was clearly a Romany, although she fiercely denied it. She had been sentenced for theft and prostitution. She always returned, at almost regular intervals, in spring or autumn, in quite a wretched state. She sometimes kicked up a terrible fuss, yelling day and night, so no one could get any sleep. One night when she was behaving like this I told the chief officer on duty not to beat her so much. He pulled me out of my cell and took me to see for myself that no one was even touching her. In fact, the criminal prisoners were treated very gently, "handled with gloves," as they say, or at least with restraint, so as to avoid conflicts. That wasn't always true of the men, however. I know they put them in straightjackets, even though they hid the fact from me. The warden and the medical officer often used to say in a vulgar way: "Let him shit himself, that'll tame him." And they left him for as long as two days in the dungeon.

Romanies, on the other hand, could manage very well and knew all kinds of tricks. For example, they could fake an appendicitis that looked just as described in Jiráska's textbook of surgery, with all the complicated symptoms that appear as a reaction to touch. They were masters of the so-called acute abdomen, that is, sudden abdominal disorders. They must have undergone special training in that field. They were also professionals when it came to simulating suicide and lashing veins, arteries, hanging, heavy bleeding, even from the genitals. This Romany woman was one of those who were caught out only after examination by specialists. They discovered she had a self-inflicted wound and not internal bleeding. Romanies could simulate coughing up blood from the lungs or bleeding from the main arteries. In one case a large needle had been used to pierce a vein. It was eventually discovered that the blood was coming from a wound in the nose before being spat out through the mouth. Everyone was shocked and the guards were worried, as was I. There was blood everywhere and it was only after the needle had been pulled out that it was discovered that there was really no internal bleeding. They used various methods to inflict wounds on themselves: they swallowed nails, glass from the window, bits broken off spoons. Some of them had had so much practice that hardly anything happened to them. They relied on medical help. They wanted to get into hospital or anywhere else where escape would be easier.

Our official doctor was originally M. W., a Jew, I believe. She was exceptionally decent to me, although she wasn't much liked by others. It was in about 1957 that she found I had tuberculosis, and prescribed extra meat rations. Of the other doctors outside the prison, I should also like to mention Ján Gunčaga, who, I believe, had returned from prison and was absolutely delighted when he met me the first time. He immediately made an appointment for me at the municipal hospital to have blood and liver tests and other examinations. He sought every opportunity for us to talk. In his room at the hospital, which he didn't allow the medical officer to enter, we talked a great deal and he showed me his works and publications. Later, his wife acted as our neurologist.

For specialist ear, nose, and throat examinations they began to send us Dr. Marica Kálayová, née Smídová, the sister of my best friend at primary school and for some of the time at secondary school. How she had grown and matured from the little girl I had known! She also used to come to the prison surgery to give a second medical opinion. It was a great pleasure to see such people.

Many specialists valued my professional opinion. I think I was quite well read at that time and in step with the latest medical findings. For that reason they often invited me to take part in consultations. It took a long time for the medical officer to understand that we got all the medical instruments (for example dental forceps, X-ray films, which were in short supply then) as "written-off equipment" mainly thanks to my friendly relations with these doctors. He realized this when he began to go for them himself. They always asked after me and he never came off so well as he did when he went with me. In the end we had a whole series of instruments that we could use for pulling out teeth and roots, although I had no one to teach me and I had only had the opportunity to observe a dentist twice, when I stole a look at how he worked. I did it in prison only when the patient couldn't bear the pain any longer and I couldn't arrange for him to be taken to the dentist in town. But I still didn't know how to deaden the nerve in the lower jaw. It was only when I was in the Prokop labor camp that I learned that properly, along with drilling and the extraction of roots.

It's interesting that even the warders began to come to me to have teeth extracted; I don't know why. Without wanting to, I made our own medical officer, R., suffer quite a bit when he came to me with a broken root. But I must say, he was quite brave. I refused to carry out an extraction for another medical officer, F., on the grounds that he had official, specialized doctors for that. He wanted to show me he could force me to do as he wished, and he sat down in front of the mirror and gripped his tooth with the forceps, without an anaesthetic. He began to twist the tooth and to pull it out. He got his own way, because when I saw his bulging eyes, I had to extract the tooth myself.

In 1957 I had quite a serious attack of sciatica, the compression of a nerve or intervertebral disc in the spine. I almost cried out in pain. Even morphium was no help, or very little. That's why it is nonsense to use morphium to expose malingerers, because it is not always effective. Special medicines, such as Pyrabutol injections, and a hard bed were more effective. I managed to get a table in my room and I lay on it for about a month on one or two folded blankets. It really was effective.

After work, or in the morning, when the medical officer was at a meeting, I could do what I liked. Then the isolation cell had great advantages. It forced me to study, read, meditate, spiritually enrich myself if I didn't want to go mad. Saturdays and Sundays seemed particularly long; I sometimes caught myself postponing my spiritual regeneration exercitations and meditations. I was no longer able to force myself to concentrate as I had before. I usually started with whatever was most difficult when I was studying or meditating, and this later proved useful as an established method. At that time it was Chinese. When F. sent me the book, the governor allowed me to have it, being the only language except Russian that was not considered dangerous. To their minds it was even "progressive." Chinese was so hard that on several occasions I flung the book across the room in anger. It took me months to make head or tail of it. Where what should be and how to read it.

It was such mad drudgery, but I kept reminding myself that our Professor Kolakovič always used to stress the need to master languages, and he himself learned them too. I knew that at any other time or outside prison I wouldn't find time for it, and that at least the basic form of some of these hieroglyphs and how to read them would perhaps remain in my head in case I should ever need it. If I remember rightly, I learned about seven or eight hundred symbols, but I needed at least three thousand. I gradually worked through two textbooks, but people forget what they learn very quickly if they don't revise and use it. What a difference it is now, when it is possible to buy textbooks with recordings of pronunciation.

My program of study also included a number of professional medical textbooks. I used to copy extracts from journals, for example from Praktický lekár, Vnitřní lékařství (The General Practitioner, Internal Medicine), from Časopis lékařů českých and Bratislavské lekárske listy (Journal of Czech Doctors, The Bratislava Medical Journal). I was now allowed a pen, whereas in Mírov I had only a pencil. I was also allowed a watch. I thought up a number of inventions for my specialization as a dermatologist. For example, a simplified, practical "dermatobiopter," as I called it, that is, special scissors for making excisions, cutting out a small piece of skin, because modern diagnostic methods in dermatology are based on histology. I wanted to make it possible for histological diagnoses to be carried out using just one instrument instead of a complicated surgical procedure. I wanted the excision and the application of a clip to close the wound (preferably metal) to be done at the same time, once the skin had been deadened. When I was able to get hold of specialist literature, I saw that these considerations had been logically correct, for in the meantime a foreign firm had come up with such an instrument.

I also thought up some improvements for cross-country skis, to make it easier to walk uphill or on the level. This was because I enjoyed skiing, but I didn't like waiting in a queue for the ski tow. I preferred spending more energy walking uphill. It would save money, too. Another invention I thought of was intended to lessen the risk of injury in the event of a car crash.

I spent the most time — months, in fact, while on remand — thinking about the choice of a so-called "priority" (preferential) international language, that would unite people and save us the trouble of learning several languages if we want to hold our own in the face of world competition or travel around the world at all.

Flu epidemics, which broke out from time to time in the prisons and camps, were usually very unpleasant. Even when kept in isolation, people came into such close contact that nearly everyone caught the virus sooner or later. I once had pneumonia with extremely high temperatures. Even though I am a doctor, I could do nothing to help myself and I was left practically to my own devices. I could not get to the window in the door, there was no one to hand me water or medicines. If I remember rightly, it was penicillin that helped me then, but it left me with diarrhea and exhausted. But they didn't assign anyone to my cell to look after me at least a little.

In this prison I also experienced several campaigns inspired by the programs of political functionaries. One of these, for example, was the "kulak" campaign. Everyone who disagreed with the regime and who owned a bit of land was labelled a "kulak." Then there were the prostitutes. It was a very sad and painful sight to see whole sections of the prison crammed with dozens of fifteen- to eighteen-year-old morally degenerate girls with venereal diseases and vulgar language. They didn't usually behave in a vulgar way towards me, however. Just once, at New Year's, one of them wrote an immoral poem, and the medical officer was very amused by the way I condemned such things.

Adolescent detainees were the saddest chapter of all. Boys from children's homes, various remand centers and reform schools, only fifteen to sixteen years old but sometimes they had already served as many as three sentence for robbery, theft or fraud. They were very self-assured, cruel, hard to control.

There was a very unusual practice in this prison. Women prisoners sometimes got five to seven days holiday, especially at Christmas. It was only later that I learned that these "democratic" holidays for women served to hide pregnancies which arose in the prison, often thanks to the guards. When a woman returned home, she would report her pregnancy and demand an abortion. (By then, as part of a general policy, they had stopped punishing abortions.) Either the women themselves demanded it or the guards, the supposed fathers, forced them into it. I reported one case to the official doctor, M., and I waited to see what stand he would take. I made no secret of the fact that I thought it absurd that the offenses and sins of the powerful should be dealt with like this. I was surprised when he had the woman brought to see him, but maybe he only did it to show he kept to his principles. He told her she could decide freely for herself what to do. As she did not insist on an abortion, he sent her, I believe, to Pankrác prison, where there was a so-called prison maternity clinic with several children, which, from the point of view of international prison rights, is an absolute absurdity: to imprison babies and children who have done no harm to anyone. But his standpoint on this case aroused in me considerable respect.

So far as I can recall my contacts with the rest of the world as a convicted prisoner, I was allowed to write one or two letters a month. I was allowed a visit about once a month. My mother was wonderful in the way she managed to learn "conspirative" methods, gazing at the guard with her eyes and secretly communicating with her mouth or fingers, so I had to laugh to see how "in her old age" she had begun to learn the tricks of criminals.

At her very first or second visit my sister Gitka thrust a bit of paper into my hand. Inside was the Eucharist. Later, however, I twice made a gesture of refusal, because I was afraid it might be desecrated. We called the Eucharist a "greeting from Uncle Julko." Uncle Julko was our name for Krébes, a chaplain from Banská Bystrica, who had had a great influence on our spiritual growth in our childhood. He was originally an engineer and now almost blind. He had had to learn the liturgical texts by heart. He gave excellent sermons, and a large number of people used to go to him for confession. They thought he wouldn't recognize them as he was blind. But that can't have any influence during confession, because the priest cannot tell who is who behind the screen, and anyway one can choose a different confessor each time.

That first password, "a greeting from Uncle Julko," which hadn't been agreed on beforehand, stuck. What a joy it was, but a worry, too. I was terrified that something would happen to it. Later I used wafer medicine capsules as the Eucharist. At that time they were made of real wheat flour, unsweetened and exactly the same in consistency as the wafers generally used for transformation during the Mass. I kept them with the rest of the medicine capsules in a locked box in a locked white suitcase with the dangerous medicines, opiates. In other prisons I used to hide the Eucharist in the spine of certain books that I knew exactly where to find in the library. True to say, during every search I was very afraid they might be desecrated. But it was certainly better than the tiny squares of bread in cigarette paper that I had in Mírov.

My premonition that God had given me the hardest trials at the beginning of my imprisonment was fulfilled. I could bear them when I was still full of strength and energy. I suspected that as time went on prison would get better. When one is almost at the end of one's strength, one should not have such a heavy burden, in case it should destroy one completely. That is why every pain or crisis was accompanied by a feeling of joy that I had overcome the worst and that the easiest would come last — freedom. Every time I went through a spiritual crisis, I promised myself that I would never reproach anyone if he failed, if he gave in. After all, I would have failed a long time before if God had not almost held me by the hand and in fact forced me to stick it out. I resolved never to boast about what I had experienced or withstood. After all, I never bore it perfectly and anyway God was exceptionally merciful to me.

I had a visit from F. She had changed considerably after being released from prison. She had served four or five years, I think. She was thinner, more nervous, but she was very glad to see me. I was so surprised that all I could say was "So you have come after all?" What I meant was: So you managed to at last? She interpreted it as meaning I hadn't wanted her to and that it was unpleasant for me. We were in the warders' sitting room, and on that occasion I saw a television for the first time in my life.

F.'s letters began to arrive at regular intervals, and I liked her tactics very much. Under the pretence of an amorous relationship with a young man, which was something everyone understood, no matter how they hated our convictions and religion, she kept me informed about everything that was going on, especially in the Czech Republic. However, I managed to get from her a declaration that it was really only a tactic on her part, so that there would be no emotional complications at a later date. Nevertheless, there were a couple of times when I wanted to break off contacts with her, as if I had a premonition. But she always prevented me from doing so, usually with the excuse that she was in urgent need of my advice, or by persuading me in some other way. As it was, a formal handshake or embrace could not be just a formal gesture for me, but a source of pleasure and therefore also of pain.

Our parents, father in particular, had changed considerably in the meantime. Before, when everyone had criticized and condemned me, father had been the only one to visit other members of the family and our friends to tell them about my situation and explain my attitude to them. When I flatly refused to make a statement, when I rejected any concessions, protection, clemency, or conditions, he was proud of me. Now, however, obviously worn down by time, his nerves were beginning to weaken, and he himself began to organize all kinds of complaints, applications for release, parcels, advantages, concessions. My parents achieved very little this way, but for them it meant humiliation, rejection, and finally, rebuke from me, too. It only made the situation worse, because the authorities took it as further proof of obdurate hostility. Now father never ceased to put pressure on me to add my voice to his applications for a break in the sentence or leave from prison. In the end I had to warn him that if he didn't stop this, I would go my own way and break off my correspondence and contacts with my family. I didn't know how to convince him otherwise. It was unbearable and more painful than my own imprisonment to see how those near and dear to me were suffering. Only after this resolute gesture did my father and the rest of my family give in.

Once I was sitting next to some convicted prisoners in the cinema. There was someone there from Prague who had spent some time in a camp in the Jáchymov region. Together with some other prisoners, he had been preparing an exhibition in Bratislava and other large towns for the Ministry of the Interior, so I was able to gather some reliable information about my brother prisoners in the camps and how they were suffering. Once more I realized how I was stagnating in that prison, without rights, without changes, without any activity, but also without any feeling of a great common sacrifice. I was, in fact, quite well off. The food wasn't bad, the clothing reasonable, there was no comparison with my time on remand. I had sleep and employment. I was sacrificing practically nothing any more, except perhaps my freedom. There were only the limitations of space, movement, and the obligation to take orders. But that is true of almost every job, although it was somewhat more difficult where I was. That was all.

Meanwhile, my brothers and the priests as well were suffering in bunkers, punishment cells, were taking risks, dying in the mines, working as manual laborers in humiliating conditions, exhausted to the limits of their strength. They would strike, go on hunger strikes, sometimes because of drunken prison warders, and they were fighting against unbearable, illegal conditions. In short, they were fighting, while I was living a peaceful life and slowly adapting myself to it. I was gradually ceasing to testify to my convictions, I was no longer protesting. This realization and increasing isolation finally drove me to request to be transferred to a camp and to physical labor. Preferably mining deep underground. That was what everyone avoided and what they were most afraid of. But, at least for a while, I wanted my hands, legs, joints, bones, my personal risk and humiliation to express a certain solidarity and brotherhood with even the most wretched of these prisoners.

After long delays, approval suddenly came through from the Ministry. According to the internal regulations of the Ministry of the Interior, about which I learned only later, every prisoner should change prisons or camps every year, in order to prevent him from creating a certain favorable atmosphere in his contacts with the warders or civil employees.

I know that my requests upset the prison warden considerably. He made references to a woman doctor in Želiezovce who had kept making similar applications, but in his opinion, it was only blackmail on her part when she didn't get something she wanted. Apparently, when everything had been arranged, she came to him in tears, saying she had not been serious about it and begging him to keep her. In short, he wanted me to stay. Probably because things went as they should in the surgery and there were no scandals.

With the agreement of the Ministry, my place was taken by a doctor sentenced for some kind of profiteering or speculation. After the arrival of the new doctor, medical officer R. began to make me feel that he would be a benefit to the prison. He wanted to show me I was not irreplaceable, which I never thought I was. The new doctor seemed clever to me, but, as I heard later, he was only there for a few months. I don't know whether he couldn't stand it or whether they weren't satisfied with him.

So I began to pack. For the first time, I had had enough books, magazines, and notes in prison. Then the medical officer appeared. He began to sort out my things and wanted to throw most of them away, because he was afraid to leave them with me. All turned out well in the end. The prison warden had all my literature packed up separately and sealed, telling me to send a request for it from wherever I was. It was good diplomacy on his part, but it helped me enormously. Things of mine were preserved which would probably not have survived if I had had them with me.

I said goodbye with rather mixed feelings, because towards the end I could feel they would be glad to get rid of me, that someone was after me. It was probably one of the secret police or a political police agent. Surprisingly enough, so far as I discovered, they gave me a good reference. At least concerning work, not from the point of view of religious belief or political views.

This time during the transport I learned that I was going to Bytíz. They had kept it secret from me, even though I had treated nearly all of them conscientiously, against the regulations, for they should have gone exclusively to their official doctor, an employee of the Ministry of the Interior. The guard escorting me, accompanied by a dog, was regarded with terror by everyone, but he began to talk to me in a very friendly manner. The others joined in too, but maybe only because the journey would otherwise have been a terrible bore for them. When we were approaching Ilava they told me to put on a serious face and keep an official distance.

I only slept one or two nights in Ilava. Then I was escorted through Pardubice to Olomouc. For the first time I was not blindfolded at all. In Pardubice I remembered all our brave women, especially Professor Vacková. Many of them had already been released, but she remained in prison, for up to eighteen or nineteen years, I think. Eventually we arrived at Ruzyň prison in Prague. I no longer looked like a typical prisoner. After seven years in prison I was more seasoned, I had a number of heavy parcels and fairly decent-looking prison clothes. An old hand. I slept in a cell with two or three prisoners and, as before, gathered information. From there we continued on our way at about the end of April 1958, in comfortable, elegant coaches, usually labelled "Excursion," to Příbram and the camp of Bytíz.

Part III

Bytíz Labor Camp

These camps were real concentration camps. The security police were allergic to this term, but when you come to think of it, it really only means the concentration of a large number of people. The Jáchymov camps already had their own reputation. Documentary films had even been made there (*The Hell of Jáchymov*), which were said to have been shown to the American Senate. There were ten or fifteen such camps, belonging to the Jáchymov uranium mines. Each of them had one thousand five hundred to three thousand prisoners, destined for elimination. The term "MUKL" was an abbreviation for "muži určení k likvidaci" — a man destined for liquidation. Or, at least, for long years without a hope of being released even after he had completed his sentence.

In the company of our political prisoners, I soon became more modest. When they asked me what sentence I had been given, I proudly answered: "Fourteen years." This was greeted by the comment: "You people serving only a few months — what's fourteen years? You can stand for ten to fifteen years on a lightning conductor, on one foot, you don't even have to change feet." I thus discovered I had one of the lightest sentences. Most people had twenty years and more, or life imprisonment; some people had received such sentences instead of capital punishment. Most of them had already been in prison for ten years, since forty-eight. But there were prisoners who had been there even longer, from forty-five. These were the so-called "retributionists" — that is, mainly Germans and collaborators.

The first meditations were very moving. By the light of the hundreds of bright lamps of five hundred watts and more that surrounded the camp's perimeter, or under a starry sky, in silence, in the shadow of the watch towers and the guards with their machine guns and automatic rifles. It looked like a huge circus, but instead of wild beasts, there were thousands of suffering humans "behind bars," the fathers of broken, persecuted, stigmatized families, who evening after evening rejoined their children in their thoughts — children who were perhaps suffering as much as they were — and many of them wept.

Here, too, blood was shed by our martyrs, priests and laymen and maybe even some bishops, or at least their sacrifice was sweat, calluses, sickness, pain, humiliation and lack of freedom, in addition to the malign ionizing radiation from the uranium ore. They made this sacrifice for the sake of the Church and other people.

All this suffering was crowded into about twenty barracks, each housing two hundred people, with twenty crammed into each room. The "circus" covered an area of about three hundred by four hundred meters, surrounded by a double line of barbed wire fencing with hidden wires connected to the alarm system, automatic rockets, or even mines, and sniper zones with lower wire fences and various obstacles. The prisoners had to put these up themselves. The same was true of the high watchtowers for their guards and tormenters, as well as their living quarters and some rather more luxurious flats. The latter were just outside the entrance to the camp. There were also outbuildings, storerooms, vegetable gardens, and a pig farm. Near the punishment cells there were solitary confinement cells and quarantine cells for those arriving under escort. That is where they put us on arrival, and I immediately had a taste of what life was like in the labor camp barracks. There were a lot of us in one room. Some were hostile, others malicious and dangerous, but there were also some who would risk their lives for you.

Early next morning they took us off to work, building a stone wall in the farm area. After so many years of isolation in a closed prison I threw myself into this physical work with a willingness and enthusiasm that provoked considerable surprise as well as criticism and indignation from the many who relied more on the principle of "more haste less speed." In short, shirking work was a basic principle for the "mukl" — one didn't want to be overburdened with more and more work, stricter work quotas, and greater exploitation by others.

Above all everyone warned me against working in those dangerous mines and discussed with me all possible illnesses for themselves and for me to help us avoid it. They said it was terrible and dangerous. Death or disablement were common occurrences, especially among beginners. But I wanted to try just that. I wanted to know what the rest of our brothers had to suffer. To shake off at last the "privileges" of a doctor, which though sometimes very unpleasant, seemed to be advantages to the ill-informed. I wanted to extricate myself from the prison services, whose workers were sneered at as the prison nobility.

In the labor camps, however, Christians were also called the nobility and I think that was fairer. It was because they gave the impression of being joyful and free people, as if they were not in prison at all. They used to meet, laugh, sing, pray, and keep together. They grew fonder of each other day by day. It was a wonderful labor camp nobility.

On the Monday we were brought before the work committee, who assigned prisoners to the different places of work. The committee was made up of prison warders and educational, work, and political officers. Most people, with the exception of real invalids, were assigned to the mines. Only a few were fortunate enough to remain above ground. When my turn came, they asked me what I had been in civilian life. "Ah, Doctor, so you'd like to be in the infirmary, wouldn't you?" "No." "No? And what do you want?" "I'd like to try working in the mines." "Well, well!" They looked at each other. "Why did they throw you out of the prison infirmary?" "They didn't, I asked to be transferred to a camp." "What were you sentenced for?" "Catholic Action." "What's that?" "Religious societies." "So you've asked to come here so you can set them up here, too? We know all about that and we'll keep a good eye on you. Just ask what happened to your friends." That was really the worst crime—Catholic religious activities. All those suspected of it were sooner or later kept in the strictest isolation. The isolation cells in Leopoldov, Valdice, Kartouze, and Mírov were particularly notorious. That is why informers were planted in all the rooms, barracks, and places of work.

It is interesting that this antireligious attitude did not involve other religions. Protestants, Orthodox, and, above all, the sects — Jehovah's Witnesses in particular. The latter were specially privileged in comparison with the Catholics. They could happily distribute their writings, publications, Bibles, as if they were deliberately supported in order to create divisions among the Christians. Catholics, as well as other Christians, were sent back to closed jails, brought to trial again, or submitted to fresh investigations by the State Security Police.

At that time in Bytíz they were just purging the camp of the remaining priests. Before, dozens of priests, known or incognito, had been serving their sentences there.

The Mass was served "in secret" in certain barracks every Sunday. Sometimes even on work days, in the presence of fifteen to two hundred prisoners. It was hard to keep it secret, even though our meetings were well guarded by our people on duty.

My appearance before the work committee continued like this: "You've even got some kind of tuberculosis." "That's already cured." I was only taking PAS (para-aminosalicylic acid) and extra food rations. At my request, the prison doctor had reclassified me from the third to the first category. "Well, if you really want to go down the mines, you're mad, you don't know what it's like." "I do know and I want to try it. As a doctor, I don't think I can treat the miners effectively, unless I try out all the kinds of work they do, whether physical or otherwise." "Then we'll put you down there." They looked very doubtful, though, and in the end they didn't send me there, I don't know why. Whether because they wanted to keep me in reserve as a doctor, or whether they forgot, or were afraid that I would have a greater influence on the miners. Maybe it was simply that they didn't want to oblige anyone. They didn't transfer me even in response to my later demands. As it was, I discovered that they had reclassified me without my knowledge to the second category, in order to justify the fact that I was not working in the mines. Thus it happened that I never did any mining.

Only once did I manage to persuade a friend of mine, Láďa Paulů — "Střelec" — the leader of one group of miners, to take me down to the pit in secret. He got me some mining clothes and boots, a carbide lamp and a helmet, but just the very day I was to work in the mine, they took me away to another camp.

This time, though, I came away from the work committee with a feeling of exhilaration. Everyone said, "You're crazy. You'll have second thoughts when you lose a leg, an arm, or your sight." My brother Christians warned me in a similar vein. They were very much against the idea. None of them ever understood how a prisoner, and a doctor in particular, could enjoy physical work. I was very proud, though, to be a real prisoner, a manual laborer. I hadn't managed to try this before I went to prison, even though I had very much needed to understand such people's mentality, in order to be able to spread the Gospel. Professor Kolakovič always stressed: "Until you have the workers on your side, you have nothing. Your work as an apostle isn't worth much."

On Sunday, like the resourceful "mukls" we were, we secretly slipped out of the "reception" barracks and visited the camp. We went to see a film or a group of musicians. For the first time I found myself in a real penal camp, with a relatively free regimen, in the center of prison life. This was a completely different world with a life of its own. An archipelago in the middle of the sea. It took me some time to get used to it. Out of habit, being accustomed to a detention and investigation prison, I would look around to see who was following me, who was watching me. I kept expecting to be asked whom I had met and what we had talked about. This made me over-cautious and reserved at first. Theoretically, there was good reason for this, because there were plenty of informers everywhere and the Camp Commandant's office received reports about every silly little triviality. That's why the true "mukl" protected himself against the stoolies with the only weapons he had available: boycotting informers, sending them to Coventry. Some prisoners got even with informers "manually" — with their fists. In this respect, there were two things that amazed me. The first was that many Christians and decent people were among those who let their feelings run away with them and took physical revenge, though they called it "self-defense." But what amazed me even more was that people of good character, who had endured a great deal, allowed themselves to be coerced into becoming informers. At first they no doubt only answered the questions the political workers and secret police happened to ask. Just yes or no. They didn't reveal anything they could possibly keep secret. But many of them gradually lost their nerve, when after years of being in a unchanging, hopeless situation, that miraculous liberation they had counted on just did not materialize. They gave in under pressure or in the hope that they would be allowed to contact their families or protect them from persecution. They also signed on in the hope of an earlier release. They passed on information both by word of mouth and in writing, in the form of a letter put in the postbox — ostensibly to be censored, but with a previously agreed mark on it. However, as the Scriptures say, "there is nothing covered, that shall not be revealed; nor hidden, that shall not be made known." So it sometimes happened that such a letter was found before it could be put in the box. And suddenly everyone was reading it. Maybe such information was occasionally discovered on purpose, when a disciplinary officer wanted to get rid of a stoolie who had become troublesome. It was also the best means of blackmailing somebody if he didn't wish to cooperate any longer.

My first meetings with my brother Christians were marked, apart from great joy, by the caution and reserve I have already mentioned, although Vlado Jukl ("Voloďa") and I couldn't tear ourselves away from each other. People even began to seek me out of their own accord, because the news of my arrival had run ahead of me. In the clothes and supplies stores they sometimes even knew the names of those to be transported. In this way I met up with previous fellow prisoners, or with their fellow prisoners who had heard about me. I remember how in Bratislava a thirty-five-year-old man hugged me joyfully in the dark of the X-ray room. I had never seen him before, but he had been in the same prison for a long time with Ján Gunčaga. When he heard the name Krčméry, he cried out: "Are you Silvo? How wonderful!" Here was an example of the real solidarity felt by prisoners and Christians.

Various funds were created from the prisoners' scanty allowances — their "pocket-money" and every decent new arrival was given some support. That is why I found a supply of milk had already been paid for me for a whole month in advance — by Tomáš, with whom I had shared a basement cell in Příční Street in Brno. He was beside himself with joy, even though he was otherwise a serious and dignified fifty-year-old father of a large family. In fact, I had to cancel my order later because the milk didn't agree with me, although I hadn't had problems with it in the past. It must have been a side-effect of the radiation.

As soon as I had had time to look around and get used to my surroundings, I concentrated on meeting people. I made use of every opportunity, whether it was in our room, in the corridor, in the area outside which had been strictly assigned to each building, but which very few people kept to, although we could be sure that the stoolies kept a close watch to see who went where and in whose company he was often to be seen, with whom he was friendly. It was also possible to contact people on the way to work, to lunch, supper and, above all, to the roll-call. As some duty officers had problems with counting, this sometimes took hours. At such times we made the best of the opportunity to talk to whoever was next to us, or we went to stand beside whoever we wanted to talk to. After the evening roll-call it was possible, though forbidden, to talk in the lavatory, in the washroom, in the corridor, in another barracks, but this meant we had to take precautions to make sure we were not seen by the stoolies. Whoever was "on duty" in the barracks would shout "alarm" or "vermin" at the sight of a uniform approaching even from a considerable distance, but this could provoke harsh reprisals.

The most wonderful thing was that you were in contact with a large group of people and relatively free to move about and therefore you could choose your own company. Here friendships were made for life, maybe they were firmer than in any other environment, the family included. There was so much work to be done spreading the Gospels, that it was impossible to manage it all. For this reason it was very rare for an active Christian believer to experience an inner crisis or despair.

Newspapers were more readily available and there was a fair selection. From the point of view of the news, they were uniform dailies, but at least we could follow and consider political developments. We learned not only personal psychology, but the psychology of the press. We learned to read between the lines and not to take things that could cheer us up at face value. In connection with the false hopes of many prisoners, one warder had his own "maxim:" "That's just what you'd like, isn't it? To eat, sleep, squander, and wait for a coup!" But he said it in a much more vulgar way.

What was even more appreciated was that we had managed to smuggle in our own religious literature. A Missal, Bible, or at least one of the Gospels was hidden down the mine. Some people prepared liturgical texts for every Sunday by copying them through carbon paper. I realized how much these brothers risked when I myself tried to write something in the midst of the noise and continuous presence of prisoners of varied character, including possible informers. There were also a few well-hidden books under the floor-boards, the roof, and mainly in the mine shafts, or kept by civilian miners. Sometimes someone was caught and put in irons and did not return to his family, because he was once more accused of "high treason." Some people got up to all kinds of daring tricks to save our books, for example, Vojto K., then still a young boy, now the father of a family. On one occasion when two warders stopped him, he had the Scriptures hidden under his shirt. They had obviously had a tip-off. However, he charged at them, crashing his head into the chest of one of them, and flew out of the window like a shot. By the time they had raised the alarm, caught him and given him a good hiding, the Scriptures were in safe hands. He didn't give anything away.

The worst thing was when we had an informer among us, or a fellow prisoner gave in under pressure. This must have been how the hiding place under the floor of the infirmary containing about twelve books was discovered. We also had Eucharist duties, which took place at an agreed time when we were walking outside. The Eucharist was kept hidden in medicine boxes, but our friends sometimes carried it under their clothes and defended it even at the risk of torture or suddenly having to consume it. We used to have both ordinary as well as recited Masses without a priest and in small groups. With Voloďa's help we even managed to reconstruct the Eastern liturgy, which we also passed round in written form. We sung it under our breaths when walking in the yard every Sunday and often even on working days.

We had Gospel societies here, as in civilian life. They mainly involved young people. I remember Janko S., Vojto K., and Alfonz M. (nicknamed "Moki"), who composed a royal sonnet about the Ascension of the Virgin Mary.

I have a clear memory from that time of the curious atmosphere that arose in connection with the election of the new Pope. We prayed intensively for them all, but we didn't know much about Roncalli. We felt a little disappointed when he was elected, although we put our trust in the

Lord. It was a pleasant surprise He had prepared for us in the person of Roncalli — John XXIII.

There were even ecumenical groups, because we had excellent relations and good experience with all other Christians, with the exception of the Jehovah's Witnesses, who cannot be considered Christians. The Evangelicals included, for example, Novotný, Vráťa, Svačina. We used to have special joint prayers and meetings, for example at the festival of Cyril and Methodius. They were very willing to join in this commemorative prayer meeting, even though Protestants have reduced respect for the saints to the minimum. But they really were sincere brothers in this distressing situation.

We also had brief courses in philosophy, theology, and Bible studies. It was also necessary to discuss the most frequent, most burning, most topical questions, including those connected with the explanation and defense of our faith or with other disciplines. I had always given priority to the practical approach, but here the others also preferred short discussions. We divided the themes of the schooling among us, but we had to work without libraries, without materials to assist us, and that made our task very difficult, because we didn't always get a good opportunity to concentrate in silence and we had to work in secret. In the cramped conditions of our sleeping quarters or in the common rooms, it was impossible to concentrate. That is why we held short, intensive courses. In civilian life we used to call a good paper like this an "O.K." or "MLEKUP" — "mlecí kurz priekopníkov" ("crash course for pioneers," something similar to what we have now — KLAP "Kurz laického apoštolátu" ("a course for lay apostles"). I was assigned the following themes: the secret of the Holy Trinity, questions of free will and God's foresight, predestination. Later I had the theme of the origin of the world and life, including from the biological point of view, the theory of evolution, and so on.

Our closest colleagues were involved, too — Vlado Juko and Jozef Myslivec, nicknamed "Moufflon." The latter was exceptionally learned's he could improvise from memory large parts of the Eastern liturgy, of which he was a great admirer, as he was of the idea of Christianizing the East. He could deliver a homily and reflection on any topic whatsoever, with practically no prior preparation. Then there was Franta Boublík, an older, sensible, very dedicated man. However, Dr. K., the camp doctor, was a different case, the prisoners themselves nicknamed him "Vraždan" (a pun indicating "murderer, butcher"). Most of them hated him they had the impression that he didn't try much to help them, that he behaved in a high-handed way and also had the reputation of being a police informer. I was told he repeatedly refused to treat P., a prisoner who eventually committed suicide, throwing him out of the surgery, even though he had severe abdominal pains and blood in his stools. P. then hanged himself right in front of the infirmary. When I came, I was given his bed, a top bunk.

Later I learned that one of my roommates, most probably a Romany who claimed to be a political prisoner, had begun to warn my other roommates to be careful what they said in front of me, because, he said, I was probably a spy. He seemed to be very radical in his views — he used to say all communists should be hanged and so on. These radical opinions, however, were just typical of informers, because they felt safe and could afford to provoke in this way. It eventually came to light that he really was one, which was a great relief to me, because it was very difficult to defend oneself against such slander.

People were often moved around in the camp, which meant a search was carried out. We were spared this in the infirmary, because we were counted separately and the searches were of our rooms or of a whole barracks. People were either moved from one barracks to another, or two, three barracks at a time were moved. But the most frequent form was the "celotáborový stehung," where the whole camp was moved around. This happened about once every one to three months. It usually took the whole of a Saturday or Sunday and it had its own ritual.

Everyone had to line up outside with his things wrapped up in a blanket. Regardless of rain, snow, wind, or heat wave. I wanted to buy a suitcase, because I used to have to carry my things in boxes, mainly margarine boxes. But for a "beginner" prisoner it was an impossible dream. Moving began with a ruthless search, first of each of the barracks. They looked in every nook and cranny, in every straw mattress and blanket. This was followed by a body search. They piled everything into the middle of the room, or sometimes in front of the hut. It was a terrible sight. Food mixed with clothes — jam and butter together with shirts. We often had to strip naked. I was told that the guards had been fond of doing this in the winter, outside in the yard, in the wind and rain. The guards had trampled on these miscellaneous piles with their boots or they would pour water on them, ruining the coffee, tea, and tobacco.

Now they concentrated mainly on drinking glasses. They loved breaking them. This was because they could be misused as weapons or as an instrument of suicide. It was personal letters, though, that they relished most. We were allowed to have with us a maximum of one and for us this was often our most precious and most carefully hidden possession. They also destroyed family photographs and searched for "submarines" (immersion heaters, mostly not the real thing, but improvised) and mess-tins, which we held over the flames of a Petri stove in the washroom. The older prisoners had a nose for these searches, which saved most of our literature. You could get ten days "in the hole," that is, in the punishment cell, for textbooks of German or English. At one time you could have got the same for Russian, too, but by that time these were allowed in Bytíz, and Russian was even recommended and taught. I took advantage of this, which many of my fellow prisoners reproached me for harshly. They hated Russian with a hate that was really unchristian.

Languages were the most popular hobby of the intellectuals. One of my fellow inmates learned four languages well in three years. I could judge that from his French. But he slaved away at it, studying all the time: in the queue for meals, coffee, during the search before work and at work. It affected his nerves and I think he overdid it. With a slightly slower tempo and intensity it was possible to achieve the same results without damaging one's health. I was not allowed to study Chinese here, and in this camp I didn't get round to my own medical studies. On the other hand I made use of every journey, every head count, every search, every roll-call to practice conversation in foreign languages. I sometimes even repeated the prayers of the rosary on Sundays in various languages.

In about July or August I was moved to the last barracks on the left (looking uphill). It was the only one with a concrete base and it was regarded as a privilege to live there, even though it had no other advantages. One of those I remember living with there was Jirka H., who as a kind of desperate joke, founded a "Cannibals' Club." He was a kind-hearted, decent fellow, although the others often declared he was mad. The "Cannibals' Club" was a bit of escapist fun, a parody of absurd communist ideology. I can still remember several stages in the program. The first stage was to eat all your enemies, the second stage was to eat all your friends, the third stage was to eat one another. The greeting, five fingers raised with your palm outward, symbolized the eating of all the five continents. I found it difficult to believe when the security police took this seriously and investigated it, as they did another similarly absurd group, called "Harem." They treated it as an illegal organization, an anti-state group with a cover name.

In the new room I later became acquainted with another good young fellow. His name was B. and he had close connections with an unusual, at that time unofficial, Catholic movement, known by the name of God's

Work. (This was not the same as the well-known Opus Dei.) It was a society that arose as a result of the alleged appearance of the Virgin Mary to a girl named Libuša A. near Prostějov in Moravia. I met her at a later date, but I felt considerable mistrust because of the accompanying atmosphere of spiritualism and sectarianism. I was interested in the basic beliefs of the society, so I met with its leader, Vlastík S., who made a very good impression on me. Apart from a deep respect for the Virgin Mary, he was a practicing Christian and an apostle. He could be judged by the fruit he bore.

I was assigned to the construction of shaft No. 9 or 12. This was therefore work on the surface. The leader of the work gang was B. Senior and the foreman was a young alcoholic, about thirty years old. They were quite kind to me. Maybe partly because before work and during it I spent many hours advising people how to stay healthy and treat their illnesses. At first my job was to secure the loads to be lifted by a crane. The crane operator was quite a good boy, a Slovak. He was exceptionally popular because he had managed to escape from Ruzyň prison. Whole loads of bricks, concrete, and wheelbarrows had to be prepared. I did this with Karl A. He was a typical criminal prisoner and pretty inconsiderate. He did "spare" me somewhat, though. Clearly because, although I was a doctor, I did physical labor and didn't lounge around, as he said, in the camp infirmary. He was also a well-known stoolie.

I refused to do lighter work, which the gang leader and my brothers wanted to arrange for me on account of my having had tuberculosis. Later K., a carpenter, let me join his gang, erecting scaffolding. I didn't feel it was "easier" work at all, but I could earn more there. It was exhausting, dragging planks, boards, and heavy iron poles twenty meters long, which had to be shifted and lifted up to thirty meters in the air. I sweated a lot, and the heights made me feel giddy, so I moved along the scaffolding with great uncertainty and hesitation. I can't understand why I never slipped and fell. I did have an accident, however, at that time. When the scaffolding was being taken down I was supposed to make sure it didn't injure anyone on the ground. I was meant to keep clear the area where the planks fell. It was partly my fault. I was talking to someone and forgot what I was meant to be doing. One of my work mates threw a number of boards down from about the third floor without looking first. One of the planks hit me in the chest and knocked me to the ground. Fortunately the others fell a bit further away. I was in a state of shock, with a concussion and chest wounds. It was qualified as an injury at work, but I was only put on sick leave for the few hours left to the end of the shift. After that I got even worse fits of giddiness and headaches, sometimes lasting for as long as a month. My work mate was reprimanded for this and I had to speak up for him. But they criticized him for other things, too, especially that he speeded up the tempo just to make more money, while not having any consideration for other people.

Later I dug ditches for sewers, shifted soil, leveled the ground, and the like. Whenever I could, I joined Jan, from the Greek-Catholic group. He taught me to plaster, because I was doing a plastering course at the same time. Sometimes I joined "Střelec," Láďa Paulů, whom I have already mentioned before. He taught me arc welding. I have vivid memories of his teaching methods. He banged every weld with a hammer and if it wasn't firm, he gave me an "educational" slap in the face, with the comment: "Learning is suffering, you'll have to get used to that." Later, he let me join his work gang building shaft No. 10. It was possible to learn more there and earn even better wages. It was at last a complete work team where one gang built the whole building. First a garage, then a changing room and shower room, with all the work from bricklaying to plastering. It was cheaper for the firm and it was better for us, to. It avoided having to put up and take down the scaffolding three times instead of once, the radiators were covered while the plastering was being done and could be easily cleaned afterwards, and so on.

However, I could never come to terms with the fact that I had never been down a real pit and never experienced work in the galleries at different levels underground, in the chutes or on the face or veins.

The employees of the Ministry of the Interior, as I mentioned before, were given nicknames by the prisoners, some of which were very fitting and some which weren't. The Camp Commandant had, for incomprehensible reasons, the quite pleasant name of "Taťulda" (an affectionate name for "Dad"). A dreaded instructor had the nickname of "Schöne Hans," Handsome John. He really was the epitome of a handsome man, complete with mirror and comb. Then there was "Shaft horse," whose appearance earned him his name. We also had a "Black Peter" (the name of a card game). And "Mephistopheles," who was coarse and malicious. Then there was the "Frog king." "Tryskáč" ("Jet") was a man who walked terribly fast and would appear unexpectedly in one place, then another. The next elite group was the camp's staff, recruited from among the prisoners. They were careerists hated by the others and most of them were stoolies.

In this camp I had "camp money" for the first time — paper tickets used instead of banknotes. They were marked from one heller to fifty crowns, each camp having its own stamp. The majority of the prisoners, however, were only given half or a small part of their pocket money. There were big deductions for various dues and those who could preferred to send some of what they earned home.

The canteen worked properly; on occasions it was even possible to buy fruit. Some groups bought large quantities and then traded with it. We took it in turns to do the shopping for those in our room.

Under the heading of "Prisoners' Cultural Activities" all kinds of groups were organized, mainly for propaganda purposes and activity reports. We boycotted most of them, especially the educational ones, which were very much influenced by the fanatical program for re-education, full of lies, hypocrisy, and careerism. Some prisoners even refused to participate in vocational courses, such as the use of mining machinery and other courses, although I personally think that was a pity. Then there was the music society, the rhythmic group, volleyball, "legball," and basketball. After an exhausting shift a hundred, if not a thousand, meters under the ground, people would come up to the surface and then spend another two, three hours enthusiastically chasing a ball. I sometimes played volleyball, too.

I also learned a few of the basic holds and defensive throws of judo from Standa K. from the town of Písek, who was a junior champion of the Republic. We did it in secret, though, in the cellar under the kitchen. For the most part, however, there was little time for such relaxation and at that time I was pretty weak physically. When Voloďa and I wished to meet, we went to a film together. At that time television was only for the privileged. It was a technical innovation.

Meal tickets were also used as part of our "re-education." We were divided according to our performance at work into three categories. The first was for those who did not meet the work quotas. The second was for average workers and the third for those who exceeded the quotas at least 130 or 140 percent. Few people managed this, because the quotas were very high. Otherwise the food was bearable so far as taste was concerned and fairly good. Especially when we could buy something to supplement it. I concentrated most on fruit and vegetables.

The morning reveille was at five, but it differed according to the shift. The first shift was from six in the morning to two in the afternoon, the second, from two to ten in the evening, the third, from ten to six. When they were leaving or returning from work, there were very few people who showed any consideration for others who were sleeping. Maybe because they themselves were so tired. They would turn on the light, smoke, or talk. For the most part we used this time of waking for meditation or private conversation. When we went to work, those who had been mining on the night shift were just returning. We were checked at the side entrance. Everyone had to say his name and take his hat off to the guard. Then we went to our place of work along the road above the camp.

Here, too, I was in contact with a Jehovah's Witness. He was from near the Hungarian border. Unfortunately, a typical sectarian — seemingly virtuous, affable and good, but only in order to win people over to his faith. At first he pretended to be very kind and helpful, but later he showed his intolerance to the point of hatred for Christians and above all for the Catholic Church. According to their interpretation of the Apocalypse, the Church is a shameless concentration of all the filth and sins of the whole world. He introduced me to their leader, a preacher, K. The latter was only better versed in the theory and in our teachings, which is obviously the reason why he had introduced me to him, when he himself was unable to produce further arguments. However, we made absolutely no progress in our discussions. On the contrary, when we went to extremes, he confessed that he preferred materialists and atheists or even communists to Catholics. They formed cliques, supporting each other very well, in addition to working to spread their faith. They knew how to suffer bravely. They all refused to work in the uranium mines, because they refused to participate in the production of atomic weapons. For this they had to stand for hours, sometimes in their underclothes, on the snow and ice in the sniper zone. It was unusual for any of them to give in. But I am afraid that the main reason was the psychological pressure which the members of the sect put on each other. Later the security police invited the leaders of this sect over from Switzerland and made some kind of written agreement with them. They explained to them, for propaganda purposes, that the uranium was not intended for the production of weapons, but for medical purposes, for various kinds of radiation equipment for the treatment of cancer. After signing this "agreement" the Jehovah's Witnesses were not only tolerated but even directly supported in their activities — in order to make divisions among the Christians. However, this clearly showed the instability of churches not founded by Christ, because they are actually dependent on such ephemeral agreements. All their sacrifices, which may have cost many lives, were in fact wasted, because they were based on a fiction, as are their teachings as a whole.

Of course, from the very beginning they received far more lenient sentences than the Catholics. For the most part two or three years, like the "Alsatians" (the criminals), and their leaders got up to five, in exceptional cases, ten years, whereas most of our leaders were given twice this or life imprisonment.

It was interesting how arguments were used against Catholics that they must have known were absolute lies, inventions, mere propaganda. For example, they copied whole pages of Alighier Tondi's book *The Jesuits,* using it as the main argument against the Church. They forgot to add that Alighier Tondi, who wrote this book against his own Jesuits, later renounced the whole book. I saw him later in a photograph, kneeling in the Church of St. Peter, face to the ground, in penitence for allowing himself to be so misguided. For us this book was very valuable from another point of view: it contained whole passages quoted from the exercises of St. Ignatius, guidance for meditations, and also thoughts from his other writings.

A separate chapter could be written about the fatal accidents that took place in the mines. They provoked the greatest agitation. In the night, or in the early hours of the morning, they would bring back the dead body, or only what remained of it, wrapped up in a sheet on a stretcher. Everyone would come running up. Who was it? Which friend was no longer alive? It was also a reminder from God. We felt His nearness through the nearness of death. In civilian life such a reminder from God is usually lost in the clamor of superficial interests. They were often terrible accidents and nearly always they were partially caused by a loss of nerve. People who had been in prison for a considerable time in these inhuman conditions of terror and insecurity used to have long-lasting premonitions of death.

Voloďa already had an organized group here, mainly made up of natural scientists, mathematicians, and physicists, including people who had been converted or those who were preparing for conversion. He occasionally called on me to speak to them or have discussions with them. They used a well-tried "procedure." We sat around the bottom part of a bunk bed with blankets hung from the top part, so that we were hidden inside and thus relatively isolated from the disturbing surroundings. Then they made the inevitable tea in a five-liter saucepan or jar.

Some prisoners had begun to succumb to drug abuse in an endeavor to stupefy their minds, to avoid "being a human" for a while. For example, they used to smoke a "lungbuster," Taras Bul'ba pipe tobacco rolled into cigarettes, such tobacco not being intended for this purpose. They inhaled thirty to fifty of these a day. If that wasn't enough for them, they added all kinds of quite unbelievable ingredients. The old lags used to call it "kurel" — a deformation of the French word *couleur,* a thick, colored concentrate. To make the above-mentioned "tea," two or three packets of Taras Bul'ba were put in that five-liter jar, together with Pitralon after-shave, toothpaste and all kinds of medicaments, mainly Yastils (anti-asthmatic pills) which in that quantity were dangerous to a point of being lethal. Sometimes three to ten Yastils were used, if they could be got hold of. It was a mush which doped everyone to the point where his eyes bulged and he walked in an abnormal manner. We tried to help them, give them some spiritual, moral support, in order to keep them from these perversions.

Vlado and I were particularly happy when one day some friends in the escort department asked us: "Do you know Dr. S.?" And it really was S. in all his glory, but with grey hair, which he had acquired during his one or two years in the detention and investigation prison. He was very pale, as people usually were who had been in a closed prison. He rushed in on us with all his impracticability — he had only been there a week when he first came into conflict with the guards. They picked on him and began to persecute and bully him. When we first met we just hugged each other for several minutes, and then we went over and over again how the investigation had gone. We explained various written records and confessions. S. kept repeating, as if he was in a dream: "I had to tell them something. They kept wanting something, nothing was enough for them. I even confessed to the espionage center. I thought it was shameful anyway and that the truth would come out in court. And then, to be honest, I had moments when I could no longer distinguish between reality and hallucinations. To this very day, it seems to me that we sat together in some room. But it's possible that it was not an espionage center, but just some editorial office or the JOC headquarters." That was S. all over! We can be thankful, though, that God preserved him for us at least like this. His motto from his period of interrogation was passed around among the prisoners: "I'll sign everything, but I won't sign that I'll leave the Church or that I'll give up Christ."

How we three, leaders of this great movement in fact, had needed to meet! It was really arranged by God, because no matter how hard we tried, we couldn't have organized it like this in Bytíz. But as soon as we had clarified these main matters and had outlined our plans for the future, he was quickly taken away from us again.

I also came to know Pavol P., the son of a Calvinist minister, about twenty years of age. He was a deeply convinced Christian, and it could be said that we understood each other better than many Catholics. We became very close. He was also learning languages and various prayers in them. I believe he is in Switzerland now and actively working for the ecumenical movement. Stando Kosík introduced me to František S. He was very interested in the East and learned the Russian Gospel by heart from me. He had received a sentence of about eight years for some criminal offense, so he was living with the "Alsatians" in a barracks with a freer regimen.

It was very difficult to find a way of mixing with the "Alsatians." They shut themselves off from us and behaved scornfully towards us, which may have covered a great deal. For example, when winter came and we didn't have any wood to light a fire, we used to slip a few sticks into our bags and take them back to the camp with us from our places of work. (By then I, too, had a real prisoner's bag. I got it from Láďa Střelec and when I left, I gave it to Vlado Záborský.) During the search at the gate, they particularly enjoyed making us tip every single splinter of wood out of our bags and then they gathered them up for themselves, as they lived in the first barracks inside the gate.

One more interesting detail. At Christmas the criminals used to be in a particularly mawkish mood. On one occasion, one or other of them began to dream aloud in a very touching way, saying how lovely it would be now at home in their village. Silence all around, just carols and candles, the family would gather round the tree and then go to midnight Mass together. And what was the conclusion to these "reflections"? "That would be a wonderful time to burgle, wouldn't it? What a pity!"

When my sister Gabika was to have her wedding, the police received some applications to visit me. Schöne Hans, our political censor, summoned me, but we didn't come to an agreement. He wanted some compromising declaration and when I did not agree, he wouldn't allow me any visits.

But I did have at least one. My mother, probably F., but maybe Gabika, too. We met on that occasion in a special house for this purpose, quite a way from the camp. I received a greeting from Uncle Julka. (He died about that time, actually.) But afterwards I reproached myself for not making better use of that visit, because they left us to talk together quite freely, and the guard was even called away for a while. However, it could have been a trick to catch me smuggling something into the camp. After a visit there was usually a specially strict and thorough search at the gate, sometimes with disciplinary punishments.

I think my next move came just in time. I had begun to get around too much and the authorities had begun to keep too close a watch on me. I finally left Bytíz sometime between September and November 1958.

I later heard that five years after I left, part of Bytíz camp, including the kitchen and mess hall, had plunged into a pit over a hundred meters deep when the ground caved in. A number of my fellow prisoners died there, the majority of whom could not be brought to the surface or identified.

So I was transferred once more. I arrived in Ruzyň, the first "stop-off" on the way. In the meantime it had been changed into a transit prison. We slept three or four to a cell, where before they had kept one prisoner in strict isolation. I learned that I was going to the dreaded Jáchymov region and I tried to gather some information about it. The bus journey from Prague to Ostrov nad Ohří, the central Jáchymov camp, was more relaxed. I was the only one in the whole of the group under escort to be handcuffed. The kind of prisoners in jail had gradually changed. They had shorter sentences and there were few political prisoners. Towards evening I was dying to go to the lavatory. I tried in vain to persuade them I couldn't hold my urine any longer, but they didn't stop. I had with me my first cardboard suitcase, bought in Bytíz for about twenty-three crowns.

Part IV

Jáchymov District –
Prokop Labor Camp near Horní Slavkov

That night they hurried us into the escort barracks. It must have been in "C," the central camp in the Jáchymov district. In spite of my protests, the camp staff prisoners took away all my books. It was only the next day, when the barber discovered that I was a doctor and realized they might need me, that they began to behave a bit more decently. But they didn't return my books. They only changed my torn clothes for better ones. They were obviously still stealing the food intended for the new arrivals, because it was only after we complained to the Camp Commandant that we got at least minimum rations of cold food.

I immediately made friends with young Stano S. He was one of us, a Christian. He must have heard of me, because he was very open and told me all about Prokop camp, an awful place, recently reopened and said to have the worst conditions. I don't think that information was quite accurate. My long years of experience had already taught me that all camps and prisons are very much the same. One place had better food, another worse company, worse cell mates or warders, elsewhere there was more bullying or a tougher regimen. I had hardly had time to dictate some of our litanies to Stano (probably on the subject of humility), when they took him away.

When it came to "better" or "worse" camps, I adhered to one principle. If I found that the new place was much worse than the one before, I told myself: "Well, I'm a prisoner, I'm bound to find myself in worse conditions sometimes. I can't always expect things to get better." But if I had got there through my own initiative or at my own request, I reproached myself for a long time for being to blame.

A smart, dark-haired second lieutenant came to fetch me from the escort cell. The prisoners called him "Big-arsed Jojo." It was Second Lieutenant C., whom I came into contact with nearly the whole time I was there, that is, over a period of several years. We got on relatively well together, but I sometimes felt it was just a tactic on his part. At times he was very good and fair, and he stood up for me when others attacked me. But at other times he succumbed to the information and pressure of various malicious prisoners and members of the security police.

When I declared that I would act only in accordance with the principles of medical science and my conscience, he said that was how he thought it should be and that I would be under the surveillance of the official doctor. The latter was a lieutenant colonel from Plzeň, who only came to the camp once in one to four weeks. He tried to deal with everything only on paper, without the patients and sometimes even without the medical officer.

In response to my refusal to force-feed hunger strikers, he said he would deal with them in a different way. He would take them to hospital or to "C" — the central camp. But, anyway, I would see that those on hunger strike here were all good-for-nothings who just wanted to get advantages for themselves.

By then Prokop camp near Slavkov was far smaller than it had been. At the beginning of the fifties it was said to have had about two thousand five hundred prisoners. Then it was closed down and now it was being reconstructed. When I was there, it had about four to eight hundred prisoners. The inmates were no longer used in the mines. There were only gangs of building workers, who traveled under escort fifty or sixty kilometers every morning to various building sites. Some remained behind to work on the reconstruction of the camp. The fences around had to be completed, as well as the administration building, where I did a bit of plastering just for the exercise.

My arrival at the camp infirmary was somewhat depressing. New surroundings, unknown dark, dirty rooms, the staff beds were almost alongside the patients', and most of the staff were disgusted with the situation. There were still a few political prisoners, but only about ten or twenty altogether. Hardly anyone you could make friends with.

There was a dentist there already, Dr. O., a terrible pessimist. But we got on well together and he livened up a bit thanks to our friendship. He was glad he didn't have to check the food and hygiene any more, as any comments he made were just signed and nothing changed anyway. He thought his fellow prisoners and the warders were terrible louts. He was very happy to hand over these duties and retreat to his surgery, where he did as little as possible, read, and waited for a change in the situation or an amnesty.

The orderly — a prisoner named Z. — was more energetic, and it is true, he did protect the political prisoners to some extent, but, like the dentist, he tried to pass the buck and keep on the right side of everyone and to avoid any conflicts. They often did this behind my back, so I got no support from them when I tried to establish an open approach.

The very next day after my arrival, I criticized the food and the head cook threw me out of the kitchen. He denied this at headquarters and preventively filed an accusation against me, so I was immediately summoned to see a young junior lieutenant, a real swaggerer, and then a security officer, Lieutenant B. They lay into me and threatened to give me what for if I was going to make difficulties in the camp. The junior lieutenant was particularly indignant, allergic as he was to the "intelligentsia" and political prisoners, which I had the opportunity to see on several occasions after that.

A change did take place, though, in the kitchen. That loutish cook had to leave his post, although mainly because he had been getting up to all kinds of shady doings. But later, as he was obliging towards the authorities, he became a gang leader. Then he was "treated" in the camp infirmary for simulated concussion. I tried in vain to show him Christian love and forgiveness, even though it cost me considerable self-restraint, but it had no effect on his hatred and churlishness.

The treatment of prisoners improved a little after the XXth Congress of the Soviet Communist Party, but we didn't feel it much, especially as the type of prisoner coming to the camp changed — the political prisoners and other decent prisoners disappeared and violent ones began to form the majority. For us this environment was often worse than the earlier period of terror, when all decent prisoners regarded themselves as one family and lasting friendships were formed.

One assistant from the Commandant's office, a dark-haired, youngish sergeant, liked to push me around and humiliate me by insisting on the formal greeting. The medical officer, a warder named P., on the other hand, tried to make himself very "important" by reducing orders for medicines or discharging patients from the infirmary or restricting walks in the fresh air for people in the infirmary to the little space in front of it, even though everyone else was allowed to move round the camp freely.

The most dangerous person in the camp was the deputy chief security officer, Second Lieutenant H., known as "Little Tonda." (My memories of him date mainly from my second stay in Prokop.) Another was the chief security officer, Lieutenant B., "Big Tonda."

In particular I had problems with the camp service staff. This elite group of prisoners usually included the doctor, which is why I often preferred to volunteer for physical labor. They were frequently ruthless careerists and opportunists, with a considerable talent for pretense, and extremely hypocritical. Most of them held privileged positions in return for regularly passing on information and intriguing against others. They often had a more decisive say in the life of the camp than the camp administration officers. In fact they even informed on them. Either by directly reporting in person to the security or counter-intelligence officers, or in the way I have already mentioned — by putting specially marked written reports in the postbox as if they were letters for their families.

Such people included, for example, the shift foreman, C., the stores manager, L. and later T., a maintenance man, H., a canteen worker, K., later B., then some of the gang-leaders, the film projectionist, and the librarian. They all tried to get some kind of little cubbyhole for themselves, where they would have a little privacy and thus the conditions they needed for their shady activities, all kinds of secret deals, and so on.

In my work as a doctor, I had quite a few problems with them. For example, K., a maintenance man, would come and remove the door handle or lock from the surgery, because he needed it somewhere else. T. took away the boards we had managed to get hold of to repair the infirmary, by calmly passing them through the window. Next it was the wall clock that had cost us so much effort to obtain and restore to working order. These people always got their way in the end, because there was no one to stand up for me. H. abolished our "bathroom" — an improvised water heater down in the boiler room. The stores manager forced us to store the blankets and people's personal belongings that previously had been kept in the storeroom. The cooks had wanted to move into our rooms. There was always a fight over something and we usually lost anyway. It often annoyed me that I had to waste my energy on such material things. But without them it would have been impossible to achieve anything, either spiritually for myself and certainly not for others, or for the patients. As soon as I gave in over one thing, these VIPs would try to get their way with something else.

There was another fight over the voluntary helpers — the orderlies — in the infirmary. The job of voluntary helper after work hours had gradually been established. This involved serving meals, looking after and cleaning up the infirmary storerooms. At first the volunteers were a great help to us, so long as they were political prisoners. Especially K., B., and later M. as well, even though he wasn't really a political prisoner. But then the security officer began more and more often to insist on choosing the volunteers himself, because in that way he could plant informers. That meant that it was no longer important whether the volunteer was of any help, whether he was conscientious and honest, or whether, on the contrary, he endangered someone's health or life by mishandling the patients, equipment, or medical supplies.

I only had a few friends who shared my spiritual beliefs. These were above all Dunčo, whose real name was Ján Dunajský, and later Kadlečík, both of whom I subsequently visited in civilian life. Kadlečík has since died, even though he was far younger than I. He was the leader of a good gang, but even though they fulfilled the work quotas 200 percent, they were always discriminated against for their political or religious convictions. We used to see each other at least on Sundays. We would repeat the Mass together in a corner in secret.

I wanted to find myself a spiritual adviser here, too, but in this camp it wasn't possible to find one among the priests. However, I knew from my experience in civilian life that without a spiritual adviser one decided everything very subjectively, and therefore one's judgments were biased. Here in Prokop camp there was a period when not only could I not find a priest, but I could not even find one spiritually mature lay person. I hesitated for a long time, but in the end I chose a murderer to be my spiritual adviser. He was a dentist by profession and had been given eight years for murdering his mother-in-law.

Maybe this will shock some people, but his company was very useful and we helped each other considerably. I couldn't understand how such a gentle and decent person could be a murderer. However, when he recounted to me this event in his life, I was horrified to have to confess to myself that if I had been in his shoes, I don't know whether I might not have ended up doing the same. I saw quite clearly that the fact that I had been sentenced for my religious beliefs and not for a crime was more God's merciful gift than of my doing. From then on I tried to stop dividing people into good and bad, well-principled or criminal, because these are just artificial pigeonholes. To this very day I think that he was nearer to Christianity than many more conventional Christians really are.

I found it difficult there to put my heart into my work as a doctor, which should have been to help those in the camp who were really ill and suffering. But it was very difficult to pick these out from among the actors and egoists who tried to pull the wool over my eyes. It was only later that I found some kind of system for this. Experience taught me to treat almost everyone the right way. If at times I lost my temper, it was always when I was overworked, when there wasn't time to talk for any length of time to any rude and aggressive people there might be in my care. It rarely happened that a "patient" attacked me. At the most, one might grab me as if he wanted to throttle me.

I once had to use this method myself to drag a Romany out of the surgery, although I felt very bad about it afterwards. In time I learned very well how to deal with hooligans, thugs, psychopaths, and even with schizophrenics. We were the only ones who knew how to calm them down without using handcuffs or straitjackets. I sometimes tried this with hypnosis, which I also found useful. For example, with D., a terribly melancholic man who was always crying, who had repeatedly attempted suicide and didn't sleep more than one or two hours even after the strongest medicines and sleeping pills. After intensive hypnotic suggestion and posthypnotic treatment, it was gradually possible for him to do without almost everything, including medicines. He began to sleep and work.

I still had serious conflicts with the kitchen staff. Whenever I entered any critical comment in the records, the head cook, H., a real criminal, would snap at me: "It's interesting that until now everyone has been satisfied with my work. Wherever I've been everyone said I was the best cook and suddenly you don't like it. You've always got something against me. You're the first person to keep criticizing me." I expect some of the prison authorities encouraged his hatred for me. Was it just by chance that Big Tonda warned me in advance that H. would give me a good hiding? Because that is what happened the next time I wrote a critical comment about the food.

One of my first aims, that is, was to introduce a rule that would make the cooks eat what they cooked and not steal on the side and cook separately for themselves. Then they would cook food fit for human consumption for the others, too. H. calmly tore my note out of the book and wrote there that he would correct my eyesight. Immediately after this, the cooks called me down to the refrigerating room to check the meat. I saw that H. was there by himself and he had a long butcher's knife in his hand. Although my heart was pounding, I spoke to him in a calm voice, which must have disarmed him somewhat, because he put down the knife and grabbed me with his hands. He began to beat me across the face, he broke my glasses and kicked me furiously. I defended myself only by shielding myself with my arms, because from experience I knew if I resisted I could make him even more furious. What is more, if I should start fighting to defend myself, they would put us both in the punishment cells, or me in the first place. There were many who could hardly wait for any excuse to do so.

When Second Lieutenant Č. heard about this, he exploded and declared that H., the cook, would pay dearly for it. He said he had attacked a public servant while he was carrying out an official inspection. But his punishment of twenty days solitary confinement after work was only a formality. It was never imposed, because he kept finding excuses — work or illness — although he didn't show the least respect for me when one conscientious duty officer took me to examine him. But about a month later H. was replaced by another cook.

This incident helped me considerably. In particular, it gave me greater confidence and assured me that I was, after all, of some use, that I would not cover up dirty dealings or allow others to steal from the prisoners. I even won great popularity with them, and many criminals who not long before had been in the habit of shouting "repair man" after me began to greet me and praise me. They were even sorry they hadn't been there to show that scoundrel and thief what they thought of him.

In the summer of 1959 some rooms were cleared in the other half of our barracks, which made it possible to extend the camp infirmary, which adjoined them. We were very happy about this, because until then we had had hardly any privacy and we had had to study in the toilet and write on a board resting on the washbasin. The extended infirmary had about three rooms for patients confined to bed. There was also a separate isolation ward for infectious cases. However, this was not enough when an epidemic of flu, diarrhea, or jaundice broke out. Sometimes one barracks after another had to be cleared to make room for more isolation or quarantine wards. It is sad that it was only thanks to such epidemics that the authorities came to value our work, as at such times everyone had to depend on us.

There was a dentist's surgery in the infirmary which was equipped with an X-ray machine that we also had to use for X-raying bones after the usual injuries. Then there was the consultation room itself. Thanks to the changes, we also got a waiting room and a toilet for the staff, for which we scoured demolition sites in search of old sewage pipes. We were given sleeping quarters in the last room, which was next to one where some musicians practiced every day, sometimes until late at night. This got on our nerves quite a bit.

Criminals often threw their weight around in the surgery and tried to dictate what the doctor should give them. One boy from Bratislava was a typical example. He looked like a fifteen-year-old, but he was the leader of a well-organized gang, whose members did not hesitate to attack anyone, even armed police officers. One day he came in and announced: "Doctor, you'll prescribe me five days' sick leave. If not, I'll turn this room into a wood shed." By that time I already knew how to handle such people, so I just put my hands on my hips and burst out laughing. He became uneasy and began to look around him. He wanted to make some threatening gesture, break something, or the like. But suddenly everyone began to laugh. From that moment on I called him "Wood Shed," and the name stuck. That was the end of his heroic gesture. It's true, though, that many of these criminals were quite dangerous, because when they let their emotions run away with them — and especially if they were under the influence of drugs — they were capable of anything, even murder.

There were quite a lot of cultural societies here, too, although the standard was lower, because most people just wanted to get "a good mark," so they could go home on leave or be put on probation, and they did all they could to put on a good act. There were music and art societies, as well as a club for motorists, which I used to go to, too. There were also variety show and theatrical societies, but these tended to put on cheap, ambiguous performances. It was also possible to go to the cinema more often, twice or three times a week. Television became available, too, which attracted me, no doubt as a means of escape.

But the doctors were discriminated against in this respect, too. We came only after the cooks. They got everywhere easily, because they held more key positions. There were also sports clubs. We occasionally managed to get a game of ping-pong, which I played with Dr. O. (the dentist) for the exercise. I even bathed in a small, improvised swimming pool, about five by five meters. The hygiene in it was somewhat dubious. Romanies and young criminals used to jump into it in their dirty underwear and with muddy feet.

When tattooing became the fashion, it spread quickly through the prison, too, and at the beginning the authorities fought against it. Later they realized that they could turn it to their advantage and use it as a good way of identifying people. Every new prisoner was cornered by some gang or other and persuaded to let himself be tattooed. For example, on their necks they would have ZDE UŘÍZNOUT (Bite here), sometimes the same in French, ICI COUPER. Or ŞTRACH A PENÍZE JSEM NIKDY NEMIL (I have never had money or fear). These were the more respectable ones, but most of them were quite immoral and often on their genitals. There were also vulgar notices, obviously meant to ridicule, for example, VSTUPUJTE DO JZD (Join [lit. "enter"] the Cooperative Farm) tattooed next to the anus. They often paid dearly for tattoos on the eyelids — it cost some of them their sight. When they realized that in this way they were indirectly helping to identify themselves permanently, they tried to remove the tattoos with very painful injections of milk, which resulted in serious inflammation that turned into ulcers. Tattoos were registered on the back of a prisoner's health record, or on special cards attached to it; sometimes they were photographed.

I became involved in health education. Partly in the form of lectures over the camp radio, but mainly by setting up health clubs. Very few people were really interested in learning anything, though. Most of them were my friends, plus a few political prisoners. We at least tried to get to know each other better and help each other by spreading the Gospel and strengthening our friendship. The security officer, however, caught wind of this early on and began to limit attendance. When discussing conditional release the health club was not even counted as a cultural activity, but rather as an exacerbating circumstance.

I made use of health education to introduce and guide people in the direction of civilized human habits, character building, and good human relations, as well as for training medical assistants and voluntary workers for the camp infirmary. However, whenever medical officer P. had anything to do with this, he put everyone off. Some people, it is true, attended mainly in order to be able to work in the surgery, or they came for the purpose of spying.

Otherwise, fifty to a hundred "patients" used to come for "treatment" every day, most of them for trivialities, mainly to chat in the waiting room, kill time, or to pull the wool over the doctor's eyes, in short, to shirk work. I could feel sympathy in particular for those who didn't often ask for sick leave and who were more reasonable. But there were limits to what I could do, even though I had twice to three times more patients on sick leave than elsewhere. The paradox was that it was the political prisoners that P. usually tried to throw out of the infirmary. He once discharged a patient who had lain there for about five to six weeks with relapsing tendovaginitis, that is, a labor-induced torpid, stubborn inflammation of the tendon and the tendon sheath. The five, six weeks must have been suspicious, but he couldn't stop me taking him in once more.

Undoubtedly there was an awful lot that could be done for the prisoners through this work, although I always felt as if I was trapped between two millstones. From above they urged that I should be strict; the security officers kept summoning me, bossing me about, shouting at me, or calling for inspections by doctors from the Ministry of the Interior. Little Tonda was particular fond of doing this, and he accused me of covering up for idlers and malingerers. He once drove all the bed patients out to help with the hay harvest, which was in fact his own private business. I'm told he was even sentenced for it later, because twenty thousand crowns of the camp's money disappeared into his pocket.

Sometimes they ordered us to help unload linen or food from lorries. At such times we, by that I mean the medical staff, preferred to go to do it voluntarily ourselves, so they would leave at least the bed-ridden patients in peace.

Many people were saved here from certain death, suicide cases in particular. We also saved patients with sudden heart attacks, when there was no blood pressure or pulse, sometimes no breathing either. There were cases when even in such primitive conditions I found the courage to use noradrenaline and sometimes even an injection into the heart.

Another struggle for the prison doctor at the camps was the question of the health classification of prisoners. The Ministry of the Interior's official doctor usually had the final word, but the medical officer could influence the matter considerably. Later, the official doctors — Major P., Major H., and sometimes also Major Č., the director of the hospital, did their best to meet my wishes. We tried to have the third classification, the most seriously ill patients, moved to a closed prison or put in a less strenuous work category, in smaller camps. Unfortunately, one sometimes learned later that they had gone from bad to worse; even though they were assigned lighter work, the conditions were far worse. When prisoners begged to remain in our camp, we tried to classify them in a higher category.

Neurotics, melancholiacs, epileptics, and psychotics, that is, schizophrenics with depressive psychoses, formed a special category. They made up quite a high percentage of the prisoners, my guess was about 30 to 40 percent. At that time the inmates of the prisons and camps could be divided into about three groups. One group were those who had been sentenced even though they were innocent; previously these had made up over two-thirds of the prison population and most of them were political prisoners. Then there were those who really should have been receiving medical treatment, and only the remainder were criminals who may have been justly sentenced. Though in time every recidivist bore the marks of nervous disorders resulting from that artificially created, cruel environment of restricted freedom and terror. We recommended these to be transferred, too.

Unfortunately, from the surrounding camps, especially the agricultural ones, from Sírovice, Drahovice and from some six more in the near surroundings, came reports about bad conditions, worse hygiene as well as labor. In agricultural brigades in particular they worked fourteen to sixteen hours a day. Prisoners were often said to be without water or rest the whole day — without a free Sunday, in very poor, inadequate clothing. I heard about a warder who, in the burning midday heat, allowed the prisoners to drink from puddles or from the stream only "as a reward."

We tried to help the prisoners and encourage them mentally and spiritually, even though the criminals were for the most part rough, uncivilized, often malicious and unscrupulous as well; not only Christianity, but even the basic human principles were alien to them. In spite of this, they often sought me out and so far as I could find the time, I had to listen daily to "confessions," life histories, complaints, or bitter memories. Old lags, murderers included, wept from depression or when contemplating their ill fate. But there were many political prisoners, too, and so I sometimes felt almost ashamed of having a good family background and previous life in general, which provided me with great moral support that others could not draw on.

For the most part, though, my work was very monotonous. I often got down to the day's work with automatic resignation. However, I tried at least to maintain some contact with the outside world and to persevere with my studies of languages and medicine.

I gained considerable experience not only in diagnosing and treating common ailments and injuries, but even more in psychology and psychiatry — practical experience, of course, not scientific. For example, in "trickology," as I called it, in exposing malingerers. In every camp there were advanced "schools" that taught how to simulate typical symptoms of acute illnesses (sudden abdominal pains, appendicitis, etc.). Nearly all the surgeons were taken in, especially the civilian ones, and for the most part they opened the patient, sometimes in a great hurry and with insufficient preparation. If a patient managed to avoid being brought to me or one of the experienced prison doctors, he could get taken to hospital or to a civilian doctor straight from his place of work.

Even at the camp, Christmas 1958 was a typical Christmas with traditional folk decorations — a Christmas tree in the mess hall and a special supper. But this was just a formality. My real Christmas was spent with a small group of friends and then alone under the open sky in the snow and frost, when I walked along the perimeter of the camp inside the wire fences. The real, humble Christmas, in harmony with the Newly-born Babe thrust out from human society. There was "no place for us" among people, either. That evening memories softened even the most hardened of the prisoners; they became more human, approachable.

When our masters wanted to show us, often with the help of other prisoners on the camp staff, that we were the lowest of the low and that we mustn't think we had the right to anything, they forced us to leave the infirmary and our patients, as if this were not work at all. I remember we used to unload lorries of linen or building materials. I fought against this, not because of the physical exertion, which we needed, but in order to preserve at least a certain degree of autonomy, of medical authority, which they were forever trying to eliminate.

Any change as concerned care for the sick we had to fight hard for. One change was the regular visits under escort to hospitals, once or twice a month. It was also one of the few opportunities to see, for half a day, a different environment than those few wooden barracks, barbed wire, and "lookouts"—the guards' watchtowers at all four corners of the camp and also every fifty meters along the double corridor between the wire fences.

We learned new things in hospital; we often found out how to do things better. At that time I wanted very much to see Dr. Ivan Porazík, who was in the prison hospital in Vykmanov, that is, in the central camp. He, too, quickly became competent in internal medicine, radiography, and pathology — he even carried out postmortems, although he had previously been head of a histology department, that is, of a strictly theoretical specialization. He was also a much loved doctor.

I did, in fact, manage to meet him. When he saw me, his eyes lit up, but he tried to control the expression on his face so they would not notice that we knew each other. That was always dangerous. He pulled me into a kind of cubbyhole, I think it was in the out-patients' ear, nose, and throat consulting room or in the inhalation room and on another occasion in the X-ray department. After a long separation, we hugged each other and poured out a few sentences we had waited so long to utter. I can remember them, as if they were said this very day: "Silvo, I know all about you. You needn't say anything. I'm following your every step. I'm very glad you are as you are. I wasn't really one of you, I couldn't have been like you. I wasn't clear about many things in philosophy, to say nothing of religion. But now, after these experiences, I'm with you wholeheartedly. I can now understand you completely and you can count on me entirely as a Christian."

I admired the way he examined patients. He may sometimes have seemed to be a little austere, but I understood it was the only possible way to avoid being worn out by the selfish talk of malingerers, who only think of themselves and who would happily let the doctor be sent to prison again or persecuted in order to get what they wanted. He behaved very politely and his manner was friendly, but if he found there was nothing wrong with a patient, he quickly showed him out of the room: "I'm sorry, but there's nothing there. Be glad you are O.K. I've got other patients here who are suffering at this moment. I can't do anything for you just now. Surely you don't want me to be arrested again or to give you priority over those who really are suffering. I'll prescribe you some excellent drops."

By then the situation in the hospital was better overall. The doctors could come to an agreement and take in prisoners without much difficulty. After all, practically everyone who had been mining for any length of time had some symptoms of illness, which were often very serious.

As the political situation was somewhat less tense, research was being done on the influence of long periods of mining on the human organism, that is, the influence of small doses of ionizing radiation from uranium ore during physical exertion. The research was even carried out under the auspices of some official doctors from the Ministry of the Interior, who used the information for scientific studies and won great credit in the professional field.

Self-mutilation was a great problem in the camp. Some people would swallow metal objects, glass, and so on. They had to be X-rayed frequently, which meant they received an unnecessary amount of radiation. However, instead of sending them to hospital, many officers and commandants sent them to the punishment cells with a strict regimen, but they did not put them in solitary confinement, because they needed to keep a close watch on them. The prisoners had to change all their clothes regularly and they were moved from cell to cell as well, in order to prevent them from hiding objects they could injure themselves with.

The most blindly obstinate of them seemed to me to be S. He was so antisocial and lazy that he had probably never ever even held a broom. In order to avoid work, he used to put bits of indelible pencil into his eyes, which caused inflammation and destroyed the tissues, so that he was already totally blind in one eye and partially in the other. The warders tried beatings, threats, good words — nothing had any effect. I was also unsuccessful with my explanations and my attempts to understand him. But in this case, too, an unbelievable miracle happened, which confirmed my opinion that you cannot write anyone off while he is still alive.

Once, when he had managed to get himself taken to hospital, he was put in the same room as another self-mutilator, N., who was also from our camp. The latter had swallowed some spoons. They hadn't wanted to let him go to hospital for a long time and once there he tried to play the hero.

After every operation, he would tear off his bandages, pull out the stitches and open his wounds, saying he wanted to die and to hell with such a life. In this way he underwent about nine operations, one after the other, with complications and suppuration. In the end one prisoner, Dr. K., lost patience and said: "This is the last time! If you open your wounds and pull out the stitches once more, we won't look after you any more, even if you drop dead right here." That is exactly what did happen. His condition began to get worse all of a sudden, and he felt he was losing strength and nearing his end. Then at last a change took place. He began to beg to be saved, promising he would be quite a different man if he returned to the camp. He did receive very expensive medicines, dozens of transfusions, injections, antibiotics, but in vain. He died in terrible agony. His special medicines alone were said to have cost over thirty thousand crowns.

When S. saw all this, he suddenly cured himself. He was so shocked and terrified that he quickly began to behave himself and he returned to the camp with the remains of one eye. There, for the first time, he picked up a broom of his own accord and began to sweep. Everyone looked on in amazement. He didn't exactly become an angel overnight, but nevertheless he changed considerably.

The staff prisoners continued in vain trying to make me behave as the authorities wished and to compromise. In the end they began to intrigue against me in various ways. They brought accusations against me to the security officers and began to meddle in purely medical matters. Unfortunately, Dr. O. used to spend time in their company, although he emphasized that he only did it so that he would know in time what was going on and could warn me.

Fortunately, the warders and medical officers were gradually replaced, medical officer P. was moved to a factory somewhere, and the new medical officer, N., was very decent, but soft as well. For that reason many people didn't respect him. On the other hand, he often let me have a fairly free hand in the infirmary. I could introduce various reforms, new rules and regulations, and a new division of labor. He was reasonably willing to put his signature to all my suggestions.

Then suddenly one evening the order was read out for my transfer. It came out of the blue, without warning or even premonition. I learned that I was going to "C," to the central camp. I quickly destroyed everything necessary, because I presumed I was going to an investigation cell. To the dreaded, notorious Sing-sing, which was a large investigation prison of the Ruzyň type for all the Jáchymov camps. People were kept there in solitary confinement for months on end.

I didn't want to cause a stir, so I went to change my clothes and hand in my things early in the morning. As usual when I was transported somewhere, I was agitated, and it seemed strange to me that the infirmary was to be left without a prison doctor. Later I learned that an excellent doctor, Dr. Ondrejka, came to take my place. He had been in Rovnosť camp and, after a conflict with the medical officers, who had begun to throw his patients out of the infirmary, he had refused to work as a doctor and gone to work in the mines. His post was filled by a medical student, B., serving a sentence for murder. He was in a very strong position, because he had powerful uncles and also because he was an informer. Apart from this, he had the fate of many patients on his conscience. It even went so far that he "operated" hemorrhoids in the camp infirmary. He was very self-assured, and yet he produced many invalids and disabled people, and he is even said to be responsible for the deaths of some.

Part V

Jáchymov District – The Central Camp

One November evening I arrived under escort at the central camp, "C." I was surprised, because it was the first time I had not been handcuffed and they didn't take me to Sing-sing, but to the hospital. I didn't have to stand face to the wall as I had always had to before.

Prisoners dressed in white, who worked at the hospital, walked past me. One prisoner of the older generation, Vladimír Ch., took charge of me. He also worked as a doctor in Sing-sing opposite. There the State Security police ruled with the methods feared throughout Jáchymov. Ch. was very willing to inform me about everything and continued to seek my company, as I was told he had Porazík's before me. It was clear that he was looking for support, maybe even sincere friendship. He wanted to become a better person, because he was clearly disgusted by all kinds of snobs and intriguers, although he himself was too self-confident, and he knew very well how to swim with the tide in any situation. One thing about him, though, was much to be valued. He told people outright what he thought. We quickly became friends, and he helped me in many ways. Apparently he had once been a drug addict, he had tried all possible opiates and had often injected himself with overdoses that could have been fatal. It had been a miracle he got over this.

He was an acquaintance of Abbot Opasek's and other important clerical and political figures. Indeed, whenever he could, he chose the company of exceptional people and prominent personalities. Some people criticized him for his behavior while in Leopoldov, because he was believed to have collaborated with the management and the official doctor, but it was impossible for us to check the truth of this.

He often mentioned his wife Jiřinka, who formally divorced him in order to avoid the repressions that followed his imprisonment and persecution. But he said she was otherwise a faithful and wonderful person. He was very afraid he would lose her. The only thing he wanted was to return to her as soon as possible. What happened in the end? At Easter 1960 he received the sacraments for the first time, while a patient in my ward, suffering from inflammation of the pancreas. It seemed he was really serious about it, but a few years later, in civilian life, he quickly changed. He doesn't even live with his wife now, and he has another partner.

It it painful to think what has remained of our brothers, so wonderful in prison and so weak outside. I myself never cease wondering whether I really did everything I should have. Whether those friendships were, after all, only superficial or too "human," if it took no more than a couple of months away from my influence for those "devout Christians" to stop going to church on a regular basis.

That first evening they gave me a bed in the barracks for the service staff and doctors. Vladimír Ch. and I continued our conversation there, trying to discover more about each other. He was already secretly planning to arrange for me to be assigned to the ward for infectious diseases, where Dr. P., a well-known informer and legendary dilettante, had left a vacancy.

Here I at last met Vojto M., who had indirectly been our "accomplice." He did iontophoresis in the physiotherapy department and prepared various graphs and documents for Dr. Č., which helped him to maintain his position. Vojto was not as pale as when we had met on that previous occasion in the corridor of the interrogation prison, where I gave him my ration of a hundred cigarettes. He looked as if he had put on weight, but it was that unhealthy fat typical for prisoners, or more likely hypoproteinemia, hypovitaminosis — swelling from a lack of protein and vitamins.

He was still very "cautious," however, he kept avoiding us and tried not to draw attention to himself. On the other hand, he gave me some good advice: to gradually take over the initiative in the department and make a habit of reporting in person to the head physician, Dr. Č., and of signing medical records in his presence, in order to put a stop to or at least restrict the informing activities of subordinate prisoners and orderlies, who could do a lot of harm to the patients and us behind our backs.

My closest friend was probably Víťo Žák. He passed the Eucharist around to other prisoners along with texts for the Sunday liturgy. After being betrayed by Lojzo M., who was indebted to him for many things, which is why Víťo had trusted him, he was thrown into a punishment cell in Sing-sing and was then moved elsewhere. He was one of those who learned by heart the royal sonnet by Václav Renčo, "Májová za mřížemi" ("May devotions behind bars"). We often meditated together and gave each other moral support. He was a very good specialist and documentalist; he kept up to date with professional literature and prepared excerpts of the most important passages for the doctors. He was a great help to us from the professional point of view. We consulted him about everything.

I came to know many doctors, but it was difficult to find any of really good character. Some of them were serving sentences for criminal, often sexual, offenses and were said to collaborate with the security agents.

I remember at least one fairly decent one — an ear, nose, and throat specialist, F. H. He was a head physician who had been thrown out of the infirmary in Mírov, where he apparently behaved well from the spiritual and political point of view, but who, it was said, had a soft spot for money. Otherwise, he had a rather uptight, intolerant nature and a reputation for being a selfish man, maybe even an informer. That was quite shameful for a Christian believer. On the other hand, he helped many of the old lags, especially political prisoners such as František Jurák, who then worked as his assistant.

Another unusual character was M. A., head of the laboratory. It was only afterwards that I learned that he had not finished his medical studies. It was sometimes very hard to work with him and his laboratory staff as a whole. I was often at a loss to know how to make them do anything for the patients that they didn't really have to do. They were a strange group of people. They worked on the cultivation of fungi, which was a favorite occupation with the whole of the hospital, the head included. In the end I got myself involved in translating articles on this subject. It was unknown and rather difficult ground for me. I'm afraid no one really got deep into the subject, though; it was mostly for effect, which the head of the infirmary had a great weakness for. There was a tale about an "antibiotic" and an antifungal preparation, which, he claimed, the Russians had stolen from him and he couldn't patent it.

We also had a doctor from the Ministry of the Interior, Captain P., a rather inexperienced and unskillful beginner. But he tried quite hard to learn. At the outset he was very unpopular with the prisoners. I think it was mainly because he was "working-class cadre," a quickly trained manual worker and therefore really an improvised doctor. He had studied medicine after he had been working for some time, getting into university by the back door. That is why the State Security police entrusted him with the most tricky cases, which they didn't entrust even to the head of the infirmary. In spite of this, he seemed to me to be of better character than the head physician, Č, although he was sometimes a bit afraid of drawing attention to himself by standing up for the truth and for his patients.

A young official doctor of the Ministry of Interior, Major H., also joined us. I was very impressed by his directness and openness, although he behaved as if he mistrusted me at first. Once when he was examining an X-ray he openly confessed he didn't understand it. Security officers rarely confessed anything of the kind. But he minded not knowing and that is why he very soon learned more than other doctors in his position. He introduced restrictions on the food for medical staff, but he left the doctors the third food category, because he said people should also be rewarded according to their social importance. I protested against this immediately, but when I saw that all kinds of people of dubious character, including layabouts, wanted to take advantage of this, I decided it would be better to go for my extra rations and pass them on to the orderlies myself.

I particularly liked one pharmacist, P., the wife of Major Dr. P., whom I didn't often come into contact with. Considering the conditions and her position, she was a very exceptional and good woman. She was one of the best employees of the Ministry of the Interior that I have ever known. When she found herself unable to defend those in her care, Víťo and Bohuš Vraštil in particular, she chose to leave rather than compromise her conscience.

The head of the infirmary assigned me to his department, known there as the infectious ward. There were patients there with tuberculosis, infectious diseases, those kept in isolation or quarantine, those under observation, often complicated internal or neurological cases, jaundice, and skin diseases. The latter suited me in particular, because it gave me a wide range of experience and practice in my specialization. I quickly acquired the necessary training for allergies, fungal infections, and other skin diseases typical for those particular conditions and that put strain on the organism. The head left me a fairly free hand in this sphere. Only later, when Chief Security Officer J. "Little Kokta" was persecuting me, did he use to appear more often to check what I was doing., He crossed out my suggestions for therapy in an ostentatious manner. In my absence — clearly under pressure from J. — he discharged a large number of patients who were not yet cured and in general he danced more and more to his tune. In the end he took a number of measures, especially as concerned the personnel, that were against his own interests. In short, he made compromises when he shouldn't have. He wanted to please everyone and, in doing so, he often harmed those who deserved it the least.

He was also the only doctor that put me in Sing-sing of his own initiative. His complacency made him easy to offend. Of course, this suited Security Officer J. very well, and my appeal to have the whole matter investigated was ignored. It was a question of an operation, a resection of the stomach, carried out by a new surgeon, a prisoner, Dr. K., on an orderly, Ch. Because I knew from past experience that I could not rely on the laboratory findings, I sent a blood sample to be checked by the civilian laboratory. In serious cases it is the usual practice to send samples to two or three places. The head complained that I had not submitted the order for his signature, although this had never been required previously. In any case, he signed most things automatically, without even knowing what they were about. He sentenced me to three days in solitary confinement, and as the reason for my punishment he wrote that I was responsible for spoiling blood samples. This was because the result came back with the comment that the blood could not be tested because it was decayed. This was not my fault by any means. Medical Officer Second Lieutenant O. was responsible for its transportation, which he often did very carelessly.

I know, however, that the standard of the treatment given by doctors and nurses was very good. We didn't give up even in really hopeless cases, where the major or the civilian doctors had long decided it was a waste of effort. We didn't give up because these were our brothers, our fellow sufferers.

We were among the first to use corticosteroids for jaundice, with great success. We had two particularly serious cases. I remember how a store-manager from Slavkov was almost literally raised from the dead. Although I suspect only to continue informing on people. Another patient, H., was cured of typhus in a similar manner.

After barbiturate poisoning we applied two medical innovations, Megimid and Amiphenazol, thanks to which D. was saved from almost certain death. This kept others alive and, even after two to three weeks in a coma, they returned to normal life.

Eventually I set up a small laboratory here, too. We then carried out all the tests, especially blood counts and urine tests, as well as the cultivation of fungi and cerebrospinal fluid, immediately after samples were taken. I also introduced suboccipital punctures, that is, the withdrawal of fluid from the cerebral cisterna by piercing the back of the head. This was much pleasanter and less painful for the patient than the generally applied back puncture. We had no complications and we achieved good results.

I also learned how to examine bone marrow, that is, by sternal puncture (puncture of the breastbone). We made sure that the sedatives and injected local anaesthetics had worked properly, because doctors often don't wait the necessary time and the patients then suffer more. We literally used a timer and waited 15–20 minutes until it rang. I also did the smear test to discover Koch's bacillus, which causes tuberculosis. All in all, I studied a great deal here in the field of medicine — both in practice and theoretically, by translating and making excerpts.

The major made me carry out postmortems, although I tried to avoid them. It was very responsible work and I had no experience with this. In the end it was decided that either he would draw up the conclusions, or senior dissectors would come from Karlový Vary and I would only assist them. That was a great relief to me, because we had all kinds of tricky cases. There was, for example, B., from Rovnosť camp, who was found hanged. It was assumed to be suicide. The postmortem, however, showed clear signs of violence and a struggle, hematomas, blood-filled swellings on his back, broken laryngal cartilages, in other words, marks left by strangling. A similar murder was subsequently discovered at Eliáš camp as well, the motive probably being money or some kind of perversity. Maybe it was a settling of accounts.

Then there was the case of P., who committed suicide by throwing himself under a lorry at his place of work about three days before he was to be released from prison. The witnesses, however, said it looked more like a fall after suddenly fainting, or maybe he was helped by someone. The postmortem showed large visible arteriosclerotic plates on the coronary arteries and thickening. So it is possible there had been a rupture of the aorta.

Prisoners who had been mining for more than five years began to have periodic examinations, mainly a series of blood counts and bone marrow tests. They often had disorders of the inner ear and professional angioneurosis — an intestinal disorder caused by working with a pneumatic drill. Likewise, there was ischaemia of the fingers, paralysis from the vibrations of the drills and fungal infections, which at least served as some excuse to hospitalize the patient.

So far as my own physical fitness was concerned, for several months I had been learning to walk on my hands and I got quite good at it. I used to walk down the corridor before the reveille. In the afternoon I used every possible minute of my free time to play ping-pong, until Little Kokta forbade it. It was pure bullying on his part and it undermined my authority with the patients and the staff under me.

I had ideal accommodation and I felt God had me under his protection. I had a little separate cubbyhole, a tiny room in the department. It was ideal for me to meditate, secretly communicate with people, read delicate materials, even participate in the sacred Mass. There was even a shower-room next door.

The greatest miracle for me, however, was "Uncle Zavarský." Valér Zavarský was a courageous priest, a Jesuit, a specialist in art history, whom the Lord sent to the camp just a few days before my arrival. What wonderful planning that must have been for me to be able to meet him like that in the same corridor! And at last I could have in my own little room an authentic sacred Mass, with confession and Communion. Even a midnight Mass at Christmas for the first time. For the first and last time.

It was one of my most beautiful experiences. We spent the evening with the others in the barracks. We met in each others' rooms, reminisced, meditated outside in the snow under the stars. After lights out at ten we quietly prayed. And then we two observed the sacred midnight Mass in complete darkness. Only then did I truly appreciate and enjoy the beauty, profoundness, and magic of the sacred Mass and Christmas. After that I secretly made wine for him in the dissecting room from raisins extracted from Christmas cakes.

In this camp, too, I used to divide wafers or dough from white rolls intended for the Eucharist into little pieces and to wrap each little bit up in new cigarette papers, so the bits would not get dirty or crumble and they were simply consumed together with the paper. That was really exciting work.

Every afternoon I used to go for a walk, but the aim was in fact to converse with Vladimír, or with someone else. The "powers-that-be" noticed this immediately, though, kept watch and followed us, until some people were afraid to meet me often. Next came the affair with our Scriptures, which a bricklayer, Herchl, from "C," had hidden in one of the sewage shafts and later in the pharmacy, where Žák worked. Kokta was delighted to have an excuse to throw him out of the infirmary when he refused to say where he had got it from.

Little and Big Kokta were typical examples of despotism, autocracy, and terror. They were my main persecutors, even though Little Kokta often smiled to your face. I find being shouted at hard to bear, but I preferred it when he shouted. At least we knew where we stood. He was always thinking up some change in the staff, a new rule for greetings, confiscation of literature, searches, and bans. It now seems almost comic to me how once, when he could find no other excuse for being nasty, he yelled that I had not re-educated the orderly in charge of the corridor and the nurse, whom he himself had placed to spy on me.

In this atmosphere I was very glad when I occasionally met some wonderful people. One of them was S., a patient of ours who had leukemia, which may have been a result of his profession, mining radioactive ore. He was a splendid young man, a patient Christian, whom we tried very hard to save. In the end, quite exceptionally, his sentence was cut short for reasons of health. I heard that he died soon after.

I also remember Antonín Novotný from Uhliarske Janovice, with whom I agreed on a more-or-less fictitious meeting in Brno at the bus station, if we were ever released. In civilian life, however, I did meet Peter, the son of his friend Milan, on several occasions. Milan was a brave and honest man, a convert, but a little hard, often with rather exaggerated reactions as a result of damaged nerves. He, too, is no longer among the living.

I also had a chance to embrace Karel Komárek, our best friend, with whom I had worked at one time in Vrchlabsko. He was given ten years for organizing religious groups. I finally managed to get him hospitalized for a fungal disease typical for mine workers. He spent about three weeks in our isolation ward. Thanks to God we were very happy and gave each other moral support, although hardly anyone was aware that we knew each other. If they had, he would probably have been quickly discharged.

It took me quite a long time to teach people — I literally had to persuade them — not to bring me bribes. Everyone who was discharged from the hospital as well as others who came to the surgery, brought me a certain "fee," quite a large sum in camp currency, as if it was a matter of course. It amounted to a hundred to two hundred crowns a day, which under those conditions was a large sum of money. When I refused money, they pressed me to take various pullovers or sweaters, which were extremely valuable in prison. Or coffee and the like. When I resolutely refused, they were really offended. They asked me whether I thought they would squeal on me or were trying to catch me out. Later, however, it became common knowledge that I didn't accept anything, and so people sometimes tried to offer me at least a sweet or an apple, and they used to lay bets whether I would accept it. At the same time many of the prisoners working as medical orderlies and doctors, too, kept an eye out for every cup of tea or coffee that I accepted, hoping to find some offense to report to the disciplinary officer. Thanks to such tip-offs I could indirectly check that I had a clean slate, because there was no slander about me.

As in the investigation prisons and in Mírov, there were often real epidemics, avalanches of sensational news. We used to call it the "muklopress." Before every approaching state anniversary "amnesty fever" usually broke out. Especially before the anniversary of the February events or in

May on the anniversary of the end of the war, in October/November on the anniversary of the Great October Soviet Revolution, during which there were all kinds of peace meetings, conferences, and important world events.

The year 1960 was particularly marked by the most varied conjectures and speculations. Every month something was expected. Especially on the fifteenth anniversary of the republic, May 6–9. Even the employees of the Ministry of the Interior debated the possibility among themselves. Some prisoners quite literally "packed their things," but that was nothing new. However, they did begin to treat us much better than, at any other time. Even the authorities weren't sure whether or not something might happen. They went as far as to send out feelers through their informers, but as usual I made it quite clear that I would not accept an amnesty. At least in this way I burned my bridges, making it impossible for me to retreat, and thus I protected myself from vain hopes.

In the end I was one of the few political prisoners to remain. In that year, 1960, almost all my best friends left me. First they were isolated in a special barracks, where no one was allowed to go out or contact anyone. Then on May 9, 1960, they left. Valér Zavarský, Zrník, our good corridor orderly, and about eight of my patients. There was Míla Fořt (though that might have been later), Antonín Novotný, Karel Komárek (who may have left from another camp). Drs. W., Š., and Sch. left, as well as Dr. S. H. from Rovnosť, who had only come to our camp two weeks earlier, in his opinion to provide medical services after others had been released, but in the end he was released himself. He thought amnesty was out of the question for him, because he had been Beneš's doctor. Then Drs. H., B., A. and, I think, K., left. My friends included M., Dr. Ch., S., T., and K.

Amnesties were always accompanied by all kinds of exceptions and stipulations. This was clearly intentional, because it meant they could be used as they liked. They could release or detain anyone just as they pleased. A useful, vague article in the law could always be found. In fact no one had a right to anything, not even to certainty. Everything depended on a few people, who demanded complete submission and required others to serve them in their shady dealings.

I had quite a hard week, although I did my utmost to control my feelings. I think that, apart from quickening my pace when out for a walk and one question that I put to Dr. Pokorný about the formulation of the law, I gave no sign of what was going on inside me. When they asked anything, I just answered that I wanted the truth, not mercy.

It was very painful for me, however, to see my best friends leave me like this, friends I had become used to and who had been my spiritual family. Or something even deeper. After all, we had lived through so many painful events together. I was also hurt by the departure of the only priest, which meant an end to receiving the sacraments. For a while I felt like a madman, who has fixed ideas and clings to them even after he has been cured, not being able to understand that they were just hallucinations. On the contrary, he keeps swimming against the tide with fanatical paranoia, while all the others, who had previously gone along with him, had grasped at least a little bit of freedom and life.

All of a sudden, there was no one I could speak openly to, or even to show a little attention, brotherly love and fellowship, to say nothing of finding someone who had any understanding for me. This state of things remained pretty well unchanged for the rest of my time in prison. From this point of view the milder regime was almost worse than the hard one, when we all kept together and were like one "family."

After a couple of days the situation began to settle down, people were no longer all of a tremble, nervously running here and there in the vain hope that the amnesty would include them, too. Delayed releases became more and more rare. Our very thinned ranks were gradually replenished. Of course, most of the newcomers were common criminals. It's worth mentioning just a few of those I came into close contact with. As replacement for the corridor orderly and assistant nurse I was assigned an excellent prisoner, Ladislav Suchomel, an old miner, who had been in prison since he was about eighteen for "political activities." He had helped a condemned man to escape from a mental hospital, where he had been tormented and tortured. Suchomel had been in prison for almost ten years. We became quite close friends, but somehow I never managed to win his complete trust. He eluded me in particular when it came to a deeper spiritual life. On the other hand, he did us many friendly services, for example, he used to make blancmange for us. Several of us had formed a "kolkhoz"; we pooled our food and money, some people their cigarettes and tobacco as well. On Sunday we always used to make him tell us about his life, about mining and all the dramatic situations that went with it, often leading to death. I believe he worked as an excavator operator on the front face, deep down in the mines.

Another splendid young man was his best friend, Bohuš Vraštil. He was also a miner, a dear, good-natured man. He took over Víťo Žák's job as assistant in the pharmacy. He was a believer, an Evangelical, and we often discussed the question of the unification of the Church and Christians. He did not want to believe it would ever take place. He bet ten kilometers of chocolate that it was just a castle in the air. In prison there was nothing to be heard about the ecclesiastic council at that time. I was convinced that there was a real possibility and a necessity for cooperation, and therefore unification at a later date.

As time went on some other political prisoners were assigned to us as assistants. They were mostly patients. They were, in fact, the only reliable, hard-working people left. All the others were extremely unreliable, which in medicine is particularly dangerous. I remember Laco Karaba, who did physical therapy and hydropathy. Then there was Oldřich K., Karel R., who worked first in the pharmacy, then in the operating room, then in the canteen, a great enthusiast when it came to learning languages. He taught me Spanish. Then there was Břeťa K., who also found a place in the laboratory and who was the only one I was left with when J. began once more to throw out the political prisoners.

The doctors included a newcomer, Edo K., a dentist, Hugo A.; later Gejza Kauzál, a senior consultant from a surgical department in Žilina. He arrived just after a patient had been brought in already dead. A medical officer from the Ministry of the Interior in charge of an agricultural work party was obviously to blame, because he hadn't allowed him to be taken to hospital. The postmortem showed serious inflammation of the gallbladder, so the patient must have suffered greatly for at least three days without medical help. The doctor wrote a report, in which he put the blame on this medical officer, because he said he had not allowed him to be operated on. But the head of the infirmary, Č., did not want to draw attention to himself in such matters.

Dr. Kauzál used to curse technology terribly, especially tape recorders. We later wheedled out of him that tape recorders had been his downfall. At a party his friends recorded his jokes, which he was apparently capable of telling all night long. In his verdict there were at least three pages of political jokes. The warders often used to confiscate his verdict and then we could hear laughter from the next room. They were amusing themselves with the jokes for which he had been given four years. As far as I know, the main problem was that he had a beautiful collection of pictures and Persian rugs in his villa and one prosecutor decided he would get his hands on them at all costs. That is how "subversive elements" were "produced." Security officer J. and nurse M. picked on Kauzál for bullying; they kept forcing him to greet them and humiliated him in a great variety of ways. Although they were dependent on him, too. He was a conscientious surgeon. Occasionally I assisted him or injected anaesthetics in the lumbar region. He was a good friend to me, even though he once called me a greenhorn. I had disagreed with him on that occasion over a gallbladder X-ray. He was also released before he had served the whole of his sentence, maybe at the intervention of a partisan woman, Tamara, from Ťumen, whose life he had saved during the war. During the Uprising he had put her in plaster and provided cover for her escape to a safe place.

When we were saying goodbye, he was magnanimous in that he didn't forget to apologize to me: "You know, you were really right about that gallbladder. Maybe at other times, too, but that's just me, I find it hard to take back something I have already said, especially in front of people so much younger than me."

He loved cooking and he was radiant on Sunday afternoons. He liked tasting food and his figure betrayed the fact. When he was eating, his face took on such an attractive expression, that it made our mouths water, too. He often used to weep over his family, especially his children. Unfortunately, after he was released, he did not enjoy freedom for long. He used to go to operate in Banská Bystrica, where, when buying some toys for his children, he had a heart attack and collapsed in front of the shop. No one offered him so much as first aid and they even prodded him with the comment that he was drunk. This is what they said to someone who had saved many from death or disablement.

A couple of times we literally rushed in to treat a dying patient in the Department of Internal Medicine headed by Dr. Sch., while he arranged the notice boards, which were valued more by the police officers than a doctor's work.

Old Dr. Karas, a dentist about seventy years of age, was very touching. Interestingly, he was quite unpopular with the prisoners. They hated him and called him "repairman" or did everything possible to humiliate him. He was even put in the punishment cell, a fact the medical officer often boasted about. Dr. Karas wanted to do dentistry and that alone, as that was his specialization and he was quite good at it. But they didn't allow him to. He was quite timid, always worried, and he was overgrateful to me. He said I helped him to pull himself together a bit. He would have liked to stay with me, but they put him in a group doing agricultural work.

The most painful thing for him was his belief that he was responsible for his wife being imprisoned for six years and his son, Jenda, for about five. He himself had got ten years for hiding some property or for speculation. He longed to see his son, who was in a neighboring camp, at least once more in his life. But they didn't allow him a visit and so, when his son was in the same hospital for a time, everyone of good will helped them, so they could see each other and talk at least for a while.

It was terrible how all the squealers were on the alert in case they should meet by chance. How Little Tonda revelled in this situation! What was this, if not sadism? They had to hide and pretend, even though it was only a father wanting to see his son once more in his life.

Then young Jenda came to work in our laboratory, doing bacteriological and biochemical tests. He was a very gifted, capable, and courageous fellow. He very soon introduced some improvements. For example, the dilution of the cerebrospinal fluid when counting the cells. He quickly became acquainted with all the new specializations. He often used to think about the girl he had been going out with, Pavla. Later they were married and their marriage was a success. He came to visit me several times when we were out of prison, and I once visited them, too.

Once, after studying an article about microbial antigens, he decided to make a special kind of autovaccine, which he did succeed in doing. We used it on about two patients. There must have been a striking improvement in their condition. We had no idea what a sensation it would be. But at least we had another chance to confirm that our consciences were clear because the "bosses" could find nothing better than this to use against us. They began investigating it as "hazardous experiments on prisoners." All of a sudden the security officers were posing as great humanists. They — the cruellest people of those times.

I think, though, that the whole investigation was really staged to undermine the authority of the head of the infirmary, Č. His position was uncertain, thanks to the compromises he was always making and the way he gave in to J., the security officer. He tried to put all the blame on us. He said we had done it without his knowledge. In fact, he had followed the injections and reactions closely. He used to ask me about them and I used to report to him our findings. I think it was in fact my pedantry that helped us that time. I had everything written down, even on the discharge documents, which he had signed himself in his position as head. In connection with this case I was recalled from Prokop camp once more a lot later and Jenda was brought from another camp. They made as much of the investigation as they could, but we didn't want to do Dr. Č. any harm, especially as it was really a power struggle, even though he had behaved so unfairly towards us.

I don't want to leave out one interesting episode involving old Dr. Karas. His condition sometimes became critical, because of his arteriosclerosis and blood pressure, which would suddenly shoot up so high it was impossible to measure. I once managed to talk to him alone, which was arranged by his son Jenda. On that occasion he confessed that sometime in the past he had signed an agreement to cooperate with the State Security.

We knew from the outset that these fluctuations in blood pressure must have had their origins in stress, in pangs of conscience, or something of the kind. People did not like to confess such secrets. Most of them were so terrorized that they sometimes carried these secrets with them to the grave, rather than risk the security police taking revenge, if they should speak out. When I saw that he still had great faith, that he was a good man at heart, and above all, that it was his conscience that was causing the stress, we decided to try an experiment that had proved its effectiveness many times before.

We asked him: "Could you bear a week or two of terrorization, interrogation, threats, maybe some pain, too?" He said he was willing to try it. "But then you can't have second thoughts!" I advised him to free himself of that burden. The easiest thing would be to write a letter, possibly keeping a copy somewhere, in which he made it quite clear that he had been forced into this service, that he did not do it out of any conviction, but from fear and under duress, while at the same time he had tried not to harm anyone. But now he couldn't sleep because of it, he could not even live, and that is why he was recalling his signature and would refuse any further contacts and cooperation whatsoever.

Well, that was a big problem, because we knew what the security police were like and just next door was Sing-sing, where they used very cruel methods to eliminate people, so one had to be resolved to die if necessary. But the old man had had enough of worry and stress. He dug his heels in, wrote the letter and sent it.

Just as we had foreseen, the hullabaloo began. All kinds of rough as well as cunning interrogators took turns. Karas was forced to stand day and night, but he chose rather to collapse on the ground than to give in once more. In this way he put them in a very difficult position, because the only way they could solve the problem would be to execute him. But these were rather different times. They terrorized him a little longer, got him to sign that he would not tell anyone about it, and released him from their clutches.

That was a really miraculous intervention of God, because the Divine Spirit gave him strength. After that, with no further therapeutic treatment whatsoever, his state of health gradually improved, his blood pressure became normal, and old Dr. Karas grew younger, brightened up, became once more a normal person. Maybe this could be regarded as an experiment on a human being, but it was a very successful one and he was grateful to us for it for the rest of his life.

Meanwhile in the laboratory, over a period of two years, a large number of people of all kinds came and went, some of very dubious character, as was usual with the service staff of a camp. These people received considerable support from Security Officer J. One such person was F., a real dilettante, who often used to make up laboratory findings out of his head. We caught him out when in the case of one patient, Tvrdý, he kept reporting negative findings for urobilinogen every day. Tvrdý's condition got worse and worse, until it was necessary to operate on him. The evening before the operation, I secretly slipped into the laboratory and checked the liver tests for myself. I discovered that his urobilinogen was highly positive, which signalized a severely damaged liver. The operation the next day would almost certainly have cost him his life. My complaints that this irresponsible laboratory assistant, F., should be dismissed immediately were in vain; no one dared do this to a stoolie.

Once they brought a prisoner, H., to the Department of Internal Medicine, from the Lipkovický labor camp for juveniles. He had severe diarrhea. They had dried him out there for about a week, until he had fallen into a coma. Kauzál thought that it was typhus. When he was transferred to our department, we began a practically hopeless fight for his life. His delirium and coma grew worse, and neither antibiotics nor chloramphenicol did anything to help. Only after we added a new medicine based on corticoids, still little known then in civilian life, did a change take place, and the Italian injections of chloramphenicol, which we had managed meanwhile to get hold of, suddenly began to have an effect.

After fourteen days, during which the patient was unconscious, we let out a sigh of relief when a vulgar curse was heard from his lips. It was only later that we discovered what a devil we had saved. A coarse, degenerate, malicious young fellow. Even so, it seems to me that later he did improve just a tiny little bit.

It wasn't long before Little Kokta intervened again and assigned a well-known stoolie, F. S., to me as a medical orderly. We got on fairly well together, but I was aware of continuous interference. The head of the infirmary would suddenly appear without warning, check everything, and discharge a large number of patients who didn't like F. S., didn't give him bribes, or who had come into conflict with him. He also threw out those who didn't look seriously ill.

F. S. tried very hard to make a good impression on me. He refuted all my suspicions that he was a squealer, but there was really no doubt about his dishonesty. Whenever I carried out an unexpected inspection of his work I found evidence of careless, underhanded, or fraudulent behavior. We had a couple of quarrels over sterilization. He happily gave patients gastric tubes that had already been used for gallbladder patients. He only did it when he thought I wasn't looking. What can you do with a person like that who has the life of his patients in his hands? Because of his irresponsibility I was afraid to carry out suboccipital punctures of the cerebral cisterna. Once a patient almost died.

One elderly patient's stomach acid had to be tested with histamine. I asked him: "Do you know how to do it?" "Of course." Only later did I realize that he "knew" how to do everything and that he never asked. To make certain, I told him where the exact procedure was described and I repeated the main things: — 0.1mg of histamine to 10kg of weight, a maximum therefore of 0.5 to 0.7mg of histamine. The next day I happened to be somewhere near, when I suddenly heard this "nurse" shout: "Doctor, quick!" "What did you give him? How much histamine?" I looked at the syringe, in which there were still about three milliliters. About six to seven ampules, each of one milligram. "Good God!" I shouted, and I could already see the patient passing away in a deep coma, with an irregular pulse and breathing. "Quick, quick, an antihistamine!" I immediately injected him with everything possible, antihistamines, adrenaline, one after the other, everything I could. We were in a real sweat before he began to come to.

I didn't want to use this episode against S., because I saw he was very shaken and I hoped it would teach him a lesson. But when I caught him once more giving patients unsterilized gastric tubes and he lied to my face, I saw I could no longer take responsibility for this. I told Major Č. that I would rather leave than continue to work with him. Little Kokta then solved the problem very "diplomatically." He sent S. to work as an independent "doctor" for a party of farm laborers....

Towards the end of my stay there, the situation was quite unpleasant and difficult. Little Kokta began a systematic campaign against the political prisoners. He encouraged informing, hypocrisy, and intrigues more and more. He also took a dislike to young Karas, because he was my best fiend. But Kokta misjudged him completely. Honza had the courage to write a complaint to the Ministry; he asked to see the camp commandant of the whole of the Jáchymov district, who even agreed he was right and dealt with him very decently. It is true that J. eventually succeeded in having him transferred, but at his new place of work in Prokop camp, the head of the infirmary was very kind to him when he learned that it was Security Officer J. he had been persecuted by.

In prison everything could in fact be done in two ways. Openly, heroically — what is there to be afraid of? I stand by what I say, let everyone know it. It often had a better effect, or at least a quicker and more wide-reaching one, but for the most part it was very short-lived. A person in fact exposed himself and in so doing, he handed all his friends, or other people with whom he came into contact, over to the enemy. He could then go on working as before only if the officers kindly allowed him to. In time they managed to tie a person's hands and take from him even that minimum of prison "freedom."

The other way, which I usually chose, was discreet and individual. It was, however, very time-consuming and difficult. You had to keep coming up with ideas, making plans, in order to meet someone without attracting attention or in order to do something with somebody. Many people thought this method was cowardly. Why shouldn't we openly declare our faith, even in front of the security officers and political functionaries? But it was possible to work like this secretly all the time. This method could not really be eliminated in any way. Individually, one by one, it was possible to speak to everyone.

Just in the middle of another flu epidemic, at the beginning of 1962, they "threw me out" of the camp. I didn't even have time to say goodbye properly. The head of the infirmary, Dr. Č., didn't say a word to me and I didn't thank him, either. It all seemed unfair somehow. I don't think I even discovered where I was going, and he avoided confronting me by turning off the corridor just as I was leaving for the transport.

I had been thinking for some time, though, that it was high time to change camps. The atmosphere in the camp, and in the infirmary in particular, was already unbearable. Apart from that, I already wanted to be transferred to physical work.

Part VI

Jáchymov District – Prokop Labor Camp (for the second time)

When they brought me back to Prokop, I noticed several changes. In the camp infirmary I was to take the place of "Doctor" B., who was to be transferred to the infectious ward I had left. B. always stressed his expertise when it came to surgery, but he passed on to me a patient who had been bedridden for over a month with a swollen leg after an accident, and he made a point of assuring me that there was no need to X-ray him. His bones were intact. From the clinical point of view as well as from the X-rays, I had my doubts. After another X-ray I immediately found quite an extensive fracture, with a displacement of the bones on the fibular, outer side of the ankle, which had been caused by walking on it meanwhile. This usually meant the patient would remain an invalid.

B. had chosen a teacher of natural sciences, said to have committed sexual offenses, to work as a male nurse. The latter was his right-hand man. He did most of the work and B. only supervised. It was inevitable we should come into conflict, because he wrote prescriptions himself and occasionally even cancelled my prescriptions and instructions. Nevertheless, when I compare him with other medical assistants, he was reasonably good. All my "masters" were quick to recommend that I should take his advice and follow in the footsteps of my predecessor, B.

The only person to oppose him was the dentist, F. M., who had been convicted of fraud about thirty-seven times. He was very clever, so at the beginning I was quite inclined towards him. He took me under his wing from the outset in an ostentatious, almost theatrical manner, and he made a point of supporting me. He stressed his friendship with "Vlado" Stercul, whom he called "Dear Vlado." This misled me, as well as the fact that he seemed to support me against "the opposition." It really took me quite a long time to realize that he was a real squealer and fraud and, what is more, he excelled at squeezing money out of prisoners, robbing them of all their valuables and rations. We used to call the competitive fight to do this, typical of informers, "BOK" — "Boj o korytá" (lit. "the fight for the trough").

At headquarters, Lieutenant S., an ardent hunter and forester, still held the post of Commandant. When attacks or intrigues against me were too obvious and unconvincing, he would speak up for me. But the soul of the camp was still Lieutenant Č., now a rival to the security officers, that is, to Little Tonda and his followers. The latter hardly ever missed an opportunity to humiliate me, shout at me, or force on me people who did their best to undermine my authority.

Big Tonda usually kept more in the background, but when he did intervene, he always showed himself again in a very negative light.

Gradually the whole atmosphere changed in the camp, because the political situation outside changed from drastic Stalinism to more civilized Khrushchevism. Although those who had been living in the camps for years did not feel its immediate effects to any great extent. The rough, supercilious, illegal behavior of many of the warders and police officers was toned down and occurred only on exceptional occasions.

The difference between present and previous practices was to be seen in one such episode. I and two voluntary workers, N. and H., were put in a punishment cell for having more blankets on our beds than we should. This was no doubt cleverly arranged by our dentist, M. He must have quickly thrown the extra blankets from the cupboard onto our beds. When we complained, however, the head of the infirmary had us released and Č. gave us permission to use one or two more blankets. However, Little Tonda insisted all evening that we had deserved our punishment and that we would be treated likewise in future.

When the army dismissed its surplus officers, some of them became prison guards or security officers. These were rather different, more decent people. Several of them came to work as medical officers in our camp. I had prayed very hard for a change of medical officers, especially on the occasion of Pope John XXIII's address, and I thought for some time that my prayer had gone unheard. Now Lieutenant Š. arrived from the army. Also a new economic manager, Lieutenant K., a new commander of the guards, and, above all, a new psychologist, a lieutenant, a truly good-hearted man. Using new methods, he was quite good at winning over cynical hooligans and recidivists. But very soon the VIPs drove him out of their midst and he was transferred to Karlový Vary.

It wasn't long before I experienced my third flu epidemic in prison. Lieutenant Č. gave me a lot of support with enforcing hygienic and anti-epidemiological measures, sometimes even overdoing it. It meant extreme exertion without rest, sometimes long into the night or even until morning. In the end I got a fever myself. I must have developed pneumonia from the flu, but I couldn't lie down, seeing men around me — some of them really big strong fellows — completely exhausted, with failing circulation and sometimes unable to breathe.

In these critical times an improvised X-ray machine helped me greatly. I was thus able to diagnose about twenty cases of pneumonia. We did not have a single death, whereas we heard that in the hospital outside they usually had ten or twelve postmortems a week. This was at last an opportunity to demand to be given some kinder, more decent helpers in the infirmary. So I was able to get the first patients cured of flu to act as my assistants.

It was then I chanced on Kurt Anderle and, what is more, Láďa Suchomel, who was transferred from "C" camp. I could happily entrust him with a whole barracks that had been taken over as a temporary infirmary. Meeting Láďa once more was wonderful, but we left private conversation until the evening. We then walked together through the snow beyond the last barracks close to the barbed wire fence. Then I became acquainted with Standa M. He came to the surgery with an abscess in his mouth. After some time he began to talk things over with me, clean up and generally make himself useful. I once let out a sigh in his presence, saying I really could do with one reliable person as a voluntary assistant, but that there was no hope, because Little Tonda didn't even want to let Láďa Suchomel do it. He took this up immediately and said he'd try to arrange it himself. The very next day he told me the matter was looking promising. This should have seemed suspicious to me, but I was glad to have two helpers at last who were on my side.

Láďa really was a help to me as a man and as a Christian. Honest, courageous, and conscientious. I considered Standa to be a person who must have certain connections with "the powers-that-be." Sometimes it really was a help. Nevertheless, one day Little Tonda threw Láďa out, almost at an hour's notice, and then I tried to get Standa transferred as well, because his initial diligence had vanished once he had managed to get himself posted to the infirmary.

After this, several more assistants came and went. I remember Ladislav P., for example, who had experienced a terrible tragedy. Two of those most dear to him, his wife and daughter, committed suicide after his arrest, because they could not endure the cruel treatment they received from the security police. Although he himself was later acquitted of all serious charges. He changed a great deal during those few months of imprisonment and often wept whenever he thought of them.

There was also a German, Hary Deimling, who later changed his name to Bureš, a young man of about twenty-five. Once, when one of his family died, he came to me in tears, asking me to help him. He came to be very dependent on me. He suffered from deep depressions and I had to use hypnotic suggestion a couple of times, with quite good results. But I had to stop this, because our dentist, M., began to meddle and interfere. Some of the officers even began to accuse me of homosexuality. This was, indeed, the only accusation they could use against me that would spoil my reputation and against which it was practically impossible to defend oneself. In this respect, however, the priests were far more vulnerable.

I became quite friendly with some of the patients. I got Messinger out of the punishment cell on account of his gallbladder. I treated him for a long time and even kept him out of Big Tonda's clutches, so that in the end the head of the infirmary had to speak in my defense. Tonda was investigating Messinger for alleged machinations involving his workers' wages. They went so far as to bring him to court for the crime of sabotage, but in the end Lieutenant Č. also stood up for him. Messinger defended himself with almost fierce determination because such fresh charges in prison usually put one in an absolutely hopeless position. There was no opportunity to defend oneself and there was nothing easier than to find (for a reward) two false witnesses among the criminals.

On many occasions I spoke up for intolerant patients, people who subsequently caused me quite a bit of trouble. This made me wonder whether I was acting sensibly.

One of the first things I did was to resuscitate a prisoner who had tried to hang himself. He said he had done it because he couldn't bear the pressure put on him by Tonda, for whom he acted as an informer. He was subsequently very grateful to me, but the other prisoners continued to hate him. He hanged himself on the site of a porcelain factory under construction in Slavkov, but he was fortunately cut down very quickly. I got there by car and then on foot through the mud. It took me the whole morning to resuscitate him. The ambulance arrived several hours later. He would have been dead long before that.

In 1964 the canteen was taken over by a very thin prisoner, a good-hearted man, but he obviously didn't know how to manage the accounts and, above all, how to protect himself against swindlers from the Ministry of the Interior. Apparently, they used to borrow things or take goods without paying for them and then denied they had them. An investigation was started with stocktaking and a new trial. The stocktaking revealed a deficit and the real debtors wanted to put the blame on him. The old man crept into the toilet in the cellar and in desperation he literally committed hara-kiri. He took a long, sharp kitchen knife and stabbed himself in the stomach and liver, partly cutting through them, and sliced through two ribs up to the heart. It looked an absolutely hopeless case, that could only be sewn up with long stitches, as after a postmortem, and put in a coffin. Yet one couldn't just leave it at that. An ambulance came, the medical officers put him in it, and after continuous infusions and injections, a regular pulse even began to appear and the patient showed stronger signs of life. I was furious, however, when the doctor in the surgical ward in Sokol declared: "What can we do? Cover him up with a sheet, there's no hope for him." I protested that the patient had already been resuscitated and blood had been ordered. So, very unwillingly, obviously only to avoid trouble, with so many witnesses around, they set to work. In spite of the antibiotics, they expected severe blood poisoning and shock. Nevertheless, I heard he recovered.

I met with a similar approach of a civilian doctor in the case of our chief maintenance man H., who had so promptly "taken care" of our bathroom, in other words, had abolished it. The poor man came to a very tragic end, and it was impossible to avoid seeing in it God's intervention. He was about forty years old and drank about fourteen cups of coffee a day. Sometimes as many beers, too. It was really only the VIPs who could afford that. One day, when he was playing football, he collapsed and began to suffocate. When they brought him into the surgery, I could see he was in a bad way. He was a bluish-purple color, hardly breathing, and his pulse was very weak. I began to resuscitate him, even using the kiss of life, but in vain. The civilian doctor we called in from the emergency department didn't even take a proper look at him. She was glad he was already dead. She just commented that I could have injected adrenaline, and when we named all the drugs we had injected him with, she was very surprised: "What more do you want?" I realized then what the standard of the health service was in civilian life.

Unfortunately, I had scratched my mouth while giving the kiss of life. A few days later a little boil appeared, accompanied by severe swelling of the lymphatic glands. Considering H. had a serious venereal disease, I was compelled to give myself about ten injections of penicillin. In fact, for the most part, I had to look after my own health myself. The worst thing was when I had an abscess below one eye. The nurse didn't have the courage to puncture it and scrape it out, so in the end I had to do it myself, in front of a mirror. About ten centimeters of drainage gauze went into it. However, I discovered that picking it out gently with pincers is sometimes more painful than radically scraping it out with a spoon.

For some time after the departure of M., the dentist, I was again the only dentist in the camp. I gained experience with extractions, the administration of local anaesthetics, the use of various forceps, the surgical removal of roots. With the primitive equipment at my disposal I learned to do simple fillings. On Saturdays I devoted all my time to dentistry and, when necessary, every evening, too. Later S., the prosecutor, began to come to me, even though I tried to dissuade him. His first filling did in fact fall out, and I felt very unhappy about it, because every failure could be regarded as deliberate.

In one of our discussions, he claimed that the Church was more successful than they were at reforming criminals, not because it was nearer to the truth, or because it had better moral principles, but because it had more experience with educating people. I then asked him why, therefore, people had to be educated by those who had less experience than, for example, the Salesian monks, and clearly with far worse results. When I refused to carry out some dental treatment, he always used to say: "Don't philosophize, drill and get on with it!" I was well aware of the fact that he could regard any complication as deliberate on my part.

M., the dentist, always used to boast that if a patient gave him nothing, he would drill his teeth so that he'd remember it for the rest of his life. It was probably this difference in approach to our patients that brought me such success. When I once reproached M. for drinking coffee when he had a waiting-room full of patients, he snapped back: "I'll deal with that in no time." He began to pull out teeth and drill so ruthlessly and painfully that the patients yelled. When all the patients in the waiting-room had disappeared, he just commented: "Look how quickly I get through my work."

Sometime in May 1962 we were caught up in the second wide-ranging amnesty, including political prisoners. But again there were so many exceptions that only about ten people went home from our camp. Of these only a couple were political prisoners. However, some were my friends, for example Kurt Anderle. On this occasion, too, it happened so quickly, that we hardly had time to say goodbye properly.

In the meantime mining gangs and camps were gradually being abolished. The last of them was Rovnosť, which, I'm told, was ploughed over, to make it impossible to find where it had once stood. Some farm work camps were abolished, too, and the average age of those who came to our camp got younger and younger. Theft became more common even within the camp, as well as punishment for it in the form of "blankets." This was how the thieves took revenge on a thief. They threw a blanket over him, so he couldn't testify as to who was more active, and then they beat him up mercilessly. Some of these thieves were brought to the surgery, bruised and swollen, with slight concussion. Even so, this didn't cure them of kleptomania.

It didn't take me long to come to a certain understanding with them; I learned how to talk to them, how to deal with them. Most of them were the kind of youths who did not respect anyone's authority. Neither God's, nor their parents', teachers', or priest's. Nevertheless, they were unconsciously looking for it and it wasn't really so difficult to win them over. These young car thieves trusted me to such an extent that they gave me "professional training." They taught me how to open our Skoda cars with a simple screwdriver, without damaging the doors or bodywork, and they even tested me. But as I have had no practice, I have long since forgotten how, which I may regret, because it might come in useful for my own car.

People also sought me out as a partner for ping-pong. I was the third or fourth best player, even though I was twenty years older than the young prisoners. As soon as I began to win, the spectators would begin to shout: "Do bučiny makovej!" (What nonsense!) because it was a phrase I used to vent my feelings. When even Little Tonda began to play with me I knew at once that some political concession, probably an amnesty, was around the corner. He suddenly became "human," he forced himself to adopt a conciliatory tone, he tried to win me over. But when I didn't manage to let him win a game, he hated me all the more.

As we were the camp with the most lenient regime, in which there were prisoners with the lightest sentences or the remains of sentences, there were still quite a few attempts to escape. Some were quite imaginative. I remember how on an earlier occasion, in Bytíz, one prisoner escaped in a lorry by hiding in an enormous wooden reel for cables. They used other tricks, too. A prisoner would stay behind after work and sleep in the snow in a ditch, in the hay, under a barracks, and so on.

When an escape was announced, there was always a great commotion and all the officers had to report for duty, even if they were on leave. A real hunt was organized, with the army and dogs. They were all furious at being disturbed during their leave or free time, and they tried to catch the escapees as soon as possible, which they usually managed to do. Meanwhile, the prisoners had to stand for a roll call for hours on end, sometimes the whole night. When they caught the runaways and brought them back, they were usually well and truly beaten up. They escorted them in handcuffs, threw them into the punishment cell, and brought them before the court once more.

Towards the end of my imprisonment, there was a very painful incident. Three boys wanted to escape. They were alone in the barracks with a young warder. They pounced on him, hit him on the head about fourteen times with the blunt end of an axe, and then cut his throat with a big knife. By God's grace, it was just that which saved him. It had the same effect as a tracheotomy, thus freeing the respiratory tract, which was full of blood. They then crawled through the wire fences. The guard must have been asleep, because they were quite a distance away before he fired at them.

The escape and the accompanying circumstances caused a great stir. Little and Big Tonda were in their element. They spent days investigating, even wanting to know who said what to whom about it. They even put those who did not condemn the escape in the punishment cells. They turned it into a political scandal. They caught the escapees after about three days. Fortunately, they were caught by soldiers, because the security police would probably have beaten them to death on the spot. I heard that one of them was executed or condemned to death.

I still kept up a correspondence with our close friend F., although I emphasized from the outset that it was a purely friendly relationship for the purpose of exchanging information, and she knew that I had taken an oath of celibacy. Later I began to be afraid there was a certain change in her feelings for me. She became more and more attached to me. But whenever I stressed that my position had not changed and would not change, she assured me that she was aware of that. She asked whether I wanted to know how many times I had repeated it. However, she claimed that whenever she wrote to me or visited me, she "became a better person." She said that if she let a long interval pass, she found herself in difficulties.

This seemed to me to be typical of a person in love. I tried in vain to postpone her visits, to break off contacts with her. It was always very painful for her and she did not agree with me. At the same time she must have experienced more than one bitter moment and even humiliation, thanks to my friends. They used to pass on "my" messages, that she shouldn't send me anything any more, because I anyway received "bigger and better" parcels from my family. It seemed incredible to me; she must have felt very hurt and I really did not wish anyone to offend her, even unwittingly.

However, it was clear that we could not go on like that. She clung to me more and more, while she neglected others, or avoided them. I saw that she was more and more tense, and I was sorry I had not put an end to our relationship earlier. I realized that I had underestimated a woman's emotional side and that I should have done this at the very outset.

When I finally refused to invite her to visit me, she suddenly came without permission and, if I remember rightly, by herself. She was very upset and declared that if I refused to see her, she would come anyway. On October 26, I wrote to my mother, asking her to find out discreetly what was the matter with her and to help her if necessary to keep her from doing anything impulsive. I wrote her a last long letter (an instructor censoring it privately for me), in which I explained everything to her once more and insisted that we stop writing to and seeing each other, because it was obviously doing her considerable harm. Maybe it was rather resolute, if not mean, on my part, but I said I would send back every letter she wrote to me in the future. She tried to answer on December 20, and then, after wishing me a happy Christmas, she stopped writing.

The whole affair was very painful for me, but I couldn't see any other way out. She soon married and isolated herself from me. After a long interval, I recently wrote her an urgent letter, asking her to forgive me if I had hurt her in any way and I was delighted by her reply. She wrote that I need not think about the matter any more or apologize. She said she did not feel any bitterness towards me, or anything of that kind.

Life in prison continued to change. An even greater number of the prisoners were given conditional release, many were allowed "holidays." Prison sentences were divided into three categories, with our camp being included in the first (most lenient) category. We had first offenders with the most privileges. The complicated rows of barbed wire were abolished, as were the notices in the firing zone that declared they would shoot without warning. All that remained was a simple fence covered with canvass about three meters high, closely interwoven with barbed wire.

Although there was a generally more relaxed atmosphere in the camp, the letters I wrote were always inspected by Little Tonda, and he picked out the letters that arrived for me. He was surprised that I wrote so few replies and so in the end I had to put my letters in the postbox instead of having them censored by certain instructors who didn't hold them back, as I didn't want to expose them to persecution.

The number of political prisoners decreased all the time. I learned that many of our associates and fellow workers had been released from prison. Amnesties, conditional release or pardons, especially from the President, became more and more frequent. It was clear they wanted to rid themselves of political prisoners in the eyes of the world — prisoners they had always claimed did not exist. Suddenly I found myself wondering whether there was any longer any point being in jail, whether my Don Quixote attitude was futile. Perhaps I really could do more outside than under continuous observation and control.

Employees of the Ministry of the Interior began to visit me more and more frequently. Warders and administrative officers kept trying to persuade me to apply for conditional release, like most of the other political prisoners. Once the Commandant himself visited me and said: "You are the least trouble for me in the camp. On the contrary, I'm glad you are here, because I have no problems with the camp infirmary. But, in all fairness to you, I feel it my responsibility to tell you that if you submitted an application for conditional release, I see no reason why it should be rejected."

Even the "ferocious" prosecutor S., who had been infuriated by my "obstinacy, hate, and futile heroism" ("In that case, you'll drop down dead here!"), when he had tried to persuade me previously, now played another tune: "Why you, as a Christian, should take others into consideration. You know very well that you can hardly defend your position or achieve your aim from here. In the past there were all kinds of miscarriages of justice. We know this and we are trying to put them right. While you are here every complaint or protest can be intercepted by any idiot." He was right there!

When I continued to turn down their suggestions, they began to offer me a holiday, so that I would get a taste of freedom, of civilian life. They thought that after twelve years I couldn't even imagine what freedom was like. I had become a kind of "professional prisoner." There was probably some truth in that, even though I tried to keep in contact with the outside world as much as I could through the mass media and discussions with people. In the end I decided to please them and I agreed to go on holiday. Up to that moment I had always rejected the idea, even though most of the inmates had been outside many times.

And so, on November 16–17, 1963, I left the barbed wire behind me for the first time. In the company of relations, and dressed in civilian clothes, I went to Slavkov. It was after more than twelve years in prison. It was a strange feeling. I kept looking over my shoulder to see who was following me. I asked them to tell me if I behaved in a strange manner. I went into a shop, I tried on a coat, we settled down in a hotel room.

Very soon Dr. C. (a former colleague and prisoner from the hospital) arrived and we chatted until the evening and even late into the night. The next day we went to church in Karlový Váry. There I met another of my former fellow prisoners and my boss, Dr. Ž. I also met Vendo Vaško, who had been released quite a long time before that. In the afternoon Dr. C and I listened to records, mainly of that wonderful negro Mass with tamtams, Missa "Luba."

I arrived back in prison at about midnight, just in time. But I almost paid dearly for that. They could have considered me a runaway. There was a blizzard and I had walked on foot across the fields, getting lost on the way.

After my return my monotonous program began to change somewhat. I would begin, about an hour before the reveille, with meditation in the X-ray room, and then I would stoke up the infirmary fires in all the four to six stoves that burned coke and briquettes. Then I concentrated on my studies in the isolation ward. I started with Chinese, continued with English and medicine. I also worked on the paper I mentioned earlier, entitled "The Remedy," about a universal international language, which I finished on December 26, 1963, on St. Stephen's day. I had brought back from outside two chapters of the Gospels, Matthew 23 and 24, and I learned them by heart. I had also brought the Eucharist, which I took only on Sundays and feast days, otherwise just spiritually.

I began to fight for my written documents. Verdicts, notes. It was a sign of better times that on January 18, 1964, I received them. My notes had been preserved intact at command headquarters for the very reason that they had been confiscated. Little Tonda had once declared that I would never be able to get hold of them, because they were state property and only they could decide what should be done with them. Maybe they would use them for further charges.

I hurriedly copied them out and had them smuggled out of the camp. The final speech, the appeal, complaints. I also wrote the draft of a complaint about an infringement of the law. It was six sides long and on June 10, 1964, during a holiday in Prague lasting eight days, I sent it by post to the Ministry of Justice.

During this second holiday, I visited many friends as well as former fellow prisoners in Karlový Vary and Prague. Then I visited Bratislava. This first time, after my long imprisonment, it seemed different, strange to me, although the center of the town had not yet changed very much. It was like watching a film. And at home? They all wanted to see me. Gitka and Ferdo and their children, Vlado's family. They took me everywhere by car, because I didn't know my way in the new streets. It seemed strange to me that in a family with four people who had been in prison, nearly all of them had cars. How the world had changed! And hadn't we changed? And what about them?

At Gitka's I also met old Martin Klempa, who had been in an interrogation cell with me in the Palace of Justice and whom we called "father." As he had done every year since that time, he brought my family some of his wine, together with that toothpaste in which he had smuggled some of my messages out of prison. We probably mentioned it over the phone, because there was a great fuss about it afterwards. Martin, his daughter, son-in-law, and wife were questioned. When they found the toothpaste, it was too late anyway. The note, written in Castelani's antifungal solution, could not be deciphered.

I also met my friends there, we went to Mariánka and prayed the Thanksgiving prayer. I hugged Jožo Špát, I visited the Jukls. I was photographed for the first time with the whole family, apart from Karol, who was abroad, and my brother's little daughter, Mária. I saw so many new faces it was hardly possible to exchange a few words with everyone. But this holiday came to an end, too.

I returned to the camp late in the evening and quickly hid the Eucharist and documents I had brought with me. I wanted to fulfill one more undertaking. To sing the praises of Mary, the servant of the Lord. For my meditations about the miracle of Mary — the Mother, Sister, Lady and yet Servant, had given me so much strength, had saved me so many times from depression and despair!

After that interrogation of Martin Klempa on account of the smuggled message, the situation again took a turn for the worse. They didn't allow my brother or Ferdo (my brother-in-law) to visit me. It's true my father and mother were given permission, after a two-month interval, but we couldn't even go to Slavkov to celebrate my fortieth birthday and father's seventieth. I was glad to be able to give them my reflections on the Virgin Mary at least in outline, hidden among descriptions of foreign medicines.

Although the situation seemed worse, my father told my mother to have a good look around her in the hotel in Slavkov, because maybe they were there for the last time. And that is how it was. When I was in Bratislava I had promised, probably purely out of obedience, that if they wanted to release me before the feast of Christ the King [the last Sunday in October] I wouldn't resist and insist on being in prison any longer.

From my point of view, I felt sure that I was being led along such a radical road because it was God's will. However, I didn't want it to look as if I was trying to show I was superior to the others. How these compromises pained me, though! After all, I had only nine months left to the end of my sentence. To tell the truth, I had not believed for a moment that my condition could be fulfilled "before Christ the King."

At the beginning of October I received a "blue summons" to the lower military court in Karlový Vary. The sitting was to be held in Prokop camp in Slavkov. The date was set for October 21. If I did not appear before the court, I would have to pay a five-hundred-crown fine and be brought there by force. I suddenly realized that the contents of the envelope did not refer to the complaint I had submitted about an infringement of the law, but concerned my conditional release, which I had not applied for. At that moment, I wanted to obliterate my signature from the registered mail book, but only then did I notice that it had not been sent by ordinary post, but a secretary had been sent specially from the Commandant.

All the others received these summons in the normal way from the duty officer or through the official post. Everyone shrugged his shoulders, saying they knew nothing about it. They said that neither the camp nor the prosecutor had submitted the proposal. Or maybe they just didn't want to confess that it was an order from above.

The warders and prisoners began to lay bets as to whether I would accept it. I kept my thoughts to myself, but with the help of L. K., a Hungarian friend, I prepared a very radical written refusal, which I wanted to read out to them at the sitting.

When on St. Ursula's Day [October 10] the senate began to discuss my release, I objected that I had not requested it and if my family had done so, I did not agree with it. I wanted to read out my explanation for my refusal to accept conditional release. The chairman presiding at the hearing, an oldish lieutenant colonel, just smiled affably and asked me to put it aside and just tell them what I wanted. I insisted on reading it out, so that my words could not be misinterpreted once more in a negative way. So he let me read it out. He listened and asked for it to be attached to my file (see Document No. 22, p. 180 above). Then he began to persuade me that this was not a question of my guilt or innocence. As I fulfilled the conditions, they could release me even against my will.

Then Mr. D., our cultural worker, read out my reference from the camp headquarters. Another surprise. It was extremely positive and praised my work. Once more I declared that I would not accept a release. In spite of this the chairman said: "It won't make any difference anyway. Take him away while the court confers." Shortly after, they read out their verdict, which said I was to be released. If you wish to appeal against this verdict, you can draw the matter out a few days at the most, because not even a higher court can decide otherwise, as the reasons will be the same."

I protested against the assertion that I had improved, and I claimed that it was not true at all, that I was the same as before, only the conditions had changed. "Don't try to catch me out. It's a question of principle, which is quite clear." Then they led me out. I was still undecided, though.

At this point Little Tonda couldn't keep his temper any longer and declared: "If you don't pack your things by lunchtime, I'll put you in handcuffs and if necessary I will carry you out of the gates myself. It will be my last pleasure so far as you are concerned!"

I think he considered me a great nuisance at the camp, because all the new prisoners used to come to me for advice on legal questions and other matters. They sought support from me when laws were broken, and especially at moments of crisis.

Thus, with a strange feeling of defeat, with expectations as well as sadness, I began to pack my things. I said goodbye to friends, acquaintances, hooligans, thieves, and warders. And to those thirteen, at least from the Christian point of view, beautiful years of my life. Even though they were spent behind bars and barbed wire.

When arranging the formalities in the "Pentagon," that is, at the head office, they already treated me as a free citizen. As with everybody else, they gave me "a little formality" to sign — that I would keep silent about everything I had learned in the course of the investigation and while serving my sentence. That is a very wide concept. In the first place it includes the inhumanity and illegality of the state investigation and of the prison organs. A breach of this would, I was told, be considered to be high treason and espionage. I refused to sign. The official was terribly angry. "Everyone has to sign it! Do you think you are an exception?" "I can't sign it." "Then you'll stay here." "That's exactly what I want. Leave me here. I'll unpack." At this point he hesitated and brought in Lieutenant Č. He began to smooth things out: "Comrade, call in Captain K., or another of the instructors and write a statement that in your presence he was given full instructions, but that he doesn't want to sign. That'll do." But in the end they didn't do even that. The chairman of the military court even confirmed that I had done the right thing, because he characterized it as one of the old, illegal practices.

That evening I arrived in Slavkov and I said goodbye to the pharmacist there, who had very often sent me her regards. I spent the evening and the next day in Karlový Vary and the following days, especially the festival of Christ the King, in Prague.

I protested once more to the High Court against the claim that I had improved and insisted on submitting an appeal. This was rejected, too, on the grounds that some law stated that no one can appeal to their own disadvantage.

I cannot fail in conclusion to thank and give praise to our Lord, who allowed me to experience all this. He accompanied me through this purgatory in such a wonderful way, that it sometimes seemed like heaven. I have probably never made so few mistakes and sinned so little as after my arrest. I would probably never have been able to do so much good as I did in the prisons and camps. In particular I thank Mary, the Mother of God, that I could discover there her great mission and that she was always at my side, ready to intercede for me.

Once more I repeat that my purpose in writing this was not some kind of dubious elevation of myself. I write out of obedience and also in order that — in the opinion of others far more important than myself — the grace and gifts that the Lord might want to confer on others should not remain hidden. And also that I, too, might help to bear witness to the important history of the Church and of our nation and make it more difficult for it to be repeated or distorted in the future.

About the Author

Silvester Krčméry, Sr., was born in Trnava on August 5, 1924. He spent his childhood and youth in Banská Bystrica where he completed his secondary education in 1942.

He then studied at the Medical Faculty in Bratislava, continued in Paris (with practical work in Morocco), and finished in Prague, where he graduated from Charles University in 1948. In 1949, he began work as a dermatologist in Košice.

He was highly influenced by Professor Kolakovič whom he had met in 1943. Later, he and Vladimír Jukl became part of the so-called Ko-lakovič "Family," working at spreading the Gospel in Slovakia and the Czech lands.

He organized the evangelization of students, especially medical students in Prague, and workers in the border regions in the Czech lands, mainly in the Diocese of Litoměřice.

In 1951, during his basic military service, he was arrested for lay apostolate activities. He was in interrogation imprisonment for three years, and on June 24, 1954, was convicted of treason by the military court in Trenčín and sentenced to fourteen years in prison. He spent these years in various prisons (Banská Bystrica, Mírov, Ostrov nad Ohří) and in concentration labor camps.

After his release, in 1964, he worked in Bratislava for twenty years as a doctor and specialist in radiodiagnostics.

From the time of his release, he and some friends renewed their apostolate work in the former Czechoslovakia within the framework of the "underground church," and he and Vladimír Jukl founded "Fatima," a secular institute of which Dr. Krčméry was the first director.

He constantly worked for the evangelization of students, apprentices, drug addicts, alcoholics, the homeless, and prisoners.

On September 10, 2013, Silvester Krčméry died in Bratislava.

About the Publisher

The Crossroad Publishing Company publishes Crossroad and Herder & Herder books. We offer a 200-year global family tradition of books on spiritual living and religious thought. We promote reading as a time-tested discipline for focus and understanding. We help authors shape, clarify, write, and effectively promote their ideas. We select, edit, and distribute books. With our expertise and passion, we provide wholesome spiritual nourishment for heart, mind, and soul through the written word.